WOMEN, WRITING
AND THE PUBLIC SPHERE, 1700–1830

In this interdisciplinary volume, an international team of special-
ists examines the dynamic relation between women and the public
sphere in the period 1700 to 1830. Drawing on literary and visual
evidence, contributors highlight the range and diversity of women's
cultural activity, from historiography, publishing and translation to
philosophical and political writing. *Women, Writing and the Public
Sphere* examines the history of the public spaces women occupied,
raising questions of scandal and display, improvement, virtue and
morality in the context of the production and consumption of
culture by women. The contribution of educated women to the
British Enlightenment and the role of translation and exchange
between European intellectual movements in shaping ideas of
nationhood is also addressed. This book offers a comprehensive
account of women's philosophical and political reflections on the
nature of their place in the public sphere.

ELIZABETH EGER is Research Fellow at the Eighteenth Century
Centre at Warwick University. She is the editor of *Selected Works of
Elizabeth Montagu* (1999) and a contributor to *Women's Poetry in the
Enlightenment* (1999) and *The Cambridge Guide to Women's Literature in
English*.

CHARLOTTE GRANT is a Fellow and Director of Studies in English
at Jesus College, Cambridge. She writes and teaches in the area of
eighteenth-century studies.

CLÍONA Ó GALLCHOIR is Lecturer in English at University
College, Cork. She is co-editor with Susan Manly of volume IX of
Novels and Selected Works of Maria Edgeworth.

PENNY WARBURTON has worked as a book reviewer, archivist and
university teacher. She is a contributor to *The Cambridge Guide to
Women's Literature in English* and is currently finalising her doctoral
thesis, 'Women Writing on Economics: Aesthetics, Writing and the
Economy, 1760–1833'.

WOMEN, WRITING
AND THE PUBLIC SPHERE,
1700–1830

EDITED BY

ELIZABETH EGER,
CHARLOTTE GRANT,
CLÍONA Ó GALLCHOIR AND
PENNY WARBURTON

CAMBRIDGE
UNIVERSITY PRESS

CAMBRIDGE UNIVERSITY PRESS
Cambridge, New York, Melbourne, Madrid, Cape Town, Singapore, São Paulo

Cambridge University Press
The Edinburgh Building, Cambridge CB2 2RU, UK

Published in the United States of America by Cambridge University Press, New York

www.cambridge.org
Information on this title: www.cambridge.org/9780521771061

© Cambridge University Press 2001

First published 2001
This digitally printed first paperback version 2006

A catalogue record for this publication is available from the British Library

Library of Congress Cataloguing in Publication data

Women and the public sphere: writing and representation 1700–1830 / edited by
Elizabeth Eger, Charlotte Grant, Clíona O'Gallchoir and Penny Warburton
p.   cm.
Includes bibliographical references.
ISBN 0 521 77106 4 (hardback)
1. Women in public life – Great Britain – History.   I. Eger, Elizabeth.

HQ1391.G7 W66 2001   305.42′0941–dc21   00-031285

ISBN-13 978-0-521-77106-1 hardback
ISBN-10 0-521-77106-4 hardback

ISBN-13 978-0-521-02580-5 paperback
ISBN-10 0-521-02580-X paperback

Contents

List of illustrations   *page* vii
List of contributors   ix
Preface and acknowledgements   xii

Introduction: women, writing and representation   I
Elizabeth Eger, Charlotte Grant, Clíona Ó Gallchoir and Penny Warburton

PART I   WOMEN IN THE PUBLIC EYE

1   Coffee-women, *The Spectator* and the public sphere in the
early eighteenth century   27
Markman Ellis

2   Misses, Murderesses and Magdalens: women in the
public eye   53
Caroline Gonda

PART II   CONSUMING ARTS

3   The choice of Hercules: the polite arts and 'female
excellence' in eighteenth-century London   75
Charlotte Grant

4   Representing culture: *The Nine Living Muses of Great Britain*
(1779)   104
Elizabeth Eger

5   A moral purchase: femininity, commerce and abolition,
1788–1792   133
Kate Davies

PART III LEARNED LADIES: FROM BLUESTOCKINGS TO
COSMOPOLITAN INTELLECTUALS

6 Bluestocking feminism   163
   Gary Kelly

7 Catharine Macaulay: history, republicanism and the
   public sphere   181
   Susan Wiseman

8 Gender, nation and revolution: Maria Edgeworth and
   Stéphanie-Félicité de Genlis   200
   Clíona Ó Gallchoir

9 Salons, Alps and Cordilleras: Helen Maria Williams, Alex
   von Humboldt and the discourse of Romantic travel   217
   Nigel Leask

PART IV THE FEMALE SUBJECT

10 The most public sphere of all: the family   239
   Sylvana Tomaselli

11 Theorising public opinion: Elizabeth Hamilton's model of
   self, sympathy and society   257
   Penny Warburton

12 Intimate connections: scandalous memoirs and epistolary
   indiscretion   274
   Mary Jacobus

Bibliography   290
Index   313

Illustrations

1 Frontispiece to James Miller's comedy *The Coffee-House A*   *page* 40
*Dramatick Piece. As it is Perform'd at the Theatre Royal in Drury
Lane* (London: J. Watts, 1737). Reproduced by permission
of the Syndics of the Cambridge University Library.

2 Hogarth, *The Harlot's Progress*, Plate 1. © The British Museum.   77

3 Simon Gribelin (after Paolo de Matthaies), *The Judgement of
Hercules* (1713), in Anthony Ashley Cooper, Earl of Shaftesbury,
Characteristicks of Men, Manners, Opinions, Times, 3rd edn
(London: John Derby, 1723). Reproduced by permission of
the Syndics of the Cambridge University Library.   79

4 Edward Fisher (after Joshua Reynolds), *Garrick between Tragedy
and Comedy* (1762). © The British Museum.   89

5 Angelica Kauffman, *Self-Portrait: Hesitating Between the Arts of
Music and Painting* (1791). Oil on canvas. Reproduced by kind
permission of the Winn Family and The National Trust
(Nostell Priory, Yorks).   90

6 Johann Zoffany, *The Academicians of the Royal Academy* (1772).
Oil on canvas, 100.7 cm by 147.3 cm. Reproduced by kind
permission of The Royal Collection. © 1999, Her Majesty
Queen Elizabeth II.   91

7 Hannah Rush, *Compartment with Cattle* (1758). Reproduced by
kind permission of the Royal Society for the encouragement
of Arts, Manufactures and Commerce.   93

8 James Barry, *The Distribution of the Premiums to the Society of Arts*.
Mural, 462.28 cm by 360.68 cm. Fifth picture in *The Progress
of Human Knowledge and Culture* (1777–1783). Reproduced by
kind permission of the Royal Society for the encouragement
of Arts, Manufactures and Commerce.   96

9 Ackermann (after Pugin and Rowlandson), *The Society's 'Great
Room'* (1809). Reproduced by kind permission of the Royal

Society for the encouragement of Arts, Manufactures and
Commerce. 98

10 Richard Samuel, *The Nine Living Muses of Great Britain*. Oil on
canvas, 132.1 cm by 154.9 cm. Exhibited at the Royal Academy,
1779. By courtesy of the National Portrait Gallery, London. 105

11 Frontispiece to Thomas Heywood, *Nine Bookes of Various
History Concerninge Women* (1624). Reproduced by kind
permission of the Syndics of the Cambridge University
Library. 110

12 Page (after Samuel), *The Nine Living Muses of Great Britain*
(c. 1778). Engraving, 12.5 cm by 10 cm. In *Johnson's Ladies'
New and Polite Pocket Memorandum for 1778*. © The British
Museum. 112

13 Angelica Kauffman, *Self-Portrait in the Character of Painting
Embraced by Poetry* (1782). Oil on canvas. The Iveagh Bequest,
Kenwood. By kind permission of English Heritage. 120

14 G. S. and I. G. Facius (after Angelica Kauffman), *Sappho
Inspired by Love*. Published by Boydell, 1778. © The British
Museum. 121

Contributors

Kate Davies is Lecturer in English at the Centre for Eighteenth Century Studies at the University of York. She has published essays on Catharine Macaulay and on Emma Hamilton's 'attitudes' and is the co-editor of *Consuming the Past in Contemporary Culture* (Shaftesbury: Donhead, 1998). Her current projects include a critical reader on language and eighteenth-century ideas of empire, and a book on gender, republicanism and sentimentality in eighteenth-century Britain and America.

Elizabeth Eger is Research Fellow at the Warwick Eighteenth Century Centre, University of Warwick, working on The Luxury Project. She is editor of *Selected Works of Elizabeth Montagu* (London: Pickering & Chatto, 1999) and has contributed to *Women's Poetry in the Enlightenment*, ed. Isobel Armstrong and Virginia Blain (London: Macmillan, 1999). She is now writing a literary and cultural history of women's intellectual identity in the long eighteenth century: 'Living Muses: Women of Reason from Enlightenment to Romanticism'.

Markman Ellis is Senior Lecturer in the School of English and Drama, Queen Mary and Westfield College, University of London. He is the author of *The Politics of Sensibility* (Cambridge University Press, 1996), and *The History of Gothic Fiction* (Edinburgh University Press, 2000). He is currently working on a study of poetic genre and the representation of empire in the late eighteenth century.

Caroline Gonda is Newton Trust Lecturer in the Faculty of English and a Fellow of St. Catharine's College, Cambridge. Her publications include *Reading Daughters' Fictions 1709–1834: Novels and Society from Manley to Edgeworth* (Cambridge University Press, 1996), and articles on Sarah Scott, Mary Shelley, contemporary Scottish lesbian writing, and lesbian theory. She is currently working on a study of relations between poetry and narrative, c.1760–1830.

Charlotte Grant is a Fellow and Director of Studies in English at Jesus College, Cambridge. She is editor of the forthcoming *Flora*, vol. IV of

Literature and Science 1660–1832 (London: Pickering & Chatto), and is currently working on a book on the visual culture of sensibility.

Mary Jacobus, formerly Professor of English and Women's Studies, Cornell University, is now Professor of English at the University of Cambridge. She has written widely on Romantic literature, psycho-analysis and feminism. Her books include *Reading Women* (London: Methuen, 1986), *Romanticism, Writing and Sexual Difference* (Oxford: Clarendon, 1989) and *First Things* (New York and London: Routledge, 1995).

Gary Kelly is Professor of English at the University of Alberta, Canada. He has written widely on the Jacobin novel and women's writing. His books include *Revolutionary Feminism: The Mind and Career of Mary Wollstonecraft* (London: Macmillan, 1992) and *Women, Writing, and Revolution 1790–1827* (Oxford: Clarendon Press, 1993). He has recently acted as General Editor for *Bluestocking Feminism: Writings of the Bluestocking Circle*, 6 vols. (London: Pickering & Chatto, 1999).

Nigel Leask is a Fellow of Queens College, Cambridge and Lecturer in the English Faculty. He is the author of *The Politics of Imagination in Coleridge's Critical Thought* (Basingstoke: Macmillan, 1988), *British Romantic Writers and the East: Anxieties of Empire* (Cambridge: Cambridge University Press, 1992) and numerous articles on Romantic literature. He has recently completed a study of exotic travel writing and antiquarianism entitled ' "From an antique land": Romanticism, Colonialism, and the Curious Travel Account'.

Clíona Ó Gallchoir is a graduate of University College Dublin, and received her PhD from Trinity College, Cambridge. She is a lecturer in the department of English at University College Cork. She is co-editor, with Susan Manly, of Edgeworth's *Helen*, vol. IX of *The Novels and Selected Works of Maria Edgeworth* (London: Pickering and Chatto, 1999).

Sylvana Tomaselli is a Fellow of Hughes Hall, Cambridge and an affiliated lecturer in the History Faculty. As an intellectual historian working principally on the Enlightenment, she has written on a variety of subjects, including mind–body dualism, the self, political and population theories and the conjectural history of woman. 'Intolerance, the Virtue of Princes and Radicals', in Ole Grell and Roy Porter, eds., *Toleration in the Enlightenment* (Cambridge University Press, 1999), is her most recent publication.

Penny Warburton is completing a doctorate on 'Women writing on economics: aesthetics, utility and the economy, 1760–1833'. She has worked as a book reviewer, contributed to reference works on women writers, and has taught widely in the area of Romantic literature and eighteenth century studies at Cambridge University and other institutions.

Susan Wiseman is Reader in English at Birkbeck College, University of London. Her books include *Women, Writing, History: 1640–1740*, edited with Isobel Grundy (London: Batsford, 1992).

Preface and acknowledgements

The editors would like to thank all those involved in the preparation of this volume. We first worked together in organising a conference held in Cambridge in June 1996, 'Women and the Public Sphere, 1700–1830', and are grateful to all those who attended this event, where many of the following essays originated. We are also grateful to the Cambridge institutions which funded the conference: The Judith E. Wilson Fund, Faculty of English; King's College; Trinity College; and The MacArthur Foundation. Many individuals contributed to the conference and the ongoing dialogue it inspired: we would like to thank all our contributors to this volume, and also Chris Roulston, Leah Price, Charlotte Sussman and Emma Donoghue. Emma Francis, Nick Harrison, Anne Janowitz, Moynagh Sullivan and John Shaw all read versions of our introduction and offered invaluable advice and encouragement.

We are grateful to the Eighteenth Century Centre, University of Warwick; Jesus College and King's College, Cambridge; and University College Dublin and University College Cork, for providing supportive environments in which to work. We would also like to thank the following libraries and their librarians: the British Library; Cambridge University Library; the Huntington Library, USA; the London Library; University of Warwick Library; and Susan Bennett of the Royal Society of Arts library.

For permission to reproduce illustrations we would like to thank the Syndics of the Cambridge University Library; the British Museum; the Winn Family and the National Trust; Her Majesty Queen Elizabeth II; the Royal Society for the encouragement of Arts, Manufactures and Commerce; the National Portrait Gallery, London; and English Heritage.

Lastly, we would like to thank Jocelyn Pye, our copy-editor, and our editor, Linda Bree, for her encouragement and invaluable advice throughout the course of this project.

Introduction: women, writing and representation

Elizabeth Eger, Charlotte Grant,
Clíona Ó Gallchoir and Penny Warburton

> Women of literature are much more numerous of late than they
> were a few years ago. They make a class in society, they fill the
> public eye, and have acquired a degree of consequence and appro-
> priate character.
>
> Maria Edgeworth, 1795[1]

> To be pointed at – to be noticed & commented upon – to be sus-
> pected of literary airs – to be shunned, as literary women are, by
> the more unpretending of my own sex: & abhorred, as literary
> women are, by the more pretending of the other! – My dear, I
> would sooner exhibit as a rope dancer.
>
> Mary Brunton, 1810[2]

Women's place in the public sphere has been debated throughout history
and is still the subject of controversy. The language of public and private
spheres has been a central organising trope for women's historiography
and for feminist theory: indeed, Carole Pateman claims that the dichotomy between public and private is, 'ultimately, what the feminist movement is about'.[3] The categories of public and private have been
interpreted as equivalent to those of male and female and understood
in terms of an ideology of separate spheres.[4] Critics and historians have
frequently allowed this binary distinction to pass as quasi-natural and
somehow explanatory of the inequalities between men and women,
often neglecting the fact that it is born out of the commercial founda-
tions of modern society.[5]

Historicised accounts of the emergence of clearly differentiated
private and public realms locate the eighteenth century as a period of
transition, moving from a time of comparative freedom for women into
a world of separate spheres, in which men occupied the public sphere of
work while women became increasingly restricted to the private sphere
of the family. Historians Leonore Davidoff and Catherine Hall have

1

complicated this model, pointing out the importance of an ideology of domesticity for both sexes in constituting their class identity.[6] However, it is only very recently that there has been any focus on women's activity in the wider public sphere.[7] While the emergence of a literary and political public sphere has been seen as definitive of eighteenth-century culture, there has been remarkably little investigation of contemporary responses to its development and scant acknowledgement of women's contribution to its character. As Linda Colley has pointed out in her recent study of British nationhood during this period, separate sexual spheres were being increasingly prescribed in theory at one and the same time as they were being increasingly broken down in practice.[8] The aim of this volume is to attend to the complex history of the public/private distinction by focusing on women's relation to the public sphere between 1700 and 1830.[9] The contributors approach this question from a variety of angles, using literary and visual sources in their exploration of the sexual politics of writing and representation in an age of cultural expansion and political transition.

Our epigraphs from Maria Edgeworth and Mary Brunton were written towards the end of a period which witnessed a substantial rise in the number of women participating in an expanding print culture.[10] Edgeworth and Brunton both emphasise the visibility of women writers: for Edgeworth, they 'fill the public eye', whereas for Brunton, to publish involves the risk of being a spectacle, an 'exhibition'. By the beginning of the nineteenth century contemporary opinion was increasingly ambivalent towards women who were active in the literary public sphere. Whereas Brunton alludes to the dominant negative stereotypes of a 'public woman' (a rope dancer being only a few degrees removed from a prostitute), Edgeworth asserts that for women to be acknowledged publicly as writers is dignified and indicative of progress. These very different reactions to female publication raise issues of inclusion, visibility and agency that remain the subject of debate. We are still in the process of adjusting our eyes to a vision of the past very different from that which previously held sway, as history is rewritten to include the stories of women, to make them visible once more. Feminist historians and literary scholars have begun to assess the nature and impact of the female contribution to eighteenth-century culture, to education, journalism, the theatre, literature, politics and poetry. Women were often the leaders of intellectual networks of exchange.[11] While there is significant interest in their literary activity, women's contribution to the broader picture of cultural transformation has tended to be neglected; there remains a danger that their work is understood as occupying its own sphere of values, separate from the mainstream tradition. In focusing on women's relation to the public sphere, this volume aims to demonstrate the more radical potential of feminist scholarship to question received paradigms of knowledge, to inspire new methods of research and transform our perceptions of the past.[12]

The conventional critical notion of separate spheres, for example, immediately appears problematic and inaccurate if approached through the contemporary writings of women. Edgeworth and Brunton's descriptions of literary women are taken from published texts which demonstrate the overlap between public and private. Brunton's letter to Mrs. Izett was published in the preface to her novel *Emmeline*, written by her husband after her death in 1818. Edgeworth's text is presented as a collection of private letters between two gentlemen, but is clearly intended to reach a public audience interested in the question of female education. Elements of disguise and deprecation in the author's self-presentation suggest the tension surrounding her cultural authority. While this volume emphasises the role of women as producers of culture, it also explores their relationship to the public gaze; in doing so, it inevitably challenges any theoretical or interpretative model of the period which constructs the public and private as mutually exclusive categories.

THE PUBLIC SPHERE IN THEORY AND HISTORY

The period covered by this volume has been characterised as an age of grand narratives, often interpreted as the crucible of the modern age. Between 1700 and 1830 ideas of political representation and national identity were transformed, and the powers and scope of public authority redefined. While scholars have long explored the emergence of concepts of the self in this period, only recently have the gendered nature of such developments come to the fore. Political historians have started to analyse the gender assumptions within the intellectual and political structures of the period and to offer powerful new readings of women's political writings.[13] It is important to consider what politics and the public might have meant to women living in a society that severely restricted their legal and political representation.

Before discussing the relevance of historiographical debates over the 'public sphere' in practice and theory, it is perhaps useful to sketch a background to political notions of rights and representation in our period. Arguments over the nature of the British constitution stemmed from the impact of the Glorious Revolution of 1688, which thwarted the Catholic James II's attempts to establish an absolute monarchy. The invasion by William of Orange and subsequent change of ruler resulted in the creation of new constitutional, financial and religious settlements, all of which were driven by pragmatism but nevertheless established the broad principle of toleration and individual liberty. Eighteenth-century commentators generally saw the Revolution as a reassertion of historic liberties rather than a break with the past.[14] Whig historians viewed it as an important moment at which the rule of law and parliamentary government were extended and continued. As Paul Langford has written, the question of whether the Glorious Revolution could be repeated was a hotly disputed point: 'No government, even an unimpeachably Whig government, wished to encourage further Revolutions. Whig Churchmen played a notable part in rendering the Revolution a unique necessity, a freak in the history of freedom, dictated by the aberration of a popish, absolutist king. Oppositions preferred to maintain the status of the Revolution as living history, a perpetual warning to posterity and a precedent for similar action in future.'[15] At the centenary of the Revolution in 1788 the court of George III made no attempt to claim it for political purposes, and it was left to more radical opponents of the government to draw significance from the occasion.

Locke's *Two Treatises on Government*, published in 1689, provided an attempt to justify and analyse the revolution in retrospect. While the historical accuracy of his account of events is still disputed, his work marked an important departure in political and constitutional thought by focusing on contract rather than authority in his discussion of political rights. Locke was provoked to write his *Treatises* by the publication of Sir Robert Filmer's *Patriarcha, or the Natural Power of Kings* (published in 1680), an extreme statement of the view that a king's authority over his subjects was like that of a father over his family. Locke denied that anybody could exercise authority by right, arguing that a ruler must depend upon the trust invested in him by the political community, which could remove its trust if the ruler failed to comply with its interests. By placing sovereignty in the people, Locke moved beyond the norms of Whig thought, which remained governed by the relationship between the Lords, the Commons and the king. Several political theorists and philosophers of the twentieth century have traced the origins of civil society in Locke's contract theory (and in the thought of his seventeenth-century predecessors), which presented civil society as a universal realm which potentially includes all people.

Feminist political theorists, however, have taken issue with standard accounts of liberal thought which have excluded women from their story. Carole Pateman has pointed out the potential dangers of ignoring sexual difference in approaching political difference: 'Political theorists argue about the individual, and take it for granted that their subject matter concerns the public world, without investigating the way in which the "individual", "civil society" and "the public" have been constituted as patriarchal categories in opposition to womanly nature and the "private" sphere. The civil body politic created through the fraternal social contract is fashioned after only one of the two bodies of humankind.'[16] As she points out in her discussion of the seventeenth-century controversy over political right, women seized on the contradiction of an 'individualism' and a 'universalism' which insisted that women were born into subjection and their subjection was 'natural' and politically irrelevant.[17] In 1700, Mary Astell famously asked: 'If *all Men are born free*, how is it that all Women are born slaves?'[18]

Women were critical of the inequalities embedded in the secular notion of a civil society from its inception and early definition. By the time of the American Declaration of Independence and the French Declaration of the Rights of Man, new definitions of human equality and political freedom still failed to include women.[19] Despite the urgent rhetoric of progressive thinkers, the rights of man were not conceived of as universal. Although some argued that political rights should be extended to more and more of the male population, few countenanced the idea of women's rights. Mary Wollstonecraft's *Vindication of the Rights of Woman* argued that full citizenship should be extended to all. However, it would be over a century before women could exercise their right to vote. This volume aims to explore what 'representation' might mean to the constrained subject, and to try to perceive the 'public' through contemporary female eyes.

The nature and implications of such profound political transformation cannot be considered apart from transformations in the nature of the public. The period of the Enlightenment has been seen to embody a transitional ideology between a pre-industrial, aristocratic culture and an industrialised, commercialised culture, in which the idea of the public was inevitably contradictory and ambiguous. While in certain contexts the term 'public' was used in its current sense, to refer to a mass of citizens, it could also be used in its more classical form, to distinguish a body of educated people, usually men, from the mass of common people, 'the vulgar'. As Iain Pears notes, the term was used in both senses throughout the eighteenth century, and artists and writers were often faced with the problem of aiming their work simultaneously at two groups of people, aware of the benefits of addressing a wider, commercial public and yet anxious to retain the respect of the intellectual élite.[20] It might be argued that there was inevitably some convergence between these two senses of the 'public' and that a wider and more discerning reading public evolved in tandem with an explosion of journalistic activity.

Addison's contributions to his influential journal, *The Spectator* (1711–12), encouraged the idea that learning should be sociable and accessible to both sexes. He famously proposed that philosophy should be discussed in public: 'It was said of Socrates, that he brought Philosophy down from heaven, to inhabit among Men; and I shall be ambitious to have it said of me, that I have brought philosophy out of Closets and Libraries, Schools and Colleges, to dwell in Clubs and Assemblies, at Tea-Tables, and in Coffee-Houses.'[21] Addison describes scenes where men and women could meet and exchange ideas through the pursuit of conversation, then a highly sophisticated art of communication in which women's civilising role was often stressed. Women published guides to conversation which emphasised the moral and improving role of what Hannah More termed 'the noblest commerce of mankind'.[22] The essays in this volume implicitly chart a history of public spaces in which, among other things, the polite art of conversation was defined and contested – the coffee house, St James's Park, Vauxhall Gardens, Mrs Montagu's salon, the Society of Arts, the Royal Academy and the Parisian salon of Helen Maria Williams. The contributors explore women's representation in and of those public spaces. In diverse ways, they engage with and question the view that as the period progressed, British culture was increasingly predicated on the exclusion of women from a public sphere which assumed greater and greater significance as courtly and aristocratic power declined.[23] Our trajectory is from issues of visibility and scandal in part one, 'women in the public eye', through questions of improvement, virtue and morality raised by women's production and consumption of culture in 'Consuming arts', to the realm of intellectual endeavour in 'Learned ladies'. Here, discussions of the cultural authority of the Bluestockings and the phenomenon of a female political historian are followed by essays on 'Cosmopolitan intellectuals', which explore the role of translation and exchange between European intellectual movements in shaping ideas of nationhood. Women inevitably experienced tensions between their allegiances to their sex, nation and profession. The final part of the book, 'The female subject', addresses women's philosophical and political reflections on the nature of their place in the public sphere towards the end of our period, focusing on the culmination of female self-analysis in Mary Wollstonecraft's work of the 1790s.

This volume presents a rich and dynamic model of the relation between the public and the private. By highlighting the range and diversity of women's participation in the public sphere, it takes issue with the majority of theorists of the public sphere, who have tended to exclude women from their story. Jürgen Habermas's *The Structural Transformation of the Public Sphere – An Enquiry into a Category of Bourgeois Society* is perhaps the fullest and most influential account of the emergence, development and decline of a public sphere within early modern Europe.[24] Originally published in 1962, and conceived partly in reaction to the pessimism of the Adorno school towards the Enlightenment and the public use of reason, his account attempts to recover the benefits of public discourse and debate which resulted from the realisation of a bourgeois public sphere. It is both a historical and a sociological account in which we can read the seeds of his later project to determine the necessary conditions for democracy. The *Structural Transformation* was published in English in 1989, nearly thirty years after its original publication. It has already had a major impact within the fields of politics, history and feminist theory.[25] Habermas's work fuses disparate lines of enquiry into a remarkably powerful narrative of sociostructural transformation.[26]

Habermas defines the public sphere as a forum in which members of the public could meet with one another to debate rationally the affairs of state. He describes it as an intermediary space, between the intimate sphere of the family and the official sphere of the state – a space free from prejudice and separate from the government, in which authority was held up to public scrutiny and the 'common good' of the people was debated. In his paradigmatic account, Habermas places great emphasis on a number of new, mainly urban institutions such as the salons, coffee-houses and taverns that flourished in eighteenth-century society. While he acknowledges the presence of women in the public sphere as readers, his attitude to them is always ambiguous. At times he appears to welcome the gradual exclusion of women, as a necessary prelude to the process whereby debates within the republic of letters assumed an increasingly political function, as in the following discussion of English coffee-houses:

Critical debate ignited by works of literature and art was soon extended to include economic and political disputes, without any guarantee (such as was given in salons) that such discussions would be inconsequential, at least in the immediate context. The fact that only men were admitted to coffee-house society may have had something to do with this, whereas the style of the salon, like that of the rococo in general, was essentially shaped by women. Accordingly the women of London, abandoned every evening, waged a vigorous but vain struggle against the institution.[27]

The inaccuracy of Habermas's assumption that only men were admitted to the coffee-house is compounded by his assumption that female opinion was inconsequential whereas male opinion was of value to the public sphere. His allusion to salon culture is a necessary reminder that he adhered to a historical narrative in which the dominance of aristocratic models (and their implied accessibility to women) gave way to a society characterised by men of the professional and commercial middle classes. In developing his account, Habermas emphasises the role of male property-owners in the formation of the public sphere, omitting women altogether from its developments, as he does in his description of an idealised realm of print culture with clear political functions.

Habermas's useful description of the organisation of public space in modern life has also acted to constrain our vision of those spaces. Recent research has demonstrated the diverse ways in which women could own property in the period, enlarging our sense of their legal power.[28] There has also been greater acknowledgement of women's role in cementing civic virtue through their charitable work, an important aspect of public life, which reaches beyond the walls of the salon. Revisionary accounts of Habermas's work have criticised its unitary and disembodied account of the bourgeois public sphere. John Brewer and Lawrence Klein have both argued that it may be more accurate to think of public and private as being shifting, multivalent categories, rather than mutually exclusive. Brewer has demonstrated that the polarities of public and private are to a great extent interpenetrating, arguing, for example, that the letter form which we associate with the rise of the individual and the private self was also widely used to present political arguments in the public realm of print.[29] Lawrence Klein, pursuing a slightly different approach, locates a number of different eighteenth-century publics other than the state and Habermas's idealised realm of print culture, identifying a civic public sphere, an economic public sphere, and an associative public sphere of social, discursive and cultural production.[30] According to Klein, 'there is no one "public/private" distinction to which interpretation can confidently secure itself'. He concludes that 'the gender of these eighteenth-century "publics" cannot be determined by an a priori commitment to the publicity of men and the privacy of women'. However, like many critics of Habermas, Brewer and Klein seem in danger of merely multiplying alternative counter-public spheres, which inevitably remain in a competitive relation to the over-arching concept of the dominant bourgeois public sphere.[31]

Women in the public eye

Several essays in this work take issue with Habermas's rigid categorisation according to gender, complicating his interpretation of the relation between intimacy and publicity through detailed attention to the relation between gender and literary genre.[32] Markman Ellis opens part one of the volume with a forceful critique of Habermas's account of the coffee-house as a masculine space. He demonstrates how, in relying on nineteenth-century accounts of the eighteenth-century coffee-house, Habermas cemented an already nostalgic and gentrified model of its character. Through his careful readings of the memoirs of contemporary 'coffee-women', Ellis offers a very different model of coffee-house sociability from Habermas, in which the moral reform of manners is replaced by a world of scandal and gossip, purveyed by the problematic and frequently transgressive figure of the coffee-woman.

Habermas's focus on a morally useful model of public opinion neglects the more unruly and negative forces of the public, whose appetite for gossip was perhaps keener than its desire to effect political change. Caroline Gonda investigates women's visibility at the borders of respectability, asking whether, if 'bad women' are 'necessarily public', all women's public appearances are therefore shadowed or tainted. She addresses the phenomenon of two pairs of women in the 1750s: the Murderesses Blandy and Jeffries, and the beautiful Gunning sisters who were 'linked not only by their place in contemporary gossip, but also by their status as spectacle, as objects of the public gaze'. Gonda contrasts these notorious couples with the 'fair penitents' of the Magdalen Hospital whose titillating presence oscillated between conventional realms of public and private. Prostitutes, frequently termed 'public women', were 'reformed' and incarcerated in the Magdalen Hospital, where they remained, paradoxically, on public display. Gonda uses these examples to argue against any easy identification of women's presence in the public eye with an assumption of agency or achieved status.

However, it would be wrong to imply that women were only the object of public opinion. They could simultaneously act as the subject, object and predicate of gossip. As writers, women were also, of course, the manipulators of public opinion. Eliza Haywood, editor of *The Female Spectator*, was aware of the necessity of balancing instruction and entertainment in catering for her readers' needs:

I flattered myself that it might be in my power to be in some measure both useful and entertaining to the public; and this thought was so soothing to those remains of my vanity, not yet wholly extinguished in me, that I resolved to pursue it, and immediately began to consider by what method I should be most likely to succeed: To confine myself to any one subject, I knew could please but one kind of taste, and my ambition was to be as universally read as possible: from my observation of human nature, I found that curiosity had more or less a share in every breast; and my business, therefore, was to hit this reigning humour in such a manner, as that the gratification it should receive from being made acquainted with other people's affairs, should at the same time teach every one to regulate their own.[33]

Haywood's concern to 'hit the reigning humour' by providing gossip and current affairs without sacrificing the moral benefits of individual instruction shows a shrewd awareness of the potential pitfalls of public opinion.[34] Her effort to combine virtue and instruction with pleasure was matched in the reigning visual culture of her time. While Ellis and Gonda emphasise scandalous aspects of women in the public eye, Grant, Davies and Eger address the relation between moral virtue and visibility for the female sex.

Consuming arts

Although women who were deemed to have transgressed their proper social boundaries were often the targets of satire and gossip, in different contexts representations of women served to symbolise the civilising influence of cultural exchange, and thus their centrality to the progress of culture. Recent historical work has explored the emergence of a critical reading public and the wider consumption of culture in a commercial age.[35] The influence of civic humanism in art and letters has been given particular attention and has provided invaluable routes into thinking about the relation between art and society in this period. While several influential cultural and historical studies have emphasised the links between virtue, commerce and the arts in the eighteenth century, these accounts have tended to ignore women.[36] Only very recently have scholars turned their attention to the role of women in the formation of aesthetics during this period, stressing women's contribution, as the subjects and objects of representation, to an evolving national culture.[37] Representations of women in the visual arts were crucial to society's self-construction and self-perception.

Part two of the volume, 'Consuming arts', examines how women were seen to constitute elements of a virtuous and visible public. Charlotte Grant looks at the way in which both the early spaces for the public display of contemporary art in London, Vauxhall Gardens and the Foundling Hospital, negotiated issues of virtue and vice. She argues that in the early art institutions, anxiety surrounding representations of the female body is compounded by art's desire to represent itself as virtuous and distinct from the dangerous effeminating effects of luxury. She charts a split in the second half of the century: while the Royal Academy can be seen through Reynolds's *Discourses on Art* to have embraced a civic humanist distrust of commerce, the 'de-moralisation' of the luxury debate in works such as Hume's 'Of Luxury' of 1752 (retitled 'Of Refinements in the Arts' in 1758) is reflected in the transactions of the Society for the Encouragement of Arts, Manufacture and Commerce, which, from the 1750s, promoted women as producers of 'the polite arts'.

Elizabeth Eger also examines the links between culture, commerce and the representation of women in this period. She focuses on the contemporary women portrayed by the painter Richard Samuel in 1779 in *The Nine Living Muses of Great Britain*, 'an act of embodiment' which 'suggests in itself the rise of the woman writer's professional activity during the eighteenth century'. Eger discusses this large-scale allegorical conversation piece alongside contemporary accounts, including James Barry's *Letter to the Dilettanti Society* of 1798 and Hume's 'Of Refinement in the Arts', to suggest that 'the painting can be read in the context of a widespread concern to justify the growth of the arts in an increasingly commercial and imperialistic context'. Her essay suggests the richness and diversity of cultural capital created by women in this period.

Kate Davies takes up these themes of femininity, commerce and virtue in the context of constructions of women's role in the anti-slavery debates. She suggests that the ease with which abolition artefacts, such as poems, and, above all, Wedgwood's cameo of the supplicant slave, become objects of commercial desire, jeopardises women's ability to hold a purely 'moral purchase' on the anti-slavery debates. She argues that it is only with the abolition movement's decision to boycott the products of the slave trade that the discourse of abolition is able to free itself from the dangerous associations both of luxury and the feminised and rejected 'bastard sensibility'. Thus Davies demonstrates how the figure of the feminine shifts from embodying the benevolence of the anti-slavery lobby, through association with the discredited image of self-indulgent sensibility, to its 'embeddedness in the potential corruptions of commerce'. She argues that femininity is positioned by the language of abolition on the cusp of two notions of the private: namely, the sphere of commodity exchange and social labour and that other private sphere of familial, intimate, and what Habermas terms 'purely human' relations. Davies's analysis of Anna Barbauld's anti-slavery poem, *Epistle to William Wilberforce Esq.*, reveals the inherent tensions involved for the female poet in personifying commerce as a figure of corrupted femininity.

From our various discussions of the tensions between women's moral agency and visibility, we progress to an exploration of their self-conscious incursions into the public sphere as writers.

WRITING AND REPRESENTATION

As our epigraphs from the works of novelists Mary Brunton and Maria Edgeworth illustrate, then, as now, women writers were often seen as a distinct class, a literary breed apart. Brunton's remarks indicate the extent to which the phenomenon of women's writing and their increasingly *self-conscious* cultural activity was greeted with new injunctions against immodesty and unfeminine public display. The self-consciousness of women's activity is evident in Edgeworth's remarks, which speak of literary women as a 'class', with 'consequence' and a definable 'character'.

The emergence of notable numbers of women writers in this period has been acknowledged in recent decades, and since the 1980s important critical work has reshaped the familiar map of eighteenth-century and Romantic culture. It is understandable that much of this work has focused on the novel, given that, as Jane Spencer showed in her ground-breaking study *The Rise of the Woman Novelist*, in the case of the novel women were the dominant force in the marketplace as readers and writers.[38] The strong critical association of women and the novel in the eighteenth century has tended, however, not just to obscure their activity in other media and genres, but to determine interpretations of their cultural activity and social position. Critics such as Spencer and Nancy Armstrong who have worked extensively on women novelists are concerned with the connections between literature and the history of sexuality. Both critics stress that the new cultural power of women beginning in the mid-eighteenth century was part of the consolidation of middle-class hegemony. Although women writers gained acceptance and prestige, becoming the spokeswomen for cultural change, these critics argue that they did so only by constructing a discourse that 'reformed' women by locking them into a 'disciplinary' domestic sphere. Catherine Gallagher has summarised this approach:

Armstrong identifies a discursive break prior to the 1740s: on the 'before' side is the aristocratic model of woman, political, embodied, superficial and amoral; on the 'after' side is the middle-class model, domestic, dis-embodied, equipped with a deep interiority and ethical subjectivity.[39]

The definition of the domestic woman writer is extended into the Romantic period by Anne Mellor, who argues that figures as diverse as Anna Barbauld, Felicia Hemans and Mary Shelley exhibit an 'ethics of care' in their writings.[40]

Conscious that critical narratives which rely on the novel tend to reinforce the separation of domestic and public spheres, this volume stresses the diversity of women's literary and broader cultural endeavour, emphasising genres and areas which have not received much attention in the past, such as memoirs, history-writing, criticism, publishing, translation and correspondence. This focus is indebted to the work of historians, literary critics and anthologists who have begun to chart the ways in which women's active contribution – as writers, readers, patrons, printers and publishers – was integral to the steady rise of a professional print culture and the re-negotiation of the role of the writer in relation to a commercial public. Numerous anthologies of women's writing in the period have appeared, generating critical interest in their formative contribution to the development of different literary genres.[41] Anthologies of poetry by women, in particular, have brought to light the diversity and wealth of talent previously obscured from view. Andrew Ashfield, in the preface to his *Romantic Women Poets*, points out that 1,402 first editions by women were published between 1770 and 1832.[42]

Harriet Guest has argued persuasively that professionalisation of their talents offered women the possibility to reclaim respectability for the notion of virtuous femininity, which had gained the taint of corruption in the vogue for consuming the novels and fashions of the culture of sensibility.[43] While women were largely denied property rights and treated as property in the marriage market, their writing was at least one thing they could own. Historians Jan Fergus and Jamie Ferrar Thaddeus argue that women's entry into writing was primarily an economic choice:

Of the few professions open to women, acting was the most lucrative, but it was self-promoting and flamboyant – and hence morally suspect. Writing alone offered the promise of decent wages without demanding a lengthy apprenticeship or even a remarkable genius – and a writer's gentility might survive relatively undamaged.[44]

Individual cases may be cited as exceptions or counter-examples, but the statement is borne out not simply by the fact that women such as Mary Wollstonecraft, Hannah More, Charlotte Smith, Elizabeth Inchbald, and Elizabeth Carter all relied on their literary earnings, but also by the views they expressed with regard to their writing. Catharine Macaulay's pamphlet, *A Modest Plea for the Property of Copyright* (1774), makes explicit the link between the professionalisation of writing and the emergence of a middle class increasingly determined to assert independence.

At the time Macaulay wrote there were four chief methods by which authors published their works: subscription, fee for limited copyright, profit-sharing, and publishing on commission (whereby the author assumed responsibility for repaying the capital if the book did not make a profit).[45] She argues for perpetual copyright partly on the grounds that otherwise 'independent men not born to estates will be prevented from using their talents for the benefit of mankind' and that none would write except 'men in opulence, and men in dependence'.[46] She urges the reader to support the right of authors to perpetual ownership of their works as a vital means of subsistence: 'If a man is deprived of the necessary lucrative advantage by the right of property in his own writings, is he to starve, or live in penury, whilst he is exerting, perhaps, vain endeavours to serve a people who do not desire his services?'[47] She ends by appealing to Lord Camden to 'settle the lucrative advantage of authors for their writings on a permanent footing; and thus to encourage useful literature, by rendering it convenient to the circumstances of men of independent tempers to employ their literary abilities in the service of their country'.[48]

Recent research has revealed that women were also active in the trades related to a rising professional literary (and literate) class: Anne Yearsley, the 'milkwoman poet', set up a circulating library; Susanna Duncombe, daughter of the artist Joseph Highmore and a close friend of Elizabeth Carter and Hester Chapone, was an engraver and book illustrator;[19] others were involved in the book trade as printers and publishers.[50] Women played an important role in extending literacy levels over the course of the century, demonstrating profound concern for education in a broader social context.[51] Women whose work features in this volume, such as Anna Barbauld, Catharine Macaulay and Hannah More, published a series of innovatory educational writings which built on the moral teachings of their Bluestocking predecessors. Macaulay's essay on copyright reveals that imperatives which were in some sense peculiar to women writers served and advanced a literary culture which was becoming increasingly conscious of its social role and national context. Writers who can earn income from their work, it is implied, will be directed towards 'usefulness'; their talents are 'to benefit mankind', and, even more tellingly, will be 'in the service of their country'. As we have suggested, the professionalisation of writing was of immediate material concern to many women. Equally crucial was the claim that the public intervention of women *in particular* by means of writing was conducive to public virtue.

'*Learned ladies: from Bluestockings to cosmopolitan intellectuals*'

What was the nature of female intellectual authority in our period? Despite the manner in which some feminists have cast the Enlightenment as a monolithic patriarchal movement,[52] there is strong reason to suspect that what we have come to regard as the Enlightenment public sphere was in fact constituted and defined by women as well as men.[53] As several historians have recently reminded us, the Enlightenment was not only an intellectual configuration but also a living world, whose ideas varied according to the social, national and economic conditions of its life.[54]

Gary Kelly opens part three with a contribution on 'Bluestocking feminism', which describes the ways in which women of the Bluestocking circle sought to remodel intellectual culture in order that women could achieve participation. In this activity, they coincided with a movement towards the advancement of moral virtue and 'gentry capitalism'. Kelly argues that this search for new forms of intellectual exchange and self-fashioning led to an experimentation with literary forms which has not received adequate recognition. He provides a useful survey of the didactic and critical writings of the Bluestockings, arguing further that their work was appropriated and institutionalised in a reprogrammed ideology of domesticity in the aftermath of the French Revolution. Kelly foregrounds a compelling instance of women's own promotion of a modernising project, which in this case was predicated on mixed-gender sociability.

From the social politics of Bluestocking assemblies, we move to women's intervention in the political sphere. Susan Wiseman explores the ambiguity inherent in women's relationship to discourses of republicanism, offering a timely critique of contemporary studies of the influence of civic humanism in constructing a public sphere of civic virtue.[55] Wiseman argues that Macaulay's career indicates the dynamic relationship between public and private, inviting us to complicate Habermas's sense of the public sphere as demarcated by critical reason used by 'private people' whose participation was guaranteed by propertied citizenship. She shows how Macaulay's particular brand of republicanism shaped her eight-volume *History of England from the Accession of James I to that of the Brunswick Line* (1763–83). Arguing that the close if disavowed relationship that existed between history and its 'shadows' (i.e. memoirs, secret histories, counter-histories) provides a means of reading the relationship between Catharine Macaulay and the public sphere, Wiseman charts the shift from respect to denigration in public responses to Macaulay's life and work. She concludes that in the history of Macaulay's career we see the political sphere acting harshly to exclude a hybrid figure created by its own confusions and pressures.

Nigel Leask and Clíona Ó Gallchoir each address the figure of the cosmopolitan female intellectual, exploring the conflicting relationship between gender, nation and the literary sphere in the decades following the French Revolution, revealing the complex ways in which women could represent their country or, in the case of Helen Maria Williams, capitalise on their position of exile. Nigel Leask explores a complementary meeting of actual and imagined public spaces, concentrating on Williams's translation of the Prussian traveller Alex Von Humboldt's *Personal Narrative of Travels to the Equinoctial Regions of the New Continent* (1814–29) into English, a project on which she worked for more than a decade. Leask argues that in addition to translating Humboldt, Williams played a crucial part in the conception and production of his work in her role as Parisian *salonnière* and proprietor of one of France's major printing businesses. Leask suggests that claims of the wholesale exclusion of women from public life in France following the Revolution fail to take account of women such as Williams, who continued to exercise an important cultural role. Whilst acknowledging the strength of the gendered representation of translation in the period, Leask asserts that 'the picture of post-revolutionary Williams which is emerging is hardly that of a woman confined to the domestic sphere'. He considers the literary relationship between Williams and Humboldt in relation to the revision of sensibility in the Romantic period, the role of gender in the constitution of knowledge, and the discourse of Romantic travel narratives.

Clíona Ó Gallchoir examines Maria Edgeworth's responses to the life and work of the French writer Stéphanie-Félicité de Genlis, who initially provided a model of the woman writer for Edgeworth, but who in the Revolutionary period became associated with sexual and political scandal and intrigue. Edgeworth's *Letters for Literary Ladies* (1795), which is structured as a correspondence between two gentlemen and alludes specifically both to Burke's *Reflections on the Revolution in France*, and Wollstonecraft's *Vindication of the Rights of Woman*, has been regarded as a lukewarm defence of women's rights to learning and to publish. Ó Gallchoir argues that Edgeworth had a particular stake in maintaining an ideal of Enlightenment cosmopolitanism in an increasingly nationalistic age. The construction of national character, which could be deployed usefully by British women, was not available to the Anglo-Irish Edgeworth. In *Letters for Literary Ladies* and subsequent works she sought to balance the rejection of improper interference in the 'masculine' sphere of politics with an argument in favour of women's interest in and contribution to matters outside the narrowly defined private sphere. Ó Gallchoir's account of Maria Edgeworth engages with the gender implications of national identity and reveals that women writers were aware of the potential limitations of the emergent ideology of national character in so far as it prescribed 'appropriate' behaviour for women and confined them to a purely domestic sphere.

The female subject

The essays in part four draw together evidence, implicit throughout *Women and the Public Sphere*, which problematises the identification of the private with the domestic sphere and the family. Sylvana Tomaselli and Penny Warburton both examine female interventions into the eighteenth-century philosophical and political discussions about the nature and scope of the public domain. Tomaselli contends that the family has always been a subject of central significance within the different traditions of political writing from the conjectural history to the female biography. Moreover, she argues that the family was of particular importance to Mary Wollstonecraft. According to Tomaselli, Wollstonecraft called for a utopian future state in which there would be no separation between the spheres of public and private; instead, within a mixed society both men and women would carry out patriotic, civic duties. In practice, for most women, this would entail a role as enlightened and nurturing mothers who would raise their children into decent citizens. Thus the family is of central concern to Wollstonecraft's political agenda, an argument which gains importance if one considers the later role of the family in political rhetoric – whether in the nineteenth century's advocation of the domestic or in recent battles between left and right.

Warburton's essay takes issue with Habermas's description of the political public sphere as one which legally and factually excluded women. She argues that Elizabeth Hamilton's reflections on public opinion, formulated via a critique of Adam Smith's *Theory of Moral Sentiments*, form one example of a specifically female engagement with the political. Through a series of close readings Warburton shows how for Hamilton, dismayed by a perceived decline in public standards of morality, conscience cannot be imposed from within by any 'impartial spectator' but must be enforced from without by the laws of God, the only just tribunal.

Finally Mary Jacobus explores Habermas's opposition between intimacy and indiscretion, arguing that while epistolarity may channel subjectivity towards publicity, it equally tends to unsettle assumptions about the discursive relations of private and public spheres. Using the example of Wollstonecraft's *Letters to Imlay* she shows how letters can become a site of fictional instability in which, far from being instruments of self-knowledge, they uphold illusions at any cost, even that of suicide.

It is appropriate that the volume closes with a fresh look at Mary Wollstonecraft, whose *Vindication of the Rights of Woman* is perhaps the most famous statement of woman's place in society for our period. In it, Wollstonecraft makes use of literary and philosophical texts in marshalling her argument, referring directly to her female precursors, including the educational works of Macaulay, Barbauld and Hester Chapone.[56] She addressed an audience aware of a female literary tradition. One of the intentions of this volume is to suggest new approaches to Wollstonecraft, and the *Vindication* in particular, by offering a fuller sense of its cultural context. Mary Wollstonecraft saw the condition of women as the true and only starting point of political and social change. Two centuries after her death, the relationship between the civic and intimate spheres of life remains an unresolved subject of debate.

NOTES

1 Maria Edgeworth, *Letters for Literary Ladies*, ed. Claire Connolly (London: Everyman, 1993), p. 7.
2 Mary Brunton, from a letter to Mrs. Izett (1810) quoted in her husband's preface to her posthumously published novel, *Emmeline* (Edinburgh: Manners and Miller, 1819), p. xxxvi.
3 Carole Pateman, 'Feminist Critiques of the Public/Private Dichotomy', in *The Disorder of Women: Democracy, Feminism and Political Theory* (Cambridge: Polity Press, 1989), p. 118.
4 For a useful and stimulating discussion of these issues, see Leonore Davidoff, 'Regarding some "Old Husbands' Tales": Public and Private in Feminist History', in *Worlds Between: Historical Perspectives on Gender and Class* (Cambridge: Polity, 1995). See also Amanda Vickery, 'Golden Age to Separate Spheres: A Review of the Categories and Chronology of Women's History', *Historical Journal* 36. 2 (1993), 383–414.
5 See Joan B. Landes, ed., *Feminism, the Public and the Private* (Oxford and New York: Oxford University Press, 1998). In her introduction to this valuable collection of essays, Landes points out that there has been a lively debate between those who attributed the public/private split to capitalism and the modern organization of society and those, like Sherry Ortner and Michelle Zimbalist Rosaldo, who saw the division as a feature of all human societies. See Michelle Zimbalist Rosaldo, 'Woman, Culture and Society: A Theoretical Overview', in Michelle Zimbalist Rosaldo and Louise Lamphere, eds., *Women, Culture and Society* (Stanford, Calif.: Stanford University Press, 1974). For a contrasting view see Juliet Mitchell, *Women's Estate* (New York: Pantheon, 1972).
6 Leonore Davidoff and Catherine Hall, *Family Fortunes: Men and Women of the Middle Class, 1780–1850* (London: Hutchinson, 1987).
7 Historians are beginning to investigate women's political agency during this period. See, for example, Linda Colley, *Britons: Forging the Nation 1707–1837* (London: Pimlico, 1994), chapter 6: 'Womanpower', pp. 237–83; Amanda Foreman, *Georgiana, Duchess of Devonshire* (London: HarperCollins, 1998); Kathryn Gleadle and Sarah Richardson, eds., *The Power of the Petticoat: Women in British Politics, 1760–1860* (Basingstoke: Macmillan, 2000); and Hannah Barker and Elaine Chalus, eds., *Gender in Eighteenth-Century England: Roles, Representations and Responsibilities* (Harlow: Longman, 1997).
8 Colley, *Britons*, p. 250.
9 Ludmilla Jordanova describes the public/private distinction 'as an artefact whose long life history requires careful examination'. Quoted in Davidoff, 'Old Husbands' Tales', p. 227.
10 Moira Ferguson has described the rate of increase in publication by women in English between 1660 and 1800 as 'a major cultural phenomenon'. See John W. Yolton et al., eds., *The Blackwell Companion to the Enlightenment* (Oxford: Blackwell, 1991), pp. 294–300. See also Vivien Jones, ed., *Women and Literature in Britain, 1700–1800* (Cambridge: Cambridge University Press, 2000).

11 In the French context, see the work of Dena Goodman, 'Enlightenment Salons: the Convergence of Female and Philosophic Ambitions', *Eighteenth Century Studies* 22 (1998–9), 329–50. See also The Folger Collective on Early Women Critics, eds., *Women Critics 1660–1820* (Bloomington and Indianapolis: Indiana University Press, 1997).

12 See Martha Nussbaum, 'Through the Prism of Gender: How Scholarship about Women's Lives is Changing our Understanding of the Past – and the Present', *The Times Literary Supplement*, 20 March 1998, pp. 3–4.

13 See Hilda Smith, ed., *Women Writers and the Early Modern Political Tradition* (Cambridge: Cambridge University Press, 1998). See also Anna Clark, 'Gender and Politics in the Long Eighteenth Century: A Review Essay', *History Workshop Journal* 48 (Autumn 1999), 252–7.

14 See John Miller, *The Glorious Revolution*, 2nd edn (Longman: London and New York, 1997).

15 Paul Langford, *A Polite and Commercial People: England 1727–1783* (Oxford: Clarendon Press, 1989), p. 681.

16 Carole Pateman, 'The Fraternal Social Contract', in John Keane, ed., *Civil Society and the State, New European Perspectives* (London and New York: Verso, 1988), pp. 101–29, p. 102. See also her longer study of the origin of political right and contract theory, *The Sexual Contract* (Cambridge: Polity Press, 1988).

17 Pateman, 'The Fraternal Social Contract', p. 108.

18 Mary Astell, *Some Reflections Upon Marriage*, in *Political Writings*, ed. Patricia Springborg (Cambridge: Cambridge University Press, 1996), p. 18.

19 See Marilyn Butler, ed., *Burke, Paine, Godwin and the Revolution Controversy* (Cambridge: Cambridge University Press, 1984).

20 See Yolton et al., eds., *The Blackwell Companion to the Enlightenment*, p. 431.

21 *The Spectator* 10, in Donald F. Bond, ed., *The Spectator*, 5 vols. (Oxford: Oxford University Press, 1965), vol. I, p. 44.

22 Hannah More, 'Bas Bleu, or Conversation. Addressed to Mrs Vesey', *Selected Writings of Hannah More*, ed., Robert Hole (London: Pickering and Chatto, 1996), p. 32, line 251. See also Hester Chapone, 'On Conversation', *The Works of Mrs Chapone, containing Miscellanies in Prose and Verse* (Dublin, 1775), vol. II, essay 2. For an interesting discussion of women's role in shaping the art of conversation, see Lawrence Klein, 'Gender, Conversation and the Public Sphere', in Judith Still and Michael Worton, eds., *Textuality and Sexuality* (Manchester: Manchester University Press, 1993), pp. 100–15.

23 Our focus on urban spaces implicitly raises a question about the nature of women's access to the public. Was it more difficult for women to participate in the public sphere away from the town? Recent work by social historians would suggest not, although there are interesting contrasts to be made and more research is required in order to draw any conclusions. See John Brewer, *The Pleasures of the Imagination: English Culture in the Eighteenth Century* (London: HarperCollins, 1997), part 6, 'Province and Nation', and Amanda Vickery, *The Gentleman's Daughter: Women's Lives in Georgian England* (New Haven: Yale University Press, 1998).

24 Jürgen Habermas, *The Structural Transformation of the Public Sphere: An Inquiry into a Category of Bourgeois Society*, trans. Thomas Burger (Cambridge: Polity Press, 1992). Habermas wrote the work as his 'Habilitationschrift' (post-doctoral thesis), and it was originally published in German under the title *Strukturwandel der Öffentlichkeit.*

25 See for example, Craig Calhoun, ed., *Habermas and the Public Sphere* (Boston: Massachusetts Institute of Technology, 1992); Bruce Robbins, ed., *The Phantom Public Sphere* (Minneapolis and London: University of Minnesota Press, 1993); *Eighteenth Century Studies* 29. 1 (1995); Johanna Meehan, ed., *Feminists read Habermas – Gendering the Subject of Discourse* (London: Routledge, 1995).

26 See Thomas McCarthy's introduction to *The Structural Transformation of the Public Sphere*, pp. xi–xiv.

27 Habermas, *The Structural Transformation of the Public Sphere*, p. 33.

28 See Susan Staves, *Married Women's Separate Property in England, 1660–1833* (Cambridge, Mass. and London: Harvard University Press, 1989) and Amy Erickson, *Women and Property in Early Modern England* (London: Routledge, 1993).

29 John Brewer, 'This, That and the Other: Public, Social and Private in the Seventeenth and Eighteenth Centuries', in *Shifting the Boundaries – Transformation of the Languages of Public and Private in the Eighteenth Century*, eds., Dario Castiglione and Lesley Sharpe (Exeter: University of Exeter Press, 1995).

30 See Lawrence E. Klein, 'Gender and the Public/Private Distinction in the Eighteenth Century: Some Questions About Evidence and Analytic Procedure', in *Eighteenth Century Studies* 29 (1995), 97–109.

31 See, for example, Anne Mellor, 'Joanna Baillie and the Counter-Public Sphere', in *Studies in Romanticism* 33 (Winter 1994), pp. 559–67.

32 See Kate Davies's analysis of female abolitionist literature and Mary Jacobus's acute exploration of the ways in which epistolarity unsettles assumptions about the discursive relations between private and public spheres. For an incisive overview of the feminist critique of Habermas, see Joan Landes, 'The Public and the Private Sphere: A Feminist Reconsideration', in Meehan, ed., *Feminists Read Habermas*, pp. 91–116.

33 Eliza Haywood, *The Female Spectator* (London, 1748), p. 3.

34 Her important contribution to the journalistic culture of her time also belies the masculine model of the press offered by Habermas, whose 'world of letters' only vaguely acknowledges female readers and excludes women writers altogether. See Ros Ballaster et al., *Women's Worlds: Ideology, Femininity and the Woman's Magazine* (London: Macmillan, 1991), and Iona Italia, 'Philosophers, Knight-Errants, Coquettes and Old Maids: Gender and Literary Self-Consciousness in the eighteenth-century Periodical (1690–1765)', (unpublished PhD dissertation, University of Cambridge, 1997).

35 See, for example, Neil McKendrick, John Brewer and J. H. Plumb, eds., *The*

Birth of a Consumer Society: The Commercialisation of Eighteenth-Century England (Bloomington: Indiana University Press, 1982); Anne Bermingham, 'Elegant Females and Gentleman Connoisseurs: The Commerce in Culture and Self-Image in Eighteenth-Century England', in Anne Bermingham and John Brewer, eds., *The Consumption of Culture 1600–1800. Image, Object, Text* (London and New York: Routledge, 1995), pp. 489–514; John Brewer, *The Pleasures of the Imagination: English Culture in the Eighteenth Century* (London: HarperCollins, 1997).

36 See, for example, John Barrell, *The Political Theory of Painting from Reynolds to Hazlitt: 'The Body of the Public'* (New Haven and London: Yale University Press, 1986); Istvan Hont and Michael Ignatieff, eds., *Wealth and Virtue: The Shaping of Political Economy in the Scottish Enlightenment* (Cambridge: Cambridge University Press, 1983); and David Solkin, *Painting for Money: The Visual Arts and the Public Sphere in Eighteenth-Century England* (London and New Haven: Yale University Press, 1993).

37 Robert Jones, *Gender and the Social Formation of Taste in Eighteenth-Century Britain* (Cambridge: Cambridge University Press, 1998); Marcia Pointon, *Strategies for Showing. Women, Possession, and Representation in English Visual Culture, 1665–1800* (Oxford: Oxford University Press, 1997).

38 Jane Spencer, *The Rise of the Woman Novelist: From Aphra Behn to Jane Austen* (Oxford and New York: Oxford University Press, 1986).

39 Catherine Gallagher, *Nobody's Story: The Vanishing Acts of Women Writers in the Marketplace, 1670–1820* (Berkeley: University of California Press, 1994), p. xx.

40 Anne Mellor, *Romanticism and Gender* (New York and London: Routledge, 1993).

41 Andrew Ashfield, ed., *Romantic Women Poets, 1770–1838* (Manchester: Manchester University Press, 1995), and *Romantic Women Poets, 1788–1848*, vol. II (Manchester and New York: Manchester University Press, 1998); Jennifer Breen, ed., *Women Romantic Poets, 1785–1832: An Anthology* (London: Everyman, 1992); Paula Feldman, ed., *British Women Poets of the Romantic Era: An Anthology* (Baltimore: Johns Hopkins University Press, 1997); The Folger Collective on Early Women Critics, eds., *Women Critics 1660–1820* (Bloomington and Indianapolis: Indiana University Press, 1995); Roger Lonsdale, ed., *The Oxford Book of Eighteenth-Century Women Poets* (Oxford: Oxford University Press, 1989); Jerome McGann, ed., *The New Oxford Book of Romantic Period Verse* (Oxford: Oxford University Press, 1993); Janet Todd, ed., *A Wollstonecraft Anthology* (Cambridge: Polity Press, 1989); Robert W. Uphaus and Gretchen M. Foster, eds., *The 'Other' Eighteenth Century: English Women of Letters, 1660–1800* (East Lansing: Colleagues Press, 1991). See also Elizabeth Eger, 'Fashioning a Female Canon: Eighteenth-Century Women Poets and the Politics of the Anthology', in Isobel Armstrong and Virginia Blain, eds., *Women's Poetry in the Enlightenment: The Making of a Canon, 1730–1820* (London: Macmillan, 1999), pp. 201–15.

42 Andrew Ashfield, ed., *Romantic Women Poets 1770–1838: An Anthology* (Manchester: Manchester University Press, 1995).

43 Harriet Guest, 'The Dream of a Common Language: Hannah More and Mary Wollstonecraft', *Textual Practice* 9.2 (1995), 303–23.

44 Jan Fergus and Janice Farrar Thaddeus, 'Women, Publishers, and Money, 1790–1820', *Studies in Eighteenth-Century Culture* 17 (1987), 191–207, p. 191.

45 See Terry Belanger, 'Publishers and Writers in Eighteenth-Century England', in Isabel Rivers, ed., *Books and their Readers in Eighteenth-Century England* (New York: St. Martin's Press, 1982), pp. 5–25.

46 Catharine Macaulay, *A Modest Plea for the Protection of Copyright* (Bath: Edward and Charles Dilly, London, 1774) p. 37. For an excellent discussion of Macaulay's political writings see Susan Staves, '"The Liberty of a She-Subject of England": Rights Rhetoric and the Female Thucydides', *Cardozo Studies in Law and Literature* 2 (1989), 161–83.

47 Macaulay, *A Modest Plea*, p. 40.

48 Macaulay, *A Modest Plea*, p. 46.

49 See the entry on Duncombe (1725–1812) by Jaqueline Riding in *Dictionary of Women Artists*, ed. Delia Gaze, 2 vols. (London and Chicago: Fitzroy Dearborn Publishers, 1997), vol. 1, pp. 473–5. Dunscombe's husband was John Duncombe, author of *The Feminead, or Female Genius, A Poem* (1757), which is discussed in chapter four.

50 Recent research is uncovering their extensive involvement in all areas of the literary marketplace. See, for example, Tamara L. Hunt, 'Elizabeth Nutt: An Eighteenth-Century London Publisher', *Antiquarian Book Monthly* (December 1996), 20–4; and Paula McDowell, *Women of Grub Street: Press, Politics, and Gender in the Literary Marketplace, 1678–1730* (Oxford: Clarendon Press, 1998).

51 See Vivien Jones's indispensable anthology, *Women in the Eighteenth Century: Constructions of Femininity* (London: Routledge, 1990), chapter 3: 'Education'.

52 See Pauline Johnson, 'Feminism and the Enlightenment', *Radical Philosophy* 63 (1993), 3–13.

53 See Barbara Taylor, 'Work in Progress: Feminism and the Enlightenment, 1650–1850. Research Agenda for a Comparative History', *History Workshop Journal* 47 (Spring 1999) 261–72.

54 See Dorinda Outram, *The Enlightenment* (Cambridge: Cambridge University Press, 1995); Ludmilla Jordanova and Peter Hulme, eds., *The Enlightenment and Its Shadows* (London: Routledge, 1990); and Roy Porter and M. Teich, eds., *The Enlightenment in National Context* (Cambridge: Cambridge University Press, 1981).

55 J. G. A. Pocock, *The Machiavellian Moment* (Princeton and London: Princeton University Press, 1975). See also his *Virtue, Commerce and History* (Cambridge: Cambridge University Press, 1985).

56 Wollstonecraft referred to Barbauld's essays in a positive sense, as well as to the notorious example of her poem 'To a Lady, with some Painted Flowers'. She also included several of Barbauld's short moral tales for children in her *Female Reader* (1789).

PART I

Women in the public eye

Coffee-women, 'The Spectator' and the public sphere in the early eighteenth century

Markman Ellis

The coffee-house has a privileged status in accounts by historians and sociologists of the early eighteenth century, in which it figures as the paradigmatic social institution of the profound and various transformations in English society in this period. The most significant argument is that advanced in Jürgen Habermas's *The Structural Transformation of the Public Sphere* (1962, translated into English 1989), an account which has been repeated and elaborated by an influential range of critics in the Anglophone world, such as Eagleton, Hohendahl, and Stallybrass and White.[1] In Habermas's account, the public sphere is founded in its simple accessibility to individuals, who come together without hierarchy in an equality of voice. He stresses the role of 'new institutions' in the formation of the bourgeois public sphere, and identifies the coffee-house as its first, and to some extent paradigmatic, institution. Through their discussions, first of literature and later of news and politics, the individuals who assemble in the coffee-house come to form a new public culture. Habermas sees the new moral essays and literary criticism associated with periodicals like *The Spectator* as central to this discursivity. The coffee-house encourages such discussion through its institutional and spatial character, by facilitating a social interaction that disregards status, fosters the toleration of a broad range of discussion, and is accessible to all. As many critics have suggested, Habermas's account does not pay sufficient attention to the exclusionary mechanisms that are simultaneously at work within the public sphere, which do not allow the participation of the greater mass of the population: the lowest stations of life and women.[2] Here the coffee-house is again a curiously apt example, Habermas finds, because it too was not ordinarily available to these majorities. The coffee-house was 'shaped', in Habermas's term, by the sociability of men, and 'the fact that only men were admitted to the coffee-house society may have had something to do with' the extension

of coffee-house debate to include not 'inconsequential economic and
political disputes'.[3] As the lived experience of women was excluded, the
universality that Habermas accords to the public sphere was largely conceptual. Women are instead confined to the 'private sphere', attached to
the house, regulated by a domestic ideology under the mastery of the
husband and the father. The coffee-house, to contemporaries, was one
of the most characteristic aspects of eighteenth-century London,
although as they noted, it was also an innovation. Anthony Hilliar's
fictional Arab visitor to London, Ali-Mohammed Hadgi, remarked that
the English 'represent these coffee-houses as the most agreeable things
in *London*' – although he himself found them 'loathsome, full of smoak,
and much crowded'.[4] Henri Misson, a French traveller, in London in
1698, remarked that the coffee-houses, which were 'very numerous in
London, are extremely convenient. You have all Manner of News there:
You have a good Fire, which you may sit by as long as you please: you
have a Dish of Coffee; you meet your Friends for the Transaction of
Business, and all for a penny, if you don't care to spend more.'[5] As
Misson emphasises, the London coffee-house was a business, which
served coffee and provided newspapers for its customers, at a certain
level of comfort and at a price to entice them to return. The manner in
which they did this was notable, however. Coffee-houses specialised in
developing a particular type of sociability. Customers were attracted not
only by the beverage, but by the prospect of other like-minded men in a
convivial social space. Contemporaries argued that the coffee-house
inculcated a virtuous model of sociability through its discursive regime:
'Good Manners and commendable Humours are here infused into Men
by the contemplation of the Deformity of their contrarie's.'[6] Contemporary visual representations in or of coffee-houses reinforce this
picture. The most widely reproduced image, 'Interior of a London
Coffee House' (c. 1705) demonstrates how the architecture established
and confirmed the sociability of the coffee-houses.[7] The coffee-room is
here portrayed as a single large space with long communal tables round
which the clients sat on benches, although other images depict the provision of more private booths. The assembled men appear to be conversing over the news-sheets: conversation competes with private
reading or writing. Around them work the coffee-boys, or waiters, taking
the coffee-pots from the fire to the customers and fetching clay pipes
from a chest. Presiding over the scene, behind the 'bar', is the coffee-
woman.

The Spectator famously uses the coffee-house as a model for its convivial moral conversation. As Richard Steele declared in *The Spectator* 10 (Monday 12 March, 1711), the periodical was part of a plan to urbanise philosophy and reform a corrupt public culture. Mr Spectator famously declared: 'I shall be ambitious to have it said of me, that I have brought Philosophy out of Closets and Libraries, Schools and Colleges, to dwell in Clubs and Assemblies, at Tea-Tables and in Coffee-houses.'[8] The coffee-house plays a significant role in *The Spectator*'s project, not only as a metaphorical site but also as a potential agent of moral reform. In *The Spectator* 49 (Thursday 26 April, 1711), Steele explores the social space of the coffee-house by charting the ebb and flow of customers through the day in Mr Spectator's favourite coffee-house.[9] He discerns some subtle distinctions between the types of men who frequent the coffee-house at different times of the day, and uses these differences to launch an argument about the most desirable model of sociability. Early in the morning he sees a group who, rejecting commercial hours, assemble to read newspapers and discuss government policy. These coffee-house politicians, as they were often known, depart when the day grows too busy and their negligent dress becomes embarrassing. They are supplanted by 'Men who have Business or good Sense in their Faces, and come to the Coffee-house either to transact Affairs or enjoy Conversation'. Between the extremes of these two groups Mr Spectator finds men suited to his moral project. These men are content 'to be happy and well pleased in a private Condition' – seeking neither political advancement nor the sordid scenes of commerce – while not neglecting 'the Duties and Relations of Life'. 'Of these sort of Men consist the worthier Part of Mankind; of these are all good Fathers, generous Brothers, sincere Friends, and faithful Subjects . . . These are the men formed for Society, and those little Communities which we express by the Word *Neighbourhoods*.'[10] Identifying such men as the best of men and the rightful inhabitants of the midday coffee-house, Steele consciously revises the character of the coffee-house in his own reformative image.[11] In his vision, the coffee-house becomes the 'Place of Rendezvous to all . . . thus turned to relish calm and ordinary Life'. Over this charmed group presides the imaginary figure of Eubulus: a rich man who lives modestly, a man of wisdom and influence who holds no political or judicial office, a man who lends money to his friends rather than calculating the highest rate of return.

The 'Authority' of Eubulus extends over all in 'his little Diurnal Audience', and each in turn becomes his own Eubulus in the coffee-house. 'Nay, their [the coffee-drinkers'] Veneration towards him is so great, that when they are in other Company they speak and act after him; are Wise in his Sentences, and are no sooner sat down at their own Tables, but they hope or fear, rejoice or despond as they saw at the Coffee-house. In a word, every Man is *Eubulus* as soon as his Back is turn'd.'[12]

Steele's model of the 'Eubulus effect' is a key component of his project of the moral reform of public culture: as Norbert Elias suggests, a notion of self-consciousness in the emulation of others is the motor of early modern self-fashioning.[13] The coffee-house regime of unregulated egalitarianism is here subsumed by another argument, in which the coffee-house environment enables men to achieve their mannered self-fashioning into the rational and polite residents of the new sentimental society. The coffee-house is made the model by which *The Spectator*'s moral project is achieved. The argument, however, also suggests a precise and powerful reform of the coffee-house. The men of the coffee-house derive their entertainment 'rather from Reason than Imagination: Which is the Cause that there is no Impatience or Instability in their Speech or Action. You see in their Countenances they are at home, and in quiet Possession of the present Instant, as it passes, without desiring to Quicken it by gratifying any Passion, or Prosecuting any new Design.'[14] Eubulus's new coffee-house is the site of rational and quiet discussion that does not raise men's passions, where no wild schemes are conceived and no unchecked flights of discourse occur.

The coffee-house transformation of manners renders its public space a more private and sentimental arena (the 'home' or 'neighbour-hood'). The structural privatisation of the public sphere into the sentimental division of the 'neighbourhood' is managed according to a model celebrating values associated with and derived from the construction of femininity: politeness, virtue, orderliness, propriety, decorum (a model that is supplemented by the masculine Enlightenment characteristic of rationality). This new polite model is intimately associated with the conversational social space of the coffee-house.[15] However, the process is only available to men: although the essay refers to 'Mankind', a term which might apply to both men and women, the 'worthier part of Mankind', as we have seen, is detailed as 'all good Fathers, generous Brothers, sincere Friends, and faithful Subjects'. The construction of femininity fills a central but paradoxical role in the civilising process.

The evidence of contemporaries, in fact, suggests that the coffee-house was often anything but quiet, polite and business-like, and, more-over, that this disputatious stimulation was a signal source of the customer's interest in attending the coffee-house. The unruly element was described in terms of babble, noise and smokiness, argument and faction. A diverse array of figures articulate this counter-culture coffee-house, amongst whom might be numbered the gambler and card-shark, the drunkard duellist, the projector (a promoter of mad-cap schemes), the philosopher and literary critic (given to extreme opinions), the but-tonholer (one who literally seizes the observer by the buttonhole, in order to secure undivided attention) and the coffee-woman. The next section of this essay gives an account of this rival view of coffee-house manners. The various text types surveyed here, such as essay, drama, tract and criminal biography, adopt another model of sociability to construct the coffee-house (one that is vulgar, popular, subversive, grotesque and sexual). My account focuses on the coffee-women, not just in the inter-ests of brevity, but because the figure of the coffee-woman, by also ani-mating the issue of gender, has the greatest power to disrupt Habermas's model of the public sphere.

WOMEN OF THE COFFEE-HOUSE

As a number of commentators have noted (Bramah, Clery and Pincus especially), there were some women in coffee-houses, although all these writers tend to suppose that women in coffee-houses express the interest of their gender.[16] Steven Pincus particularly rejects 'the claim that women were excluded from the coffee-houses' – although on closer examination his argument that women were welcome as clients of coffee-houses is justified by just three examples, at least two of which are not clear.[17] As all three commentators signal, however, the most common reason for women to be in the coffee-house was as workers. Many women 'kept' coffee-houses in the period, some of which were named after them, for example Anne Blunt, proprietor of Blunt's Coffee-House, Cannon Street, in 1672;[18] Widow Wells, proprietor of Mrs Wells Coffee-House in Scotland Yard, between 1696 and 1712;[19] Jenny Man, proprietor of Jenny Man's Coffee-House in Charing Cross, in 1712;[20] Jane Rudd, who as proprietor of Widow Rudd's Coffee-House in the Haymarket was found bankrupt in May 1731;[21] and Mrs Edwards, proprietor of Daniel's Coffee-House in Temple Bar and later Edward's Coffee-House in Fleet Street, in 1739.[22]

A woman was not, it seems, unusual in a coffee-house: indeed, to contemporaries, they were ubiquitous. The Grub Street satirist Tom Brown commented in 1702 that 'Every Coffee-House is illuminated both without and within doors; without by a fine Glass Lanthorn and within by a Woman so *light* and *splendid*, you may see through her with the help of a Perspective. At the Bar the good man always places a charming Phillis or two, who invite you by their amorous Glances into their smoaky Territories, to the loss of your Sight.'[23] Critics and competitors of the coffee-houses argued that the coffee-women tempted men into their businesses. The coffee-men, they complained, 'take Care always to provide such tempting, deluding, ogling, pretty young Hussies to be their Bar-Keepers, as steal away our Hearts, and insensibly betray us to Extravagance'.[24] The beguiling flirtation of the coffee-women offered their sexuality as a commodity alongside the addictive bitter liquid. Leya Landau argues that the association of the coffee-women with deception and trickery, as the 'naive customer is gulled into parting with his money', equates their influence with prostitution.[25] A Swiss visitor to London, César de Saussure, remarked that many coffee-houses were 'temples of Venus', or brothels: 'You can easily recognise the latter, because they frequently have as sign a woman's arm or hand holding a coffee-pot. There are a great number of these houses in the neighbourhood of Covent Garden; they pass for being chocolate houses, and you are waited on by beautiful, neat, well-dressed, and amiable, but very dangerous nymphs.'[26] Ned Ward's fictional country visitor in *The London Spy* (1698) observed the working life of two prostitutes in the coffee-vaults of the Widow's Coffee-House.[27]

It is clear, then, that women were not unknown in the coffee-house of eighteenth-century London, but their presence requires a more complex model of social interaction than that proposed by Habermas. The erasure of hierarchy in the coffee-house observed by Habermas and eighteenth-century commentators is overlaid by another kind of status difference that recognises and reads gender and sexuality. In the engraving noted earlier, 'Interior of a London Coffee House' (c. 1705), Emma Clery has argued that the spatial organisation of the room reinforces a gendered structure clearly demarcating the woman's space from that of the men. To underline this, the woman proprietor (or servant) is separated off from the customers in a little booth, or bar. Rather than simply affirming a masculine sociability, the coffee-house proposes a fractured sociability riven by significant gender difference, within which the coffee-woman is figured as a subversive sexual renegade.

One such coffee-woman is noted in *The Spectator* 87 (Saturday 9 June, 1711), in a letter purporting to be from a coffee-woman maligned for flirtatiousness, probably composed by Laurence Eusden.[28] This letter directs us back to an earlier essay by Joseph Addison examining the vanity and coquetry of women he calls '*Idols*', whose aim is 'to gain Adorers' and 'to seduce Men'.[29] These women concatenate anxieties about luxury, gender, promiscuity and immorality. In *The Spectator* 87 Steele returns to the topic of the '*Idols*'. The letter contributed by Eusden points to the deforming influence of female beauty (and coquetry) in the marketplace, using the example of a beautiful coffee-woman. 'There are in six or seven Places of this City, Coffee-houses kept by Persons of [the] Sisterhood [of *Idols*].'[30]

These *Idols* [of the coffee-houses] sit and receive all day long the Adoration of the Youth within such and such Districts; I know, in particular. Goods are not entered as they ought to be at the Custom-House, nor Law-Reports perused at the Temple, by reason of one Beauty who detains the young Merchants too long near Change, and another Fair one who keeps the Students at her House when they should be at Study.[31]

The adoration inspired by these coffee-women drives young men to suicide, perverting the proper operation of the market (as the lovelorn customers accept poor-quality coffee) and worse, 'poison[s]' the conversation of those 'who come to do Business, and talk Politics' – presumably because the force of love (figured as 'Heartburnings') perverts the masculine discourse of the assembly.[32] Eusden sees coquetry (and women) as a poison, 'a Ratsbane', to the coffee-house sociability, which ought properly to be orderly, conversational, convivial and homosocial.

Steele returns again to the coffee-woman 'Idol' in no. 534, (Wednesday 12 November, 1712), in an essay composed of miscellaneous letters to Mr Spectator, most of which address the topic of flirtation in courtship. The correspondent, signing herself Lucinda Parly, claims to be a 'Bar-keeper of a Coffee-house' in 'the Condition of the Idol'. From the women's point of view, of course, the disruptive impetus of seduction flows the other way across the bar. The assiduous courting of her Gentleman wooer is comically phrased in the language of a military siege, like that of Uncle Toby's approach to Widow Wadman in Sterne's *Tristram Shandy* (1760–8). However, her erstwhile lover keeps her from her business (her tea grows weaker), and destroys his own trade in the law: 'while we parly, our several Interests are neglected'.[33] Behind the ironic badinage one might detect a note of barely suppressed sexual harassment, and conclude that the coffee-woman places the Spectatorial coffee-house sociability under considerable and revealing pressure. This is explored in depth by some later texts that consider the coffee-women in more detail.

THE VELVET COFFEE-WOMAN

The first such text is *The Velvet Coffee-Woman* (1728), a 46-page biography of Anne Rochford, the eponymous velvet coffee-woman. As the subtitle signals, the text promises to relate *The Life, Gallantries and Amours of the late Famous Mrs. Anne Rochford*.[34] The text, in short, is something between a whore's biography and a scandalous memoir. After a supposedly virtuous upbringing, and a briefly successful business career as a property developer,[35] an unexplained turn in her fortunes, referred to as the 'Vicissitudes of Female-Affairs',[36] forced Rochford to become the proprietor of a coffee-house in Charing Cross,[37] and to turn prostitute. These occupations are seen as nearly synonymous, referred to by the concealing cognomens of 'Obliging Lady' or 'Lady of Industry'. Here, she seems to have found her mettle. As her biographer pronounces, Ann Rochford 'had something *Strong* in her *Diversions*, loved to associate chiefly with Rakes, and affected *Masculine Pleasures*', such as drinking games and gambling.[38] Her coffee-house became a fashionable and reputable business. Macky, in his *Journey Through England* (1723) reports that at 'About Twelve the *Beau-Monde* assembles in several Chocolate and Coffee-houses: The best of which are the *Cocoa-Tree* and *White's* Chocolate-Houses, St *James's*, the *Smyrna*, Mrs. *Rochford's* and the *British* Coffee-Houses, and all these so near one another, that in less than an Hour you see the Company of them all.'[39]

She earned her cognonym – 'the Velvet Coffee-Woman' – after her role in a notable public scandal: a 'noble Peer' introduced her, dressed in velvet, with two other women to the King's court in the guise of ladies of virtue, wealth and merit. In fact, all three were 'coffee-women' (or proprietors of coffee-houses) and prostitutes or coquettes (women of 'Intrigue'). Each '*Coffee-Lady*' played her part well at court, and in a witty stroke, pretended to represent the opinion of a lobby close to their heart (reflecting the interests of the customers of their coffee-houses). One of the coffee-women argued the case of the officers of the army, another the Scottish clans, while Nanny Rochford argued 'the Cause of Love'.[40] The narrative hints that Rochford's pleading earned her the special favour of the King, who allowed her to open a 'polite *Cabaret*' in the Palace mews, and thus caused her to leave off 'retailing *Coffee, Tea and Chocolate*'.[41]

MOLL KING: THE COFFEE-WOMAN AS SEXUAL OUTLAW

Another coffee-woman's biography, *The Life and Character of Moll King, Late Mistress of King's Coffee-House in Covent-Garden* (1747?), relates the history of Moll King, born in 1696 in Vine Street, the daughter of a shoe-maker and a market-seller.[42] After working as a market-trader and a servant, she married (in the Fleet) a fallen gentleman, Thomas King (called 'Smooth'd-Fac'd-Tom'[43]) when she was fourteen years old.[44] Moll soon left her husband, seduced by a man named Murray, after which she became a common prostitute, 'one of the gayest Ladies of the Town', a friend of notorious whores like Nanny Cotton and Sally Salisbury.[45] Moll however returned to her husband, who was working as a waiter in a 'bawdy-house' in Covent Garden, and, with the profits from a nut-stall, they opened a small coffee-house in the market-place (then a raggle-taggle collection of single-storey market stalls). The coffee-house was known as Tom King's Coffee-House until he died in 1739, and thereafter, Moll King's.

The Kings' coffee-house, on the south side of the Market opposite Southampton Street, was a mean concern, described as 'a little House, or rather Hovel' where they sold coffee and tea. 'In this House they first set out with making Coffee at a Penny a Dish for the Market People, and Tea and Chocolate in Proportion.'[46] Established prior to 1732 at least, their business grew rapidly, and though it encompassed two of the surrounding Houses, there was still 'hardly room to accommodate their Customers'. Because their main customers comprised their fellow market-sellers, this coffee-house kept odd hours, opening at one or two o'clock in the morning, especially on market days in the fruit season. As these hours and these parts were also the favourite 'Rendezvous' of 'young Rakes, and their pretty Misses', the Kings' coffee-house became their 'Office to meet at, and to consult of their nocturnal Intrigues'. The coffee-house gained a certain notoriety. In Fielding's prologue to his *Covent Garden Tragedy* (1732) he asks, 'What rake is ignorant of King's Coffee-House' – but while he was confidant of rakes, he was less sure of readers' comprehension, and so added a footnote which explained that it was 'A Place in *Covent-Garden* Market, well known to all Gentlemen to whom Beds are unknown'.[47] It became a place where assignations were made, 'famous for nightly Revels, and for Company of all Sorts', where 'Every Swain, even from the Star and Garter [nobility] to the Coffee-House Boy [waiter], might be sure of finding a Nymph in waiting',[48] and it 'was at midnight resorted to by all the Bucks, Bloods, Demireps and Choice Spirits in London'.

> At *Tom King*'s you might see every evening Women of the Town the most cele-brated, and dressed as elegant as if to sit in the stage box at an Opera. There you were sure also of meeting every species of human kind that intemperance, idleness, necessity, or curiosity could assemble together.[49]

Here the free mixing of status groups brought about a different kind of non-hierarchical intercourse from that imagined by Habermas. In George Stevens's Ned Wardian 'Authentic Life of a Woman of the Town' (1788), the sociability of the coffee-house is rough and bawdy, characterised by 'riots, bowls breaking, shrieking, murder, and such like amusements' and articulated by linguistic muddle as 'pell-mell, higgle-de-piggle-de'.[50] The sociability of King's Coffee-House was, then, uncomfortably close to a brothel, for which Moll King was repeatedly prosecuted.

> Here you might see Ladies of Pleasure, who appear'd apparelled like Persons of Quality, not at all inferior to them in Dress, attended by Fellows habited like Footmen, who were their Bullies, and wore their Disguise, the more easily to deceive the unwary Youths, who were so unhappy as to Cast their Eyes upon these *deceitful Water-Wag-Tails*.[51]

Moll defended herself from prosecution for running a bagnio or brothel, on the grounds that there were no beds in the house, though not always successfully.[52]

Moll King had a provocatively transgressive femininity, crossing and destabilising boundaries that the period spent much energy in making and maintaining.

> She made a great Distinction between Industry and Vice; for she was a Woman well acquainted with the World, both in low and genteel Life, had not her love of Wealth led her on to do such Things as were highly inconsistent with Morality, and very unbecoming her Sex.[53]

Her coffee-house was transgressive not only because of its character as a place of resort for the sexual underworld, but also for its promiscuous mixture of high and low status groups. The 'witty Beaus' who frequent the coffee-house perceive the transgressive company of the female host as a part of the entertainment offered by the house, enjoying '*a Dish of*

Flash *with* Moll'. As the text delineates, 'flash' is an underground criminal lexicon, which the text examines in a witty dialogue composed of almost impenetrable cant terms and phrases, imagined to be spoken by Moll and a customer (although the dialogue is a reprint of an untraced earlier text, *The Humours of the Flashy Boy's at Moll King's*).[54] That flash discourse is characteristic of the coffee-house conversation further identifies the coffee-house sociability, in this instance, as criminal, immoral and low. The Kings' coffee-house (which was known ironically as 'Moll's Fair Reception House', and elsewhere as 'King's College') is clearly a different sort of coffee-house from that celebrated in the Habermasian model, with a significantly different and more subversive regime (boisterous, sexually promiscuous, heterosexual, status-obsessed and heterodox).

The Kings' coffee-house features in Hogarth's 'Morning' plate from *The Four Times of the Day* (May 1738). The plate is located in a snow-covered Covent Garden Market, where Hogarth contrasts the morning ritual of two groups of residents: an old and pious woman heading into the church (St Paul's Covent Garden) for her morning devotions, accompanied by her scruffy house-boy, and a riotous group of revellers outside Tom King's Coffee-House, at the centre of which is a beautiful young prostitute being fondled by a gentleman, and around which crouch dishevelled beggars seeking alms and warming themselves next to a sputtering fire. The setting, offering a prospect across the bustling market, is dominated in the top right by the architectural contrast Hogarth draws between the cold neo-classical facade of the Palladian church and the shambolic hovel that is the coffee-house, through whose open door one can see only more riotous revels (a violent altercation, in fact).[55] Hogarth has relocated the coffee-house, across the market, in order to underline the ideological difference implied in the contrast. To Hogarth, the coffee-house has a boisterous sociability equated with promiscuity, tumult and poverty: a carnivalised sociability, more popular than polite.

The evidence about the coffee-women suggests, then, that it was conventional for women to act as proprietors of coffee-houses. Their presence changed the modes of sociability available within the coffee-house. Many contemporaries report that the flirtatious discourse engendered by their presence was an integral part of the coffee-house experience. These women, as I have argued, were unruly ciphers of a sexuality elsewhere repressed by the hegemonic masculinity of coffee-house sociability. They were also women of business, although Ann Rochford called herself a 'bar-slave', suggesting that not all work in the coffee-house was glamorous[56] (the coffee-woman's role might, however, have included management, keeping accounts and stock control, as well as making and serving coffee). Coffee-house keeping was, then, one of the occupations that widows might have followed: an avenue of business activity and in a sense somewhat emancipatory. Yet this does not seem to have necessarily implied that they were in possession of financial independence or economic agency. There were many impediments, both legal and cultural, to women engaging in business, as many historians have noted. Indeed, as Elizabeth Kowaleski-Wallace has argued, femininity was perceived as antithetical to business, and as such, all kinds of women's businesses were repeatedly equated with prostitution.[57]

The coffee-women were purveyors of gossip and scandal (their 'Calling' was 'both for *Coffee* and *Intrigue*', as *The Velvet Coffee-Woman* says). To many contemporaries they were dangerous sexual nonconformists: sexually promiscuous, if not actually prostitutes or procurers. Henry Fielding, in *Joseph Andrews* (1742), offers a miniature recapitulation of the criminal version of a woman's coffee-house keeping. On his travels, Parson Adams encounters a hypocritical Squire, renowned for encouraging the ambitious poor only to deceive them in time. Amongst his victims is 'a young Woman, and the handsomest in all this Neighbourhood, whom he enticed up to London, promising to make her a Gentlewoman to one of your Women of Quality: but instead of keeping his Word, we have since heard, after having a Child by her himself, she became a common Whore; then kept a Coffee-House in Covent-Garden, and a little after died of the French Distemper in a Gaol'.[58] The coffee-woman, in short, presents us with a fascinating ambiguity: on the one hand, she is figured as a masterless criminal in the feminine underworld, akin to a prostitute. On the other hand, as an unconventional self-mastering woman, the coffee-woman is a subversive figure, possessed of a kind of empowered femininity.[59] The whore's narrative offers the representation of a woman who refuses to identify with any of the sanctioned ideas within the dominant constructions of femininity (patriarchal or sentimental). The coffee-woman retains some of the worrying power of the whore, a power that is enhanced by her presence within the nominally homosocial masculinity of the coffee-house (where she stands behind her bar as both spy and subversive).

Reading the coffee-woman as a sexual radical, however, presents considerable difficulties. The radical posture of the coffee-woman as masterless woman may be an impolite fiction for more pernicious forms of sexual predation, like that of the madam who 'runs' a brothel. *The Life and Character of Moll King* suggests that coffee-house keeping was an offshoot of the sex industry, with the coffee-woman one of the pimped professions. Moll King relates the practice of Mr Haddock, a notorious brothel-keeper: 'of all the Slaveries he impos'd on unhappy Women, by taking Coffee-Houses, and putting them into them as Mistresses, for which they paid sometimes three Guineas a Week, but seldom less than two; and if they could not make good their Payments, the Marshalsea Prison was their next Quarters'.[60] In this view, coffee-women were coerced into coffee-houses by organised crime, victims of the sex industry. In this material, the trope of the coffee-woman expresses the transgressive characteristics of the new coffee-house sociability. The Spectatorial coffee-house aims to reject and eliminate the coffee-woman from its ordered and decent interior, for the reason that her sexuality disrupts the coffee-house's sense of its own prestige and status. The coffee-woman, however, does not entirely go away, as can be seen in James Miller's sentimental comedy *The Coffee-House* (1737), where the coffee-house, improbably, is recast as the scenario for the development of a transgressive tale of romantic love.[61]

JAMES MILLER'S COMEDY *THE COFFEE-HOUSE* (1737)

The Coffee-House is set entirely within the coffee-room of a coffee-house owned by a widow, Mrs Notable.[62] Under the watchful gaze of the 'The Widow in the Bar'[63] a group of regulars assemble, including a scrivener, an officer, a poet, a politician, a fox-hunter, a 'solemn beau', a law student and a comic actor called Cibber, played by Colley Cibber himself. These men are made the subject of a gentle satire on the follies of their conversation, behaviour and aspirations, which depicts them engaged in various activities (backgammon, writing verse, reading newspapers, smoking). Their conversation swirls around diverse topics – such as the conduct of the war in the Balkans, the quality of the poet's verses, the propriety of cheating at games, the quality of a castrato's voice – elaborating a scene of convivial social engagement, mixing professions and occupations. The light satire effectively masks the combative quality of their disagreements, in which an injured party may profess rage but is seen to forget it almost immediately. The masculine social environment, then, conforms to the Spectatorial model of the convivial coffee-house, even as the satire appears to criticise it.

The romantic love plot that structures the comedy disrupts the convivial homosociality of the coffee-room. Mrs Notable's daughter Kitty is

a beautiful and sprightly young woman, and although it is not made explicit, it seems that Mrs Notable has raised her to affect genteel status. Kitty has in any case inspired the love of Hartly, 'a Gentleman of the Temple' or law student. As his friend Gaylord remarks, 'But for a Gentleman to marry a Coffee-Man's daughter – 'Sdeath!, 'tis a Scandal'. Hartly, however, replies that 'upon balancing the Account', he finds she is doubly attractive, as she stands to inherit the coffee-house. 'I am a Gentleman and poor; she a Coffee-Girl, and Rich; why, if I have her money for my gentility, troth, I think 'tis a good Bargain.'[64] The bar separates the world of women from that of men, but it also encodes social distinctions of rank. The two are eventually married, which comes as no surprise, but only at the end. The plot extends their lovelorn separation by exposing the widow's schemes to marry her daughter to Harpie, an ugly old man made rich by his work as a scrivener. He comes 'gallanting' in old-fashioned and overly formal dress, which the other men dishevel. His address to Kitty, composed in ornate and formal legal diction, leaves her speechless with mirth. He is eventually conned by Gaylord into thinking he has injured Cibber in a fight. To conceal this criminal scandal, Harpie agrees to withdraw his suit and Mrs Notable agrees to Kitty's marriage to Hartly.

In the course of the play, Kitty upsets a number of conventions of virtuous behaviour in the coffee-house, where she transgresses distinctions of status and gender. The most extensive of these occurs when she plays at being a coffee-house proprietor: she comes into the coffee-room and finding the bar empty, decides to get into it. In the bar she comments 'Lah! how pure it is to sit here, and have all the fine gentlemen crowding about one, one saying This, and another saying That; one doing one pretty Thing, and another Pretty Thing.'[65] After the men re-enter the

Figure 1 Frontispiece to James Miller's comedy *The Coffee-House A Dramatick Piece. As it is Perform'd at the Theatre Royal in Drury Lane* (London: J. Watts, 1737). The interior of a coffee-room, as depicted in Miller's play, which was performed at the Theatre-Royal in Drury Lane in January 1738. In the coffee-house, the assembled gentlemen drink coffee, converse and play backgammon in the booths (visible beyond the figures in the plate), while Mrs Notable serves coffee and other drinks from behind the bar (unseen), aided by her coffee-boys. The plate depicts a moment in the final scene: to the left, Widow Notable, mistress of the coffee-house, is consoled by Mr Harpie, a scrivener; while in the background Miss Kitty is conversing with her betrothed, Mr Hartly, a gentleman of the Temple, with whom Kitty proposes to establish a coffee-house that admits women. Presiding over the scene is Mr Gaylord, an officer, who has pretended to murder Mr Cibber, an actor at the Comedy (played by Colley Cibber), so as to persuade Mrs Notable to give her daughter's hand to his friend Hartly.

coffee-room, Kitty continues to play coffee-woman by serving her male admirers. This scene only works as scandal, yet it is not entirely clear how this scandal operates: clearly, it is not a scandal for a woman to serve coffee, but it is for a woman who aspires to gentility, innocence and virtue. Kitty here conflates the sentimental construction of femininity and the unruly femininity of the coffee-woman, a conflation the play experiences as a nervous kind of satire.

The play concludes with marriage, but ends with yet more evidence of Kitty's perverse disposition. After marriage, she suggests to Hartly that they could continue to run the coffee-house.

——But Mr *Hartly*, must I quite leave our Coffee now? I wish you'd keep a Coffee-House, with all my Heart I do; you shou'dn't have any Trouble in it, my Dear; I could serve all the Gentleman with what they want, and I shou'd love to do it dearly too!

Hartly nervously agrees that they could, although it would certainly halt his gentlemanly pretensions. But as she concludes, Kitty has a more radical proposal: 'I'll tell you what, Mr. Hartly, we'll have a Room for the Women too, if you will . . . By the Stars! and so we will; for 'tis an unreasonable thing that Women should not come to the Coffee-House.' Kitty's proposal for a coffee-house for young ladies seems to throw the play's conservative closure into limbo. Her revised female coffee-house wears the appearance of a polite and genteel environment (a reformed coffee-house sociability reorganised along sentimental and feminised principles). But this re-gendering is ambiguous, as the play suggests it would be something more akin to a brothel, a place which would create gossip and scandal: 'there would be more News stirring there in a Week, than there is now in six Months.'[66]

Miller's *The Coffee-House* deliberately invokes the trope of the coffee-woman, but does so in order to suppress it. The character of Mrs Notable, through her unseemly recapitulation of the convention of the avaricious widow, recalls clearly enough the unruly coffee-woman. The behaviour of the women, and that of their male customers, continually threatens to spill over into more bawdy material, even as it is disciplined by Miller's irony. Over the unruliness of the coffee-women, Miller lays the girlish coquetry of Kitty, for whom the coffee-house is space for the play of light-hearted courtship wit. Miller's comedy thus attempts to curtail the disruptive power of the coffee-woman by essentialising her subversive status under the rubric of an unthreatening female coquettishness. Transposing the female sexuality of the coffee-woman onto the widow's beautiful daughter allows the subversiveness of the bar-crossing romance to dissipate into the polite fictions of dramatic comedy. Generic convention is deployed here as a powerful force to shape and repress the unruly coffee-woman familiar from the whore's biography.[67]

CONCLUSION: THE SPECTATORIAL SUPPRESSION OF THE UNRULY IN THE STRUCTURAL TRANSFORMATION OF THE PUBLIC SPHERE

There is not space in this essay to trace exhaustively the consequences for Habermas's argument of the repression of unruly material from the coffee-house model of sociability. Instead, the intention is to historicise how *The Spectator's* polite model of sociability came to acquire its hegemonic force in the history books through the later eighteenth and nineteenth centuries (a hegemony it always claimed to have through its universalising posture). One could pursue and defend the argument that coffee-houses did become more polite and refined through the course of the eighteenth century. A trajectory of polite reform can be traced in the mid-eighteenth century in the tendency of coffee-houses to adopt explicitly exclusive regulations. This took two main forms: coffee-houses like the Baltick and Lloyd's transformed themselves into business associations, where subscribers alone were given access to a coffee-room where business deals could be transacted and highly specialised information disseminated.[68] Other coffee-houses, like White's and Almack's, followed a similar subscriber-led transformation into clubs open only to a highly selective membership, largely appropriated by a distinctive high-status social group and specialising in one particular form of socialising, such as high-stakes gambling.[69] Even 'regular' coffee-houses seem to have adopted a quieter and more restrained model of sociability. However, there is also some solid evidence that the popular coffee-house survives this process of polite refinement. Iain McCalman's work on the convivial debating clubs of the ultra-radical political underground of the 1790s has argued that not only did the coffee-house serve as the site where the clubs could meet, but the type of communal activity and democratic discussion engendered there provided 'the preferred institutional model' for revolutionaries.[70] Yet despite the continuing heterogeneity of the coffee-house experience, the construction of the coffee-house in official culture came increasingly to represent the coffee-house only in its polite mode.

As the coffee-house declined in importance in late eighteenth-century society, its representation became increasingly nostalgic, and the preserve of historians. By the early nineteenth century, nostalgia for the Spectatorial coffee-house sociability was pronounced. A correspondent identified by the Spectatorial cognonym 'Harry Honeycombe' remarks in the *New Monthly Magazine* (1826), that 'As I never pass Covent Garden . . . without thinking of all the old coffee-houses and the wits, so I can never reflect, without impatience, that there are no such meetings now, and no coffee-room that looks as if it would suit them.' Instead, society now congregates in the pew and the box (church and theatre), which Honeycombe describes as a kind of confinement. He regrets the passing of the old coffee-house, where 'there was a more humane openness of intercourse', and where 'Hostility might get in, but it was obliged to behave itself.'[71]

Victorian historians of the eighteenth century continue this process of nostalgic re-evaluation of the coffee-house.[72] Macaulay, in his *History of England* (1848–55) describes the coffee-house as a 'most important political institution' in its day, one of 'the chief organs through which the public opinion of the metropolis vented itself', equivalent to a 'fourth Estate of the realm'. In Macaulay's estimation, the coffee-houses were the daily resort of every man of the upper or middle class, from which nobody was excluded by rank, profession, religious or political opinion. In a reprise of the *Spectator*'s Eubulusian argument, he claims that the 'gregarious habit' instilled by the coffee-house made it 'the Londoner's home'.[73] Leslie Stephen's *English Literature and Society* (1903) similarly explores the role of the coffee-house in the formation of a new state public culture through its ability to commingle 'the political and the literary class' in a 'characteristic fraternisation', even though his representation of the coffee-house admits of much disputatious rowdiness. Stephen's coffee-house plays a central role in the formation of a literary critical 'tribunal' in which men of the middling state might learn to make judgements and take a place in political life.[74]

The nineteenth-century reconstruction of the coffee-house seems to have some significant points of similarity with that of Habermas. As a student of his footnotes realises, Habermas appears to have used their research to formulate his account of the coffee-house, a reliance that is, in the end, rather significant. Habermas relied on a restricted range of generalist secondary texts on the English coffee-house: making reference to English research by Stephen, Trevelyan and an anonymous, untraced nineteenth-century popular historian,[75] and two German works (both of which are heavily dependent on the nineteenth-century research of Timbs and Robinson).[76] It is likely he did no primary research.[77] It is, of course, unsurprising that Habermas's work on the coffee-house is under-researched (the work the book does is theoretical, as is appropriate in a *Habilitationsschrift*, or post-doctoral dissertation, submitted to a philosophy department). However the manner in which his research is weak is central to the success of his argument.

Habermas's account of the coffee-house, filtered through the Victorian coffee-house historians, reflects the model of sociability of the Spectatorial reformed coffee-house, even while it recognises the existence of texts, like *The Women's Petition*,[78] that might offer a more unruly model. Habermas's own work was completed, of course, in the 1950s, and in it one might recognise the influence of the post-war coffee-house renaissance. In the 1950s, the coffee-house, in the new guise of espresso bar, underwent a profound phase of renewal. The espresso bar relied on new technology – Achille Gaggia had patented the modern espresso coffee machine in Italy in 1946 – but its real revolution was cultural; it defined an innovative model of sociability to attract, define and refashion a distinct social identity.[79] This 'coffee-bar craze' was closely associated both with high modernist art practices and practitioners, and the emergent popular youth culture. The sociability of the espresso bar was identified as international, cosmopolitan and sophisticated, allying itself with the post-war new world order (managing to be both European and modern, but dissociated from the extreme politics and militarism of the immediate past). In part it did this by cloaking itself in the counter-culture mystique of beat-poets, teenagers and youth rebellion – characterised, satirically, in 1957 by Angus Wilson as the 'espresso-bar rebellion'.[80] Perhaps for the first time since the 1690s, the coffee-house was associated with a reforming and convivial sociability, one in which women were, however, conspicuously central. The new coffee-bar, like the old coffee-house, thus establishes curious but by no means impotent analogies with Habermas's wider project in *The Structural Transformation of the Public Sphere* in establishing an understanding of a liberal democratic theory that might coherently apply in post-war West Germany.

NOTES

I am grateful to the following for their advice and comments: Ava Arndt, Emma Clery, Elizabeth Eger, Charlotte Grant, Marian Hobson, Leya Landau, Miles Ogborn, Chris Reid, Vanessa Smith and Carol Watts.

1 Jürgen Habermas, *The Structural Transformation of the Public Sphere: An Inquiry into a Category of Bourgeois Society*, trans. Thomas Burger (Cambridge: Polity, 1989); *Strukturwandel der Öffentlicheit* (Darmstadt and Neuwied: Hermann

Luchterhand Verlag, 1962). Peter Hohendahl, *The Institution of Criticism* (Ithaca: Cornell University Press, 1982); Terry Eagleton, *The Function of Criticism* (London: Verso, 1984), p. 9; Peter Stallybrass and Allon White, *The Politics and Poetics of Transgression* (London: Methuen, 1985), pp. 80–118.

2 Joan B. Landes, *Women and the Public Sphere in the Age of the French Revolution* (Ithaca: Cornell University Press, 1988); Janet Siltanen and Michelle Stanworth, eds., *Women and the Public Sphere: A Critique of Sociology and Politics* (London: Hutchinson, 1984). Habermas has responded to these criticisms in 'Further Reflections on the Public Sphere', in Craig Calhoun, ed., *Habermas and the Public Sphere* (Cambridge, Mass. and London: The MIT Press, 1992), pp. 421–62, p. 423.

3 Habermas, *Structural Transformation*, pp. 32–3, 36–7. Habermas does not use the term 'sociability', which is here understood to mean the character or quality of being sociable or engaging in friendly intercourse.

4 Anthony Hilliar, *A Brief and Merry History of Great Britain, Containing an Account of the Religions, Customs, Manners, Humours, Characters, Caprice, Contrasts, Foibles, Factions &c., of the People. Written originally in Arabic by Ali-Mohammed Hadgi* (London: J. Roberts, J. Shuckburgh, J. Penn and J. Jackson, 1730), p. 22.

5 Henri Misson de Valberg, *Mémoirs et observations faites par un voyageur en Angleterre* (La Haye, 1698); trans. John Ozell, *Memoirs and Observations in his Travels over England. With some account of Scotland and Ireland. Dispos'd in Alphabetical Order* (London: D. Browne et al., 1719), pp. 39–40.

6 M. P., *A Character of Coffee and Coffee-Houses. By M.P.* (London: John Starkey, 1661), p. 9.

7 *Interior of a London Coffee House* (c. 1705), British Museum. This plate is widely reproduced; see for example Peter Earle, *The Making of the English Middle Class: Business, Society and Family Life in London, 1600–1730* (London: Methuen 1989), pl. 8. See also Emma Clery's discussion in 'Women, Publicity and the Coffee-House Myth', *Women: A Cultural Review* 2.2 (1991), [168]–77.

8 *The Spectator* 10 (Monday 12 March, 1711), in Joseph Addison and Richard Steele, *The Spectator*, ed. Donald F. Bond, 5 vols. (1st edn 1965; Oxford: Clarendon Press, 1987), vol. I, p. 44.

9 Addison and Steele, *The Spectator*, vol. I, pp. 208–11. The coffee-house is not named, but is said to be near the Inns of Court.

10 Addison and Steele, *The Spectator*, vol. I, pp. 209–10.

11 Angus Ross writes of 'the revolution in habits and manners which *The Tatler* and *The Spectator* helped to bring about' (in his introduction to *Selections from The Tatler and The Spectator* (London: Penguin, 1982), p. 52. *The Spectator*, even to near contemporaries, is associated with the introduction of a new and innovative social organisation: Johnson says the periodical had a role in establishing 'the minuter decencies and inferior duties' and in regulating the 'practice of daily conversation'.

12 Addison and Steele, *The Spectator*, vol. I, p. 211.

13 Elias argues that 'the compulsion to check one's own behaviour', through shame and embarrassment, drives the 'structural transformation of society'

into its 'new pattern of social relationships'. Norbert Elias, *The Civilising Process*, trans. Edmund Jephcott (1st edn 1938; Oxford: Blackwell, 1994), p. 66. See also Scott Paul Gordon's account of a more aggressive 'controlling gaze' in *The Spectator*, in contradistinction to the gentle and polite 'Work of Reformation' articulated in this essay. 'Voyeuristic Dreams: Mr. Spectator and the Power of Spectacle', *The Eighteenth Century* 36, 1 (1995), 3–23.

14 Addison and Steele, *The Spectator*, vol. 1, p. 210.

15 See Lawrence Klein, 'Coffeehouse Civility, 1660–1714: an aspect of post-courtly culture in England', *Huntingdon Library Quarterly* 59.1 (1997), 30–51.

16 Edward Bramah, captions in the Bramah Tea and Coffee Museum, Maguire St, London (1996); Clery, 'Women, Publicity and the Coffee-House Myth; and Steven Pincus, '"Coffee Politicians Does Create": Coffeehouses and Restoration Political Culture', *Journal of Modern History* 27 (1995), 807–34.

17 Pincus, '"Coffee Politicians"', pp. 814, 815. Thomas Bellingham records in his Diary in 1689 that he had met 'with several women in the coffee-house', but he doesn't comment what he thought of them or their morals; see Anthony Hewitson, ed., *Diary of Thomas Bellingham* (November 1688, Preston 1908), p. 44. Robert Hooke dined with Robert Boyle and his sister Lady Ranelagh at Man's Coffee-House; Henry Robinson and Walter Adams, eds., *The Diary of Robert Hooke, 1672–1689* (London, 1935), entry for October 2, 1675, p. 184. Pincus's claim that Martha Lady Giffard, the sister and biographer of Sir William Temple, was a 'habituée' of the coffee-house is also built on slim evidence: the text he cites does not claim that she was in the coffee-house, but that Swift, in 1710, had heard that one of her servants (the mother of his beloved Stella) had enquired in the coffee house for her; Julia G. Longe, *Martha Lady Giffard: Her Life and Correspondence (1664–1722)* (London: George Allen, 1911), pp. 250–1.

18 Bryant Lillywhite, *London Coffee-Houses* (London: George Allen & Unwin, 1963), no. 147, p. 127.

19 Lillywhite, *London Coffee-Houses*, no. 1501, pp. 635–7.

20 *Flying Post*, November 6–8, 1712, quoted in Lillywhite, *London Coffee-Houses*, no. 624, p. 625.

21 Lillywhite, *London Coffee-Houses*, no. 1531, p. 647.

22 *London Evening Post*, 16–18 October, 1739, quoted in Lillywhite, *London Coffee-Houses*, no. 331, p. 188.

23 Tom Brown, 'Amusement VIII', originally in *Amusements Serious and Comical, Calculated for the Meridian of London* (London, 1702), how in *The Works of Mr. Thomas Brown. Serious and Comical, in Prose and Verse*, 4 vols., 5th edn (London: Sam Briscoe, 1715), vol. III, pp. 71–2.

24 *The Case between the Proprietors of the News-Papers and the Coffee-Men of London and Westminster* (London: E. Smith, 1729), p. 12.

25 I am grateful to Leya Landau for allowing me to read an early version of her dissertation chapter, '"Men of Business, or Men of Pleasure": The London Coffee-House', in 'Reading London: the Literary Representation of the City's Pleasures, 1700–1782' (unpublished PhD dissertation, University College, University of London, 1999).

26 César de Saussure, *A Foreign View of England in the Reigns of George I & George II: the letters of Monsieur César de Saussure to his Family, translated and edited by Madame Van Muyden* (written 1729, first edn London: John Murray, 1902), pp. 164–5.

27 [Edward Ward], *The London Spy Compleat, in Eighteen Parts*, 2nd edn (London: J. How, 1704), part II, pp. 25–32. It is unclear which coffee-house Ward is referring to, but there was a Widow's Coffee-House in Devereaux Court, located off the Strand near the Temple (Lillywhite, *London Coffee-Houses*, no. 1973, p. 746).

28 T. T. [Laurence Eusden?], 'Letter to Mr Spectator', Addison and Steele, *The Spectator*, vol. I, p. 372. Laurence Eusden (1688–1730) was named by Steele as a contributor to *The Spectator* (no. 555), but there is no textual evidence for Nichols's attribution, which, however, may be based on oral tradition (John Nichols, Thomas Percy and John Calder, eds., *The Spectator*, 1788–89, 8 vols.).

29 *The Spectator* 87, Saturday June 9, 1711, in Addison and Steele, *The Spectator*, vol. I, pp. 312–13.

30 Nichols suggests that Eusden was inspired by the female proprietor of The Widow's Coffee-House in Devereaux Court, noted above.

31 Eusden(?), *Spectator*, No. 88, Bond, I, p. 371.

32 Addison and Steele, *The Spectator*, vol. I, pp. 371–2. In the case of the coffee-woman 'Idol', the issue of female coquetry is overlaid with an anxiety about status inconsistency (that a servant might seduce a gentleman).

33 Addison and Steele, *The Spectator*, vol. IV, pp. 407–8.

34 *The Velvet Coffee-Woman: or, the Life, Gallantries and Amours of the late Famous Mrs. Anne Rochford. Particularly I. The History of Her going by that Name; II. The Adventures of her noted Irish-Lover Mac Dermot; III. An Account of that unparallel Imposter Count Brandenburgh; IV A Funeral Oration to her Memory, and all Ladies of Industry, as well among the Grecians and Romans, as those of our own Nation* (Westminster: Simon Green, 1728).

35 Rochford was born Ann Woase, the daughter of Francis Woase (pronounced 'Voice'), a servant of the Earl of Torrington (coxswain of his boat, as well as a procurer). After the death of her mother in childbirth, Woase and Ann had lived 'at, or near, *Stangate*, in the Parish of *Lambeth*'. As a young woman she had worked in an alehouse (The Mitre, Stangate), and as a nursery maid at a merchant's house in the City of London. After her father's death, Ann Rochford's business skills became apparent, when she used her personal credit to purchase and renovate two decrepit houses belonging to her step-mother.

36 *The Velvet Coffee-Woman*, p. 33.

37 In 1713 her business, located at Charing Cross, is described as Madame Rochford's Chocolate House, and by 1724, as a coffee-house. Lillywhite, *London Coffee-Houses*, no. 1086, p. 486.

38 *The Velvet Coffee-Woman*, p. 10. Her beauty was renowned: 'In her were collected the scattered Beauties of her whole Sex. In short, She was the

PINE-APPLE of Great Britain, which includes the several Flavours of all the delicious fruits in the World' (p. 10).

39 John Macky, *A Journey Through England. In Familiar Letters. From a Gentleman Here, to his Friend Abroad*, 3rd edn (London: J. Hooke, 1723), letter 9, p. 154.

40 *The Velvet Coffee-Woman*, p. 34.

41 Ibid., p. 35.

42 *The Life and Character of Moll King, Late Mistress of King's Coffee-House in Covent-Garden, Who departed this life at her Country-House at Hampstead, on Thursday the 17th of September, 1747. Containing A true narrative of this well-known Lady, from her Birth to her Death; wherein is inserted several humorous Adventures relating to Persons of both Sexes, who were fond of nocturnal Revels. Also, the Flash Dialogue between Moll King and Old Gentleman Harry, that was some Years ago murdered in Covent-Garden; and the Pictures of several noted Family Men, drawn to the Life. To the Whole is added, An Epitaph and Elegy, wrote by one of Moll's favourite Customers, And a Key to the Flash Dialogue* (London: W. Price, [1747?]).

43 *Moll King*, p. 5.

44 Tom King, born at West Ashton, Wilts., was a scholar at Eton and at King's College, Cambridge, where he matriculated in 1713. *Alumni Cantabrigienses: a biographical list of all known students, graduates, and holders of office at the University of Cambridge, from the Earliest Times to 1900*, comp. John Venn and J.A. Venn (Cambridge: Cambridge University Press, 1924), part I, vol. III. See also *Registrum Regale: Sive Catalogus Alumnorum è Collegio Etonensi in Collegium Regale Cantabrig. per singulos annos cooptatorum* (Eton: Jos. Pote, 1774), p. 29.

45 *Moll King*, p. 5.

46 *Moll King*, p. 7.

47 Henry Fielding, 'Prologue', *The Covent-Garden Tragedy. As it is Acted at the Theatre-Royal in Drury-Lane. By his Majesty's Servants* (London: J. Watts, 1732), p. [12].

48 *Moll King*, p. 8.

49 George Alexander Stevens, *The Adventures of a Speculist; or, A Journey Through London exhibiting a Picture of the Manners, Fashions, Amusements, &c. of the Metropolis at the middle of the eighteenth century*, 2 vols. (London: for the editor, sold by S. Bladon, 1788), p. 260.

50 Ibid., p. 262.

51 *Moll King*, p. 8.

52 On 24 May 1739, 'Moll King, Mistress of Tom's Coffee House Covent Garden was brought to the King's bench to receive judgement, when the Court committed her to the King's Bench Prison Southwark, till they took time to consider of a punishment adequate to the offence of keeping a disorderly house.' Lillywhite, *London Coffee-Houses*, no. 1370, p. 596. The coffee-house was a lucrative trade which eventually made the Kings enough money to buy a country house near Hampstead in Haverstock Hill. After the death of Tom King (before 1739), Moll ran the coffee-house herself, remarried (a Mr Hoff), had her son educated at Eton, and eventually retired to Hampstead. She died in Haverstock Hill on 17 September 1747. Her

coffee-house survived her death, with its character unchecked. Tobias Smollett's *Roderick Random* (1748) equates it with a kind of brothel: at 'near two o'clock in the morning' Roderick accompanies Banter and Bragwell to 'Moll King's Coffee House, where, after [Bragwell] had kicked half a dozen hungry whores, we left him to sleep on a bench and directed our course towards Charing Cross'. Tobias Smollett, *The Adventures of Roderick Random*, ed. Paul-Gabriel Boucé (1748; Oxford: Oxford University Press, 1981), chapter xlvi, pp. 277–8.

53 *Moll King*, p. 10.

54 *Moll King*, p. 10.

55 See Ronald Paulson, *Hogarth*, vol. II: *High Art and Low, 1732–1750* (New Brunswick, N.J.: Rutgers University Press, 1992), p. 145. Paulson identifies Tom King's Coffee-House as a tavern (pp. 144, 146), which is odd, given its name, but perhaps comprehensible, given the recent hegemony of the Habermasian construction of the coffee-house.

56 *Nanny Roc—d's Letter to a member of the B—f Stake Club; In Vindication of Certain Ladies Calumniated in the Freeholder of March 9th. In the Stile of a Certain Knight* (London: J. Roberts, 1716), p. 8. The ten-page pamphlet is a reply to Addison's misogynist denunciation of 'She Malcontents' who debate politics, in which he accuses the 'Common Women of the Town' of being Tories. See 'No. XXIII, Friday March 9, 1716', *The Freeholder*, ed. James Leheny (Oxford: Clarendon Press, 1979), pp. 135–36.

57 Elizabeth Kowaleski-Wallace, *Consuming Subjects: Women, Shopping and Buisness in the Eighteenth Century* (New York: Columbia University Press, 1997), pp. 111–43.

58 Henry Fielding, *The History Of The Adventures Of Joseph Andrews, and of his Friend Mr. Abraham Adams* (1742), ed. R. F. Brissenden (London: Penguin, 1977), vol. I, book 2, chapter 17 p. 179.

59 John J. Richetti, *Popular Fiction before Richardson: Narrative Patterns 1700–1739* (Oxford: Clarendon, 1969), pp. 35–6.

60 *Moll King*, p. 20.

61 Rev. James Miller, *The Coffee-House. A Dramatick Piece. As it is Perfom'd at the Theatre Royal in Drury-Lane* (London: J. Watts, 1737). The play was performed three times: twice in January 1738, and once in September 1739 (A. H. Scouter, ed., *The London Stage*, 8 vols., Carbondale: Southern Illinois University Press, 1960–8, p. 699).

62 The play provoked a minor scandal when the customers of Dick's Coffee-House, in Fleet Street near Temple Bar, imagined a similarity between their proprietor, Mrs Yarrow, and her daughter, and the characters of the play. Dick's Coffee-House had been established in 1680 by Richard Turner, and was later patronised by Thomas Gray and William Cowper. (Gray writes to John Chute, 7 September 1741: 'Mrs Dick to whom I resorted for a dish of coffee instead thereof produced unto me from her breast your kind letter.' See Lillywhite, *London Coffee-Houses*, no. 346, p. 192). Miller denied the suggestion, claiming that the shape of the play had been borrowed from a

French source (Jean Baptiste Rousseau, *Le Caffé* (1694) in *Oeuvres Diverses*, 2 vols (London: Jacob Tonson and Jean Watts, 1723), vol. II, pp. 441–96), but he was not widely believed, as the engraved frontispiece of the comedy depicted a coffee-house interior that resembled that of Dick's Coffee-House. The customers of the coffee-house (students and residents of the Temple) went in a body to the theatre to disrupt the performance of the play (and thereafter, all of Miller's dramatic works). See entries for Miller in *Biographica Dramatica* and *DNB*. For a different account, see Landau, "'Men of Business'", where she argues that the play is primarily shaped by the censor (it was one of the first plays to be staged after the passing of the Licensing Act in 1737).

63 Miller, *The Coffee-House*, I, ii, p. 3

64 Ibid., I, i, pp. 2–3.

65 Ibid. I, ii, p. 27.

66 Ibid., I, ii, p. 37.

67 See Frank H. Ellis, *Sentimental Comedy: Theory and Practice* (Cambridge: Cambridge University Press, 1991).

68 Charles Wright and C. Ernest Fayle, *A History of Lloyd's from the Founding of Lloyd's Coffee House to the Present Day* (London: Macmillan, 1928); Hugh Barty-King, *The Baltic Story: Baltick Coffee House to Baltic Exchange, 1744–1994* (London: Quiller Press, 1994).

69 See for example John Timbs, *Club Life of London with Anecdotes of the Clubs, Coffee-Houses and Taverns of the Metropolis During the 17th, 18th, and 19th Centuries*, 2 vols. (London: Richard Bentley, 1866); and Percy Colson, *White's, 1693–1950* (London: William Heineman, 1951), pp. 20–33.

70 Iain McCalman, 'Ultra-radicalism and convivial debating-clubs in London, 1795–1838', *English Historical Review* 102 (1987), 309–33.

71 'Coffee-Houses and Smoking', *New Monthly Magazine and Literary Journal* 16 (1826), 50–2, p. 51.

72 See also G. Dood, 'Public Refreshment', in Charles Knight, ed., *London*, 6 vols. (London: Charles Knight, 1843), vol. IV, pp. 305–20; anon., 'The Clubs of London', *National Review* 4.8 (1857), 295–334; John Timbs, *Club Life of London*; and Edward Forbes Robinson, *The Early History of Coffee Houses in England, with some account of the first use of coffee and a bibliography of the subject* (London: Kegan, Paul, Trench and Trübner, 1893).

73 Thomas Babington, Lord Macauley, *The History of England from the Accession of James the Second*, 6 vols. (1848–1855) (London: Macmillan, 1913), vol. I, pp. 360–2. Macauley's footnote (p. 362n) demonstrates his reading amongst the restoration coffee-house tracts.

74 Leslie Stephen, *English Literature and Society in the Eighteenth Century* (1903) (London: Methuen, 1966), pp. 21, 23, 26.

75 Stephen, *English Literature*; G. M. Trevelyan, *English Social History: A Survey of Six Centuries from Chaucer to Queen Victoria* (London, 1944); anon., 'The Clubs of London'.

76 Helmut Reinhold, 'Zur Sozialgeschichte des Kaffees und des Kaffeehauses',

Kölner Zeitshrift für Soziologie und Sozialpsychologie 10 (1958), 151–4 (a review of Heinrich Eduard Jacob, *Sage und Siegezug des Kaffees, die Biographie eines welt-wirtschaftlichen Stoffes* (Hamburg: Rowohlt Verlag, undated), a text whose first edition (Berlin, 1934) was translated as *The Saga of Coffee: the Biography of an Economic Product* (London: George Allen and Unwin, 1935)); and Hermann Westerfrölke, *Englische Kaffeehäuser als Sammelpunkte der literarischen Welt im Zeitalter von Dryden und Addison* (Jena: Walter Biedermann, 1924). The latter is a well-researched but brief account (ninety pages) that traces the use made of coffee-houses by literary figures (Dryden, Addison, Steele, Defoe, Swift and Savage).

77 Habermas's citation of Ned Ward is sourced to a footnote in Trevelyan, *English Social History* (p. 324n), and his remarks about *The Women's Petition Against Coffee. Representing to Publick Consideration the Grand Inconveniences accruing to their Sex from the Excessive Use of that Drying Enfeebling Liquor. Presented to the Right Honourable Keepers of the Liberty of Venus. By a Well-willer* (London: no pub., 1674) do not suggest personal knowledge of the text beyond the title.

78 See footnote 77.

79 Edward Bramah and Joan Bramah, *Coffee Makers: 300 Years of Art and Design* (London: Quiller, 1989), pp. 74–7.

80 Angus Wilson, 'After the show', in *A Bit Off the Map, and Other Stories* (New York: The Viking Press, 1957), pp. 136–7.

CHAPTER TWO

Misses, Murderesses, and Magdalens: women in the public eye

Caroline Gonda

> It was my impression that these women had done something wrong, had stepped, as it were, into the limelight out of turn – too young or too old, too early or too late – and yet anyone, any *woman*, could make a spectacle out of herself if she was not careful.
>
> (Mary Russo, *The Female Grotesque*)[1]

In the spring of 1752, two women, whom I shall call for the moment 'Elizabeth' and 'Mary', are planning a retreat from the world and a new life together. Their letters look forward to the joys of peace, privacy and seclusion, in an idyllic (and ladylike) version of pastoral. 'I perpetually figure to myself our little Seat and Garden', Elizabeth writes, 'our Evening and Morning Walks, our silent and Entertaining Books, our useful and friendly Conversation: Thus Life will glide away with Ease and Innocence.' Mary, meanwhile, has already fixed on the perfect location for this delightful life:

The Place I have in View is an obscure but pleasant Village; the House is at one End, small but convenient; the Gardens not large, but rather useful than elegant, at the Bottom of which runs a little Brook, clear as Chrystal, in which you see Trout and other Natives of the watry Element glide and wantonly play; on the other side is a delightful Meadow, which yields a beautiful and extensive Prospect. I propose to have but one Servant and a Gardener, and I have got a young Lady that will be very fond to make one among us; she is a Person of very great Worth, and though her Misfortunes are not so conspicuous as ours, yet she has undeservedly had her Share, which hereafter you will know more at large. In this sweet Retreat, and with this Company, what pleasures do I not propose, being fully determined neither to visit nor be visited; for after what has happened to us, we can never expect to be on an equal footing with the rest of the World, and I believe neither of us would chuse to be insulted by it.[2]

Despite Mary's attitude to household economy and the servant question, the ladies' pastoral remains a charmingly generalised affair. That idea of a retreat into private life and female companionship, seeking asylum and

53

comfort away from the rough world, seems as if it could come from almost any point in eighteenth-century literature: from the ending of Eliza Haywood's *British Recluse* (1722) to *Sir Charles Grandison*'s proposal for Protestant 'convents' (1753–4) – a hint taken from Mary Astell's *A Serious Proposal to the Ladies* (1696–7) – Sarah Scott's *Millenium Hall* (1762) or the fragmentary ending of Wollstonecraft's *The Wrongs of Woman* (1798). The 'Misfortunes' which prompt women's retreat in those texts range from being 'crossed in love' to seduction, rape, marital cruelty, wrongful imprisonment, and betrayal by wicked guardians, faithless lovers, false friends. Mary and Elizabeth, however, are indeed more than usually 'conspicuous' in their 'Misfortunes', as Mary's next sentence indicates: 'My Trial comes on the 3d of *March*, when I expect (nay, without bad Practices it can't be otherwise) to be clear'd.'[3] For this pastoral interlude, so unremarkable in itself, appears in a context which makes it extraordinary: it comes from a volume entitled *Genuine Letters that pass'd between Miss Blandy and Miss Jeffries, Before and After Conviction*, and by the time it was published, on 21 April 1752, the supposed authors of the letters, Mary Blandy and Elizabeth Jeffries, had both been hanged for murder. The dream of privacy and protection from the insults of 'the World' could not be further from the reality of Blandy and Jeffries – two women whose lives had become very public property, and whose deaths (attracting spectators in their thousands) still more so.

In a year when Parliament passed an Act to curb the alarming increase of murders (an Act under which convicted murderers could be immediately executed and then anatomized or hung in chains), the cases of Miss Blandy and Miss Jeffries were singled out as 'Instances of the most unnatural Barbarity'. Both crimes had been committed in the home, a hideous reminder that (as one speech for the prosecution put it) 'there is no Place where Security may be depended upon, but at the same Time Persons are barring their Doors from Thieves without, they are inclosing worse Enemies within'; Blandy's poisoning of her father, and Jeffries' conspiracy with a manservant to murder her uncle and pretend he had been shot by burglars, proved that 'the nearest Ties of Kindred are no Security'.[4] Other cases of domestic murder had, nevertheless, aroused comparatively little interest; it was the combination of domestic murder and 'female cruelty' which so gripped contemporary audiences – particularly when the murderess's victim was a father or father-substitute.

Parricide, as many of the anti-Blandy pamphlets pointed out, was the ultimate outrage against human and divine law, an offence against one's

Heavenly as well as Earthly Father: 'Ev'n Nature, with a Panic Struck, /
Sickens, and scarce endures the Shock', one poem commented.[5] The
natural order totters as paternal authority – the model and foundation
of all civil and social order – is struck down. Inverting the accepted
power structure of family relations, parricide presents the destruction of
the creator by his creation, the murder by a child of 'the Author of my
Being, the very Fountain of my Life'.[6] But a parricide who was also a
daughter was something more monstrous still, given the eighteenth
century's near-obsessive idealisation of the father–daughter bond.
'Certain it is, that there is no kind of Affection so pure and angelick as
that of a Father to a Daughter', Richard Steele had written in 1712:

He beholds her both with, and without Regard to her Sex. In Love to our Wives
there is Desire, to our Sons there is Ambition; but in that to our Daughters, there
is something which there are no Words to express.[7]

The beautiful purity and tenderness of the father–daughter relationship,
however difficult it might be to define its essential quality, was a theme
to which eighteenth-century writers returned again and again. For that
relationship to be violated by parricide was unthinkable: as Catherine
Talbot wrote to Elizabeth Carter (one of many who believed that Mary
Blandy must be innocent), 'On the whole her idea is too terrible to dwell
on.'[8]

Certainly the image of the father–daughter relationship which
emerged at the trial of Mary Blandy, and in the pamphlet war surrounding the case, fell hideously short of that eighteenth-century ideal. Miss
Blandy, a woman no longer young, had been courted by a Scottish half-
pay officer with aristocratic connections, Captain Cranstoun. Her
mother favoured Cranstoun's suit, but died before her husband's opposition could be overcome. Mary's father, Francis Blandy, a well-off attor-
ney from Henley, had let it be known that his only child would have
£10,000 on her marriage – a strong temptation to the impecunious
Cranstoun. Only after Mr Blandy's death did it emerge that he was
worth less than £4,000. Mr Blandy's hostility to Cranstoun may have
had some connection with his own lie about the extent of Mary's
fortune; it certainly had a lot to do with the fact that Cranstoun already
had a wife and child – or, as Cranstoun himself asserted when the news
broke, a mistress and bastard – living in Scotland. In order to soften Mr
Blandy's hostility to his prospective son-in-law, Mary claimed,
Cranstoun had sent her a supposedly harmless 'love-powder' which she
had duly put into her father's water-gruel. Mr Blandy subsequently died

of arsenic poisoning; traces of arsenic were found in the gruel; and, following detective work by the servants and by the eminent Dr Addington, who had attended Mr Blandy in the last stages of his illness, Mary was arrested for her father's murder.

The prosecution made great play of Mr Blandy's character as 'a Father . . . the most fond, the most tender, the most indulgent that ever lived', a father who 'with his dying breath forgave' his daughter and tried to shield her from prosecution.[9] Mary, by contrast, appeared as a monstrous daughter, who cursed her father for a rogue, a villain, and a toothless old dog; the hostile maidservant, Betty Binfield, reported with considerable relish that she had heard Miss Blandy say, '*Who would grudge to send an old Father to Hell for 10,000 l.* Exactly them words.'[10] Mary was caught in a double bind: accepting the Crown's version of her father's character weakened the 'love-powder' argument, but trying to excuse her alleged remarks by pointing out Mr Blandy's volatile and violent temper only reinforced the case against her as a daughter needing to be free of her difficult father. 'Who could bear to lighten herself, by loading a Father?', Richardson's Clarissa had asked in rather different circumstances, some years earlier; the Blandy case suggested that whether or not the daughter could bear to do it was not the question.[11] Culturally the thing was an impossibility.

The jury took only five minutes to find Mary Blandy guilty; and her own published *Narrative* of the events leading to her father's death failed to win the Royal clemency she had hoped for. Insisting to the last that she was merely the innocent, though fatal, instrument of her father's death, Mary Blandy was hanged at Oxford on the 6 April 1752. One account of the execution estimates the number of the crowd to be about 5,000, 'many of whom, and particularly several Gentlemen of the University, were observed to shed Tears. . . . Contrary to what is observed at other Executions, there was almost a profound Silence during the Time of this.'[12]

Elizabeth Jeffries' execution, like the rest of her case, was a less decorous affair than Mary Blandy's (at least as it appears in that account). According to *The Gentleman's Magazine*, more than ten thousand people 'assembled . . . early in the day, where galleries were erected, and rooms hired at considerable prices', only to find that the execution was happening elsewhere in Epping Forest rather than in Walthamstow. Despite this, 'such prodigious crowds of spectators came to all parts of the road' from the gaol 'and to the place of execution, as were never known in the county before'.[13] Unlike Mary Blandy, whose coolness on the scaffold

won her supporters even at the last, Miss Jeffries suffered a series of convulsion fits, as she had done during her trial. But then, Blandy's supporters might claim, she had not Blandy's consciousness of innocence to
sustain her. And, though her crime was not the heinous one of parricide,
it was little better; had not her rich, childless uncle adopted her at the
age of five, made her his sole heir, and 'behaved in every Respect to her
as an indulgent Father'?[14] It was true that some people claimed that her
uncle had then debauched her at the age of fifteen (or sixteen); that she
had had two children by him, of whom one, 'a fine Boy', was still living
(or that he had sent her to Portsmouth to lie in, where she miscarried,
then made her have an abortion when she became pregnant a second
time).[15] But in any case, the pamphleteers insisted, 'Miss was of a very
vicious and wicked Inclination naturally'.[16] Certainly no one seems to
have thought of the incest as offering either an excuse for Jeffries' murderous behaviour or a psychological insight into it. Incest was just one
more sordid element in the already squalid Jeffries case, with its enquiries into the state of Miss Jeffries' linen on the night in question and its
belowstairs intrigue (the manservant, John Swan, confessed that the
motives for murder included 'an apprehension that Miss was with child
by [him]').[17] Though the two cases were frequently compared by newspapers, magazines, and pamphlets, the Jeffries murder did not produce
anything like the flood of publications unleashed by Mary Blandy's case
– Authentic, Full, Secret and Genuine Histories, trial transcripts, even a
play (*The Fair Parricide*). Elizabeth Jeffries' story gained additional notoriety from its similarities to Mary Blandy's; but a year after the executions, new pamphlets debating Blandy's guilt or innocence were still
appearing.

In the sense that Miss Blandy and Miss Jeffries formed a kind of gruesome double-act, representing the extreme of women's public disgrace,
they had their curious counterpart in a sister-act which played out the
extreme of women's public success. For, in the spring of 1752, two young
women named Maria and Elizabeth were raised by marriage as high
above the common lot of women as Mary Blandy and Elizabeth Jeffries
were plunged by murder below it. The Gunning sisters, penniless Irish
beauties who had been drawing crowds and stopping traffic since their
arrival in London in 1750, had finally bagged a brace of coronets:
Elizabeth, the younger, becoming Duchess of Hamilton and Brandon in
a romantic midnight marriage on Valentine's Day; and Maria, with
more fitting pomp and circumstance, marrying the Earl of Coventry
three weeks later 'at his Lordships' [*sic*] House in Grosvenor Square'.[18]

Certainly in the minds of contemporaries the two apparently very different pairs of women were linked. 'Since the two Misses were hanged, and the two Misses were married, there is nothing at all talked of', complained Horace Walpole's friend, Lady Gower.[19] The beautiful Misses and the murderesses are linked not only by their place in contemporary gossip, but also by their status as spectacle, as objects of the public gaze.

From the very first, the Gunnings' combined appeal drew crowds on a grand (and often inconvenient) scale. Writing in June 1751, Walpole describes them as

two Irish girls of no fortune, who are declared the handsomest women alive. I think their being two, so handsome and both such perfect figures, is their chief excellence, for singly I have seen much handsomer women than either: however, they can't walk in the park, or go to Vauxhall, but such mobs follow them that they are generally driven away.[20]

Nine months later, after the two spectacular marriages, Walpole writes:

The world is still mad about the Gunnings: the Duchess of Hamilton was presented on Friday; the crowd was so great, that even the noble mob in the Drawing-Room clambered upon chairs and tables to look at her. There are mobs at their doors to see them get into their chairs; and people go early to get places at the theatres when it is known they will be there. [21]

Gunning mania was not confined to London; Walpole notes that 'such crowds flocked to see the Duchess Hamilton pass, that seven hundred people sat up all night in and about an inn in Yorkshire to see her get into her post-chaise next morning', and that 'It is literally true that a shoemaker at Worcester got two guineas and an half by showing a shoe that he was making for the Countess, at a penny apiece.'[22]

The Gunnings not only *attract* mobs, it seems; where necessary, they create them. Even the courtiers in the Royal drawing-room become 'the noble mob', casting Court manners to the winds and clambering on the furniture to gawp at the beautiful Duchess. The Gunnings and the gazers are inseparable in the popular imagination: it seems only fitting that Maria's marriage to the Earl of Coventry should be greeted with an Epithalamium from a poet styling himself 'Peeping Tom', invoking the legend of Lady Godiva and casting the new Lady Coventry as her natural successor:

> The wanton Casement stands at jar,
> At first she shines a distant Star:
> And now I take a nearer View;
> How blest, who thus shall peep at you![23]

What the Countess made of this impudent effort is not recorded; but her own attitude (and her sister's) to being the object of all eyes was ambivalent, to say the least. Following another incident in the Park, a satirical poem describes Maria as petitioning the King to intervene:

> Then straightway to Court she betakes her: –
> 'I'm come, Sir, to make my complaint;
> I can't walk the Park for your subjects,
> They stare without any restraint.'
>
> 'Shut, shut up the Park I beseech you;
> Lay a Tax upon staring so hard;
> Or, if you're afraid to do that, Sir,
> I'm sure you will grant me a Guard!'
>
> The Boon thus requested was granted:
> The Warriors were drawn up with care;
> 'With my slaves and my Guards I'm surrounded,
> Come, stare at me now if you dare!'[24]

According to Horace Bleackley, in his biography of Elizabeth Gunning, Maria did indeed seek and was granted her escort from the Brigade of Guards; whereupon she paraded for two hours of a summer evening in St James's Park, 'obliging every one to make way and exciting universal laughter . . . Naturally, the mob was more numerous and more curious than ever, and several of the most demonstrative were arrested by Justice Fielding's men for disorderly conduct.'[25]

The King's soft-heartedness (or soft-headedness) towards Lady Coventry is all the more remarkable given her notorious *faux pas* at their first meeting, when he had asked her which of the sights of London she most wanted to see, and she replied that what she really longed to see was a Coronation. Her early death from consumption in 1760 meant that she missed George III's Coronation in 1761; another satirical poem describes her in Elysium, asking Pluto for a passport so that she can see the ceremony, but rejecting it when she learns that she must remain invisible throughout:

> Nay, nay, quoth the Countess, if that be the case,
> I will stay where I am – Here's your passport again;
> A fig for the sight, if concealed one's fine face:
> I'd rather see nothing than not to be seen.[26]

The poem about the mobs in the Park had suggested that rank had increased Lady Coventry's self-importance:

> Indeed, if I were but Moll Gunning,
> They might have done just as they chose;
> But now I am married to Covey,
> They shall not thus tread on my toes.[27]

An early anecdote of Walpole's, however, suggests that even as 'Moll Gunning' and her sister, the beauties were apt to stand on their dignity – with, at times, very undignified results:

As you talk of our beauties, I shall tell you a new story of the Gunnings, who make more noise than any of their predecessors since the days of Helen, though neither of them, nor anything about them, have yet been *teterrima belli causa*. They went t'other day to see Hampton Court; as they were going into the Beauty Room [i.e. the room in which the Kneller portraits of Beauties from the reign of William III are kept], another company arrived; the housekeeper said, 'This way, ladies; here are the beauties.' The Gunnings flew into a passion, and asked her what she meant; that they came to see the palace, not to be showed as a sight themselves.[28]

The Gunnings' protest against being made a 'sight' for tourists itself becomes a comic part of the Gunning mythology; for these two women, attempts to control their representation in the public sphere meet with at best a limited success. Mary Blandy, with so much more at stake, had still less good fortune: her bids to represent herself on her own terms to the public – in her conduct after arrest, her speech at the trial, and her two pamphlets, the *Narrative* and *Miss Mary Blandy's Own Account* – served mainly to intensify public feeling against her, and to sharpen the sense of just how appalling her crime had been.

'Who could have thought that Miss *Blandy*, a young Lady virtuously brought up, distinguished for her good Behaviour and prudent Conduct in Life . . . should ever be brought to a Tryal . . . for the most desperate and bloodiest kind of Murder . . . ?' asked one of the opening speeches for the Crown. The judge, passing sentence, echoed that sentiment: 'One should have thought, your own Sense, your Education, and even the natural Softness of your Sex, might have secured you from an Attempt so barbarous and wicked.'[29] Instead, Mary's status and upbringing aggravated her guilt; and her behaviour in prison was merely an unfortunate reminder of those advantages in life which she had so wickedly abused.

A contemporary pamphlet shows her drinking tea in gaol and reports that she had taken her own tea-chest with her when arrested, its canisters 'all most full of fine Hyson, which she said would save her some Money'.[30] Such cool attention to detail and economy surely marks her out, the pamphlet implies, as a calculating murderess; but tea-drinking is only one of the unsuitably ladylike pursuits in which she indulges while awaiting trial:

Her Behaviour in Gaol from the first has been very serene and calm; but she did not appear so deeply and sincerely affected as could be expected for one in her Circumstances, she always drinking Tea twice a Day, sometimes walking in the Keeper's Garden with a Guard, and playing at Cards in the Evening; refusing to be seen by any Persons, except her own Particular Friends, who first sent in their Names, and then but very few.[31]

At the gallows, Mary Blandy's stoic calm would belatedly make her a heroine; here, the least sinister thing it betokens is a lack of proper filial feeling. Her refusal to be seen, too, far from indicating a gentlewoman's natural desire for privacy, becomes a sign of arrogance: how dare a criminal presume to set the terms on which she may be viewed?

Mary had already suffered repeated violations of her privacy and her dignity; but so, it could be argued, had the whole Blandy household, its secrets and quirks indecently exposed to public view by the trial proceedings as well as the pamphleteers. As in the Jeffries case, a rupture of relations in the private sphere turns 'little Family Affairs' (to borrow Mary Blandy's description of her quarrels with her father) into public property, and forces women into the glare of that fierce light that beats upon a scaffold.[32] Mary Blandy, trying to the last to keep intact the dignity of her own body, is reported to have said 'Gentlemen, don't hang me high for the sake of decency' – a not unreasonable request at a time when women's basic undergarment was a shift, and hanging itself a protracted process in which one might 'dance upon the rope' for half an hour or so. Her attempt to protect her body from further violation in death was, in any case, unsuccessful:

In about half an hour the body was cut down, and carried thro' the croud on the shoulders of a man with her legs exposed very indecently, for two or three hundred yards, to a neighbouring house, where it was put into a coffin.[33]

The longing for privacy and freedom from the insulting gaze of the world, so poignantly represented in those so-called *Genuine Letters* I quoted at the start, could scarcely have found a harsher conclusion.

The Murderesses' presence and performance in the public sphere of the courtroom and the scaffold both indicates and reinforces a disruption of contemporary ideals about women's place in the private sphere – the setting which supposedly reveals the true nature and character of women. The beautiful Misses, on the other hand, take the supposed epitome of female success in the private sphere (making a good marriage, becoming wives and mothers) to excess – and therefore into the morally dubious realm of female spectacle. As Lady Gower's equation of Misses hanged and Misses married suggests, the fact of female spectacle can trump the reasons for being spectacular. The line between being spectacular and making a spectacle of oneself is in any case – as the many Gunning anecdotes show – a perilously thin one.

Female readers desirous of emulating the Gunnings' spectacular success were to become the target of an Awful Warning in William Dodd's novel, *The Sisters*, first published in 1754. The Gunnings are never mentioned by name, but their recent triumphs hover over Lucy and Caroline Sanson's dreams of gaining fame, fortune, and titled husbands by flaunting their beauty in the London marriage-market. Dodd's novel presents an increasingly popular cautionary tale of the mid-eighteenth century: the horrific fate of the fallen woman, moving through seduction and betrayal to prostitution, gross physical injury, and death. Lucy's dreams of public glory lead her to the point where she no longer has a private life: she is 'thrown upon the common', without even a roof over her head once venereal disease has made her 'unfit for trade . . . forced, amidst many other fellow-sufferers, to wander about half naked, and in the night croud amongst them, to warm her miserable limbs, and to defend themselves from the severity of the skies.'[34] Only the approach of death allows her to regain a shadow of her former substance in the private sphere, in that obligatory sentimental scene, the reunion of a distracted father with his lost and fallen daughter:

'Said she not, *my father!*' cried the old unhappy man; 'said she not, *my father!* – hark! let me listen! Poor miserable object, that in this distress and sorrow hast but even now called me father! One word more, and I have done – speak one word more and I will be no farther curious – say thou art my daughter – and there needs not another syllable to burst my heart-strings – they are already cracking!' She groaned, she wept; and, with a voice that would have melted stone, she said – 'I am thy daughter! thy most wretched daughter! – Oh, my father, my dear distressed father!' With vehement haste, he threw himself on the floor by her side; and, unable to speak, uttered sounds far more pathetick and expressive than all speaking.[35]

Mr Sanson's already tottering reason is unable to bear the shock of reunion with his horrifyingly altered daughter; echoes of *King Lear* come thick and fast as he plummets into madness, and Lucy's death is closely followed by his own. That reunion scene is played over and over again in eighteenth-century narratives of the fallen woman; Dodd's novel itself offers a condensed version, in the story of the ragged, penitent prostitute whom Lucy has earlier refused to help. This unnamed woman is so deeply affected by her reunion with her bankrupt, imprisoned and dying father, who sends for her in order to give her his forgiveness and paternal blessing, that she miscarries. Her purpose in approaching Lucy and her fellow courtesan, Charlotte, she explains, is not only to solicit their charity but to reclaim them by her example: 'such as you are, I once was; such as I am, if you recover not yourselves immediately, you surely will be'. Despite Charlotte's rude dismissal ('beggars must never presume to be teachers. Pray trot, good Madam penitence'), the 'poor penitent prostitute' haunts both Lucy and the novel.[36]

Given his interest in the figure of the penitent prostitute and the fate of the fallen woman, it was perhaps appropriate that Dr William Dodd, the author of *The Sisters*, should have become a regular (and very popular) preacher at the Magdalen Hospital, or Magdalen House, the charitable institution for reception and reform of fallen women, established in 1758. Gerald Howson, in his biography of Dodd, *The Macaroni Parson*, suggests that

Dodd's theatrical temperament was perfectly suited to this particular institution. Magdalen House . . . flourished because it was continuously the object of malicious gossip. People, including the wicked old Earl of Sandwich, who regarded all charities as boring and would normally never be seen near such a place, came to the chapel on Sundays to have a look at the girls. Dodd preached, and the collection dishes brimmed with £1300–£1400 a time . . . . When Sterne preached at the equally deserving Foundling Hospital . . . the most he ever squeezed out of the public was £160.[37]

Like the Misses and the Murderesses, the Magdalens were powerful attractors of crowds. All sorts and conditions of people (and both sexes) came to watch the Magdalens, respectably and uniformly dressed, weeping and praying. H. F. B. Compston, historian of the Magdalen Hospital, notes that 'Early guides to London show that the chapel was popular' as a tourist attraction, and suggests that 'Royalty had encouraged, and may have created, a Magdalen *vogue*.'[38] He also quotes (as many others do) Walpole's account of a visit to the Magdalen in the company of Royalty (Prince Edward):

This new convent is beyond Goodman's Fields, and I assure you would content any Catholic alive . . . . The chapel is small and low, but neat, hung with Gothic paper and tablets of benefactions. At the west end were inclosed the sisterhood, above an hundred and thirty, all in greyish brown stuffs, broad handkerchiefs, and flat straw hats with a blue ribband, pulled quite over their faces. As soon as we entered the chapel, the organ played, and the Magdalens sung a hymn in parts; you cannot imagine how well. The chapel was dressed with orange and myrtle, and there wanted nothing but a little incense, to drive away the devil – or to invite him. Prayers then began, psalms, and a sermon; the latter by a young clergyman, one Dodd; who contributed to the Popish idea one had imbibed, by haranguing entirely in the French style, and very eloquently and touchingly. He apostrophized the lost sheep, who sobbed and cried from their souls – so did my Lady Hertford and Fanny Pelham, till I believe the City dames took them both for Jane Shores.[39]

After the service, the Royal party was given tea by 'the lady abbess, or matron', then taken to the refectory, where, Walpole writes,

all the nuns, without their hats, were ranged at long tables ready for supper. A few were handsome, many who seemed to have no title to their profession, and two or three of twelve years old: but all recovered and looking healthy. I was struck and pleased with the modesty of two of them, who swooned away with the confusion of being stared at – one of these is a niece of Sir Clement Cotterel . . . I kept my countenance very demurely, nor even inquired whether among the pensioners there were any *novices* from Mrs. Naylor's.[40]

Walpole's jokes about nuns and novices rely on the familiar double meaning of 'nunnery' as brothel – these young women have got themselves from one nunnery to another. As Walpole describes it, a visit to the Magdalen House is anyway a somewhat equivocal affair: it seems likely that he is not the only one keeping his 'countenance very demurely'. Everyone – including the two swooning Magdalens – is behaving just as they should.

But although the Magdalens are being (in the Gunnings' phrase) 'showed as a sight', the distinction between spectacle and spectators is not as clear as it seems at first. As the 'lost sheep' sob and cry 'from their souls', the aristocratic female audience sheds tears of sympathy, 'till I believe the City dames took them for Jane Shores'. For the City dames (or perhaps one should say, for Walpole?), Lord Hertford's lady and Judy O'Grady are sisters under the skin. (I had never thought of 'Jane Shores' as rhyming slang before, but perhaps I am the last to know.) Sympathy as an act of generous imagination comes dangerously close to fellow-feeling of quite another kind. The Magdalens' ritual performance of penitence and self-abasement draws at least part of its female audience in as participants, as performers themselves, blurring the boundaries between fallen women and fine ladies. The presence of Sir Clement Cotterel's niece suggests that, in one case at least, the boundary has already been crossed.

The Magdalen House redomesticates women who have entered the public sphere in the sense of 'coming upon the town'; through penitence, useful work, and regularity of life, it refits women for their proper place in the home, aiming to return them to the private sphere. Yet this process becomes itself a very public spectacle, and, as Ann Van Sant suggests, the women's individual and private histories are suppressed (a sign in all the wards of the second hospital building read 'Tell your story to no-one'), to make way for a public, 'representative fiction' of the Magdalen. That fiction appears not only in the 'Magdalen narratives', by Dodd and others, which Markman Ellis discusses in *The Politics of Sensibility*, but also in what Van Sant calls the 'theater of pathos' created by the chapel services. 'As they played the pathetic role of repentant prostitute before a public audience, they became more thoroughly what they played.'[41]

This public spectacle of reform also went some way towards solving one of the Charity's main problems, outlined by Dodd in *An Account of the Rise, Progress, and Present State of the Magdalen Hospital*. Introducing 'An Authentic Narrative of a Magdalen', the story of 'A. F.', Dodd explains that the Magdalen House cannot, like other charities, point to its most lasting successes, since reformed women 'would wish, doubtless, to steal through the world silent and unknown . . . . Let therefore, such remain in that decent privacy which they desire'. Those women who 'return to vice', however, Dodd regrets,

will necessarily be public; and indeed every bad woman will bring, or attempt to bring an opprobrium upon the House; while no counterbalance can be had from the public and becoming conduct of those, who persevere in the paths of virtue.[42]

The story of 'A. F.' can be told because it is successfully completed; reconciled to her estranged father after her reform in the Magdalen House, she has died a Christian death, expiring 'with blessings on the Charity, as the great means of her salvation'.[43] In general, however, the Magdalen ideal is fulfilled by penitents who return silently to the private sphere, leaving their stories to be shaped and ventriloquised by others in 'Authentic Narratives' and 'Original Letters'. Meanwhile, the Magdalen's 'theatre of pathos' displays as product what can only be in process: a performance which, inevitably, must try to prove its authenticity through ritual repetition.

Questions of authenticity are inevitably raised by the representations of all three sets of women I have been discussing in this essay. It is not merely a case of which writings (or visual representations) we decide to accept as authentic among so many – all those secret histories, candid accounts, original and genuine letters, full and authentic narratives – though the number and variety of representations is clearly a complicating factor. (Mary Blandy's many pamphlets, for example, are hedged about with publishers' authenticating devices – title pages proclaim that the originals in Miss Blandy's handwriting are available to public view at the publishers', or that the account is followed by a declaration of authenticity signed by Miss Blandy herself in Oxford Castle Gaol in the presence of *two* clergymen.)

Questions of authenticity are also clearly related to female *performance*: Mary Blandy's behaviour in gaol or at the scaffold, the Gunnings' supposed desire to avoid being 'showed as a sight', the Magdalens' penitence and the aristocratic ladies' tears, may betoken an 'authentic' female virtue, or one that is only assumed. If female virtue is coded as that which is private and silent (as it seems to be in Dodd's *Account*), must women's public virtue be a contradiction in terms, something which cannot be proved as true but only exposed as false construction or 'acting'? Is the 'public sphere' in some sense always already a stage, and therefore an improper space for women or a space only for improper women? If 'bad women' are 'necessarily public', are all women's public appearances shadowed or tainted?

For aristocratic women, one might argue, being in the public eye, being on display, is part of their duty as daughters or as wives. Women *are* written into the ceremonial script of state occasions in particular, even if they are present as functions rather than as persons, their individuality subsumed in rank. The Gunnings marry into a life of performance and show; as Duchess and Countess they should necessarily be a decorous part of whatever spectacle they attend. What their detractors complain of is their failures in decorum – they become the Wrong Kind of Spectacle.

A prime example of this appears in an anonymous satire of 1773 called *A Mob in the Pit*, attacking Elizabeth Gunning, now Duchess of Argyll, for her behaviour at the theatre.[44] The Duchess, 'bent for once to be completely odd', has given up her box 'to try if she can sit / With vulgar Souls, and mob it in the Pit'; but, finding that 'place to her high Greatness was denied', attempts publicly and noisily to reclaim the box from its now rightful occupants, mesdames Harrington and Paget. The supposed star of the show, Mlle Heinel, finds herself caught up in a different drama as Paget appeals to her 'for the truth'; despite her tearful confirmation of Paget's claim, Heinel is unable to make peace as the

Duchess's tantrum carries all before it. Here, once again, the boundaries between (female) spectacle and (female) spectator are dangerously blurred, though the performance is neither tragedy nor sentimental comedy, but burlesque: Heinel herself is 'bribed from France / By Macaronis, dying for a dance'. The audience, as it turns out, is the right one for both the scheduled and the unscheduled spectacle:

> The crouds that throng, this Phoenix to behold,
> Widows, and wives, and virgins – young, and old,
> Of every sex, condition, and degree,
> From w——s profess'd, to W——s of Quality;
> . . .
> From batter'd *H*————*n*, and blasted *V*—*e*,
> To every tatter'd drab of Drury-Lane:
> . . .
> Sudden in all this bustle, noise, and din,
> *A*————*ll*'s puissant Duchess marches in.

Once again, Elizabeth Gunning becomes the focus of mob attention, though it is interesting to note that this mob is described as entirely female (and largely disreputable). In theory, the Duchess's offence is that she has first abandoned, then attempted to regain, her aristocratic elevation. In fact, however, the poet seems to suggest in his closing address to her, the Duchess (if behaviour is anything to go by) may unwittingly have sought her rightful place when she tried to 'mob it in the Pit':

> Such has thy conduct been – reflect, and say,
> Is it not justice boldly to convey
> The story to the public ear, and show
> To all the world, what all the world should know,
> Tho' lifted, by the Beauty of a face,
> From vile Plebeian to Patrician race,
> That, spite of Titles, Dignity, and Fame,
> The paltry Breed of *G-nn-gs* is the same?

There is a curious tension in this poem: the difference between 'w——s profess'd' and 'W——s of Quality' is clearly of degree, not kind, with both drabs and duchesses appearing as ciphers. And yet the poem needs a sense of the very real difference between 'vile Plebeian [and] Patrician race' in order to condemn the Duchess as 'Thou self-created Creature'. In fact, the Gunnings' origins were not as humble as this suggests: their mother was an Honourable and their father, though poor, was a gentleman and a landowner of sorts in Ireland (with a useful bog into which creditors tended to disappear).[45] Nevertheless, the

Gunnings, like Heinel, offend against proper categorisation: Heinel is unfavourably compared with the stars of tragedy ('our British Roscius') and comedy (lacking 'BARRY's grace') and can only 'strut, and flourish with her Legs and Arms'. The Duchess, too, is a creature of burlesque (it is significant, I think, that the old story about the sisters' being on the verge of becoming actresses if they had not made those spectacular marriages should have clung so tenaciously to the Gunnings throughout their careers). The 'paltry Breed of *G-nn-gs*' can produce only grotesquely parodic performances of aristocratic demeanour. Like all those Gaiety Girls marrying up a century or so later and effortlessly out-Duchessing Duchesses, the Gunnings had to be even more aristocratic than the aristocracy. And yet, as the poem and the events it describes suggest, the division between the Gunnings and the mob, spectacle and spectator, may always have been a false one.

I have been using metaphors of theatre and performance fairly freely here, but some implications of those metaphors need to be addressed. To the extent that these women were actors on a public stage, it was mostly not to a script of their own making, or under their own direction and management. This is most obvious in the case of the Magdalens, but it's also true of the Murderesses and even of the beautiful Misses. When these women do try to assume direction or provide their own script, the result is generally either ridicule or catastrophe. Performance metaphors are sometimes used as if women's presence centre stage, in the limelight, what you will, in itself confers power on women or is some kind of feminist triumph.[16] That usage forgets that in the end the real power always lies with the audience and that what lies beyond the theatre lights may just as easily be a barrage of rotten tomatoes and dead cats – or, more grimly in the case of Mary Blandy, an unimpressed jury's verdict of Guilty. Women's presence in the public eye – as Mary Blandy, Elizabeth Jeffries, the Gunnings, and the niece of Sir Clement Cotterel all in their different ways discovered, and demonstrate, is not automatically a cause for celebration.

NOTES

1 Mary Russo, *The Female Grotesque: Risk, Excess and Modernity* (New York and London: Routledge, 1994), p. 53.
2 *Genuine Letters that pass'd between Miss Blandy and Miss Jeffries, Before and After Conviction* (London: J. Scott, 1752), pp. 20, 21–2.
3 Ibid., p. 22

4   *The Genuine Trial of John Swan and Elizabeth Jeffreys, Spinster, for the Murder of her late Uncle Mr. Joseph Jeffreys of Walthamstow in Essex* (London: C. Corbett, [1752]), p. 4.

5   Verses from a contemporary engraving, 'Miss Molly Blandy, Who with her own & her Sweetheart's Contrivance did Barbarously and Inhumanly Poison her own Father for his Estate. Taken from the Life in Oxford Castle', reproduced in William Roughead, ed., *Trial of Mary Blandy*, Notable English Trials series (Edinburgh and London: William Hodge, 1914), facing p. 112.

6   *The ****-Packet Broke-open; or, a Letter from Miss Blandy in the Shades Below, to Capt. Cranstoun in his Exile Above* (London: M. Cooper, 1752), p. 6.

7   *The Spectator* 449, 5 August 1712.

8   *A Series of Letters between Mrs. Elizabeth Carter and Miss Catherine Talbot*, 4 vols. (London: F. C. and J. Rivington, 1809), vol. II, p. 76.

9   *The Tryal of Mary Blandy, Spinster; for the Murder of her Father, Francis Blandy, Gent. At the Assizes held at Oxford for the County of Oxford, on Saturday the 29th of February, 1752 . . . Published by Permission of the Judges* (London: John and James Rivington, 1752), pp. 45–6.

10   Roughead, ed., *Trial*, p. 98.

11   Samuel Richardson, *Clarissa*, 7 vols. (London: S. Richardson, 1747–8), vol. II, p. 69.

12   *Miss Mary Blandy's Own Account of the Affair between Her and Mr. Cranstoun from the Commencement of their Acquaintance in the Year, 1746. To the Death of her Father, in August 1751. With all the Circumstances leading to that unhappy Event. To which is added, An Appendix. Containing Copies of some Original Letters now in Possession of the Editor. Together with An exact Relation of her Behaviour whilst under Sentence; and a Copy of the Declaration signed by herself, in the Presence of two Clergymen, two Days before her Execution. Published at her dying Request* (London: A. Millar), p. 63.

13   'Historical Chronicle for March 1752', *The Gentleman's Magazine* 22, p. 141.

14   *The Genuine Trial of John Swan and Elizabeth Jeffreys*, p. 5.

15   See, for example, *The Gentleman's Magazine* 22, 141; *The Whole Tryal of John Swann, and Elizabeth Jeffries, for the Murder of her Uncle . . . Second Edition. To which is added, The voluntary Confession of Elizabeth Jeffries, since her Conviction; as also an Account of her incestuous Living with her Uncle, and her Motives for murdering him* (London: M. Cooper, 1752); *Authentick Memoirs of the Wicked Life and Transactions of Elizabeth Jeffryes, Spinster. Who was Executed on Saturday, March 28, 1752, On Epping-Forest, near Walthamstow. For Being Concerned in the Murder of her late Uncle, Mr. Joseph Jeffryes* (London, 1752), p. 38.

16   *Authentick Tryals of John Swan, and Elizabeth Jeffryes, for the Murder of Mr. Joseph Jeffryes of Walthamstow in Essex; with the Tryal of Miss Mary Blandy, for the Murder of her own Father. To which are added, The Particulars relating to those horrid Murders; the Behaviour and Dying Speeches of the Criminals; and whatever else is to be relied on as a true History of those memorable Offenders* (London, 1752), p. 58.

17   *The Gentleman's Magazine* 22, p. 141.

18 Letter from John Gunning, 5 March 1752, quoted in Ida Gantz, *The Pastel Portrait: The Gunnings of Castle Coote and Howards of Hampstead* (London: The Cresset Press, 1963), p. 46.

19 Horace Walpole, letter to Henry Seymour Conway, 23 June 1752 OS, in *The Yale Edition of Horace Walpole's Correspondence*, ed. W. S. Lewis, 48 vols. (London: Oxford University Press, 1937–83), vol. XXXVII, p. 342. The same letter reports the gossip that 'Lady Coventry has miscarried of one or two children, and is going on with one or two more, and is gone to France today' (vol. XXXVII, p. 341).

20 Walpole, letter to Horace Mann, 18 June 1751 OS, in *The Yale Edition*, vol. XX, 260.

21 Walpole, letter to Horace Mann, 23 March 1752 OS, in *The Yale Edition*, vol. XX, 311–12.

22 Walpole, letters to Horace Mann, 13 May and 27 July 1752 OS, in *The Yale Edition*, vol. XX, 317 and 324.

23 *Peeping Tom to the Countess of Coventry. An Epithalamium* (Dublin: S. Price, [1752]).

24 Quoted in Gantz, *The Pastel Portrait*, p. 62; attributed to Horace Walpole.

25 Horace Bleackley, *The Beautiful Duchess: Being an Account of the Life and Times of Elizabeth Gunning, Duchess of Hamilton and Argyll* (London: John Lane, The Bodley Head and New York: Dodd, Mead, 1907; reprinted 1927), p. 84.

26 Quoted in Bleackley, *The Beautiful Duchess*, p. 98.

27 Quoted in Gantz, *The Pastel Portrait*, p. 62.

28 Walpole, letter to Horace Mann, 31 August 1751 OS, in *The Yale Edition*, vol. XX, 272.

29 *Tryal of Mary Blandy*, pp. 9, 46.

30 *A Genuine Account of the most Horrid Parricide committed by Mary Blandy, Spinster, upon the Body of her Father Mr. Francis Blandy, Gent. Town-Clerk of Henley upon Thames, Oxfordshire . . .* (Oxford: C. Goddard 1751), p. 13.

31 Ibid., p. 15.

32 *Tryal of Mary Blandy*, p. 30.

33 'Historical Chronicle for April 1752', *The Gentleman's Magazine* 22, p. 189.

34 William Dodd, *The Sisters; or, the History of Lucy and Caroline Sanson, Entrusted to a False Friend* (1754), 2 vols. in I (London: Harrison, 1781), p. 134.

35 Ibid., p. 151.

36 Ibid., pp. 56–7.

37 Gerald Howson, *The Macaroni Parson: A Life of the Unfortunate Dr Dodd* (London: Hutchinson, 1973), p. 43.

38 H. F. B. Compston, *The Magdalen Hospital. The Story of a Great Charity* (London: SPCK, 1917), p. 151.

39 Walpole, letter to George Montagu, 28 January 1760, in *The Yale Edition*, vol. IX, pp. 273–4.

40 Walpole, in *The Yale Edition*, vol. IX, 274.

41 Ann Jessie Van Sant, *Eighteenth-Century Sensibility and the Novel: The Senses in Social Context* (Cambridge: Cambridge University Press, 1993), pp. 33, 36.

See also Markman Ellis, *The Politics of Sensibility: Race, Gender and Commerce in the Sentimental Novel* (Cambridge: Cambridge University Press, 1996); and Sarah Lloyd, '"Pleasure's Golden Bait": Prostitution, Poverty and the Magdalen Hospital in Eighteenth-Century London', *History Workshop Journal* 41 (1996), 50–70.

42 [William Dodd,] *An Account of the Rise, Progress, and Present State of the Magdalen Hospital*, 5th edn (London: W. Faden, and sold at the Hospital, St George's-Fields, 1776), p. 35.

43 Ibid., p. 43.

44 *A Mob in the Pit: or, Lines addressed to the D—ch-ss of A————ll* (London: S. Bladon, 1773).

45 See Frank Frankfort Moore, *A Georgian Pageant* (New York: E. P. Dutton, 1909), p. 109. Moore writes that 'The topography of the district was notoriously puzzling to the officers from the Dublin courts.'

46 See e.g. Judith Butler, *Bodies that Matter: On the Discursive Limits of 'Sex'* (New York and London: Routledge, 1993), and its derivatives.

PART II

Consuming arts

The choice of Hercules: the polite arts and 'female excellence' in eighteenth-century London

Charlotte Grant

ye Art of Drawing is absolutely necessary in many Employments, Trades, and Manufactures . . . Encouragement thereof may prove of great Utility to the public.

Minutes of the Society of Arts[1]

'No taste can ever be formed in manufactures.

Sir Joshua Reynolds, 'Discourse I'[2]

Art requires and imagines a series of publics in its various practices from production through display to viewing.[3] Works of art are viewed in particular contexts; the organisation of those contexts, the history of spaces, and their controlling institutions constitute an essential part of any consideration of art's publics. This essay traces women's representation in the public sphere of art in eighteenth-century London. I examine two related pairs of contexts for the viewing of contemporary British art in London: Vauxhall Gardens, in Vauxhall, and the Foundling Hospital in Lamb's Conduit Fields in the 1740s; and the two major hosts of exhibitions from the 1760s onwards: the Society for the Encouragement of Arts, Manufactures and Commerce, site of the first exhibition of contemporary British artists in 1760, and the Royal Academy, founded in 1768.

Public exhibitions joined shows and spectacles as part of the 'material pleasures' on offer to London's consumer society.[4] As with other forms of public pleasure, the display of art provoked a series of anxieties, focusing in particular on the moral implications of sensual pleasure. As a consequence, theorists and practitioners were keen to stress the usefulness or moral qualities of the art they produced and promoted. However, it was also acknowledged, as expressed here by Alexander Gerard, that: 'Great sensibility of taste is generally accompanied with lively passions. Women have always been considered as possessing both in a more eminent degree than men.'[5] Referring to Gerard, Stephen

75

Copley draws attention to the problem this poses both for civic humanism and for polite culture:

The humanist tradition cannot find any place for women in the ranks of its
active citizens. In contrast . . . the position of women in polite culture is ambiguous, as they are offered 'simultaneous enfranchisement and restriction'[6] in
polite texts that appear at first sight committed to the celebration of thoroughly
'feminized' values. Nowhere is this clearer than in the area of taste, and in the
practice and appreciation of the fine arts.[7]

Not only is this a problem posed by women, but, as I hope to show, it is
also a problem partly solved by women's involvement – as exemplified
by Elizabeth Montagu's representation in James Barry's mural for the
Society of Arts.

  John Brewer's examination of 'the emergence of an overtly commercial "high" or "polite" culture in the "public sphere"' draws attention to
the fact that 'women's periodicals . . . sentimental comedy and "she
tragedy" in the theater, conversation pieces and domestic portraits in
painting, even the funereal sculpture of Roubillac . . . were seen as especially catering to female taste'.[8] Anxious contemporary critics saw this
pattern of cultural consumption as leading to the feminisation of culture
in general. Brewer argues that 'the seductive woman is analogous to the
culture of which she is a part'. Thus in a public sphere in which culture
is sold as commodity, and that culture is feminised, culture is figured as
a whore:

As Hogarth well knew, it is in the image of the prostitute that all the greatest
anxieties about eighteenth-century culture – its debasement into a trade or business, its association with sexual license, its ambiguous status as a realm of sensuality, sense, or reason, and its potential to privilege women – are to be found.[9]

  Hogarth's Harlot provides a starting point. The pirating of *The
Harlot's Progress*, the first of his 'modern moral subjects', prompted
Hogarth to put an act through Parliament in 1735 protecting the copyright of engravers. Thus, the story of the woman as commodity is
claimed by Hogarth as his commercial property in the marketplace. In
the first plate (figure 2) the innocent Moll Hackabout arrives from the
country, and is shown between an unresponsive priest and a bawd,
Mother Needham, who is eyeing her up for her client, Colonel
Charteris.[10] As Ronald Paulson has noticed, this innocent poised
between the church and prostitution, between a compromised virtue
and vice is a re-working of the theme of 'Hercules at the Crossroads'.[11]
In the original legend of the 'Choice of Hercules' as told by Xenophon

Figure 2 Hogarth, *The Harlot's Progress*, Plate 1.

in his *Memoirs of Socrates*, Hercules was confronted by two beautiful women before beginning his labours, one offering a life of ease and pleasure, the other a life of duty and labour for mankind. Petrarch introduced the idea of Hercules thinking over his choice at a parting of the ways. Paintings by Carracci, Veronese and Poussin show him as a male nude between two women.[12] The gender of personifications of virtue and vice is unstable in the seventeenth century: in an English version of *The Choice of Hercules* from George Wither's *A Collection of Emblems* of 1635, virtue or wisdom is a man, carrying a book and shown with Hermes' *caduceus* or herald's staff. This reference to Hermes, messenger of the gods, reinforces the idea that wisdom or virtue function as the path to the gods. Pleasure is an old woman holding up the mask of youth, who appears to have a devil's tail, and is associated with emblems of death: a scull and crossbones, and a cut flower in a vase.

John Barrell and David Solkin have established an early eighteenth-century representation of *The Judgement of Hercules*, which reverts to showing two women, as the paradigmatic image for the period; it encapsulates the attempts of theorists to raise the intellectual profile of contemporary painting, to locate painting in the realm of virtue rather than luxury.[13] This representation was painted by Paolo de Matthaeis (and engraved by Simon Gribelin), based on instructions from the third Earl of Shaftesbury (figure 3). The engraving first appeared in Shaftesbury's *Characteristicks* of 1714, which included his *Notion of the Historical Draught or Tabulature of the Judgement of Hercules*. It serves to illustrate Shaftesbury's argument in favour of a shift from emblematical representation towards a more rational iconography.

Shaftesbury's version shows a well-muscled Hercules deciding between virtue and pleasure or vice, represented as two alluring females. His head is turned towards the woman on the left who, decently dressed, is pointing to the path of virtue which is winding, rocky and steep, but ultimately rewarding, since it leads man nearer to God. She, rather than Hercules, is pointing. Her sword and helmet suggest that she represents Minerva (also goddess of the arts, and thus a doubly suitable subject for Shaftesbury's purposes). Hercules' body language is complicated, his body leans to the right, towards a minimally dressed woman who fawns at him from the floor, tempting him to her cave of vice with its items of faintly oriental luxury. This representation encodes a lesson about eighteenth-century attitudes to landscape: virtue's landscape is open, and will offer the wide prospect of control; vice's landscape is enclosed, an artificial-looking bower, the foliage and the artifacts oriental and luxurious.[14] In Hogarth's version there is a neat gender inversion of most eighteenth-century representations of Hercules since the chooser is a woman, and her two possible destinations, Charteris and the priest, are male.

The 1740s saw a shift in cultural formation recognised by Sir Ellis Waterhouse. Taking Richardson's novel *Pamela* (published 1740) as paradigmatic, he identifies an alliance of virtue and a 'newly powerful social group – the literate bourgeoisie with the mode of sensibility', and names the decade 'the bourgeois sentimental decade'.[15] He uses this characterisation to draw analogies with Vauxhall Gardens and the Foundling Hospital.[16] Hogarth was instrumental in introducing the display of contemporary art into both. We can read these two spaces as reflecting the dichotomy of Hercules' choice: vice and virtue, public and private, cast as pleasure and charity or, perhaps more specifically, the pleasures of social interaction leading to the vice of dissipation, compared with the pleasures of benevolence leading to the virtue of charity.

These two interlinked options form the uneasy core of the literary

Figure 3 Simon Gribelin (after Paolo de Matthaies), *The Judgement of Hercules* (1713), in Anthony Ashley Cooper, Earl of Shaftesbury, *Characteristicks of Men, Manners, Opinions, Times*, 3rd edn (London: John Derby, 1723).

culture from which Waterhouse borrows his term 'sentimental'. Sensibility may be founded on the rock of moral sense, but the sentimental frequently comes perilously close to foundering on the rocks of sensuality. Richardson's *Pamela* charts Mr B.'s attempts at seduction, which are thwarted by Pamela's virtue. Her triumph of sensibility is registered in the sublimation of his illicit desire into respect and matrimony. This exploration of the sublimated possibility of the erotic in the pleasures of benevolence is also key to other fictions, for example Yorick's encounters in Laurence Sterne's *A Sentimental Journey* (1768). Contemporaries were alive to these ambiguities: an anonymous portrait of Sterne shows him ogling nude female sculptures, and representations of sentimental heroines typically exploit the ambivalent erotic appeal of virtue in distress.[17]

Vauxhall Gardens (described at the turn of the eighteenth century as a 'rural brothel') struggled hard to convert its licence for licentiousness into a licence for pleasure. The ambiguity persists in at least some of the few surviving of the original fifty supper-box paintings commissioned by

Jonathon Tyers around 1740 as part of his programme of redesigning the gardens as a polite pleasure ground. Among the paintings were versions of Joseph Highmore's *Pamela* paintings. Few Vauxhall supper-box paintings survive, but one which does is Francis Hayman's *May Day or the Milkmaid's Garland*, one of the Vauxhall images which, as Solkin suggests, seeks to render comic or sentimental the unruly popular manifestations of carnival.[18] Similarly, Hayman's *The Play of See Saw* shows the innocent on the brink of 'falling'. The verses by L. Truchy attached to the engraving published in 1743 make this obvious:

> When at the top of her advent'rous Flight
> The frolick Damsel tumbles from her Height:
> Tho her Warm Blush bespeaks a present Pain
> It soon goes Off – she falls to rise again;
> But when the Nymph with Prudence unprepared,
> By Pleasure sway'd – forsakes her Honours Guard:
> That slip once made, no wisdom can restore,
> She falls indeed! and falls to rise no more.

'Pleasure' lures the 'Damsel' into trouble. Despite being cleaned up by Jonathon Tyers and enjoying patronage by Frederick Duke of Wales, Vauxhall kept its reputation for sexual danger. In Fanny Burney's *Evelina* (1778), the heroine suffers the most frightening attempt on her virtue in Vauxhall when, in search of 'a little pleasure', her insufficiently genteel cousins lead her into one of the 'dark walks'. They become objects of unwelcome notice, and, separated from her cousins, Evelina is accosted by a group of youths who assume her to be an actress or worse. She is apparently rescued by an acquaintance, Sir Clement Willoughby, who exclaims: 'Is this a place for Miss Anville?' but then takes advantage of her situation, attempting to lead her off where they 'shall least be observed'.[19]

The second major venue for the display of contemporary British art in the 1740s was the Foundling Hospital, where Hogarth organised a group of artists to decorate the general court room. Established by Thomas Coram in 1739, the hospital cared for abandoned children, training them as useful members of society. As a friend of Coram, and one of the first Governors, Hogarth marshalled artists to donate works to the institution, among them large history paintings which featured acts of charity – for example his own *Moses Brought before Pharoah's Daughter* (1746) and Highmore's *Hagar and Ishmael* (1746).[20] These paintings encourage emulation, but also fulfil a commercial function: they advertise the artists' skills to potential clients among the wealthy supporters of the hospital. André Rouquet suggested in 1755 that 'this exhibition of skill, equally commendable and new, has afforded the public an opportunity of judging whether the English are such indifferent artists, as foreigners, and even the English themselves pretend.'[21] They are images of virtue, biblical exempla, but given the origins of the foundlings (illegitimate and other abandoned children) vice is never far away. Solkin describes the Foundling as an example of the 'privatisation of virtue': 'part of the process by which the central values of civic humanism were redefined to meet the ideological require-ments of a modern commercial policy', which registers what Barrell describes as the confusion of the distinctions between public and private virtue.[22] This public/private distinction is typically mapped onto a male/female opposition; but as the essays (and specifically the introduc-tion) in this collection suggest, the assumption of gendered 'separate spheres' is not consistent for the period. The public/private distinction is also already challenged in some civic humanist discourse; for example, the inscription from a monument in York Minster to the honourable Thomas Watson Wentworth, who died in 1723, reads:

> HIS VIRTUES WERE EQUAL TO HIS DESCENT:
> BY HIS ABILITIES HE WAS FORMED FOR PUBLICK,
> BY INCLINATION DETERMINED TO PRIVATE LIFE:
> IF THAT LIFE CAN BE CALLED PRIVATE,
> WHICH WAS DAILY EMPLOYED
> IN SUCCESSIVE ACTS OF BENIFICENCE
> TO THE PUBLICK.[23]

'Acts of benificence' require money, and charity functions to justify com-merce, but in civic humanist discourse commerce itself threatens to overthrow the concerns for public good.

This argument is clearly demonstrated in *An Estimate of the Manners and Principles of the Times* (1757) by John Brown, who also wrote *Essays on the Characteristics of the Earl of Shaftesbury*. Brown charts the slide of politeness into viciousness: 'We are rolling to the Brink of a Precipice that must destroy us'; a precipice formed by 'gross luxury' and 'effeminacy'.[24] He identifies three stages of commerce. The first is characterised by its social aspect: it 'supplies mutual Necessities, prevents mutual Wants, extends mutual Knowledge, eradicates mutual Prejudice, and spreads mutual Humanity'. The second is where he locates the arts: the 'middle and more advanced Period . . . provides Conveniences, increaseth Numbers, coins Money, gives Birth to Arts and Science, creates equal Laws, diffuses general Plenty and general Happiness'. It is only the third stage, with

which Britain is threatened, which raises problems: 'it brings in
Superfluity and vast Wealth; begets Avarice, gross Luxury, or effeminate
Refinement among the higher Ranks, together with general Loss of
Principle' (pp. 152–3). Luxury is anti-social; it is vain and selfish, and
threatens effeminacy. Here too 'active religious Principle is lost thro' the
attentive Pursuit of *Pleasure*'. Further danger follows. Not only practical
belief, but also what Brown terms '*speculative* Belief' will suffer since, due
to the spread of leisure and literature, vice now has a voice: 'because
Leisure and *Literature* having opened the Field of *Disputation*, Vice as well
as Virtue will of course arm herself with every Weapon of Preservation
and Offence' (p. 166). Vice and Virtue are here personified and, as in
Shaftesbury's *Judgement Of Hercules* image, gendered female. Brown
directly links the desire for commodities to this abandonment of honour
and describes it as doubly 'unmanly':

Instead of the Good of others, or the Happiness of the Public, the object of
Pursuit naturally sinks into some unmanly and trifling Circumstance: The
Vanity of Dress, Entertainments, Equipage, Furniture, of course takes
Possession of the Heart. (pp. 170–1)

In Brown's argument commerce finally becomes incompatible with the
public spirit:

In the commercial State, Avarice represents *Wealth*, in the mixed state
Effeminacy represents *Pleasure*, as the *chief Good*. Both these Delusions tend to
the Extinction of public Spirit. (p. 174)

Art is traditionally seen as evidence of society's improvement or
'refinement', but, as suggested by Brown, refinement is a contentious
issue when it raises the spectre of luxury. The debate on luxury, to which
Brown's text belongs, is complex and characteristically employs a gendered vocabulary. In classical rhetoric, women are doubly associated
with luxury: presumed to have an innate desire for ornament, they are
associated with physical or bodily pleasures; they represent the animal
side of humanity, rather than the rational or intellectual. A society which
indulges in the pursuit of luxury risks becoming 'soft'; its men turning
away from virtue, specifically martial virtue, towards a life of ease and
pleasure, frequently represented as effeminisation.[25]

This language, found in Pliny, Juvenal and later Machiavelli, reap-
pears in the eighteenth century in the discourse of civic humanism,
where, as in Brown's *Estimate*, anxiety about the encroachment of luxury
focuses on the increasing commercialisation of eighteenth-century
society. The alternative strand in the luxury debate, instead of seeing

luxury as emblematic of the decadence and impending destruction of society, accepts it as beneficial to society's development. Christopher Berry charts a 'de-moralisation' of the luxury debate through Barbon, Mandeville, Hume and Adam Smith, which challenges the distrust of luxury central to civic humanism.[26] One effect of this challenge is to broaden the category of those understood to be in a position to exercise taste from landowners to include the urban 'middling sort', and women.

The anxieties about commerce and its dangerous effect on the 'public Spirit' are reflected in and contested by the early alliances of artists in England. The Royal Academy pursued a number of functions laid out in its 'Instrument of Foundation' signed by George III on 10 December 1768. Item one states that:

> The said Society shall consist of 40 Members only, who shall be called Academicians of the Royal Academy; they shall all of them be artists by profession at the time of their admission, that is to say, Painters, Sculptors, or Architects, men of fair moral characters.

Engravers were not originally included, although they were allowed in as associate members in 1770. The two major functions of the Academy relate to the setting up of Schools of Design and an annual exhibition. Item 17 of its 'Instrument of Foundation' decrees: 'There shall be an Annual Exhibition of Paintings, Sculptures and Designs, which shall be open to all artists of distinguished merit; it shall continue for the public one month.' One of the aims of the annual exhibitions was to raise money for charity: 'Of the profits arising therefrom, two hundred pounds shall be given to indigent artists, or their families.'[27] Thus the 'Instrument of Foundation' recognises the professional status of the artists (who are presumed to be male, although two in fact were female) and discusses the education of young artists, the conditions of public exhibition and the provision of charity.

These were also the predominant concerns of earlier artists' groups. The first major English academy of drawing and painting from life opened in 1711, under the governorship of Sir Godfrey Kneller. It was taken over by Sir James Thornhill, foundered, and later re-opened in St Martin's Lane in 1720. After Thornhill's death William Hogarth took over in 1734–5 and life classes were held there until after the opening of the Royal Academy. One early plan to found an 'Academy for Painting and Sculpture' is remarkable in its acceptance of both commerce and pleasure. In his plan 'laid before the Society of Arts . . . in 1755' Sir Henry Cheere stated that: 'Pleasure Profit, Fame are the great Ends of every pursuit publick or Private . . . A Love of Pleasure is Implanted in every Heart, as the Necessary Sweetner of Life; and Consequently, can never be reprehensible, but when Irregular or Inordinate.' He suggests that 'Of all pleasures those excited by Works of Art and Genious, are of the most Innocent, the most refined, and the most Laudable kind', and uses the idea of public utility to motivate his argument: 'Thus the more Attention we bestow upon the Arts, and the quicker Relish we Acquire for them, the more Enlarged the province of pleasure becomes; And what is equally worthy of Consideration, the pleasure of Individuals thus derived and Obtained becomes so many Inexhaustible sources of profit to the Public.'[28] Cheere's proposals for an Academy were not accepted by the Society of Arts. Instead the Society became involved via Hogarth's committee of practicing artists. Hogarth organised a committee of artists to meet every year on 5 November at the Foundling Hospital for an artists' dinner. It was at this meeting in 1759 that a general meeting of all Artists 'to consider of a proposal for the honour and advancement of the Arts' was called. Unlike the later Royal Academy foundation charter, this call specified a much wider definition of Artists: 'all Artists in the several branches of Painting, Sculpture, Architecture, Engraving, Chasing, Seal-cutting, and Medalling'.

At the subsequent meeting held on 12 November 1759 in the Turk's Head Tavern in Gerard Street, Soho, a committee was chosen to make arrangements for an annual exhibition of 'the Present Artists'.[29] The aim of the exhibition appears to have been two-fold: firstly to gain public recognition, and secondly to raise money from visitors to the exhibition for charitable purposes. At the next meeting, on 22 December 1759, a 'proper room for the Exhibition' was sought and 'the room belonging to the Society for the Encouragement of Arts etc having been proposed' it was decided that 'Application be made to the Noblemen and Gentlemen of the Society for obtaining the said room'; and on 19 January Samuel Johnson's help was enlisted in writing to the Society of Arts.

The Society for the Encouragement of Arts, Manufactures and Commerce (known by its short title, the Society of Arts) had been founded at a meeting held in Rawthmell's Coffee-House in Henrietta Street, Covent Garden on 22 March 1754. The Society's founder, William Shipley, was a Northampton drawing Master, and his co-founders were not other artists in London, but two peers: Lord Folkestone and Lord Romney; four fellows of the Royal Society: Henry Baker, the microscopist and Gustavus Brander, both also Fellows of the

Society of Antiquaries, Revd Dr Stephen Hales, a divine and naturalist, and James Short; the other four were Husband Messiter, a surgeon, John Goodchild, a linen draper, Nicholas Crisp, jeweller and pottery manufacturer and Charles Lawrence, profession unknown.[30]

One fundamental difference in the aims of the Society of Arts and the later Royal Academy is demonstrated by my opening quotations. Reynolds asserts in his first *Discourse* (2 January 1769):

An Institution like this has often been recommended upon considerations merely mercantile; but an Academy, founded upon such principles, can never effect even its own narrow purposes. If it has an origin no higher, no taste can ever be formed in manufactures; but if the higher Arts of Design flourish, these inferior ends will be answered of course.[31]

When, in the same *Discourse*, he celebrates the opening of the Royal Academy, a place where 'the Polite Arts may be regularly cultivated' as 'an event in the highest degree interesting, not only to the Artists, but to the whole nation' he makes a strong claim for its importance to the public. The Society of Arts had indeed been supporting 'the Polite Arts', but specifically within a context of commerce. If Reynolds' Royal Academy *Discourses* embrace the civic humanist distrust of commerce (although Reynolds describes the King as promoting 'the Arts, as the head of a great, a learned, a polite, and a commercial nation'), then the Society of Arts reflects the opposite pole in the luxury debate as articulated variously by Mandeville, Smith and Hume.

Hume's essay 'Of Luxury', first published in his *Philosophical Discourses* of 1752, reappeared after 1758 re-titled 'Of Refinement in the Arts'. Following an emphasis on the role of context and the importance of perception in establishing meaning familiar from his philosophy, Hume opens up the possibility of luxury being a positive force in society:

Luxury is a word of an uncertain signification, and may be taken in a good as well as in a bad sense. In general, it means great refinement in the gratification of the senses; and any degree of it may be innocent or blameable according to the age, or country, or condition of the person.[32]

Hume argues that progress in the mechanical and in the liberal arts are necessarily linked:

Another advantage of industry and of refinements in the mechanical arts, is, that they commonly produce some refinements in the liberal; nor can the one be carried to perfection, without being accompanied, in some degree, with the other. The same age, which produces great philosophers and politicians, renowned generals and poets, usually abounds with skilful weavers, and ship-carpenters. (p. 277)

In Hume's account an increase of trade and advancement in arts will bring about an increased sociability, which explicitly includes both men and women:

Particular clubs and societies are every where formed: Both sexes meet in an easy and sociable manner; and the tempers of men, as well as their behaviour, refine apace. So that, besides the improvements which they receive from knowledge and the liberal arts, 'tis impossible but they must feel an increase of humanity, from the very habit of conversing together, and contributing to each other's pleasure and entertainment. Thus *industry, knowledge*, and *humanity*, are linked together by an indissoluble chain, and are found, from experience as well as reason, to be peculiar to the more polished, and, what are commonly denominated, the more luxurious ages. (p. 278)

While there seems to be no causal relation between Hume's essay and the founding of the Society of Arts two years later, the values of the Society are close to this vision of 'industry, knowledge, and humanity' linked and motivated by a positive account of the effects of luxury on society.

The Society's activity focused on the establishment of annual prizes or 'premiums' for specific types of innovation or achievement. The first such measure was 'to consider, whether a Reward should not be given for the finding of Cobalt in this Kingdom'; the second for the 'Cultivation of Madder'. The need to import these pigments was a pressing concern for both artists and the manufacturing trades. The third proposed premium is surprising:

It was likewise proposed, to consider of giving Rewards for the Encouragement of Boys and Girls in the Art of Drawing, and it being the Opinion of all present, that ye Art of Drawing is absolutely Necessary in many Employments Trades, and Manufactures, and that the Encouragement thereof may prove of great Utility to the public, it was resolved to bestow Premiums on a certain number of Boys or Girls under the Age of Sixteen, who shall produce the best pieces of Drawing, & shew themselves most capable, when properly examined.[33]

Unlike the Society of Artists and the Royal Academy, the Society of Arts seems to have been committed from the outset to encouraging young girls as well as boys to produce drawings.

There were various problems between the artists and the Society negotiating the terms for an exhibition in 1760. The artists wanted to charge an admission fee, which would have had a dual function: to raise funds for charity, and to exclude impecunious and therefore undesirable members of the public. The Society refused. Instead catalogues were sold at a cost of sixpence each. A total of 6,582 were sold, leading to estimates for attendance of over twenty thousand visitors during the period 21 April to 8 May.[34] As feared, the officers of the Society of Arts found it hard to control the behaviour of the public. Unused to a free exhibition, people were apparently unruly and disordered despite the presence of extra servants instructed to 'exclude all persons whom they shall think improper to be admitted, such as livery servants, foot soldiers, porters, women with children etc. and to prevent all disorders in the Room, such as smoaking, drinking etc., by turning the disorderly persons out'.[35] Fights ensued and windows were broken.[36]

A further problem was that the exhibition coincided with the display of drawings which had won premiums offered by the Society of Arts: 'The drawings chosen for exhibition were framed and mounted at the Society's expense and hung on the walls of the meeting-room for the inspection of members of the Society and their friends.'[37] These works, by young apprentice artists, were still on display during the exhibition, which led to confusion. Some members of the public assumed that the works which had gained prizes were the 'best' works present, rather than the 130 works by professional artists including Reynolds, Richard Wilson, Francis Hayman etc.. In the following year application was again made to the Society of Arts, with the proviso that, as phrased by Johnson:

The Artists being desirous that the Pictures drawn for the prize should be removed, lest any man should a second time suffer the disgrace of having lost that which he never sought. The Exhibition of last year was crowded and incommoded by the intrusion of great Numbers whose station and education made them no proper Judges of Statuary or Painting, and who where made idle and tumultuous by the opportunity of a shew.[38]

This again is a conflict of opposing possible responses to what an earlier committee meeting describes as 'the Arts of Elegance'. The public experience of the exhibition hovers between virtue, expressed through the charitable donation exercised through the purchase of the catalogue, and vice in the form of idle, tumultuous and presumably pleasurable disorder.

The Society refused these conditions, insisting that the premium paintings remain on view and that this exhibition of the 'productions in the Polite Arts' be 'free and open to the Public at proper Hours and under proper regulations'. The majority of the artists chose instead to show at a room in Spring Gardens. This group received a Royal Charter as the Incorporated Society of Artists in 1765, and the most prominent of their members went on to found the Royal Academy in 1768. A smaller group continued to show at the Society of Arts and became known as the Free Society of Artists.

There are two versions of the 'Choice of Hercules' motif by Academy artists which redescribe the choice in terms of possible art forms or genres, thereby rejecting the moral dichotomy of Shaftesbury's image, and perhaps registering the triumph of the rhetorical de-moralisation of luxury. Reynolds's *Garrick between Tragedy and Comedy* (figure 4) was shown at the Society of Artists in 1762 as *Mr. Garrick, between the two Muses of Tragedy and Comedy*. Unlike Hercules, Garrick on this occasion clearly takes the more pleasurable option, whilst apologising to a rather stern Tragedy. Through an inversion of the relation of landscape to figure Reynolds suggests that his is an aesthetic rather than a moral choice. Comedy stands in front of the open prospect, the more noble landscape associated in Shaftesbury's image with virtue. Tragedy is shown in the enclosed space, previously associated with vice, but here rendered sublime. The overall mood is playful: Garrick, the great tragic actor, was also renowned for his versatility. Maria Edgeworth refers to this painting in *Belinda* (1801), where Belinda and Mrs Delacour dress in masquerade costume as Comedy and Tragedy. Marriot, Lady Delacour's maid, is described as 'standing in distress like Garrick, between tragedy and comedy'.[39] The two characters swap costumes before entering the masquerade, thus confusing Clarence Hervey, who, like Garrick, is caught by the appeal of both women. The novel also exploits comparisons of virtue and vice: Belinda compared with Mrs Freke, Lady Percival with Lady Delacour.

The *Self-Portrait: Hesitating Between the Arts of Music and Painting* (figure 5) by Angelica Kauffman continues the iconography, but as a woman between women the choice is rather different. Although Kauffman uses the image to explore the choice between two of the polite arts, the background (occluded interior on the left and temple of virtue on top of a hill), in contrast to Reynolds' *Garrick*, retains the hierarchy of landscape in Shaftesbury's image, with the suggestion that painting is the more morally uplifting choice.

The two female founding members of the Royal Academy, Mary

Figure 4 Edward Fisher (after Joshua Reynolds), *Garrick between Tragedy and Comedy*
(1762)

Moser and Angelica Kauffman, always appear somewhat anomalous. In his 1968 history of the Royal Academy, Sidney Hutchison writes: 'It will be noted that there were two women but no others were elected till the 1920s.'[40] Zoffany's well-known painting of *The Academicians of the Royal Academy* (figure 6) exhibited at the Royal Academy in 1772 commemorates the gift in 1771 from George III of rooms in Old Somerset House on the Strand to house the Schools of the Academy. It shows the Academicians assembled in the students' rooms, but Angelica Kauffman and Mary Moser are present only as portraits on the right-hand wall. Like the casts of classical statues and the male life models, they are rendered as objects to be viewed, although no one seems to notice them, so that they seem rather to haunt the gathering like ghosts at a feast. The explanation of their relegation to portrait representations is usually linked to the presence of two nude models.[41] However, this image is a *capriccio*.[42] It is not the Academicians who would have been present

Figure 5 Angelica Kauffman, *Self-Portrait: Hesitating Between the Arts of Music and Painting*
(1791). Oil on canvas.

during a life class, but the students of the Royal Academy schools. Were
Zoffany to have painted the life class, there would have been no women
artists present, since there were no women students at the Academy.
There were, however, female models, and conditions for their presence
were laid down in 1769:

No student under the Age of twenty be admitted to draw after the Female
Model, unless he be a married Man . . . 'No Person be admitted (except the
Royal Family) during the time the Female Model is sitting.[13]

Moser and Kauffman were, it seems, isolated figures. However, if we
return to the history of the premiums offered by the Society of Arts then
a context for these two women emerges.

As is clear from its full title, The Society for the Encouragement of
Arts, Manufactures, and Commerce saw painting and the 'fine' or 'polite
arts' in a continuum with those skilled practices which were specifically
designed to further manufacture and commerce. In 1754 the Society's
first premiums list consisted of four awards, in 1755 twelve, 1756 twenty-
two, 1757 sixty-three, 1758 more than a hundred, and by 1764 there were

Figure 6 Johann Zoffany, *The Academicians of the Royal Academy* (1772). Oil on canvas, 100.7 cm by 147.3 cm.

364 awards. Initially premiums for different awards were listed in order of introduction;[14] after 1758 the list was divided up into categories: Agriculture; Chemistry; Colonies and Trade; Manufactures; Mechanics; and the Polite Arts. The category of Polite Arts was the major area in which girls were awarded premiums. Robert Dossie offered a useful definition of the 'polite arts' in 1782:

> By POLITE ARTS, according to the sense in which the expression is used by the Society, are meant, those which depend on fancy and taste; and are called by others the FINE ARTS.[15]

The relation between the term 'polite arts' and 'fine arts' is charted by Lawrence Klein:

> 'politeness' came to be applied to modes of expression more formal than social intercourse. In expressions such as 'polite learning', 'polite arts', and 'polite letters', 'politeness' became an ascription of certain areas of intellectual and literary endeavour and expressiveness . . . 'polite arts' covered this ground in English until the later development of the term 'fine arts'.[16]

Dossie talks of the Society organising '*public exhibitions* of all works of taste' (p. 32) and states that: 'The Society . . . early offered premiums in a general way to the youth of both sexes, to encourage their application to the study of designs for weaving and ornaments.' Dossie places further emphasis on the fact that 'in 1766, they also offered a premium of fifty guineas for the best patterns for weavers, by persons of any age or sex' (pp. 33–4).

The category of Polite Arts grew rapidly from two premiums in 1754 out of a total of four premiums offered, to 106 premiums out of a total of 364 in 1764. The first two premiums in 1754 were for 'the best Drawings, by Boys and Girls under the age of Fourteen Years' and 'the Best Drawings, by Boys and Girls between the ages of Fourteen and Seventeen'. The classes became more specialised, and in 1756 the following category was devised:

> The Candidates, allowed to be near the Age of 20, were to produce *Fancy Designs*, and *Compositions* of *Ornaments*, with *Flowers*, *Fruit*, and *Foliage*, *after Nature*. Such drawings were meant to be of use to *Fabrics* and *Manufactures*.

Dossie notes further that in 1757 this class, 'very suitably, became a field of contention for young ladies' (vol. III, p. 398). Under the growing category of 'Premiums Relating to Manufactures' there were also a high proportion of premiums awarded to women, especially in relation to designs for fabrics.[17]

Figure 7 Hannah Rush, *Compartment with Cattle* (1758).

Categories continued to be expanded, and the lists of prize-winners include many otherwise unknown young women artists. Initially the entrants from 'youths' and 'young ladies' were judged in the same categories – but from 1757 onwards separate categories were established. This seems to have been the result of a petition:

A Petition of sev.l young Ladies and Girls (who have offered themselves as Candidates for the Drawing Premiums) was presented and read, setting forth the great Disadvantages they are under in Drawing in the same class with the Boys, and that if the Society should think proper to give Premiums to be Drawn for, by their sex only, Numbers would offer themselves as Candidates, who are now intimidated.[18]

This anxiety, usually interpreted as referring to girls' unwillingness to share physical space with boys, refers rather, I would argue, to the sharing of a single 'class' of premium.

Successful premium drawings by women which survive include numerous 'Compositions of flowers', designs for commodities such as Hannah Chambers' *Design for a Candelabra* of 1757, and the purely decorative such as Hannah Rush's *Compartment with cattle* of 1758 (figure 7).

Mary Moser won premiums in 1758 and 1759 and a silver medal in
1759 'as a further Reward for her extraordinary merit'. The minutes
note the decision that 'the Drawing produced by the above Miss
Moser be handsomely framed and glazed'.[49] It still hangs in the
Society's buildings today. As Marcia Pointon has pointed out, Mary
Moser transferred her allegiance to the Royal Academy from 1768.[50]
Mary Moser's father was George Michael Moser, a founding member
of the Royal Academy and first Keeper of the Academy Schools
(shown in the Zofany painting (figure 5) putting the model's hand into
the rope loop); like her, many of the young women artists who received
prizes were the daughters or sisters of artists. Sarah Kirby, who won a
second share for '*The best fancied Designs*, to serve as *Patterns for
Manufactures*, by Girls under 17 Years' in 1757, was the daughter of
Joshua Kirby, author of *Dr. Brook Taylor's Method of Perspective Made Easy*,
for which Hogarth produced his satire on false perspective as a frontispiece.[51] Sarah Kirby knew both Hogarth and Gainsborough, met
Dr Johnson at Reynolds's house and later had a successful career as an
author and educator.[52] She continued to enter the competitions after
her marriage, listed as 'Miss Sarah Kirby, now Mrs Trimmer' in 1758,
when she won a third share of the premium for 'Original *Compositions
of Ornaments*, with Beasts, Birds, Fruit, and Flowers, *after Nature*, for
Embroiderers, Manufacturers, &c. the general Subjects *from Prints after
Baptiste*; by either Sex under 18 Years'.[53] On this occasion, although the
premium is listed as being 'by either sex' the male and female prize-
winners are listed separately. Similarly, Mary Vivares, a first-prize
winner in 1761, is listed as 'Daught. of Engrav.', and Mary Pingo, who
won prizes in 1758, 1759, 1761 and 1762 came from a family of medal-
makers.[54]

Another refinement took place in 1757 with the introduction of premiums for the genteel.[55] The first honorary Gold Medal was won in 1758
by the Hon. Lady Louisa Augusta Greville, daughter of the Eighth Earl
of Warwick, for a drawing of *A View of the Priory of Warwick*, and the following year she won again with a drawing of *The Ruins of Netley Abbey*. In
the same year she also won an Honorary Premium for etching. Overall
the Honorary Premiums were won consistently more often by women.
The scope of women's achievement as recorded in Dossie and in the
Register of the Premiums and Bounties Given by the Society is significant, but has
disappeared from view until recently.[56] Helen Clifford, writing in 1997,
quotes the *Register*'s approval of improvement in 'the lower branches of

the Polite Arts such as Drawings of Patterns for Silk-Weavers and Callico-Printers', and asks: 'As the girls took the majority of prizes in these categories, can we conclude that their contribution to this national design initiative was comparably great?'.[57] It seems clear that women's contribution was significant; perhaps earlier historians' failure to recognise the extent to which these categories of the Society's premium awards came to be dominated by women comes from a lack of interest both in 'female excellence' and in industrial design aimed at a luxury market.

Women's contribution to the Society was, however, recognised by contemporaries. George Cockings's extraordinary poem in praise of the Society of Arts describes it as 'instituted solely for the Public Good', records the fact that 'the Society from their first Institution have given great Encouragement to Persons of either Sex, for Designs in Architecture . . . &c.', and praises female honorary prize winners:

> Th' ennobled Fair Ones emulously glow,
> And condescend their pencil'd Works to show;
> they likewise claim the Honorary Prize,
> On Fame's bright Summit fix their sparkling Eyes.[58]

In 1777 James Barry undertook to paint a series of six pictures for the Society of Arts' Great Room depicting 'the Progress of Human Knowledge and Culture'. In his notes to the pictures Barry states: 'I have . . . endeavoured to . . . illustrate one great maxim or moral truth, viz. that the obtaining of happiness, as well individual as public, depends upon cultivating the human faculties.'[59]

Barry's paintings reinforce the logic of the pro-luxury argument. He places 'Commerce, or the Triumph of the Thames' opposite 'Orpheus' and 'A Grecian Harvest-Home'. The fifth painting shows 'The Distribution of Premiums in the Society of Arts' (figure 8) diagonally opposite the third painting: 'Crowning the victors at Olympia', thus suggesting that the Society's premiums which encourage innovation in the fields of art, manufacture and commerce are the contemporary equivalent of the reward of achievement at Olympia. A young female prize-winner is shown in the middle of the image, a younger girl admiring her medal draws attention to the blue ribbon on which the medal hangs around the older girl's wrist. The blue ribbon provides a visual link to 'Olympia', where the young athletes are also shown wearing blue ribbons. Barry casts the Society's annual prize-giving as an act of civic

Figure 8 James Barry, *The Distribution of the Premiums to the Society of Arts*. Mural, 462.28 cm by 360.68 cm. Fifth picture in *The Progress of Human Knowledge and Culture* (1777–1783).

virtue. Moreover, at the centre of this fifth image he places an example of female virtue, Mrs Montagu, applauding female industry:

Towards the centre of the picture is a distinguished example of female excellence, Mrs. Montagu, who is earnestly recommending the ingenuity and industry of a young female, whose work she is producing. (pp. 73–4)

Mrs Montagu had joined the Society in 1758, the year her husband inherited extensive estates in Northumberland which included coal mines. Montagu was both an enthusiastic patron of art, and closely involved in manufacture; she became increasingly involved with the mines and took over their running after her husband's death.[60] Barry shows her as an ideal patron, and as a suitable model for emulation:

Near Mrs. Montagu stand the two beautiful duchesses of Rutland and Devonshire . . . Between them I have placed that venerable sage, Dr. Samuel Johnson, who is pointing out this example of Mrs. Montagu, as a matter well worthy their grace's most serious attention and imitation. (p. 74)

The female prize-winner promoted by Mrs Montagu is holding a bale of cloth; clearly she, unlike the 'successful boy' on the right, has won one of the premiums associated with manufacture. James Barry's work embodies the allegiance between art and commerce sought by the Society of Arts, which was offered as an ideal by David Hume. I would argue that it is the acceptance and de-moralisation of luxury encoded in this allegiance which allows for the inclusion of women as producers and patrons in the Society of Arts, and their celebration at the centre of Barry's painting. This public representation of a named woman as a patron of art, displaying the work of an unnamed female artist (herself on display to two different publicly visible women of fashion), is a challenge both to the Royal Academy's occlusion of female artists, and to subsequent art history's acceptance of Reynolds's implicit assumption that if art is to be virtuous and embody the public spirit it must necessarily eschew the commercial and its dangerous tendency towards effeminisation. If we turn away from the Royal Academy, another public for art emerges, one which embraces both commerce and female industry, as suggested by Ackermann's 1809 image of 'The Society's "Great Room"' (figure 9). Under Barry's murals the young female prize-winners are clearly visible, picked out in white. The Society of Arts provided a unique context for young women artists facilitated by the link accepted by the Society between commerce and 'the polite arts'. The premiums offered by the Society for young women artists complicate our current model of the relation

Figure 9 Ackermann (after Pugin and Rowlandson), *The Society's 'Great Room'* (1809).

between women and 'the public spirit' in the practices and discourses of eighteenth-century art.

NOTES

I am grateful to Elizabeth Eger, Markman Ellis, Richard Hamblyn and Charlotte Sussman for reading and commenting on this paper; to Susan Bennett at the Royal Society of Arts for her suggestions and her generosity in guiding me round the archive of the RSA; to the staff and readers of the Huntington Library, California, and to Helen L. Bing, who made my visit there possible.

1 22 March 1754, Society Minutes (RSA Archives), p. 3; quoted in Derek Hudson and Kenneth Luckhurst, *The Royal Society of Arts 1754–1954* (London: John Murray, 1954), p. 8.

2 Sir Joshua Reynolds, 'Discourse 1 Delivered at the Opening of The Royal Academy, January 2, 1769', in *Discourses on Art*, ed. Robert R. Wark (New Haven and London: Yale University Press, 1975), pp. 13–21, p. 13.

3 I am using 'art' here, anachronistically, in the modern sense. The Royal Academy is concerned to distinguish fine art from other eighteenth-century uses of the term 'art' to mean skill or technique, as opposed to 'science' meaning an abstract body of knowledge; the Society of Arts encodes an acceptance of that link with skills and techniques in its full title: The Society for the Encouragement of Arts, Manufactures and Commerce.

4 On the growth of public amusements see Roy Porter, 'Material Pleasures in the Consumer Society', in Roy Porter and Marie Mulvey Roberts, eds. *Pleasure in the Eighteenth Century*, (Basingstoke: Macmillan, 1996), pp. 19–36.

5 Alexander Gerard, *An Essay on Taste, with three dissertations on the same subject. By Mr. De Voltaire, Mr. D'Alembert, F.R.S. Mr. de Montesquieu* (London: A Millar, 1759), p. 200.

6 Kathryn Shevelow, *Women and Print Culture: The Construction of Femininity in the Early Periodical* (London: Routledge, 1989), p. 2.

7 Stephen Copley, 'The Fine Arts in Eighteenth-Century Polite Culture' in John Barrell, ed., *Painting and the Politics of Culture: New Essays on British Art 1700–1830* (Oxford: Oxford University Press, 1992) pp. 13–37, p. 25.

8 John Brewer, '"The Most Polite Age and the Most Vicious" Attitudes towards Culture as a Commodity: 1660–1800', in Ann Bermingham and John Brewer, eds., *The Consumption of Culture, 1600–1800: Image, Text, Object* (London and New York: Routledge, 1995) pp. 341–61, pp. 341, 356. For an analysis of Roubillac, Brewer refers to Ronald Paulson, *Breaking and Remaking: Aesthetic Practice in England 1700–1820* (New Brunswick and London: Rutgers, 1989) pp. 231, 244.

9 Brewer, 'The Most Polite Age', p. 358.

10 Jenny Uglow points out that 'Hogarth told the French commentator Jean André Rouquet that the clergyman . . . was Moll's father.' Jenny Uglow, *Hogarth* (London: Faber, 1997) p. 201.

11 Ronald Paulson, *Emblem and Expression: Meaning in English Art of the Eighteenth Century* (London: Thames and Hudson, 1975), pp. 38ff.

12 Annibale Carraci, *Hercules at the Crossroads*, c. 1596, ceiling painting for Camerino, Palazzo Farnese, Rome; Paolo Veronese, *The Choice of Hercules*, c. 1578–81, Frick Collection, New York; Nicolas Poussin, *The Choice of Hercules*, mid-1630s, Stourhead, Wiltshire.

13 John Barrell, *The Political Theory of Painting from Reynolds to Hazlitt: 'The Body of the Public'* (New Haven and London: Yale University Press, 1986). Barrell draws on Pocock's version of civic humanism; see J.G.A. Pocock, *The Machiavellian Moment: Florentine Republican Thought and the Atlantic Tradition* (Princeton: Princeton University Press, 1975); and *Virtue, Commerce and History* (Cambridge: Cambridge University Press, 1985). On Barrell's use of Pocock see Andrew Hemingway's review of Barrell's *Political Theory of Painting*, 'The Political Theory of Painting without the Politics', *Art History* 10.3 (1987), 381–95 (p. 383). David H. Solkin, *Painting for Money: The Visual Arts and the Public Sphere in Eighteenth-Century England* (New Haven and London: Yale University Press, 1992) follows Barrell, but his version of the public is also heavily influenced by Habermas; Jürgen Habermas, *The Structural Transformation of the Public Sphere*, trans. Thomas Burger (Cambridge: Polity Press, 1989).

14 See John Barrell, 'The Public Prospect and the Private View: The Politics of Taste in Eighteenth-Century Britain', in *The Birth of Pandora and the Division of Knowledge* (Basingstoke and London: Macmillan, 1992), pp. 41–63.

15 Sir Ellis Waterhouse, 'The Bourgeois Sentimental Decade: 1740–1750', in *Three Decades of British Art 1740–1770* (Philadelphia: American Philosophical Society, 1965), pp. 1–23.

16 Waterhouse, 'Bourgeois Sentimental Decade', p. 2. Richardson's *Pamela* provided the source for the first series of contemporary English history paintings: Joseph Highmore's sequence of twelve paintings from *Pamela* from 1744 is reproduced in *Manners and Morals* (London: Tate Gallery, 1987) cat. nos. 134–45.

17 The portrait of Sterne (1761) is reproduced in Harrison R. Steeves, *Before Jane Austen: The Shaping of the English Novel in the Eighteenth Century* (London: George Allen & Unwin, 1966). For the appeal of distress see: R. F. Brissenden, *Virtue in Distress: Studies in the Novel of Sentiment from Richardson to Sade* (London: Macmillan, 1974); Susan Staves, 'British Seduced Maidens', *Eighteenth Century Studies* 14 (Winter 1980–1), 109–34; Markman Ellis, '"Recovering the path of virtue": The Politics of Prostitution and the Sentimental Novel', in *The Politics of Sensibility: Race, Gender and Commerce in the Sentimental Novel* (Cambridge: Cambridge University Press, 1996), pp. 160–90. Examples include Emily Atkins in Henry Mackenzie's *The Man of Feeling*, and Sterne's Maria, twenty paintings of whom were exhibited and/or engraved between 1777 and 1819, including two versions by Wright of Derby in 1777 and 1781, and one by Angelica Kauffman in 1777. See also G. J. Barker-Benfield, *The Culture of Sensibility: Sex and Society*

in *Eighteenth-Century Britain* (Chicago and London: University of Chicago Press, 1992).

18 Hayman's painting is in the Tate Gallery, London; see Brian Allen, *Francis Hayman* (Yale University Press, 1987) cat. no. 32, pp. 110–11, illustrated p. 111; and Solkin, *Painting for Money*, pp. 139–42. On Vauxhall's images see also T. J. Edelstein, *Vauxhall Gardens* (New Haven: Yale Center for British Art, 1983).

19 Fanny Burney, *Evelina* (1778), ed. Edward A. Bloom (Oxford: Oxford University Press, 1982), pp. 193–206. Miles Ogborn describes a contemporary account of a woman compromised by unwanted attention in the 'Vauxhall Affray' in *Spaces of Modernity: London's Geographies 1680–1780* (New York: The Guilford Press, 1998) especially pp. 116–57.

20 On Hogarth's involvement in the Foundling Hospital, see Uglow, *Hogarth*, chapters 16 and 21.

21 André Rouquet, *The Present State of the Arts in England* (1755) ed. R. W. Lightbown (London: Cornmarket Press, 1970), p. 27.

22 Solkin, *Painting*, p. 169; Barrell, *Political Theory*, p. 55.

23 The monument, still visible in York Minster, was designed by William Kent and made by Guelfi.

24 John Brown, *An Estimate of the Manners and Principles of the Times* (London: L. Davis and C. Reymers, 1757), p. 15. Page numbers for further references to this edition will be given in the text.

25 See G. J. Barker-Benfield, 'The Question of Effeminacy', in his *The Culture of Sensibility; Sex and Society in Eighteenth-Century Britain* (Chicago and London: Chicago University Press, 1992), pp. 104–53.

26 Christopher Berry, *The Idea of Luxury, A Conceptual and Historical Investigation* (Cambridge: Cambridge University Press, 1994), p. 121.

27 Royal Academy papers, Royal Academy Archives.

28 'A Plan for an Academy for Sculpture and Painting laid before the Society of Arts by Sir Henry Cheere in 1755', in Dr Templeman's Transactions, vol. I: 1754–58 (RSA Archives), pp. 32–48.

29 It is interesting to note the locations of meetings of artists' groups: evidence of taverns as well as coffee-houses facilitating sociability and the establishment of public bodies. See Ellis's discussion of coffee-house sociability in chapter 1 above.

30 D. G. C. Allan, *William Shipley Founder of the Royal Society of Arts: A Biography with Documents* (London: Scolar Press, 1968), p. 54.

31 Sir Joshua Reynolds, *Discourse 1 Delivered at the Opening of The Royal Academy, January 2, 1769*, *Discourses on Art* ed. Robert R. Wark (New Haven and London: Yale University Press, 1975), p. 13.

32 David Hume, 'Of Refinement in the Arts', in *Essays Moral Political and Literary* (Oxford: Oxford University Press, 1963), pp. 275–88. p. 275. Further page references to this edition will be given in the text.

33 22 March 1754, Society Minutes (RSA Archives), p. 3 quoted in Derek Hudson and Kenneth Luckhurst, *The Royal Society of Arts 1754–1954* (London: John Murray, 1954), p. 8.

34 The artists were left with a balance, of which £100.00 was invested in annu-
    ities; this and the remaining £3 16s were resolved 'to be apply'd to the
    advancement of the Academy' (Papers of the Society of Artists, p. 120,
    Solkin, *Painting*, p. 175) rather than towards charity as had been the stated
    intention.

35 Hudson and Luckhurst, *Royal Society of Arts*, p. 37.

36 Allan, *William Shipley*, p. 72; 'Affair of the Porter', 10 May 1760, Committee
    Minutes (1758–60) (RSA Archives), p. 27.

37 Hudson and Luckhurst, *Royal Society of Arts*, p. 34.

38 8 Dec 1760, *Society of Artists Papers* (RA Archives) published (with emenda-
    tions) as 'Papers of the Society of Artists of Great Britain', *The Walpole Society*
    6 (1917–18), 113–30 (p. 122).

39 Maria Edgeworth, *Belinda*, ed. Eiléan Ni Chuilleanain (London: Dent, 1993)
    p. 14. Reynolds' painting was popular and often reproduced, see Nicholas
    Penny, ed., *Reynolds* (London: Royal Academy of Arts, 1986) cat. no. 42.

40 Sidney C. Hutchison, *The History of the Royal Academy 1768–1968* (London:
    Chapman and Hall, 1968), p. 47.

41 This is the view expressed by Ilaria Bignamini and Martin Postle: 'While it
    was never specified that the two female members of the Academy, Mary
    Moser and Angelika Kauffman, were forbidden to study from the model,
    their portraits on the wall in this work, rather than in the room itself, suggest
    that it would have been deemed improper for them to have done so.' *The
    Artist's Model; Its Role in British Art from Lely to Etty*, ed. Martin Postle and
    Joanne Wright (Nottingham University Art Gallery, 1991), cat. no. 5, p. 42.

42 Marcia Pointon suggests that 'It should also be noted that these portraits fall
    within a long tradition for the representation of absent but venerated
    members of a body through *imago clipeata.*' *Strategies for Showing: Women,
    Possession, and Representation in English Visual Culture 1665–1800* (Oxford:
    Oxford University Press, 1997), p. 165. See also Marcia Pointon, *Hanging the
    Head: Portraiture and Social Formation in Eighteenth-Century England* (New Haven:
    Yale University Press, 1992), pp. 65–6.

43 RA Council Minutes, vol. 1, p. 19 (RA Archives).

44 D. G. C. Allan, 'Artists and the Society in the 18th Century: (ii) Members
    and Premiums in the First Decade, 1755–64', *Journal of the Royal Society of Arts*
    (March 1984), 271–5 (p. 275).

45 Robert Dossie, *Memoirs of Agriculture and other Oeconomical Arts*, 3 vols. (London:
    J. Nourse, 1782), vol. 1, p. 32.

46 Lawrence Klein, 'The Third Earl of Shaftesbury and the Progress of
    Politeness' *Eighteenth Century Studies* 18.2 (1984–5), 186–214, (pp. 200–1).

47 See Helen Clifford, 'Key Document from the Archives: The Awards of
    Premiums and Bounties by the Society of Arts', *Royal Society of Arts Journal*
    (August/September 1997), 78–9 (p. 78).

48 21 January 1756, Society Minutes (RSA Archives), p. 84.

49 14 February 1759, Society Minutes (RSA Archives), p. 146.

50 Marcia Pointon, *Strategies for Showing*, pp. 145–6.

51 On Joshua Kirby see Ronald Paulson, *Hogarth*, 3 vols. (press, 1993), vol. III: *Art and Politics*, esp. pp. 60–1.

52 See entry on Sarah Kirby, *DNB* (Oxford: Oxford University Press, 1995).

53 Dossie, *Memoirs*, p. 408.

54 Ibid., p. 412. On the Pingos see Christopher Eimer, *The Pingo Family and Medal-Making in Eighteenth-Century Britain* (London: British Art Medal Trust, 1998).

55 Dr Templeman's Transactions, vol. I: 1754–8 (RSA Archives), pp. 115–16.

56 Alicia C. Percival, 'Women and the Society of Arts in its Early Days', *Journal of the Royal Society of Arts* 125 (Dec 1976–Nov 1977) 266–9; 330–3; 416–18.

57 *A Register of Premiums and Bounties given by the Society instituted at London for the Encouragement of Arts, Manufactures and Commerce* (London: 1778), p. 54; Clifford, 'Key Document', pp. 78–9.

58 George Cockings, 'Arts, Manufactures, and Commerce: A Poem' (London: printed for the Author, 1768), p. 6.

59 James Barry, *An Account of a Series of Pictures in the Great Room of the Society of Arts, Manufactures, and Commerce, at the Adelphi* (London: Printed for the Author by William Adlard, Printer to the Society and sold by T. Cadell in the Strand, 1783), p. 40.

60 I have been unable to trace any reference to Montagu joining the Society in her correspondence for the year 1758 held by the Huntington Library, although it is clear that her husband's inheritance greatly increased their wealth; the RSA holds a letter dated 22 January 1770 recording her proxy vote.

CHAPTER 4

Representing culture: 'The Nine Living Muses of Great Britain' (1779)

Elizabeth Eger

If any one should start a query, why the ancients, who reasoned so deeply, should, in their personifications of the sovereign wisdom, have chosen Minerva a female; why the Muses, who preside over the several subordinate modes of intelligence, &c. are all females; and why the conversation of the serpent was held with Eve, in order that her influence might be employed in persuading Adam; such queries could have been well and pertinently answered by the eloquent, generous, amiable sensibility of the celebrated and long-to-be-lamented Mary Wolstonecraft [sic], and would interweave very gratefully with another edition of her Rights of Women [sic]. Her honest heart, so estranged from all selfishness, and which could take so deep and generous an interest in whatever had relation to truth and justice, however remote as to time or place, would find some matter for consolation, in discovering that the ancient nations of the world entertained a very different opinion of female capabilities, from those modern Mohomaten, tyrannical, and absurd degrading notions of female nature, at which her indignation was so justly raised.[1]

In his *Letter to the Dilettanti Society*, first published in 1798, James Barry reflects wistfully on a culture that transmitted its highest aesthetic values to the world through the symbolic figures of women. Pondering the question of why women were chosen to personify wisdom, knowledge and intelligence in the past, he thinks immediately of his contemporary, Mary Wollstonecraft, a prolific writer and a woman of almost iconic cultural standing. Barry is writing in the year after her death, at a point when her reputation was most controversial.[2] He refers to her as the upholder of truth and justice, both virtues traditionally portrayed as feminine icons, imagining her possible relish in recognising the elevated position of women in ancient myth.[3] Considering his own artistic status in an increasingly commercial context, Barry attempts to view the muses, those ambiguous figures of mythical women, through the eyes of

Figure 10 Richard Samuel, *The Nine Living Muses of Great Britain* (c. 1779). Oil on canvas, 132.1 cm by 154.9 cm.

a real and public woman. In alluding to the muses he is viewing their forms afresh, imagining a world in which women's capabilities are fulfilled and recognised. His reflections convey the ongoing tension between real and symbolic female figures as depicted in the realms of literature, the visual arts and philosophy, raising questions relating to women's extensive involvement in their culture during the eighteenth century.[1] There is a two-way relationship between writing about women and writing by women, representations of and by women, which the allegorical figures of the muses embody.

The purpose of Barry's *Letter to the Dilettanti Society*, as summarised by William Pressly, was to establish that the Royal Academy of Arts was 'no longer capable of accomplishing its original intention of improving public taste' and that therefore Barry 'was appealing to another society, the Dilettanti, to undertake this patriotic duty in its place'.[5] Barry's concern to find a justification for his art can be seen in the context of an emerging discourse surrounding the public purpose and commercial utility of British culture. His letter is both a specific complaint and a more general reflection on the place of art in society. His desire to find a method of defining and representing the civic virtues of the arts was often expressed through feminine figures, to which he referred constantly in visual and literary terms. Cultural historians have tended to characterise the development of the fine arts in Britain as the expression of inherently masculine and classical theories of the place of art in a just society, focusing on the public man of virtue to the exclusion of his female counterpart.[6] As John Barrell has shown in his invaluable discussion of British theories of painting in the period, the discourse of civic humanism was complicated during the course of the century. The constitution of 'The Body of the Public' was shifting according to social and political changes which were closely related to the discussion of the aesthetic and social fabric of the nation. Barrell characterises the development of this discourse as inherently masculine. He argues that history painting was a genre which addressed the public man of virtue through the portayal of heroic actions carefully selected from the past. The less prestigious genres of portrait painting and nature drawings were reserved for women, both as the consumers and the producers of art. Similarly, the effects of luxury and commerce were characterised as dangerously weakening and effeminate.

Barrell's thesis draws too neat a distinction between aesthetic categories in relation to gender, neglecting models of society that proposed the advancement of women and promoted their civilising force in society.[7] As Barry's reflections on Minerva and the muses suggest, women were present in the minds of artists as more than just abstract figures or passive consumers – many felt the need to represent real heroines who might form models of behaviour for contemporary women (and perhaps even men). There is much evidence to suggest that the hierarchical divisions in the fine arts were far less rigid than is often implied, and that women were involved in the development of aesthetic theory, both as the topic and the initiators of critical discussion and artistic representation. Recent research into the exhibition catalogues of the Academy has revealed that many women artists exhibited regularly.[8] Their work includes history painting as well as portraits and depictions of flowers. I will argue that Enlightenment discussions of the fine arts (and their public) not only acknowledged the contributions of both sexes to a model of social progress but also promoted the cultural achievements and moral virtues of women as integral to its future definition and development. As Barry suggests, to acknowledge women's cultural and intellectual standing is a mark of advanced civilisation. His belief that the symbolic role of women in their culture might relate to their real capabilities and potential was shared by several advocates of female education during the period. Barry raises questions relating to the inclusion, visibility and agency of woman in her culture. Are women merely cast in symbolic feminine figures, abstracted and idealised, or can they inhabit these forms in a more direct and positive sense?

Richard Samuel's painting *The Nine Living Muses of Great Britain* portrays a group of contemporary women, each renowned in her chosen artistic field (figure 10). Exhibited at the Royal Academy in 1779, Samuel's portrait creates a powerful convergence of the real and symbolic figures of women. Samuel's 'muses' were Elizabeth Montagu, Elizabeth Griffith, Elizabeth Carter, Charlotte Lennox, Elizabeth Linley, Angelica Kauffman, Catharine Macaulay, Anna Barbauld and Hannah More. Together they formed an important network of intellectuals, who were involved in a diverse range of cultural activity, from writing poetry, political pamphlets, educational and moral philosophy, legal essays, novels, plays and Shakespeare criticism to performing arias and exhibiting paintings.[9] With the exception of Elizabeth Montagu, a powerful patron of the arts, they all made a living from their work. Their portrait celebrates the relationship between the arts along the lines of the classical humanist model of a harmonious society, capturing the moment when English women as a group first gained acceptance as important contributors to the artistic world.

Whereas Richard Samuel's 'Nine Living Muses' are firmly placed upon the ground, commanding respect and curiosity, earlier paintings of the mythological muses tend to depict a set of ethereal figures who symbolise abstract qualities, lofty bearers of culture who dwell on the slopes of Mount Parnassus. Versions by Raphael and Poussin, for example, seem to be set in another, golden world. Raphael's *Parnassus* gives pride of position to Apollo, playing the fiddle and surrounded by the muses. Historical and classical figures are united in a single space, as Raphael has included a group of poets at the base of the mural.[10] However, as with the allegorical figures, these are not clearly individuated or labelled, with the single exception of Sappho. A huge and impressive figure, she appears to wear an expression of defiance, which is perhaps not unrelated to the fact that she is the only historical female figure in the entire series of murals. Poussin's *Apollo and the Muses on Parnassus*, painted just over a century later, is obviously inspired by Raphael's work, adopting a similar, crescent-shaped composition. Sappho is not present however, and the only female figures depicted are the allegorical muses, who occupy the background of the painting, decorative ornaments to the cluster of active male poets who dominate the foreground of the picture. The naked nymph of the Castillian springs is sprawled languorously across the centre of the composition. Apollo is seen to be inspiring one of the poets, while the muses look on.[11]

References to a lost and glorious past, these paintings have a symbolic power that is not related to the position of contemporary women but rather celebrates an aesthetic ideal, an Arcadian idyll. Today, the muses can still be evocative of the 'timeless value' of culture to society. Few critics have considered the implications of the fact that the muses, a resonant image of cultural harmony, are female. As Marina Warner has argued in her study of the allegory of female form, their symbolic power is so universal that it seems that we are not meant to associate them with real women, let alone women artists.[12] She is correct to make this point in a contemporary sense – we have for the large part lost a sense of the individual characters and functions of the muses, let alone the possibility that they might refer to real women. The muses form an allegory of ideas, in which the personification of abstract aesthetic categories is the primary device, rather than a historical or political allegory, in which figures represent or allegorize historical personages.[13] They provide a means of picturing artistic knowledge in painting and prose, and historically have been used in connection with various metaphors of literary community or to make more general public statements of cultural refinement. Academies of learning are often adorned with statues or friezes of the muses, or Minerva, the goddess of wisdom. The muses symbolise ideals and aspirations to knowledge, as well as their attainment. Samuel, however, has painted his peers – living women who practised the arts they represent. Visitors to the Academy's exhibition would have been familiar with their recent literary, visual and dramatic achievements. *The Nine Living Muses of Great Britain* formed a contemporary model of excellence, embodying the neo-classical ideal of the sister arts.[14] Samuel and James Barry share a willingness to link the classical figures of myth with their real, contemporary counterparts.

The idea that it is possible to consider the relation between the real and symbolic forms of woman in a positive sense runs counter to the instincts of contemporary feminism. Images of the muses or muse in the twentieth century have tended to be of voiceless sources of male creativity rather than vivid practitioners of the arts. As Germaine Greer and

Margaret Homans have shown, certain male poets, such as Robert Graves, have been responsible for perpetrating the myth of the muse as an eternally feminine and passive figure of inspiration.[15] The Romantic and modernist concentration on the individual act of literary creation has tended to focus on the poet's communication with the muse as an intimate and often highly sexualised relationship, obscuring the classical tradition of representing the muses as a group of independent, active, wilful and manipulative practitioners of the arts. In classical literature the muses' judgement was absolute and they represented the standard by which artistic achievement might be measured. In Ovid's *Metamorphoses*, for example, the nine daughters of Peirus, who are presumptuous enough to challenge the muses for their position, are turned into crows in punishment for their failure in a singing contest.[16] Thus the comparison between real women and muses can be seen as an assertion of the former's artistic endeavour rather than as a portrayal of women as the passive enablers of art.

The possibility that the allegorical figures of the muses referred to real historical figures was often raised in discussions of women's education during the Renaissance and the eighteenth century. The examples of learned women of the past became a standard and popular means of providing evidence of the potential benefits to society in educating women. Thomas Heywood, in the preface to his *Generall History of Women*, published in 1657, noted that 'the invention of all good Arts and Disciplines has been ascribed to the Muses'. The frontispiece to this work is based on that in his first work, *Nine Bookes of Various History Concerninge Women* (1624), a decorative engraving of the muses in their iconological postures and clearly labelled according to their function (see figure 11). Just as men were incited to virtue by examples of great men, he wrote 'what properer object can there be of woman's emulation than the deeds of other famous women'.[17] Heywood's work is the first in a long catalogue of dictionaries and encyclopaedias of women that flourished in the eighteenth century.[18] Whether or not the feminine icon represented real women, women identified and were identified with it. Londa Schiebinger has suggested that the social contexts in which interest in the feminine icon flourished, the Renaissance court and the eighteenth-century salon, were conducive to women's intellectual advancement.[19] It is certainly true that in the eighteenth century, as more and more women participated in the creation and cultivation of polite and professional culture, the means to represent their achievement and authority tended to be found in classical myths and histories of

Figure 11 Frontispiece to Thomas Heywood, *Nine Bookes of Various History Concerninge Women* (1624).

civilization. Wetenhall Wilkes, in his *Essay on the Pleasure and Advantages of Female Literature*, published in London in 1741, asked 'If it were intended by Nature, that Man should Monopolize all Learning to himself, why were the Muses Female, who . . . were the Mistresses of all the Sciences, and the Presidents of Music and Poetry?'.[20] His question precedes Barry's comment on the injustice of contemporary society towards learned women. Marchioness de Lambert, an educational writer popular with the bluestocking writers in Samuel's portrait, reflected:

> The Muses have in all ages been the sanctuary of virtue, and the patronesses of a virtuous and honourable behaviour. May not also the fair sex with great justice thus plead with the men? 'What right have you to forbid us the study of the sciences, the finer arts? Have not our devotees to literature succeeded therin, and distinguished themselves as well in the sublime as the agreeable? And could the poetical performances of certain ladies plead the merit of antiquity, you would read them with the same admiration you do the works of the antients which you cannot help doing justice to.[21]

Women frequently made links between their mythical and real historical predecessors. Mary Hays, for example, presents women as diverse as Abassa, Catharine Macaulay, Sappho and Zenobia in the same *Dictionary of Female Biography*, published in 1803.[22]

Thus Samuel's painting can be read as belonging to a tradition that celebrated the feminine icon as a powerful example of what women might be and do. Although Samuel was a member of the Royal Academy, little is known about his life and it is assumed that he died young.[23] It is difficult to date precisely the execution of his painting. The image first appeared in the form of a print circulated in *Johnson's Ladies New and Polite Pocket Memorandum for 1778*, published by Joseph Johnson, and advertised in the *London Chronicle* for 8–11 November 1777 and other issues (figure 12). The print became extremely popular, which may have been what spurred Samuel to exhibit the original painting at the Royal Academy.[24] The importance of its subjects' literary and artistic work to a sense of national identity can be seen most clearly in the print, in which Apollo is about to crown the female figure of Britannia. She is the central and most important figure in the composition, resplendent in a traditional chariot, her laurel crown hovering above her head like a halo. The image of Britannia is still familiar today as the image of British currency, the stamp on the coins of the Royal mint.[25] In Samuel's painting, Apollo replaces Britannia, a mute and marble figure amidst the muses' colourful silks. Samuel's portrait offers an interesting inversion of *The Tribuna of the Uffizi* (1772–8), Zoffany's famous depiction of male

Samuel delin.

The NINE LIVING MUSES of GREAT BRITAIN.

Miss Carter, M.ʳˢ Barbauld, M.ʳˢ Angelica Kauffman, on the Right hand ; M.ʳˢ Sheridan, in the Middle ; M.ʳˢ Lenox, M.ʳˢ Macaulay, Miss More, M.ʳˢ Montague, and M.ʳˢ Griffith, on the Left hand.

Page Sculp.

Figure 12 Page (after Samuel), *The Nine Living Muses of Great Britain* (c. 1778). Engraving, 12.5 cm by 10 cm. In *Johnson's Ladies' New and Polite Pocket Memorandum for 1778*.

connoisseurs ogling women in the archetypal forms of Venus and Virgin (the *Venus de Medici*, Titian's *Venus of Urbino* and a Raphael *Madonna*).[26] Here the masculine figure of perfection is subject to the female gaze. Samuel's subjects form an impressive gathering, inviting comparison with various eighteenth-century portraits but remaining a unique example of a group portrait of women united by their professional status. In choosing to paint *living* muses, Samuel paid tribute to his female contemporaries, a community of artists who personified the aims of a civilized society. He both brought an allegory down to earth and raised his contemporaries to a higher plane. While Samuel's painting can be interpreted on a number of levels, it remains primarily a testament to the achievement of women in the eighteenth century as cultural standard bearers of considerable influence.

The Nine Living Muses of Great Britain should be seen in the context of contemporary aesthetic debate, providing an interesting example of contemporary efforts to advocate the importance of female involvement in social and cultural progress. The only evidence we have of Samuel's artistic aims and achievements is that provided in a lecture he gave in 1786 to the Society of Arts, Manufactures and Commerce. Here he immediately establishes his concern with the commercial and cultural improvement of the nation and the promotion of the teaching of drawing as a tool of social progress:

Independent of the gratitude I feel for the honour conferred, by your twice adjudging me the premium of your Gold Pallet, for the best original Historical Drawings, I cannot think an Essay on the utility of Drawing and Painting can be anywhere so properly addressed as to your truly respectable Society; who, sensible of how necessary a fine taste in the Polite Arts is to a commercial Nation, early promoted the practice of Drawing and Painting, by appropriating a considerable part of your funds to the rewarding of such Artists as excelled in the various branches of the Polite Arts: thus stimulated they aim'd at that excellence which has raised the English school to its present eminence.[27]

Samuel's lecture praises the potential of visual art to transcend language barriers in a commercial and moral project of expansion beyond the borders of England. He had been awarded a prize from the Society of Arts in 1773, for an improvement in the method of laying mezzotint grounds, and was particularly committed to finding new inventions to improve artistic methods.[28] He advocated that travellers to foreign countries should acquire an accurate skill in drawing in order to bring home useful knowledge:

To such skill were we indebted to for the introduction of the curious Italian machine, first invented in Derby, for throwing of silk, for which the parliament gave a reward of fourteen thousand pounds; and there are still in Europe, machines and improvements which may become equally valuable.[29]

The silks of the Nine Muses' togas, while classical in inspiration, are perhaps Derby patterns. Women were important patrons of the burgeoning new decorative industries.[30] Samuel's manifesto presents the development of the fine arts as the privileged distinction of a civilized society. He quotes Lord Kames: 'A just taste in the fine arts, derived from rational principles, is a fine preparation for acting in the social state with dignity and propriety.'[31]

In such a society, the social and cultural position of women was an important indicator of the level of civilization acquired. Their role as the producers and consumers of fine art and literature was important to the definition of Britain's status as a commercially successful and culturally sophisticated nation. In this spirit, George Ballard boasted, 'it is pretty certain, that England hath produced more women famous for literary accomplishments, than any other nation in Europe.'[32] The close affinity between commerce and the arts during the eighteenth century is perhaps charted most clearly in Hume's *Essays, Moral, Political and Literary*. In two essays, 'Of Commerce' and 'Of Refinement in the Arts' (originally entitled 'Of Luxury'), he maintains the importance of the mutual relation between private and public prosperity. He argues that the refinement of the arts and the industries associated with luxury goods is necessary to the general advancement and happiness of mankind, and that a taste for refinement in the arts and a thirst for knowledge progresses towards the creation of a community of cultural consumers:

The more these refined arts advance, the more sociable men become; nor is it possible, that, when enriched with science, and possessed of a fund of conversation, they should be contented to remain in solitude, or live with their fellow-citizens in that manner, which is peculiar to ancient and barbarous nations. They flock into cities; love to receive and communicate knowledge; to show their wit or their breeding; their taste in conversation or living, in clothes or furniture. Curiosity allures the wise; vanity the foolish; and pleasure both. Particular clubs and societies are everywhere formed: Both sexes meet in an easy and sociable manner; and the tempers of men, as well as their behaviour, refine apace.[33]

Hume emphasises the role of both sexes in creating his model of sociable commerce. Not only are women integral to the public good, but the private and the public are mutually interdependent:

But industry, knowledge and humanity, are not advantageous in private life alone: They diffuse their beneficial influence on the *public*, and render the government as great and flourishing as they make individuals happy and prosperous. The increase and consumption of all the commodities, which serve to the ornament and pleasure of life, are advantageous to society; because at the same time that they multiply those innocent gratifications to individuals, they are a kind of *storehouse* of labour, which, in the exigencies of state, may be turned to public service. In a nation where there is no demand for such superfluities, men sink into indolence, lose all the enjoyment of life, and are useless to the public, which cannot maintain or support its fleets and armies from the industry of such slothful members.[34]

Thus the traditionally conceived effeminate characteristics of luxury are translated into a useful source of industry rather than remaining a wasting influence with associations of greed and vice. The domestic site is an important counter in the national economy, creating a demand that must be supplied.

Returning to Samuel's painting in the light of Hume's discourse, we can see *The Nine Living Muses* as a model of productivity and industry. Samuel links Britain's moral and social progress directly to its cultural and economic status. Each implies the other in a mutually beneficial relationship, in which he aims to educate his receptive audience:

If the art of painting was considered either as an object of elegant speculation, or the means of polishing and softening our manners, we could not esteem it too highly; but the utility is far more extensive. To painting we are indebted for the pleasing enlargement of our minds, by which we look back to ages past, view the customs, manners, and even the persons of the ancients; which by painting become as familiar to us as if they were still living.[35]

In *The Nine Living Muses of Great Britain*, Samuel realises his belief in the didactic potential of painting as a medium for communicating 'the pleasing enlargement of the mind'. The classical figures of the muses are made familiar in the living forms of Samuel's renowned female contemporaries.

On first glancing at Samuel's painting one receives an abstract sense of female unity and achievement. Reading more closely we can realise the more complex nature of its message. Samuel was representing culture to the cultured, his work being exhibited in the recently founded Royal Academy, at the first exhibition to be held in the larger and grander Somerset House, designed by William Chambers, architect to George III. In merging reality and myth through the living bodies of his contemporaries, he performs an exercise in flattery and advertisement that also complies with the theoretical standards of high art as espoused by the Academy's first President, Joshua Reynolds. *The Nine Living Muses* is emblematic of Britain's cultural status and also suggestive of the emergence of a new female and feminine republic of letters. Samuel's painting can be interpreted as a representation of women's achievement in the context of Hume's 'storehouse of labour'. The centrality and high status of the muses' combined artistic output illustrates the power of Britain as Europe's most highly cultured, proto-Imperial power.[36] Women become the symbolic flags of a country's pride, a practice still common today. Only recently were the 'Muses for a Modern Britain unveiled' on the front page of a national broadsheet, in which an updated image of Samuel's painting illustrated the fact that 'Britain excels at modern art, auctioneering, exploring and theatre – London's West End has twice the number of theatres of Broadway; the armed forces and inventions – Britain has won 61 Nobel prizes compared to Japan's four; gardens, the City, broadcasting, field sports and public education.'[37]

While the use of women's achievement to boost national morale may seem crude today, in an eighteenth-century context it can be seen to illustrate a more profound development in contemporary theories of the progress of civil society. It is also arguable that the blurring and merging of the real and symbolic in contemporary representations of women reflects the transitional nature of their cultural status more broadly. Like Hume and Richard Samuel, James Barry incorporated women in his vision of the public. He represented both contemporary and mythical images of the female form in his paintings and writings, including Minerva, Elizabeth Montagu, Pandora and Anna Barbauld. One of Barry's major projects was a series of murals depicting the *Progress of Human Knowledge and Culture*, painted for the Society of Arts, Manufactures and Commerce, at his own suggestion, during 1777 and adjusted and improved until 1801, the year in which he was expelled from the Royal Academy. His account of these paintings was published in 1783.[38] The murals were didactic in purpose and relied on Barry's supporting text, which draws on an eclectic selection of stories from history and myth in order to form a contemporary aesthetic and moral manifesto. In the fifth painting from the set, *The Distribution of Premiums in the Society of Arts*, he aims to make visible a community of social purpose, which, in an extensive commercial society, might otherwise be invisible (see figure 8). He introduces the painting thus:

The distribution of the Premiums in a Society, founded for the patriotic and truly noble purposes of raising up and perfecting those useful and ingenious arts in their own country, for which in many instances they were formerly obliged to have recourse to foreign nations, forms an idea picturesque and ethical in itself, and makes a limb of my general subject, not ill-suited to the other parts.[39]

Elizabeth Montagu is given a central position as a benevolent enabler of artistic progress. She had enrolled as a member of the society in 1758. Scholars have been unable to deduce much about the level of her involvement in the society, although it is almost certain that she acted as a patron.[40] There also survives an example of her own sketches in ink.[41] Barry's explanatory notes emphasise the exemplary moral virtue of Montagu, who is 'a distinguished example of female excellence, who is earnestly recommending the ingenuity and industry of a young female, whose work she is producing'.[42] Behind Montagu, surrounded by Duchesses of the realm, stands the 'venerable sage, Dr. Samuel Johnson, who is pointing out this example of Mrs Montagu, as a matter well worthy their graces most serious attention and imitation'.[43] In the background of the painting is a statue of 'the Grecian mother dying, and attentive only to the safety of her child, putting it back from her breast after which it is striving'.[44] Barry brings together a statue and the real figure of a woman in a crowded and disturbing space of bustle and competition. Woman's sacrifice is presented as a powerful resource of an advancing society, which in a double sense proceeds at her expense. His portrayal of both female figures verges on the propagandist in emphasising their role in forging a moral and virtuous society in which the arts, agriculture, manufactures and commerce are appreciated as public benefits.

Barry's model of a busy and productive society ever aspiring towards progress includes men and women and men paying tribute to women. The Society of Arts admitted women from its foundation and bestowed premiums on female artists. His painting was conceived as a very public statement of a vision which diverged from the more staid agenda of the Royal Academy, where he saw artistic excellence pursued in too narrow a fashion. His purpose is patriotic, and he is proud of Britain's achievements in the arts and commerce, aiming to present the nation's produce in all its variety, from 'white tough-iron, maps, charts, madder, chochineal, a gun-harpoon for striking whales with more certainty and less danger, English carpets, and large paper of a loose and spongey quality', to 'history, painting, and sculpture'.[45] In one of several diversions from his description of the painting, he refers to the contemporary high standard of 'criticism and philological knowledge':

What an acquisition has knowledge and literature lately received from those great luminaries that have blazed out in Scotland. Even our women, what encomiast could exceed in speaking of the perfections of many of them. I hope it will be excused me if I just point at one, who, to the shame and loss of the public, is buried in a retirement . . . actually making two-penny books for children; but the appearances may deceive us; some epic or other great work is, I trust, in hand, as the solace of retirement . . . Leisure will, I hope be found; the world of imagination lies still before her, and there is no region of it which Mrs Barbault's [sic] muse may not appropriate to itself.[46]

Barry died before Barbauld published her magisterial *Eighteen Hundred and Eleven*. His admiration for Montagu's fellow 'living muse' is further proof of the substantial power held by women in the public imagination. He laments the fact that her talents are employed in providing the 'virtuous culture of a few children' when 'talents, like her's, belong to the country at large and to the age, and cannot, in justice, be monopolized, or converted into a private property.'[47] Women constituted an important part of a new consumer society, freshly aware of the improving force of culture. They played a vital role in Barry's argument for broadening the terms on which taste was decided, for expanding the narrow standards of the Academy.[48]

However, women were not only icons of national pride. They were involved, at least to some extent, in the processes of definition taking place in new cultural institutions.[49] Samuel has chosen the painter Angelica Kauffman to represent his own art. In his composition, she replaces the figure of Urania, muse of Universal Vision, thus giving a particularly high status to painting.[50] Kauffman was a founding member of the Royal Academy of Arts in 1768, soon after she arrived in England, after training in the studios of Italy.[51] She was responsible for some of the ceiling decorations of the Royal Academy's new quarters in Somerset House in the Strand, where they moved to in 1780. Kauffman was assigned four oval paintings of allegorical images which represent the four components of painting: 'composition', 'invention', 'colour' and 'design'. These are depicted as female figures, based on Ripa's *Iconologia*.[52] They were set into the ceiling of the Council Chamber around a central painting by Benjamin West that represented *Nature*, the *Three Graces* and the *Four Elements*.

Kauffman was most famous in her lifetime for succeeding in the genre of history painting, which had traditionally been conceived of as a male activity, as contemporary reviews of her work frequently remark. The *London Chronicle* of May 1777 reported on her painting of *Calypso Mournful after the Departure of Ulysses*, exhibited at the Royal Academy annual exhibition:

Miss Kauffman still maintains her character as one of the first history-painters of the age; and so strong is the turn of her genius to that sublime branch of art, that while most of the male pencils in the kingdom are employed in portraits, landscapes &c. she gives us, every succeeding year, fresh proofs of the vigour of her mind by producing something excellent in the historical way.[53]

Here we find a direct inversion of twentieth-century received wisdom in relation to the sexual division of labour in the eighteenth-century art world. Kauffman's historical works were extremely popular and received several glowing reviews, which often admire her 'masculine and daring spirit' in choosing such heroic subjects, comparing this phenomenon with the idea of a woman poet writing epic and heroic compositions as opposed to sonnets and epigrams.[54] She exhibited numerous portraits and history paintings during her years in London and even after her return to Italy in 1781. In 1771 the artist Mrs Delany wrote: 'This morning we have been to see Mr West's and Mrs Angelica's paintings

. . . My partiality leans to my sister painter. She certainly has a great deal of merit, but I like her history still better than her portraits.'[55]

Recent historical research into the life and work of Kauffman has resulted in a major retrospective exhibition of her paintings, engravings and porcelain designs, which stressed the professionalism and diversity of her oeuvre.[56] Here I will briefly address her self-portraits and portraits of female icons, considering her work as an important example of how women artists represented themselves in the cultural context I have described. Her *Self-Portrait: Hesitating Between the Arts of Music and Painting,* 1778, provides a fascinating comparison with Samuel's painting, with which it is almost exactly contemporary (figure 5). She hovers between a choice of two versions of herself, two muses. She has implanted herself in the position usually occupied by Hercules in the period's traditional topic of painting, 'The Judgement of Hercules', in which he makes the difficult choice between vice and virtue.[57] Contrast with Paolo de Mattheis's version of this painting reveals the provocative nature of her adoption of Hercules' powerful position of choice (figure 3). Here Kauffman asserts herself in the public sphere of painting at the Royal Academy with a direct and forceful sense of purpose.

In her *Self-Portrait in the Character of Painting Embraced by Poetry,* 1782, Kauffman portrayed herself with portfolio and brush in the personification of Painting embraced by Poetry, her Sister Art, who is identified by the standard attributes of laurel wreath, winged temples and a lyre (see figure 13). This image expresses her allegiance to the ideal of *ut pictura poesis* (as is painting, so is poetry) expressed in Horace's *Ars Poetica*. Both arts require learning to create images in words or pictures that will instruct as well as delight the mind and eye. An individual response to the issue of professional selfhood, Kauffman's self-portrait reveals her awareness of the doubleness involved in being a woman painter in the traditionally masculine sphere of classical history painting. By placing herself as the artist she both breaks with the traditional image of the male artist being inspired by a female muse and ensures her status as a practitioner of high art.

Kauffman's powerful portrait, *Sappho,* painted and exhibited at the Royal Academy in 1775, creates a striking vision of the female poet, her left hand pointing at the scroll upon which she writes with her right. The original painting, a richly coloured work in oils, was engraved by the Facius brothers for Boydell in 1778 (figure 14).[58] Peter Tomeroy has argued that the painting was probably intended as a veiled self-portrait.[59] Gill Perry supports this view, arguing that Kauffman's borrowed

Figure 13 Angelica Kauffman, *Self-Portrait in the Character of Painting Embraced by Poetry* (1782). Oil on canvas.

identity as Sappho allowed her to work within a conventional academic system of symbolic or allegorical personifications of women: 'When the "academic" female artist was both subject and object of representation she was enabled to speak largely through the careful manipulation of forms of symbolic representation.'[60] As Perry points out, Kauffman's *Sappho* forms an allegorical image of inspiration which breaks with the symbolic codes established, for example, in Poussin's *Inspiration of the Epic Poet*, in which Apollo inspires a young poet to write while a languorous muse looks on.[61] Kauffman perhaps intended to paint herself as an image of inspiration for other women. She certainly offered generous financial and moral support to younger female artists. She assisted Maria Cosway and Rosa Florini, her cousin. She also encouraged the talent of

Figure 14 G. S. and I. G. Facius (after Angelica Kauffman), *Sappho Inspired by Love.* Published by Boydell, 1778.

Georgiana Keate, the daughter of her friend the poet George Keate, who wrote an enthusiastic encomium to Kauffman, in which he describes how 'The historic muse unfurls her scroll.'[62] Her bold self-portraits formed an engaging demonstration of her participation in the higher genres of academic art.

Sappho's role as a contemporary model of inspiration can be further illustrated in the several translations and impersonations of her work by women writers.[63] Mary Robinson's Preface to her translation, *Poems from Sappho to Phaon* (1796), argues for recognition of her generation of female authors, whom she views as advancing into the light of reason and freed from the shackles of slavery:

It is in the interest of the ignorant and powerful, to suppress the effusions of enlightened minds: when only monks could write, and nobles read, authority rose triumphant over right; and the slave, spell-bound in ignorance, hugged his fetters without repining. It was then that the best powers of reason lay buried in the dark mine; by a slow and tedious process they have been drawn forth, and must, ere long, diffuse an universal lustre: for that era is rapidly advancing, when talents will tower like an unperishable column, while the globe will be strewn with the wrecks of superstition . . . I cannot conclude these opinions without paying tribute to the talent of my illustrious country-women; who, unpatronized by courts, and unprotected by the powerful, persevere in the paths of literature, and ennoble themselves by the unperishable lustre of MENTAL PRE-EMINENCE![64]

Robinson acknowledges the power of her female contemporaries as a growing body of professionals. In her later essay, *A Letter to the Women of England, on the Injustice of Mental Subordination* (1799), published under the psuedonym Ann Randall, she lists over two dozen prominent female literary critics, most notably Anna Barbauld and Clara Reeve, as well as essayists, historians, biographers, translators and classical scholars. She concludes that the best novels since those of Smollett, Richardson and Fielding have been produced by women: 'and their pages have not only been embellished with interesting events of domestic life, portrayed with all the elegance of phraseology, and all the refinement of sentiment, but with forcible and eloquent, political, theological and philosophical reasoning'.[65]

Women were aware of and often enjoyed their sense of belonging to an age in which their fame was in the ascendent. When Elizabeth Montagu spotted the printed version of Samuel's 'Nine Living Muses of Great Britain' in *Johnson's Ladies New and Polite Pocket Memorandum for 1778* (figure 11), she immediately wrote to her closest friend, Elizabeth Carter:

Pray do you know, that Mr Johnson, the editor of a most useful pocket book, has done my Prose head the honour to putt it into a print with yours, & seven other celebrated heads, & to call us the nine Muses. He also says some very handsome things, & it is charming to think how our praises will ride about the World in every bodies pocket. Unless we could all be put into a popular ballad, set to a favourite old English tune, I do not see how we could become more universally celebrated. We might have lived in an age in which we should never have had ye pleasure of seeing our features, or characters, in Pocket books, Magazines, Museums, litterary & monthly reviews, Annual Registers, &c &c &c. You, who may look to future & posthumous fame, may despise the weekly, monthly, or annual registers, but for a poor Grisette of a Commentator, who only aspired to brush off a little dust & some Cobwebs with which time & filthy spiders had disgraced the Bays of a great Poet, I think it extraordinary felicity even to enjoy a little brief celebrity, & contracted fame.[66]

Montagu is proud of her fame, recognising her popular, and possibly fleeting, appeal. She seems to revel in the rapidly expanding print culture of her age, with its 'Pocket books, magazines, Museums, litterary & monthly reviews, Annual Registers, &c &c &c.' Her precise distinction between contemporary 'celebrity' and 'posthumous fame' reveals her awareness of the hierarchy governing the emerging sense of a national literary canon, in which the place of women writers was the topic of lively debate.[67] Montagu's playful humour suggests her familiarity with the professional world of letters. She is keen to enjoy the multiplicity of her representation, to become public property. A woman of independent mind and means, Montagu was concerned to promote female learning and encouraged several women's participation in the world of letters. During her lifetime she manipulated the market forces of the literary profession, for herself and on behalf of others. As leader of the 'Bluestocking circle', she was responsible for creating a literary community of both sexes which forged new links between learning and virtue in the public imagination. Female friendship and professional support were vital components in establishing the bluestockings as a group who cultivated intellectual conversation about literature, history and politics.[68] Women expressed a sense of their relation to each other, and to existing models of literary tradition, in the pages of their correspondence and through the creation of an intellectual 'salon culture'.[69]

Throughout the course of Montagu's voluminous correspondence, there are several references to the formation of literary tradition, which often take into account the different experiences of male and female authors in historical terms.[70] She wrote against a backdrop of contemporary critical discussion in which women writers, whether praised or condemned, were treated as a separate group, within or outside the mainstream of literary tradition. The subsequent occlusion of women from the annals of literary history has obscured the phenomenal interest in their growing activity during the eighteenth century itself. This

substantial increase in women writers coincided with a growth of inter-
est in their character and condition in different ages and nations.[71]
Women's achievements were often celebrated in the context of a trium-
phalist history of civilisation. Thomas Seward, in his poem 'The Female
Right to Literature', contrasted the happy position of women in
England with their sisters who were oppressed by the backward ways of
'Eastern tyrants.' He called for a more advanced education for women,
for the need to overturn custom:

> But say, Britannia, do thy sons, who claim
> A birth-right liberty, dispense the same
> In equal scales? Why then does Custom bind
> In chains of ignorance the female mind?[72]

John Duncombe picked up the strain in his longer poem, 'The
Feminead, or Female Genius,' published in 1757, which catalogues the
achievements of several seventeenth-century women writers. He also
mentions his contemporaries, including Elizabeth Carter and the
labouring poet, Mary Leapor, who is praised for her 'perpetual pursuit
after Knowledge.' His plea for recognition of these women contains an
implicit reference to the injustice of their legal position:

> Shall lordly Man, the Theme of every Lay,
> Usurp the Muses' tributary Bay;
> In Kingly state on Pindus' Summit sit,
> Tyrant of Verse, & Arbiter of Wit?
> By Salic Law the Female Right deny,
> And view their Genius with Regardless Eye?
> Justice forbid! and every Muse inspire
> To sing the glories of a Sister-Choir!

His vision of 'British Nymphs' roving through 'Wisdom's sacred Grove'
becomes more Arcadian as the poem proceeds. As seen in the preceding
discussion of visual representations of the female sex, the blurring of the
real and iconic status of 'woman' appears to be inherent in the act of
recognising her cultural achievements:

> Ev'n now fond Fancy in our polish'd Land
> Assembled shows a blooming studious Band
> With various Arts our Rev'rence they engage,
> Some turn the tuneful, some the moral Page,
> These, led by contemplation, soar on high,
> And range the Heavens with philosophic Eye;
> While those, surrounded by a vocal Choir,
> The canvas tinge, or touch the warbling Lyre.

Duncombe's zealous conclusion has a remarkable affinity with Samuel's painting, as he imagines that a great artist, such as Lely or Kneller, might immortalise their forms for future ages, just as his own verse, he tells his female contemporaries, 'shall save / Your darling Names from dark Oblivion's Grave.'[73]

While the chivalry of gentlemen critics could lapse into rather fawning tributes, women were quick to form their own more robust paeans to the 'sister-choir'. Mary Scott introduced her poem 'The Female Advocate' (1774) thus:

> It may perhaps be objected that it was unnecessary to write on this subject, as the sentiments of all men of sense relative to female education are now more enlarged than they formerly were. I allow that they are so; but yet those of the generality . . . are still very contracted. How much has been said, even by *writers* of distinguished reputation, of the distinction of sexes in souls, of the studies, and even of the virtues proper for women? If they have allowed us to study the imitative arts, have they not prohibited us from cultivating an acquaintance with the sciences?[71]

Her suggested reforms in female education are more ambitious than those of most male writers on the subject. She emphasises the need to consider the social context of 'improving women's minds in knowledge', using the recent expansion in numbers of women writers as ammunition in a wider argument about women's rationality:

> I flatter myself that a time may come, when men will be as much ashamed to avow their narrow prejudices in regard to the abilities of our sex, as they are now fond to glory in them. A few such changes I have already seen; for facts have a powerful tendency to convince the understanding, and of late, *Female Authors*, have appeared with honour, in almost every walk of literature. Several have started up since the writing of this little piece; the public favour has attested the merit of Mrs Chapone's "Letters on the Improvement of the Mind;" and of Miss More's elegant Pastoral Drama, intituled, "A Search After Happiness." "Poems by Phillis Wheateley, a Negro Servant to Mr. Wheateley of Boston;" and "Poems by a Lady," printed for G. ROBINSON in Pater-noster-row, lately published, also possess considerable merit.[75]

All in all, women writers and artists could not fail to be conscious of their growing reputation at the time Samuel chose to paint *The Nine Living Muses of Great Britain*. Their intervention in literary and artistic tradition was inevitably self-conscious, involving a sense of group identity and a commitment to women's education and in the words of Mary Hays, an interest in 'their advancement in the grand scale of rational and social existence'.[76] The future of critical reason appeared to belong to both sexes.

Samuel's depiction of nine 'living muses' can be seen as a metonym for women's involvement in the cultural world of their time, conveying at once the centrality and diversity of their public role. The painting provides evidence of the iconic status granted to 'literary women' as a collective class. The breadth and diversity of these nine women's combined achievement is perhaps remarkable to the present-day student, given the subsequent occlusion of their lives and works from the annals of literary history.[77] Their critical works address the legal rights of authors, the political rights of dissenters, the moral philosophy of the ancients, the education of young children, the literary genius of Shakespeare, Richardson and Akenside. Their original works include drama, poetry and novels. The discipline of English literature is presently occupied by questions of value and canonicity, representation and politics which can be enlivened and materially challenged by the act of reading these little-known texts. It is only by reading their works in detail, rather than merely reiterating the acts of discovery and rediscovery which were already taking place in the eighteenth century, that we can bring the muses back to life.

NOTES

I would like to thank Charlotte Grant, Richard Hamblyn and Nick Harrison for reading and commenting on several versions of this essay.

1 James Barry, 'A Letter to the Dilettanti Society', in *The Works of James Barry*, ed. Edward Fryer, 2 vols. (London: Cadell and Davies, 1809), vol. II, p. 594.

2 William Godwin's *Memoir of the Author of the Vindication of the Rights of Woman* had been published at the beginning of 1798. His frank account of her sexual freedom shocked contemporary readers.

3 For a discussion of the feminine allegory of truth, 'nudas veritas', see Marina Warner, *Monuments and Maidens* (London: George Weidenfeld & Nicholson, 1985), pp. 294–328.

4 The symbol of 'woman' and all it represents is inextricably linked to women's place in society, their rights and education. See Denise Riley, *'Am I that name?' Feminism and the Category of 'Women'* (London: Macmillan Press, 1988). Chapter 5, 'Bodies, Identities, Feminisms', pp. 96–115.

5 William J. Pressly, *The Life and Art of James Barry* (New Haven and London: Yale University Press, 1981), p. 137.

6 See, for example, John Barrell, *The Polical Theory of Painting from Reynolds to Hazlitt: 'The Body of the Public'* (New Haven and London: Yale University Press, 1986), and David Solkin, *Painting for Money: The Visual Arts and the Public Sphere* (London and New Haven: Yale University Press, 1993). This issue is discussed in this volume by Charlotte Grant and Kate Davies.

7 Recent historians of the Scottish Enlightenment have pointed out that several histories of mankind incorporated chapters on the history of women. See for example Henry Home, Lord Kames, *Sketches of the History of Man* (1774), which included a chapter on 'The Progress of the Female Sex' (during the writing of which he solicited the advice of Elizabeth Montagu). See also Sylvana Tomaselli, 'The Enlightenment Debate on Women', *History Workshop Journal* 20 (Autumn, 1985), 101–23.

8 Marcia Pointon, *Strategies for Showing. Women, Possession, and Representation in English Visual Culture, 1665–1800* (Oxford: Oxford University Press, 1997). See also the essay by Charlotte Grant above, especially pp. 88–9.

9 See bibliography for a selection of the literary works of the individual 'muses'.

10 Raphael's murals for the papal suites of Pope Julius II at the Vatican were painted at the beginning of the sixteenth century. Raphael finished *Parnassus* in 1511. See James Beck, *Raphael: The Stanza della Segnatura* (New York: George Braziller, 1993).

11 Nicolas Poussin, *Apollo and the Muses on Parnassus*, c. 1630–2, 145 by 197 cm, Museo de Prado, Madrid. See Richard Verdi, *Nicolas Poussin 1594–1665* (London: Zwemmer, in association with the Royal Academy of Arts, 1995), catalogue no. 22, p. 183.

12 Marina Warner, *Monuments and Maidens* (London: George Weidenfield & Nicholson, 1985).

13 M. H. Abrams, *A Glossary of Literary Terms (sixth edition)* (Fort Worth: Harcourt Brace Jovanovich College Publishers, 1993), p. 4.

14 See Larry Silver, 'Step-Sister of the Muses: Painting as Liberal Art and Sister Art', *Articulate Images. The Sister Arts from Hogarth to Tennyson*, ed. Richard Wendorf (Minneapolis: University of Minnesota Press, 1983), pp. 36–70.

15 See Germaine Greer, *Slip-Shod Sibyls* (London: Viking, 1995), chapter one, and Margaret Homans, *Women Writers and Poetic Identity* (Chicago: University of Chicago Press, 1980). For a recent account of the male poet's fascination with a feminine muse, see Joseph Brodsky, 'The Muse is Feminine and Continuous', *Literary-Half-Yearly* (Mysore) 32.1 (1991), 21–3.

16 Ovid, *Metamorphoses*, trans. Mary Innes (London: Penguin Classics, 1955), book 5, line 300.

17 Thomas Heywood, *The Generall History of Women, Containing the Lives of the most Holy and Prophane, the most Famous and Infamous in all ages, exactly described not only from Poeticall Fictions, but from the most Ancient, Modern, and Admired Historians to Our Times* (London, 1657). 'To the reader', A3–4. See also 'A Discourse Concerning the Muses', 77–83.

18 See, for example, George Ballard, *Memoirs of Several Ladies of Great Britain, who have been Celebrated for their Writings or Skill in the Learned Languages Arts and Sciences* (Oxford: Printed by W. Jackson, 1752); *Biographeum Faemineum, or Memoirs of the Most Illustrious Ladies of Great Britain* (London, 1766); William Alexander, *The History of Women from the Earliest Antiquity, to the Present Time; giving some Account of almost every interesting Particular concerning that Sex, among all*

Nations, Ancient and Modern, 2 vols. (London, 1779); Mary Hays, *Female Biography; or, Memoirs of Illustrious and Celebrated Women, of All Ages and Countries. Alphabetically arranged* (London: printed for Richard Phillips, 1803) 6 vols.; Lucy Aikin, *Epistles on Women* (London, 1810).

19 Londa Schiebinger, 'Feminine Icons: The Face of Modern Science', *Critical Inquiry* 1988 (Summer) pp. 661–91.

20 Quoted in Shiebinger, 'Feminine Icons', p. 684.

21 *The Works of the Marchioness de Lambert. A new edition from the French*, 2 vols. (London, 1781) p. 228.

22 Hays, *Female Biography*. Here she combines consideration of her contemporaries, including Catharine Macaulay and Mary Leopor, with real and mythical heroines of the past, such as Abassa, Héloïse and Lucretia.

23 *The Nine Living Muses of Great Britain* appears to be one of the only paintings of his to survive. He exhibited portraits and landscapes at the Royal Academy in 1774. See Royal Academy Exhibitions, Anderdon Catologue 1769–1775, annual exibition 1774: Portrait of a Gentleman, half length, (257) & Perspective View-taken from the lower end of the walks of Tunbridge Wells (258).

24 For a detailed discussion of the date of the painting see Sylvia Harcstack Myers, *The Bluestocking Circle: Women, Friendship and the Life of the Mind in Eighteenth-Century England* (Oxford: Clarendon Press, 1990), pp. 276–9.

25 For details of Britannia's various history see Warner, *Monuments and Maidens*, pp. 45–9.

26 For a fascinating discussion of this painting in relation to issues of gender see Anne Bermingham, 'Elegant females and gentleman connoisseurs: The Commerce in Culture and Self-image in Eighteenth-Century England', in Anne Bermingham and John Brewer, eds., *The Consumption of Culture 1600–1800. Image, Object, Text* (Routledge: London and New York, 1995), pp. 489–514.

27 Richard Samuel, *Remarks on the Utility of Drawing and Painting. To the Society Instituted at London for the Encouragement of Arts, Manufactures and Commerce* (London: printed by Thomas Wilkins, Aldmanbury, 1786).

28 Bryan's *Dictionary of Painters and Engravers*, new edition revised and enlarged under the supervision of George L. Williamson (London: George Bell & Sons, 1905), vol. V, p. 13.

29 Montagu Pennington, ed., *Letters from Elizabeth Carter to Mrs Montagu between the years 1755 and 1800*, 3 vols. (London: F. C. and J. Rivington, 1817).

30 See Marcia Pointon, *Strategies for Showing: Women, Possession, and Representation in English Visual Culture, 1665–1800* (Oxford: Oxford University Press, 1997).

31 Samuel, *Remarks*, p. 3.

32 George Ballard, *Memoirs of Several Ladies of Great Britain, who have been Celebrated for their Writings or Skill in the Learned Languages Arts and Sciences* (Oxford: Printed by W. Jackson, 1752), p. vi.

33 David Hume, *Essays, Moral, Political and Literary* (Oxford: Oxford University Press, 1963), p. 278.

34 Hume, *Essays*, p. 279.
35 Samuel, *Remarks*, p. 4.
36 For an interesting discussion of the arts in an imperial context, see Kathleen Wilson, 'Empire of virtue. The imperial project and Hanoverian culture, c. 1720–1785', in Lawrence Stone, ed., *An Imperial State at War: Britain, 1689–1815* (London: Routledge, 1993).
37 *The Independent*, Friday 25 October, 1996, front page. The 'modern muses' include Evelyn Glennie, Vivienne Westwood, Sarah Kirkby and Victoria Hervey-Bathurst. The photographer has not included a single writer, conveying the difference between our age and the eighteenth century in terms of the relative importance of literature to national identity.
38 James Barry, *An Account of a Series of Pictures, in the Great Room of the Society of Arts, Manufactures, and Commerce, at the Adelphi* (London: Printed for the Author by William Adlard, Printer to the Society and sold by T. Cadell in the Strand, 1783).
39 Barry, *A Series of Paintings*, p. 71.
40 See Alicia C. Percival, 'Women and the Society of Arts in its Early Days', *Journal of the Royal Society of Arts* 125 (Dec 1976–Nov 1977) 266–9; 330–3; 416–18.
41 In the private collection of David Alexander.
42 Barry, *A Series of Paintings*, p. 73.
43 Ibid., p. 74.
44 Ibid., p. 92.
45 Ibid., p. 91.
46 Ibid., p. 81.
47 Ibid., p. 82.
48 The nature of Barry's move away from the Royal Academy is exemplified through visual contrast between his *Distribution of the Premiums*, in which women participate in the model of artistic production, and Zoffany's painting of *The Academicians of the Royal Academy*, exhibited at the Academy in 1772 (see figure 7). In the latter, the absent female academicians (Mary Moser and Angelica Kauffman both founding members) are represented in oval portraits on the walls of the room in which the men are engaged in a life drawing class, from which women were excluded on grounds of propriety. The men are shown in active pursuit of their ideals, in animated poses which suggest discussion and deliberation. The women remain static and shadowy presences – sedate and unconscious onlookers outside a party which they are not permitted to attend. See Marcia Pointon, *Hanging the Head: Portraiture and Social Formation in Eighteenth-Century England* (New Haven and London: Yale University Press, 1993), pp. 66–7.
49 The complex nature of women's status in the evolving institutions of British cultural and scientific life requires further research and elaboration. While some institutions admitted women initially, such as the Royal Academy, they subsequently acted to exclude their work. In the area of science, The Royal Society refused women admission until 1923.

50 In his lecture, Samuel makes large claims for painting and drawing as superseding the power of language as a means of communication: 'Painting has an infinite advantage; for applying immediately through the medium of nature, it becomes a universal language; it is perfectly understood by the Briton, the German, the Turk or the Chinese.' Samuel, *Remarks*, p. 10.

51 See entry on Kauffman by Wendy Wassyng Roworth in Delia Gaze, ed., *Dictionary of Women Artists*, 2 vols. (London and Chicago: Fitzroy Dearborn Publishers, 1997), vol. 1, pp. 764–70.

52 Wendy Wassyng Roworth, ed., *Angelica Kauffman: A Continental Artist in Georgian England* (Brighton and London: Reaktion Books, 1992) pp. 70–1.

53 *The London Chronicle*. Thursday April 30–Saturday May 2, 1773. p. 421. Consulted in the compiled catalogue of Academy exhibition reviews held at the Paul Mellon Centre, London. Unfortunately I was unable to find a single reference to Samuel's painting, despite the fact that it appears in the exhibition catalogue for 1779.

54 *The London Chronicle*, Tuesday April 29–Thursday May 1, 1777, p. 413.

55 Mary Delany, *The Autobiography and Correspondence of Mary Granville, Mrs Delany*, ed. Lady Llanover, 6 vols. (London: Bentley, 1861–2).

56 See Bettina Baumgärtel, ed., *Retrospektive Angelika Kauffmann* (Verlag Gerd Hatje: Düsseldorf, 1999); and *Verrückt nach Angelika: Porzellan und anderes Kunsthandwerk nach Angelika Kauffmann* (Düsseldorf: Hetjens-Museum,1999).

57 See Charlotte Grant's discussion of this traditional topic of painting above, pp. 76–82, 88.

58 The painting, 132 by 145 cm, is in possession of the John and Mable Ringling Museum of Art, Florida. It is reproduced in Baumgärtel, ed., *Angelika Kauffmann*, p. 245.

59 Peter Tomeroy, 'Angelica Kauffman "Sappho"', *The Burlington Magazine*, CXIII (1971) pp. 275–6.

60 Gill Perry, '"The British Sappho": Borrowed Identities and the Representation of Women Artists in late Eighteenth-Century British Art.', *The Oxford Art Journal* 18:1 (1995), pp. 44–57 (p. 50).

61 *The Inspiration of the Epic Poet*, c. 1628–9, 182.5 by 213 cm, Musée du Louvre, Département des Peintures, Paris. See Richard Verdi, *Nicolas Poussin, 1594–1665* (London: Zwemmer, in association with the Royal Academy of Arts, 1995), colour plate 18.

62 See George Keate, *An Epistle to Angelica Kauffman* (London, 1781).

63 For a longer view of Sappho's influence on English literature, see the following excellent anthology: Peter Jay and Caroline Lewis, eds., *Sappho through English Poetry* (London: Anvil Press Poetry, 1996).

64 Mary Robinson, *Sappho and Phaon. In a Series of Legitimate Sonnets, with Thoughts on Poetical Subjects, and Anecdotes of the Grecian Poetess* (London: Printed by S. Gosnell, 1796), pp. 15–16.

65 *A Letter to the Women of England, on the Injustice of Mental Subordination* (London: T. N. Longman and O. Rees, 1799) p. 95. See her 'list of female literary characters living in the eighteenth century', pp. 99–104.

66 MO 3435, Elizabeth (Robinson) Montagu to Elizabeth Carter, 24th November, 1777. The Montagu Correspondence, The Huntington Library, San Marino, California. Unfortunately I have been unable to track down the relevant issue of Johnson's *Pocket Book*, although The British Museum do have a copy of the print which appears to have been removed from the Pocket Book. See figure 12.

67 For a fascinating discussion of the relation between the parallel developments of 'women's writing' and the national canon of literature in Britain, see: Timothy Reiss, *The Meaning of Literature* (New York: Cornell University Press, 1992). Chapter 7, 'Critical Quarrels and the Argument of Gender', pp. 192–226.

68 See Sylvia Harckstack Myers, *The Bluestocking Circle. Women, Friendship, and the Life of the Mind in Eighteenth-Century England* (Oxford: Clarendon Press, 1990).

69 The links between the two generations represented in Samuel's portrait have seldom been explored or acknowledged. The intellectual ideas of the elder circle of bluestockings had undoubted influence on the younger generation of women writers, such as Barbauld and More. For the historical significance of the salon in relation to literature, see Chauncey Brewster Tinker, *The Salon and English Letters: Chapters on the Interrelations of Literature and Society in the Age of Johnson* (New York: Macmillan, 1915).

70 See Elizabeth Eger, ed., *Selected Works of Elizabeth Montagu* (London: Pickering & Chatto, 1999), pp. lv–lxxxii.

71 See, for example, William Alexander, *The History of Women from the Earliest Antiquity, to the Present Time; giving some Account of almost every interesting Particular concerning that Sex, among all Nations, Ancient and Modern*, 2 vols. (London, 1779).

72 Thomas Seward, 'The Female Right to Literature', in *A Collection of Poems in Several Hands* (London: Printed for R. Dodsley, 1748), vol. II, pp. 295–302.

73 John Duncombe, *The Feminead, or Female Genius, A Poem*, 2nd edn (London: Printed for R. and J. Dodsley, 1757).

74 Mary Scott, *The Female Advocate; a poem occasioned by reading Mr Duncombe's Feminead* (London: Joseph Johnson, 1774), p. vi.

75 Scott, *Female Advocate*, p. vii.

76 Hays, *Female Biography*.

77 The mechanisms of such occlusion would be the subject of another paper. Scholars have detected various material instances of the exclusion of women from literary history, for example in the policies of early nineteenth-century anthologists who exluded women (and working-class men) from their monumental volumes of British poetry. Why are women forever in the process of being rediscovered? As Margaret Ezell has argued, the *Norton Anthology of Literature by Women*, edited by Sandra Gilbert and Susan Gubar, is the most eloquent and complete statement of Woolf's assertions about early women writers in her essay on Judith Shakespeare, offering a history defined by suppression and absence rather than professional presence. While Woolf referred to the period before the eighteenth century, such has

been the force of her influence in twentieth-century feminist literary criticism that her views have tended to cast a shadow on the longer history of
women's writing. By the beginning of the twentieth century several women
writers assumed that they had no significant female predecessors. See
preface to Roger Lonsdale, ed., *The Oxford Book of Eighteenth-Century Women
Poets* (Oxford: Oxford University Press, 1989); Margaret Ezell, *Writing
Women's Literary History* (Baltimore and London: John Hopkins University
Press, 1993), chapter 2: 'The Myth of Judith Shakepeare: Creating the
canon of Women's Literary history in the Twentieth Century.' pp. 39–66;
and Marlon B. Ross, *The Contours of Masculine Desire: Romanticism and the Rise
of Women's Poetry* (New York and Oxford: Oxford University Press, 1989).

CHAPTER FIVE

A moral purchase: femininity, commerce and abolition, 1788–1792

Kate Davies

In 1787 an anonymous letter appeared in *The Manchester Mercury*, arguing that women were ideal exponents of the abolition of the slave trade:

If any public interference will at any time become the Fair Sex; if their names are ever to be mentioned with honour beyond the boundaries of their family, and the circle of their connections, it can only be, when a public opportunity is given for the exertion of those qualities which are peculiarly expected in, and particularly possessed by that most amiable part of the creation – the qualities of Humanity, Benevolence and Compassion . . . If the young men, if the husbands of Manchester are so much involved in the cares of the world, in the bustle of trade, that the still small voice of pity cannot be listened to, it is the Duty, and I trust it will be the earnest inclination of the Fair Sex, in this town at least, to remind them, that some attention is due to the Humanity of our Commerce as well as to the gains of it.[1]

In suggesting that women would and should be drawn to the cause because of their characteristic 'humanity, benevolence and compassion' *The Manchester Mercury* makes certain assumptions about femininity and its specific mode of 'public interference' in the campaign to abolish the slave trade. For the writer, Manchester's 'fair sex' constitutes a sort of moral repository which is drawn on to consolidate the city's opposition to the slave trade's inhumane exchange of bodies and commodities. The limits of public interference by the 'amiable part of the creation' are clearly prescribed: femininity must only ever be visible outside the 'boundaries' of familial or domestic space if that visibility is dictated by the necessity of exerting those sympathetic and humane qualities which inhere in and are produced by that space. Since opposition to the inhumanity of the slave trade offers such an imperative, women are urged to take the 'still small voice of pity' out of the intimate 'circle of their connections' and re-situate it in a higher and more audible location somewhere above the 'bustle of trade' and the 'cares of the world'. Femininity comes to represent an authoritative moral constancy, a motionless fixity set beyond the fluctuating business and busy-ness of masculine commercial activity. For the writer, this feminine fixity seems to carry a dual regulatory function as the domestic underpinning of the marketplace and as its legitimate moral overseer. By involving themselves in the campaign to abolish the slave trade, women are apparently neither engaged in participatory politics, nor the business of commodity exchange, but simply diffuse a beneficent influence over the marketplace and the manners of men. Issuing a reminder to 'young men' and 'husbands', impelling their recognition that commerce should be humane as well as lucrative, the fair sex seems to hold a purely moral purchase on the anti-slavery debates.

Between 1788 and 1792, repeated appeals, like that made by *The Manchester Mercury*, appeared in pamphlets, poems and periodicals urging women to exercise their humanity in the extra-parliamentary campaign to abolish the slave trade. Women's sympathetic virtues were seen as ideal abolitionist characteristics: 'I cannot suppose', argued one anonymous pamphleteer, 'that there exists a female possessing a heart of sensibility, who can consider the facts I have now hinted at, without many a deep sigh, without many an earnest wish that the world may be rid of a traffic which involves in it such complicated villainy'.[2] Over these five years, hundreds of abolitionist texts flooded Britain's presses and a significant number of women wrote poems which engaged with the debate on the slave trade.[3] During the late 1780s, abolitionist activity in Britain was characterised by its eclecticism. Drawing together writers from diverse religious and political affiliations, abolition was initially a popular and distinctly uncontroversial form of public agitation. Whilst debates on colonial slavery and the slave trade necessarily and inevitably overlapped with contentious contemporary questions concerning civil rights and liberties and parliamentary reform, abolitionist writers attempted to represent their campaign as apolitical and disinterested, arguing that it proceeded from 'pure' motives of humanity rather than factional or commercial interests. One of the central tropes of abolitionist disinterestedness was the figure of feminine sympathy. In 1788, abolition had defined itself as a language of moral indignation – not political outrage – precisely through circumscribing and appropriating the characteristics of a culturally acceptable femininity. This feminine figure is the 'goddess like' woman of Cowper's 'Morning Dream', who travels from Africa to the British colonies, forcing slavers to drop their scourges in shame.[4] She appears in abolitionist images as the unthreatening personification of Liberty smiling benevolently at groups of freed slaves gathered about her feet.[5] She presides over drawing rooms and tea tables, urging her friends and relatives to abstain from the 'blood stain'd luxury' of slave-grown sugar.[6] She is seen out shopping for anti-slavery tea sets, brooches, hair pins, cushion covers, snuff boxes and fire screens. Her eyes are closed to denominational or factional interests and she inhabits a sphere of pure 'humanity', a space apparently unpolluted by the influence of commercial desire.

In what follows, I will examine how the figure of feminine sympathy and humanity became imbricated with notions of commerce and consumption in the abolition debates. Clare Midgely and Charlotte Sussman have both recently argued that abolitionism's construction of a sympathetic domestic femininity afforded late eighteenth-century women a form of political agency.[7] Here, however, I am less concerned with how far women's engagement with abolition might or might not have constituted a feminine public sphere, and I want rather to explore how a certain figure of femininity is positioned by the language of abolition on the cusp of two late-century notions of the private: namely, the sphere of commodity exchange and social labour, and that other private sphere of familial, intimate and what Habermas terms 'purely human' relations.[8] Abolitionism in the late 1780s positioned femininity and sympathy in a discursive space set beyond participatory politics and the marketplace, in a space that seemed characterised only by the moral authority of properly middle-class private virtues. However, as I will suggest, this notion of a fully privatised femininity set beyond the potential corruptions of commerce is extraordinarily difficult to sustain within the discursive context of late eighteenth-century Britain in general, and the abolition debates in particular. To examine this uneasy relationship between feminine morality and commerce I will look at how women's moral purchase on abolition, through the writing and reading of anti-slavery verse, the consumption of abolitionist artefacts and the abstention from slave-grown sugar, was represented in the late 1780s and early 90s.

The conviction that humane feeling proceeded from a space transcendent of the competing interests of civil society is a notable feature of abolitionist rhetoric during the late 1780s. Abolitionist writers and activists sought to dissociate their ideal of liberty from particular calls for rights and tended to represent their cause as a moral question set apart from divisive political issues.[9] Thomas Clarkson, for example, suggested that abolitionism was 'a kind of holy flame', which, as it burnt in the heart of the nation, obliterated political or religious distinctions: 'churchmen and dissenters forgot their difference of religious opinion, and joined hands, all over the kingdom, in its support'.[10] The apparent unanimity of conservatives and radicals, Quakers, Evangelical Anglicans and Dissenters in opposition to the slave trade meant that abolition could construct itself as a grand master discourse which, by suspending all difference in the name of humanity, would surpass all difference as well. In May 1789, William Wilberforce declared before a crowded House of Commons that the call to abolish the slave trade was not simply one political issue among many, but a moral imperative from a 'higher region':

There is a point of elevation where we get above the jarring of the discordant elements that ruffle and agitate the vale below: in our ordinary atmosphere, clouds and vapours obscure the air, and we are the sport of a thousand conflicting winds and adverse currents; but here we move in a higher region, where all is peace and clear and serene, free from perturbation and discomposure. . . on this august eminence let us build the temple of benevolence.[11]

Abolitionist sentiment was, Wilberforce argued, located in this serene space set beyond the 'conflicting winds and adverse currents' which characterised the social sphere of opinion and interest, of getting and spending. Wilberforce's temple afforded the abolitionist a viewing position which, because it was associated with the private or 'purely human' qualities of pity and sympathetic feeling, could be considered to be impartial.

Women's anti-slavery poems were initially understood to be prompted by a purity of moral sentiment, as if the scene of their writing were Wilberforce's 'temple of benevolence':

The accounts lately given to the public respecting the slave trade were horrid enough to call into vigorous exercise the amiable sensibility of the female breast. By the ladies this subject has been contemplated through the pure medium of virtuous pity, unmix'd with those political, commercial or selfish considerations which operated in steeling the hearts of some men against the pleadings of humanity. To find them, therefore, writing on it, by no means excited wonder.[12]

The ladies the *Monthly Review* describes who, moved by the horrid accounts of the slave trade, are inspired to take up their pens for the cause must be virtuous and domesticated, uninterested in the machinations of party and hold no economic investment in the trade of the Atlantic triangle. Their pity is, the reviewer suggests, a disinterested sentiment positioned outside the masculinised arena of 'political, commercial, or selfish considerations'.

This abolitionist assumption, that women were inevitably sympathetic, and that that sympathy proceeded from a space outside political faction and beyond commerce, facilitated the notion that from its sympathetic eminence femininity might function as the impartial overseer or rational observer of societal specialisms and commercial interests. By equivalence and extension, female poets might construct themselves as the global visionaries of a commercial world free from the moral stain of the slave trade, by speaking from within those very assumptions which constructed femininity as sentient, sympathetic and therefore excluded from both commerce and politics. In *The Slave Trade*, Hannah More represents herself as precisely one of those 'enlighten'd few' who are qualified to oversee and regulate a global softening process in which manners are refined, barbarism civilised, and all humanity assimilated into a commercial brotherhood of reciprocity which Britain initiates.[13]

More's poem was written hurriedly after a request by members of the Abolition Committee that she publish something to coincide with a parliamentary debate on the slave trade.[14] The poem was extremely popular, frequently cited, and probably the only poem written by a woman of this period to be included in nineteenth-century anthologies of anti-slavery verse.[15] More spends the first part of the poem validating her claims to reason and impartiality. The muse which inspires her to write is not, she argues, 'that mad liberty' associated with the volatile mob sentiment of the Gordon rioters, but a 'sober' and 'chaste' feminine presence, who regards Britain's continued involvement in the slave trade as a betrayal of those humane principles which should distinguish the national character (ll. 25, 21, 22). Throughout the poem, More speaks with the voice of moral authority, confidently representing her poetic perspective as broader in scope and more generalising than the 'failing efforts' of lesser writers (l. 55). Locating *The Slave Trade* within Wilberforce's temple of benevolence, More finds herself qualified to observe, judge and impart knowledge or instruction to the civilised and uncivilised world:

> From heads to hearts lies nature's plain appeal,
> Though few can reason, all mankind can feel.
> Though wit may boast a livelier dread of shame;
> A loftier sense of wrong refinement claim;
> Though polish'd manners may fresh wants invent,
> And nice distinctions nicer souls torment;
> Though on these finer spirits heavier fall,
> Yet natural evils are the same to all.
> Though wounds there are which reason's force may heal,

> There needs no logic sure to make us feel.
> The nerve, howe'er untutor'd can sustain
> A sharp, unutterable sense of pain.   (ll. 183–94)

Here, More appears to be making a claim for a 'natural' commonality that cuts across racial and cultural differences. However, as this passage moves through the distinctions which separate the mediated sensations of Britain's refined middle classes from the spontaneous ones of African slaves and those of the 'untutor'd' ranks of the vulgar, More generates a hierarchy of feeling, and positions herself as a polished being at the top of it. Slaves and the vulgar, More implies, experience natural evils with a sort of dumb incomprehension. The 'untutor'd nerve' feels the same pain as the 'finer spirits', but can make no sense of it. Conversely, the 'nice distinctions' that refinement bestows enables the feeler to make sense of feeling, drawing the effect of pain back to its cause. Whilst the emotions of the vulgar and those of African slaves remain at the brute level of sensation, middle-class refinement is seen to augment sense into sympathy. Through not identifying with individual suffering and attempting to make sense of pain in general, the fully 'polish'd' More aligns herself with the refined and sympathetic: a position from which she is able to assimilate the complexities of the problems of slavery in a way that slaves apparently cannot. From her privileged and supposedly impartial vantage point, she can see both the moral and economic problems of the slave trade and the solution which abolition offers.

Drawing on the tropes and associations which in other abolitionist writings linked sympathetic femininity with disinterestedness, More develops a poetic strategy which legitimates her vision of bourgeois Christian imperialism.[16] Precisely because the language of *The Slave Trade* relies on the assumption that sympathetic femininity is necessarily apolitical, a-commercial and therefore impartial, More is able to raise that language to the level of a master narrative.[17] In the latter part of the poem, More's vision expands to encapsulate an international free market of peace and plenty. Representing herself as both the qualified interpreter of the global trading body and the spokesperson of the providential design which supposedly governed it, she explains why 'thirst of Empire' is in itself a 'specious crime' (ll. 153, 154) and how the abolition of the slave trade would transform British commerce into a moralised, ameliorative philanthropy:

> Insulted Reason loathes th'inverted trade –
> Loathes, as she views the human purchase made.

The outraged goddess, with abhorrent eyes
Sees man the traffic, souls the merchandise!
Man, whom fair Commerce taught with judging eye
And liberal hand, to barter or to buy;
Indignant Nature blushes to behold
Degraded man himself, truck'd, barter'd, sold.
. . .
Then bless'd philanthropy! Thy social hands
Had link'd dissever'd worlds in brothers' bands;
Careless if colour or if clime divide,
Then, loved and loving, man had lived and died.

(ll. 170–7, 283–6)

By personifying certain concepts and making them absolutes, More makes the slave trade a fault against nature, an insult to reason, an inversion of commerce. Instead of men using their 'judging eye' and 'liberal hand' to purchase goods as they were taught, their fall into the slave trade means that it is now men themselves who are being purchased. Reason, commerce and nature are the three graces of More's moral-economic order; a harmonious, inseparable trio whose linking arms might, if the slave trade were abolished, bind the globe in the philanthropic links of an international marketplace.[18] To redress the commercial faults against and threats to the authority of More's feminine prosopopoeaia, the exchange of humans must cease and the beneficent curiosity which motivated discoverers like Cook be reinstated.[19] Linking 'dissever'd worlds in brothers' bands', commerce and colonialism would enable those characteristics More identifies as British – Christianity, philanthropy, civility – to be propagated throughout the globe.

In More's poem, as in much anti-slavery verse, abolition is the master spring of a philanthropy which would moralise and humanise all commercial exchange. Similarly, other abolitionist campaign strategies offered consumers the opportunity to moralise domestic commodity exchange through acts of philanthropic shopping. The surfeit of pamphlets and poems during the parliamentary campaigns of the late 1780s was matched by a rapid production of anti-slavery artefacts. At the height of its popularity, anti-slavery's slogans and motifs were reproduced on decorative objects to the extent that the cause became a fashion accessory.[20] Abolitionist marketing techniques, many of which were aimed specifically at women, appeared to negate the potentially irregular forces of consumer desires, or better to transform those desires into sympathetic imperatives, mingling middle-class morals with commercial culture. 'The ladies', wrote Hesther Thrale, 'now wear the Figure of a Negro in Wedgwood's Ware round their Necks, the Inscription these Words: Am I not a Man and a Brother?'[21] The black man kneeling in chains had first appeared as the logo of the Abolition Society, and Wedgwood obligingly reproduced the figure as a jasper cameo from 1787 onwards.[22] The supplicant slave was also marketed on snuff boxes, crockery, cushion covers, fire screens and fly leaves, but the cameo remained most popular as a decoration for female dress. The 'effect' of the emblem, argued Benjamin Franklin, was 'equal to that of the best written pamphlet', and the striking visual combination of the black slave and the white female consumer functioned as a powerful abolitionist advertisement.[23] As the manacled slave merged into a feminine economy of exchange at the level of ornament or accessory, he simultaneously marked out his wearers as women of thought and sentiment. Women incorporated the emblem into their own dress codes, transforming it into a sign of fashionable femininity, and the emblem reciprocally transformed women into signs of ardent abolitionist sentiment. Voicing his claim from his position on the sympathetic female consumer's clothing, the black slave's call for rights was feminised and so, to a certain extent, de-politicised. In turn, the wearers of the brooch became like the slave, a homogenised emblem of abolitionism's normative language.

Thomas Clarkson wrote that 'the ladies' wore these motifs:

> in bracelets, and others had them fitted up in an ornamental manner as pins for their hair. At length, the taste for wearing them became general; and thus fashion, which usually confines itself to worthless things was seen for once in the honourable office of promoting the cause of justice, humanity and freedom.[24]

Women's desire for and display of ornaments and trinkets could easily be interpreted in the late eighteenth century as a manifestation of the corruptions commerce engendered, since fashionable women were frequently seen as spectacular commodities themselves; signs of the fresh wants and superfluities of consumerism. But abolition's female shoppers only functioned as signs of humanity and sympathy. Reconciling feminine virtue with female consumption, the fashion for anti-slavery ornaments did not seem self-referential but purposefully benevolent, 'promoting the honourable cause of humanity and freedom'. Through their acts of morally informed consumption, women might be seen as commerce's cultural regulators. Wedgwood's cameo appeared to transform fashionable display into propriety, hinting that feminine virtue might not be at odds with shopping.

However, if, through the sympathetic purchase of abolitionist arte-facts, femininity participates in the commodification of humanity, a potential problem arises: namely, that humanity might remain always and only that – a commodity. If the slave trade was represented as the unfeeling sale of 'humanity' in the bodies of Africans, might not the buying into, or buying back of, that humanity through philanthropic shopping actually exacerbate a British anxiety about the potential cor-ruptions of commerce by relocating it onto the bodies of abolitionist women? Samuel Jackson Pratt describes the slave trade as a doubled exchange of 'humanity'; at one level, it is the sale of slaves and at another, the disposal and loss of British benevolence:

> Blush, Britain blush, for thou, 'tis thou hast sold
> A richer gem than India's mines can hold;
> Traffick'd thy soft HUMANITY away,
> And turn'd her strongest objects into prey![25]

Abolition encouraged female consumers to buy back Britain's 'gem' through moral purchases; through their sympathetic support of aboli-tion, through the writing and reading of abolitionist poems and through their display of anti-slavery artefacts. Yet the sale of those artefacts and women's consumption of sympathetic feeling in abolitionist texts para-doxically initiated another 'traffick' in humanity. When humanity becomes a fashion and those feminine characteristics of sympathy and compassion are represented as commodities, can they remain moral qualities with the same legitimacy, the same reparative function, the same connotations of disinterestedness they carried for many abolition-ists? The writer of a 1788 letter in the *Gentleman's Magazine* thought not:

Our countryman JOHN BULL has ever been the dupe of some favourite fash-ions. That of the present day is HUMANITY . . . Our poetesses, who can oppress and abuse one another when the opportunity offers, unite in opposition against oppression. Poetry and romance are racked to torture the feelings of John in behalf of his tawny kindred.[26]

The apparent unanimity of women writers in opposition to the slave trade, which was frequently cited as ultimate proof of abolition's humane and disinterested credentials, is here merely an example of fem-ininity's propensity to be swayed by the dictates of fashion. Illustrating women's irrational capacity for absorption in the luxury of feeling, female poets who take the slave trade as their subject are, according to this writer, like John Bull; the duped consumers of a transient trend. As more and more poems were written, and the nation's presses became saturated with hundreds of abolitionist texts, periodical reviewers became irritated with programmatic sentimental tropes, depictions of familial separations, national guilt, white shame and black suffering.[27] Through a repeated association of abolition with humanity, humanity with femininity and femininity with indulgence, the anti-slavery movement came to be seen by many as a cause with no other object besides the gratification of its own self-referential feelings.

Arguing in *The Theory of Moral Sentiments* that 'humanity is the virtue of a woman, generosity that of a man', Adam Smith suggested that humanity 'required no self-denial, no self-command, no great exertion of the sense of propriety'. Humanity, according to Smith, was aligned with an 'exquisite sympathy', with a spontaneity of feeling that was at odds with reflection, judgement, self-sacrifice and public-spiritedness.[28] The 'humane actions' thus prompted relied on grief, sentiment or the pleasures of emotion and might be seen as an extension of the self, or as indulgence. Generosity, on the other hand, Smith argued, was initiated through a rather more complex process of identification, and its actions entailed the partial negation or subjugation of the self to the requirements of a greater need.[29] Yet humanity was, for him, the singular symptom of a polite and commercial culture: 'Among civilised nations, the virtues which are founded upon humanity are more cultivated than those which are founded upon self-denial and the command of the passions.'[30] Thus feminised humanity, with its potential for self-absorption and the luxury of feeling, fostered desires and pleasures perhaps analogous to the desires and pleasures generated by the stimulations and possessions of consumerism. Put another way, humanity threatened to become merely the luxury which would both arouse and satisfy a feminine desire to consume.

The pro-slavery lobby argued that this humanity of sympathetic exchange carried no real weight in what was a particularly contentious debate concerning the transport of millions of Africans to the British Caribbean and their subsequent treatment on sugar plantations.[31] In this atmosphere, where pro-slavery pamphlets received as much review space as abolitionist texts; where supporters of the slave trade were praised for their 'cool sense', and its opposers excused for their feeling 'hearts'; where the 'humanity' of abolition began to look dangerously like the luxury of feeling its opponents claimed it was, abolitionists began to attempt to dissociate humanity from its negative associations with the desires and pleasures of feminine feeling and to recuperate it positively as benevolence.[32] Humanity was, according to some abolitionists, divorced from the consuming pleasures of reading sentimental anti-slavery verse, and was linked instead with the more rationally aligned qualities of self-command and Smithian generosity:

Some people seem inclined to lend an ear to tales of human woe, and feel a certain gratification in beholding the exhibitions of tragedy, or in the perusal of pathetic poetry and the like. Even the case of the oppressed Africans when represented by their favourite bards, or appearing in the form of *'The Dying Slave'* or *'The Negroe's Complaint'*, seems to possess, if not charms to please, at least powers to win their sympathetic regard. Yet the evidence delivered before the House of Commons, containing a true and faithful account of the miseries and wickedness attendant upon the traffic in their fellow creatures, unblemished by flourishes of rhetoric, undecorated with the splendid habiliments of poetry, is almost in vain recommended to their notice. Should they be prevailed upon to cast their eye over a few pages of the shocking history, they presently shut up the book – it makes them shudder . . . But let such remember, that humanity consists not in a squeamish ear . . . Humanity appertains rather to the mind than to the nerves and prompts men to real, disinterested endeavours to give happiness to their fellow creatures. It is therefore to be wished that no affectation of extreme sensibility, or real effeminacy of manners, may disincline or disqualify for the service of humanity. That extreme DELICACY which deprives us, if not of the disposition, yet of the ability to encounter suffering . . . is detrimental to its possessor and injurious to the community; it renders compassion a painful, useless thing and makes beneficence fruitless.[33]

W. B. Crafton suggests that what has formerly gone under the name of humanity is merely a form of debilitating 'DELICACY' which seeks gratification through its absorption in fictitious accounts of suffering. Dissociating 'humanity' from the indulgences of consumption, Crafton redefines it as a species of morally informed action.[34] For him, humanity is both a moral quality and an occupational vocation which impels its possessors to the performance of benevolent deeds. Crafton's was the first pamphlet to advocate abstention from slave-grown sugar after the crushing defeat of Wilberforce's abolition bill in 1791, and according to him, abstention was the abolitionist tactic which would prove beyond doubt the benevolent moral credentials of the cause. He continued:

we are now called upon to redress evils, in comparison with which, all that exist in this nation sink beneath our notice: and the only sacrifice we are required to make in order to effect it is the abandoning of a luxury, which habit alone can have rendered of importance, a luxury to which the industrious bee labours to supply an excellent succedaneum. If we refuse to listen to the admonitions of conscience on this occasion, may it not be justly inferred, that those numerous displays of humanity, of which this kingdom boasts, have not their foundation in any virtuous or valuable principle, but that to custom and ostentation they owe their origin?[35]

So, humanity can finally realise itself in action through a purposeful rejection of slave-grown sugar, and abstention becomes that self-sacrificing act of generosity which would refute inferences of abolition's self-referential 'display'. Abstention, Crafton suggests, offers abolitionists the opportunity of virtuous, moral performance through the denial of 'luxury', thereby quelling accusations of the cause's ostentatious luxuriating in feeling and sentiment.[36]

In the early 1790s, sugar seemed a contentious commodity both in moral and economic terms. Its mode of production seemed a moral affront to humanity as well as a betrayal of the ideals of Smithian political economy.[37] As a sign, it was seen to cut across the late-century vocabularies of feminine virtue and commerce, since qualities associated with sugar, such as 'luxury' and 'refinement', functioned as ambiguous indices of commercial progress or civility and were also understood to be peculiarly feminine characteristics. In circuits of polite and commercial exchange, through pamphlets and poems, over shop counters and tea tables, sugar was linked with the moral connotations of polite, middle-class femininity.[38]

Late in 1792, Samuel Bradburn calculated that the number of abstainers had risen to 400,000 and over half of this number, he asserted, were women.[39] William Allen's *The Duty of Abstaining from West India Produce* closed with an appeal to British women:

> Is it possible, sir, that the LADIES OF ENGLAND, possessing a sense of virtue, of honour and of sympathy beyond those of any other nation – is it possible for them to encourage the slave trade! Can they persist in the use of an article obtained at the expense of the lives and happiness of millions of their fellow creatures! Can they think of the connection subsisting between the consumer of West India produce and the cruel means by which it is acquired and not reject that produce! Can they hear the voice of humanity, demanding that the slave trade be abolished and yet promote the continuance of that traffic! Can they feel the mild influence of Christianity and not act upon it! Are they alive to the blessings of social life and yet dead to the pangs of parting relatives – mothers torn from their children – wives severed from their husbands – and the violation of all the tender ties of blood which this inhuman traffic occasions! IMPOSSIBLE . . . Their example in abstinence from the use of West India produce must silence every murmur – must refute every objection – and render the performance of the duty as universal as their influence.[40]

By linking women's sympathetic leverage with their responsibility as consumers, Allen makes femininity perform a dual regulatory function as the nation's moral overseer and its commercial control. Women are urged to acknowledge the causal 'connection' between themselves as humane consumers and the inhumanity of the slave trade with its related commodities. Once they recognise that connection, Allen argues, it is 'impossible' for them to continue sweetening their tea with slave-grown sugar, since the gulf between feminine virtue and the vicious commodity is too wide. Used at the tea table (a site of feminine sociability) sugar might be seen as the domestic cement of British politeness. But for Allen's female anti-saccharites, sugar is the agent of domesticity's fragmentation since its mode of production severs 'all the tender ties of human blood'. By abstaining from slave-grown sugar, then, female consumers could be seen to be drawing attention as much to their own virtue as to the horrors of the middle passage.

The moral rhetoric of abstention was ideologically potent, and seemed to assuage abolitionism's anxieties about fashionable femininity, female consumption and the desires aroused by reading sentimental anti-slavery verse. In denying itself the luxuriant temptation, domestic femininity seemed motivated by an entirely virtuous form of anti-consumption, anti-commodification. There was, apparently, no danger of humanity once again being 'traffick'd' through the bodies and feelings of women as a form of fashionable display.[41] Abstention, unlike the purchase of abolitionist artefacts, involved no ornamentation and nor did it, like the anti-slavery verses derided in the periodicals, facilitate a public exhibition of feeling and self-referentiality. The only display abstention necessitated was the entirely private display of feminine refusal at the domestic tea table.

In an essay on the slave trade and sugar consumption published in *The Watchman*, S. T. Coleridge argued that abstention was a form of benevolent action diametrically opposed to sensibility and the luxury of feeling. Mobilising a gender distinction which recalls that between humanity and generosity in Adam Smith's *Theory of Moral Sentiments*, Coleridge expresses disgust at the continuation of the slave trade and the self-satisfied moral blindness of the age:

There is observable among the many a false and bastard sensibility that prompts them to remove those evils and those evils alone, which, by hideous spectacle or clamorous outcry are present to their senses and disturb their selfish enjoyments. Other miseries, though equally certain and far more horrible, they not only do not endeavour to remedy – they support, they fatten on them. Provided the dunghill be not before their parlour window, they are well content to know that it exists, and that it is the hot bed of their pestilent luxuries. – To this grievous failing we must attribute the frequency of wars and the continuance of the slave trade . . . – The fine lady's nerves are not shattered by the shrieks! She sips a beverage sweetened with human blood even while she is weeping over the sorrows of Werther or of Clementina. Sensibility is not Benevolence. Nay, by making us tremblingly alive to trifling misfortunes, it frequently prevents it and induces effeminate and cowardly selfishness. . .There is one criterion by which we may always distinguish benevolence from mere sensibility – Benevolence impels to action and is accompanied by self-denial.[42]

Whilst benevolence here incorporates masculine judgement, self-sacrifice and productive action, sensibility promotes an effeminate selfishness, delicacy and a debilitating contraction of moral vision which impedes 'the many' from seeing beyond the 'dunghill' outside their windows. Absorbed in 'pestilent luxury', these complacent consumers fatten themselves on the produce of slave labour; their unthinking consumption supporting the continuance of the slave trade and perpetuating the commercial-moral degeneration of the age. As this passage progresses, 'the many' are reduced into the singular, corrupt figure of the fine lady, sipping her blood-sweetened beverage whilst dissolved in self-indulgent tears over imaginary sufferings. A simultaneous consumer of feeling and the produce of slavery, the female reader is, for Coleridge, the epitome of refinement's potential degeneracy.

Coleridge suggests that the corruptions of indolent sensibility, which according to his essay are the locatable source of blame for 'the frequency of wars and the continuance of the slave trade', can be combated through the performance of benevolent, self-denying acts like that of abstention.[43] However, could the spectre of corrupt and consuming feminine sensibility really be slayed through its benevolent denial of a blood-stained commodity? Might not the problems of the luxury of feeling and the luxury of consumption actually be exacerbated rather than resolved if Coleridge's fine lady sipped honey-sweetened tea and wept over the *Sorrows of Yamba* instead of those of Werter or Richardson's Clementina?[44] Maybe, since a 1790s anti-commercial discourse, like that which Coleridge deploys, had a tendency to represent *all* femininity as corrupt, delicate and consuming, bound to pleasure and gratification; not only the personification of commerce's new wants, but the degenerate motor of commercial desire.

Whilst many abolitionist writings represented commerce unambiguously as a heaven-ordained providential force and as the ultimate sign of a British civility which would be fully reconciled with bourgeois Christian morality after the cessation of the slave trade, abolition also made itself available to an anti-commercial reading; a reading which represented the slave trade, as Coleridge does above, as the most visible manifestation of the commercial and moral degeneracy symptomatic of the age. Within the vision of national progress which governs Hannah More's pro-commercial anti-slavery poem *The Sorrows of Yamba*, femininity functions as the reparative force of sympathy which would restore commerce to the bonds of a naturalised, peaceable and brotherly global reciprocity. In a more anti-commercial abolitionist poem, such as Anna Laetitia Barbauld's *Epistle to William Wilberforce Esq.*, noted by contemporaries for its forceful, pessimistic vision of Britain's inevitable decline, sympathetic femininity cannot function in the same way, and the textual anxieties generated by the degenerate force of commerce which the slave trade exemplifies, become bound up with another figure – that of a fully corrupted and diseased femininity.[45]

I want to close, then, by looking briefly at Barbauld's poem, a text which illustrates how, during the 1790s, the language of abolitionism appropriated to itself those figures of feminine corruption which characterised that decade's anti-commercial discourse.[46] In the preface to his popular anti-slavery poem, *The Wrongs of Africa*, Barbauld's friend William Roscoe explained that Britain's participation in the slave trade seemed to exemplify how 'the spirit of trade may degrade the national character.'[47] Barbauld's *Epistle* similarly represents 'the spirit of trade' as the motor force of Britain's degradation, as a monstrous contagion come to a head in the inhuman sale of human bodies. In the poem, the problem of which the slave trade is a manifestation is everywhere and nowhere, like a viral disease that has grown to such epidemic proportions that it is impossible to trace its source. Far from being a moral aberration potentially healed by Britain's civilising influence and the reparative powers of sympathy, the slave trade is just one symptom of a virus which pervades the entire commercially oriented global body; the single most corrupt instance of a more general malaise. The disease cannot be combated by attacking its most visible symptom, since this strategy (implicitly Wilberforce's) does not penetrate to the source of infection.

In the poem, feminine desires are represented in both a parallel and synechdochic relation to commerce; they are both the depraved result of commercial culture, and the degenerate imperative which impels national profiteering, international exchange and the slave trade itself. In a startling passage, the depravity which the slave trade engenders on the coast of Africa is described by Barbauld in terms of excess feminine desire and corrupt sexuality:

> injured Afric, by herself redrest
> Darts her own serpents at her Tyrant's breast.
> Each vice, to minds depraved by bondage known,
> With sure contagion fastens on his own;
> In sickly languors melts his nerveless frame,
> And blows to rage impetuous Passion's flame:
> Fermenting swift, the fiery venom gains
> The milky innocence of infant veins;
> There swells the stubborn will, damps learning's fire,
> The whirlwind wakes of uncontrouled desire.   (ll. 45–54)

Cleopatra is, of course, a familiar figure of feminine excess. Here she is Africa embodied: the fulsome temptress, the exotic seductress. With her poisonous serpents functioning as the signs of her uncontrollable sexuality, she seduces and further corrupts her European 'Tyrants'. 'Passion's flame' is thus also the unquenchable fire of commercial desire which creates the corruptions of a trade in human bodies. Sexual possession is linked with material possession, 'the whirlwind wakes of uncontrouled desire' referring both to commercial greed and corporal pleasure. In the giving over of her own body for the physical/material pleasure of merchants, Africa seems to be prostituting herself, surrendering the bodies of her inhabitants as well. But who is the possessor and who the possessed in this passage? Does Africa give herself or is she taken? Who is the source of corrupt desire, of 'vice' and 'contagion': Cleopatra, with her dangerous sexuality, or the British traders with their excessive greed? In this passage, with its underlying theme about the moral hazards of excess possession, commerce has become so sexualised and female sexuality so commercial that it is impossible to draw a distinction between them. In the sickening union between Britain and Africa, desire breeds vice, which breeds contagion and yet more vice. Because of the excess of desire in this commercial/sexual promiscuity, the encounter between Britain and Africa does not bring with it the promise of fulfilling consummation but the threat of infection instead. As the 'venom' spreads, polluting 'the milky innocence of infant veins', it becomes clear that Barbauld is comparing both the dissemination of materialist ideologies and the global movement of commerce and slavery along intercontinental trade routes with the sexual transmission of disease.[48] As Barbauld's poem moves, like a merchant ship, across continents and trade routes, she seems to be engaged in a frenzied search for a single corrupt body where blame can finally be located; someone accountable for the spread of the disease, for the inverted trade in human flesh and the corrupt desires inspired by commerce's alluring features:

> Lo! where reclin'd, pale Beauty courts the breeze,
> Diffus'd on sofas of voluptuous ease;
> With anxious awe, her menial train around,
> Catch her faint whispers of half-utter'd sound;
> See her, in monstrous fellowship unite
> At once the Scythian, and the Sybarite;
> Blending repugnant vices, misally'd,
> Which *frugal* nature purpos'd to divide;
> See her, with indolence to fierceness join'd,
> Of body delicate, infirm of mind,
> With languid tones imperious mandates urge;
> With arm recumbent wield the household scourge;
> And with unruffled mien, and placid sounds,
> Contriving torture, and inflicting wounds.   (ll. 57–70)

The figure of corrupt femininity combines both Englishness and exoticism, European commerce and Oriental luxury: she is the indolent wife of a colonial plantation owner. 'Pale Beauty' unites the softness of lassitude to a calculated hardness, embodies both 'indolence and fierceness' and her innocuously delicate femininity is commingled with a boundless capacity for cruelty and corruption. Living her days in the ease and idleness of the British Caribbean, the labour of African slaves and the profits of British sugar production have released her into the pleasures of consumption and self-indulgence. 'Diffus'd', dissipated, degenerate, she controls and subjugates her 'menial train' with 'faint whispers' and whims, wielding not only the 'household scourge' but the inequalities and oppressions of commerce and colonisation in her recumbent arm. She is both the sum of, and the spur to all commercial exchange, being both the embodiment of the leisure wealth affords, and the personification of the luxuriant desire to consume and possess which greases the wheels of the commercial machine. Reclining and displaying her femininity, 'pale Beauty' also seems to represent the alluring novelties of commerce, being the feminised object of commercial desire. Both dangerously desirous and dangerously desirable; uniting corrupt economics and false morality in her 'blend' of 'repugnant vices', she is, like commerce, endlessly desiring, self-referential, perpetually unsatisfied.

In pamphlets of the late 1780s and early 90s, the cruelty of the fashionable wives of Caribbean sugar planters to their black slaves was often cited as an example of the excessive corruption which the slave trade generated.[49] Abolitionist writings frequently contrasted the 'barbarity' of these exotic symbols of colonial desire to the stable civility of sympathetic British women. In Barbauld's *Epistle*, however, no such comparison can be made. The anti-commercial discourse she deploys requires that femininity fulfil no reparative function; requires that it, always and everywhere, be the incubus in the commercial machine. In the *Epistle*, there is no feminine 'simplicity' that is not already 'violated', no rural enclave free from infection, no recuperable form of virtuous independence, no domestic retreat from the marketplace (ll.101–103). The poem closes with the suggestion that Wilberforce's efforts to promote abolition have merely served to exonerate himself from the guilt and corruption of slavery; having 'saved himself', therefore, Wilberforce should now 'seek no more to break a nation's fall' (l. 113). For Barbauld, the future holds the necessary collapse of a Britain that breaks under the weight of its own commercial success. At the heart of the 'nation's fall' is Barbauld's synecdoche of degeneration: the figure of corrupt femininity. In *The Epistle*, commerce is feminised, and femininity is irretrievably commercial; femininity cannot, in terms of its author's anti-commercial abolitionist vocabulary, function as the source of universal sympathy, but instead, in its corrupt form, here constitutes the diseased root of the problem of the slave trade itself.

I have argued that in its apparent exclusion from the marketplace, abolitionism's figure of sympathetic femininity offered the promise of a fully privatised, domestic, 'purely human' sympathy unpolluted by commercial desire, and thus represented a moral authority set beyond societal specialisms and political interests. Exerting a beneficent influence over manners and the marketplace, this feminine figure came to signify the humanised, moralised system of international commercial exchange which would apparently be promoted by the abolition of the slave trade. In the late 1780s and early 90s, the very popularity of the abolition campaign and the mammoth overproduction of anti-slavery verses with their ubiquitous sentimental tropes, provided the pro-slavery lobby with an ideal opportunity to deride their opposers for their feminised self-indulgence. With women's consumption of abolitionist artefacts and the slippage of the meanings of 'humanity' from a disinterested sympathy to an indulgent and self-gratifying sensibility, I suggested, femininity's function as the non-participatory regulatory guarantor of bourgeois commercial morality was called into question. In the terms of the anti-commercial discourse characteristic of the 1790s, there seemed no possibility of positioning femininity in that discursive space set outside commerce's circuit of desire and demand. Illustrating femininity's embeddedness in the potential corruptions of commerce, rather than its exteriority to all forms of exchange which were not 'purely human', women's moral purchase on abolition during the 1790s threatened to become an amoral purchase. These shifts in the functions of femininity illustrate, I think, the inseparability of notions of morality and commerce within the abolition debates and also highlight the instability of the division between the private sphere of 'purely human' relations and that other private sphere – the marketplace – in late eighteenth-century British culture.

NOTES

1 *Manchester Mercury*, 7 December 1787.
2 Anon., *An Address to the Duchess of York Against the Use of Sugar* (London: no pub., 1792), p. 14.
3 Anti-slavery poems written by women during this period include: Hannah More, *The Slave Trade: A Poem* (London: T. Cadell, 1788); Ann Yearsley, *A Poem on the Inhumanity of the African Slave Trade* (London: G. G. and J. Robinson, 1788); Helen Maria Williams, *A Poem on the Bill Lately Passed for Regulating the Slave Trade* (London: T. Cadell, 1788); Eliza Knipe, 'Attomboka and Omaza', in *Six Narrative Poems* (London: C. Dilly, 1787); Elizabeth Bentley, 'On the Abolition of the African Slave Trade, July, 1787', in *Genuine Poetical Compositions on Various Subjects* (Norwich: Crouse and Stevenson, 1791); Harriet and Maria Falconar, *Poems on Slavery* (London: J. Johnson, 1788); Mary Birkett, *A Poem on the African Slave Trade Addressed to her own Sex* (Dublin: J. Jones, 1792) and Anna Laetitia Barbauld, *Epistle to William Wilberforce Esq.* (London: J. Johnson, 1791). Anna Seward was encouraged by Josiah Wedgwood to compose an anti-slavery poem, but she refused, writing that: 'I sicken at the idea of encountering the certain pains and uncertain pleasures of publication by committing this great theme to my muse, fruitful as it is in the great nerves of poetry, pathos and horror; and this, because I have no confidence that her voice would arrest the general attention.' *The Letters of Anna Seward: Written between the Years 1784 and 1807*, vol. II (Edinburgh: E. Ramsay, 1811), p. 31.
4 'But soon as approaching the land / That goddess like woman he viewed / The scourge he let fall from his hand / With the blood of his victims imbrued.' William Cowper, 'The Morning Dream: A Vision', *The Gentleman's Magazine* 58 (1788), p. 1008.
5 See, for example, Samuel Jennings, *Liberty Displaying the Arts and Sciences* (1792), reproduced in Hugh Honour, *The Image of the Black in Western Art*, vol. IV (Cambridge Mass.: Harvard University Press, 1989), part 1, p. 49.
6 Sugar is described as the 'blood stain'd luxury' in Birkett, *A Poem on the African Slave Trade*, part 1, p. 13. For an analysis of Mary Birkett's work in relation to the abstention movement see Elizabeth Kowaleski Wallace, *Consuming Subjects: Women, Shopping and Business in the Eighteenth Century* (New York:

Columbia University Press, 1997). Cowper's *Pity the Poor Africans* was printed
in a small, pocket edition on high-quality paper with a note on the flyleaf
explaining that the poem was 'a subject for discussion at the tea-table'. See
Thomas Clarkson, *The History of the Rise, Progress and Accomplishment of the
Abolition of the African Slave Trade by the British Parliament*, 2 vols. (London:
Longman, Hurst, Rees and Orme, 1808), vol. II, p. 190.

7 See Clare Midgley, *Women Against Slavery: The British Campaigns 1780–1870*
(London: Routledge, 1994) and Charlotte Sussman, 'Women and the
Politics of Sugar, 1792', *Representations* 48 (1994), 48–69. Sussman argues that
in the 1790s, 'women were accorded an innovative and influential form of
political agency by the anti-slavery movement' (p. 65). I would suggest,
however, that women's 'political agency' was broadly denied by the abstention campaign during the volatile years of the early 1790s, precisely so femininity might be seen as an apolitical, moralising agent. See also Deirdre
Coleman, 'Conspicuous Consumption: White Abolitionism and English
Women's Protest Writing in the 1790s', *ELH* 61 (1994), 341–62 for a discussion of the racial politics of anti-slavery writings during this period.

8 Jürgen Habermas, *The Structural Transformation of the Public Sphere: An Inquiry
into a Category of Bourgeois Society*, trans. Thomas Burger (Cambridge: Polity
Press, 1992). Habermas' model of an eighteenth-century bourgeois public
is predicated on a differentiation between intimate or domestic and economic spheres. Habermas suggests that the 'process of the polarisation
between state and society was repeated once more within society itself. The
status of private man combined the role of owner of commodities with that
of head of the family, that of property owner with that of "human being"
per se. The doubling of the private sphere on the higher plane of the intimate sphere furnished the foundation for an identification of these two roles
under the common title of the "private"; ultimately, the political self-under-
standing of the bourgeois public originated there as well' (pp. 28–9).
Following Habermas, it would seem that the language of abolition in the
late 1780s positioned femininity within the doubly privatised space of intimacy and humanity; a space that was necessarily represented as immune
from the exchanges and stimulations of the marketplace. As I argue,
however, this construction of a feminised 'humanity' freed from commerce
and all its possible corruptions is complicated by an elision in the abolition
debates between 'humanity' as a moral quality or benevolent imperative
and 'humanity' as a form of consumption or commodification. For related
arguments concerning the distinctions between 'private' (humanity/neces-
sity) and 'private' (commodity exchange / labour) see Nancy Fraser, 'What's
Critical About Critical Theory', in Johanna Meehan, ed., *Feminists Read
Habermas* (London: Routledge, 1995), pp. 21–55 and Carole Pateman, 'The
Fraternal Social Contract', in John Keane, ed., *Civil Society and the State: New
European Perspectives* (London: Verso, 1988), pp. 101–29.

9 See, for example, anon., *Old Truths and Established Facts; Being a Reply to a Very
New Pamphlet Indeed* (London: no pub., 1792), where it is argued that the

Committee Instituted for Effecting the Abolition of the Slave Trade was necessarily impartial since it was: 'connected with no party: of which it is scarcely possible to produce a stronger proof, than that it is composed of individuals, whose sentiments, both in religion and politicks, are known to be widely different, and whose sole cement of union is a detestation of that horrid traffick in human kind', p. 3. See also Clarkson, *History*, vol. I, pp. 255–8 and 288–9 for a discussion of how the Abolition Committee attempted to dissociate itself from reformist politics.

10 Clarkson, *History*, vol. I, p. 572.

11 *The Speeches of Mr. Wilberforce, Lord Penrhyn, Mr. Burke, Mr. Pitt &c on a Motion for the Abolition of the Slave Trade in the House of Commons, May the 12th, 1789* (London: John Stockdale, 1789), pp. 44–5.

12 *The Monthly Review* 80 (1789), p. 237.

13 'See the cherub Mercy from above / Descending softly, quits the sphere of love! / On Britain's isles she sheds her heavenly dew; / And breathes her spirit o'er th'enlighten'd few.' Hannah More, *The Slave Trade* (London: T. Caddell, 1788), lines 309–12. Further line references are given in parentheses in the text.

14 In a letter to her sister, More stressed the importance of the timing of the poem: 'if it does not come out at the particular moment when the discussion comes on in parliament', she wrote, 'it will not be worth a straw'. William Roberts, *Memoirs of the Life and Correspondence of Mrs. Hannah More*, vol. II (London: R.B. Seely and W. Burnside, 1834), p. 97.

15 See, for example, *The Anti-Slavery Album: Selections in Verse from Cowper, Hannah More, Montgomery, Pringle and Others* (London: Howlett and Brimmer, 1828) and *The Anti-Slavery Scrapbook* (London: Bagster and Thomas, 1829).

16 See Boyd Hilton, *The Age of Atonement: The Influence of Evangelicalism on Social and Economic Thought, 1785–1865* (London: Oxford University Press, 1988) for a discussion of the links between Evangelical Anglicanism and Smithian economic paradigms.

17 In her stimulating essay on women and the division of labour in Adam Smith's *The Wealth of Nations*, Kathryn Sutherland argues that whilst Smith's masculinised construction of the philosopher/overseer of the economy enables him to position himself as the 'master manufacturer' of his 'master narrative', the 'unofficial tradition of women's economic writing that emerges from the late eighteenth century', within which she includes Hannah More, precludes such a construction and such a positioning. As I suggest here, and as More's poem clearly illustrates, women in the late eighteenth century might occupy a textual position analogous to that of Smith's philosopher precisely because they could be seen as not only excluded from the division of labour, but transcendent of it. Kathryn Sutherland, 'Adam Smith's Master Narrative: Women and the Wealth of Nations', in Stephen Copley and Kathryn Sutherland, eds., *Adam Smith's Wealth of Nations: New Interdisciplinary Essays* (Manchester: Manchester University Press, 1995), pp. 97–122.

18 I take issue here with Paul Langford's comment, that 'viewed against the
   sentimental background in which it belongs, abolition takes its place among
   the manifold expressions of the new sensibility, most of which can only be
   tangentially related to economic analysis'. Paul Langford, *A Polite and
   Commercial People: England 1727–1783* (Oxford: Oxford University Press, 1992),
   p. 516. In a variety of abolitionist writings commerce and sensibility are seen
   to play mutually constitutive roles in a civilising process. See, for example,
   anon., *Thoughts on Civilisation and the Gradual Abolition of Slavery in Africa and the
   West Indies* (London: J. Sewell, 1788).

19 Although the facts of Cook's voyage and the circumstances of his death
   were known at the time More wrote *The Slave Trade*, he was still represented
   in a number of poems as the beneficent civiliser of the South Pacific. See,
   for example, Helen Maria Williams, 'The Morai: an Ode' in Andrew
   Kippis, *The Life of Captain James Cook* (London: G. Nichol and G. J. Robinson,
   1788), pp. 524–5: 'Till Cook . . .along the surges cast / Philanthropy's con-
   necting zone, / And spread her loveliest blessings round. – / Not like that
   murd'rous band he came, / Who stain'd with blood the new-found West; /
   Nor as, with unrelenting breast, / From Britain's free, enlighten'd land, /
   Her sons now seek Angola's strand; / Each tie most sacred to unbind, / To
   load with chains a brother's frame, / And plunge a dagger in the mind; /
   Mock the sharp anguish bleeding there / Of Nature in her last despair! / –
   Great Cook! Ambition's lofty flame, / So oft directed to destroy, / Led thee
   to circle with thy name, / The smile of love, and hope, and joy!'

20 On the techniques of marketing philanthropic commodities, particularly
   those of Josiah Wedgwood, see G. J. Barker Benfield, *The Culture of Sensibility:
   Sex and Society in Eighteenth-Century Britain* (Chicago and London: University
   of Chicago Press, 1992), p. 213; Langford, *A Polite and Commercial People*, p.
   668; and Neil McKendrick, 'The Consumer Revolution of Eighteenth-
   Century England', in Neil McKendrick, John Brewer and J. H. Plumb, *The
   Birth of a Consumer Society: The Commercialization of Eighteenth-Century England*
   (Bloomington: Indiana University Press, 1982), pp. 71–4.

21 *Thraliana: The Diary of Mrs Hesther Lynch Thrale, 1776–1809*, 2nd edn, ed.
   Katherine C. Balderston (Oxford: Clarendon Press, 1951), p. 714.

22 Wedgwood sent a consignment of cameos to Benjamin Franklin, writing on
   29 February 1788: 'it gives me great pleasure to be embarked on this occasion in the same great and good cause with you, and I ardently hope for the
   final completion of our wishes. This will be an epoch before unknown to
   the world, and while relief is given to millions of our fellow creatures immediately the object of it, the subject of freedom will be more canvassed and
   better understood in the enlightened nations.' Ann Finer and George
   Savage, eds., *The Selected Letters of Josiah Wedgwood* (Oxford: Clarendon Press,
   1965), p. 311.

23 Benjamin Franklin to Josiah Wedgwood, 15 May 1788, in Finer and Savage,
   eds., *Selected Letters of Josiah Wedgwood*, p. 314.

24 Clarkson, *History*, vol. II, pp. 191–2.

25 Samuel Jackson Pratt, *Humanity, or, the Rights of Nature: A Poem in Two Books* (London: T. Cadell, 1788), p. 11.

26 'Polinus', letter, *The Gentleman's Magazine* 58 (1788), p. 598.

27 Discussing the Falconar sisters' *Poems on Slavery*, a writer in the *Critical Review* remarked that 'the subject itself almost precludes any novelty of ideas'. *The Critical Review* 66 (1788), p. 151. The *Gentleman's Magazine* similarly derided a number of anti-slavery verses, and in 1789 named the slave trade as 'this almost exhausted topic'. *The Gentleman's Magazine* 59 (1789), p. 633.

28 Adam Smith, *The Theory of Moral Sentiments* (1764), ed. D. D. Raphael and A. L. Macfie (Oxford: Clarendon Press, 1976), p. 113.

29 The example Smith gives of generosity is an example of martial virtue: the young soldier sacrificing his own life for that of his officer. For a different reading of the implications of this passage see Jane Rendall, 'Virtue and Commerce: Women in the Making of Adam Smith's Political Economy', in Ellen Kennedy and Susan Mendus, eds., *Women in Western Political Philosophy* (Brighton: Harvester Wheatsheaf, 1987), pp. 44–77.

30 Smith, *Theory of Moral Sentiments*, pp. 204–5.

31 See, for example, Jesse Foot, *A Defence of the Planters in the West Indies* (London: J. Debrett, 1792), p. 2. Foot, like many other supporters of the West India interest, argues that the nation's support of abolition is a 'counterfeit humanity' that deflects Britain's attention from the problems of its own labouring poor. On this point see also James Boswell's distasteful poem, *No Abolition of Slavery, or, the Universal Empire of Love* (London: R. Faulder, 1791).

32 See *The Monthly Review*'s comments on *The Dictates of Indignation: a Poem on the African Slave Trade. By an Undergraduate*: 'his anger is prompted by his humanity. His sentiments do credit to his heart, but they are such as the muse has often repeated on this subject.' Compare this to their assessment of, for example, the pro-slavery *Observations on Slavery and the Consumption of the Produce of the West India Islands*: 'In seasons when people are hurried along by hasty prepossessions, it is pleasing to find a few individuals whose cool sense keeps them out of the croud.' *The Monthly Review*, 2nd ser. 4 (1791), pp. 469, and 8 (1792), p. 101.

33 William Bell Crafton, *A Short Sketch of the Evidence Delivered before a Committee of the House of Commons for the Abolition of the Slave Trade: To Which is Added a Recommendation of the Subject to the Serious Attention of the People in General*, 3rd edn (London: M. Gurney, 1792), pp. 19–20. Crafton's pamphlet was first published in May 1791, directly following the defeat of Wilberforce's bill in parliament.

34 In his *History*, Thomas Clarkson, like Crafton here, draws a distinction between those whose abolitionist sympathies were merely aroused through reading pamphlets and poems, and those whose sympathy was channelled into benevolent action. Clarkson discusses three types of abolitionist, who are placed in a sort of hierarchy of usefulness. At the bottom are those who simply read about and approve of abolition; placed above them are abolitionist pamphleteers (but not poets – since Clarkson seems to have a dim

view of most abolitionist poetry, save that of Cowper and Roscoe); and at the top are those whom Clarkson describes as 'actors' or 'labourers' in the cause. These distinctions run throughout both volumes of Clarkson's *History*, but see especially vol. 1, chapters 3–9.

35 Crafton, *A Short Sketch of the Evidence*, p. 20.

36 Every abstention pamphlet published during 1791–2 argued that British consumers, by revelling in the sweetness and luxury which sugar afforded, were active promoters of the slave trade. See, for example, anon., *Address to the Duchess of York*: 'It is then the buyer and consumer who form the first spring which sets in action the several engines of injustice and oppression which annually destroy several hundreds of our fellow creatures' (p. 13); Andrew Burn, *A Second Address to the People of Great Britain: Containing a New and most Powerful Argument to Abstain from the Use of West India Sugar* (London: M. Gurney, 1792): 'it is evident beyond a doubt that the consumers of sugar and rum, innocent or guilty, are actually the first and moving cause of all those torrents of blood and sweat that annually flow from the body of the negro' (p. 6); Francis Randolf, *Remarkable Extracts and Observations on the Slave Trade with some Considerations on the Consumption of West India Produce* (London: J. Johnson, 1792): 'The load of guilt bears equally upon every link of this infernal chain. . .but the first mover seems more criminal than the rest, so a larger portion of guilt may perhaps not unjustly, be attributed to the consumer' (p. 10); William Allen, *The Duty of Abstaining from the Use of West India Produce* (London: T. W. Hawkins, 1792): 'the consumer of West India produce is the principle cause, both of the continuance of the slave trade and of the prevalence of slavery' (p. 8); and William Fox, *An Address to the People of Great Britain*, 10th edn (London: M. Gurney, 1792): 'The slave dealer, the slave holder and the slave driver are virtually the agents of the consumer, and may be considered as hired by him to procure the commodity. For, by holding out the temptation, he is the first mover in the horrid process' (p. 2).

37 The Caribbean sugar monoculture was represented by abolitionists as a regressive form of agricultural production, and colonial trade monopolies and the protectionist policies of the British government towards West Indian produce were seen as mercantilist atavisms. See, for example, anon., *Remarks on the New Sugar Bill and on the National Compacts Respecting the Sugar Trade and the Slave Trade* (London: J. Johnson, 1792): 'The West India Colonies have been built on two false principles: first, slavery, with its companion the slave trade; and secondly, a reciprocal monopoly', p. 43. For other views on the sugar monopoly see anon., *The Legal Claim of the British Sugar Colonies to Enjoy an Exclusive Right of Supplying this Kingdom with Sugars in Return for Sundry Restrictions Laid upon these Colonies in Favour of the Products, Manufactures, Commerce, Revenue and Navigation of Great Britain* (London: no pub., 1792). The latter pamphlet includes details of the legislation which consolidated the monopoly dating back to the reign of Charles II. The sugar monopoly was not fully abolished until 1846.

38 See Sussman, 'Women and the Politics of Sugar, 1792'. On the cultural asso-

ciations between femininity and sugar more generally see Werner Sombart, *Luxury and Capitalism* (1919) (Ann Arbour: University of Michigan Press, 1967), p. 99; Sidney Mintz, *Sweetness and Power: The Place of Sugar in Modern History* (Harmondsworth: Penguin, 1985), pp. 139–51; Kowaleski Wallace, *Consuming Subjects.*

39 Samuel Bradburn, *An Address to the People called Methodists; Concerning the Evil of Continuing the Slave Trade* (Manchester: T. Harper, 1792), p. 15. On a journey through England in 1792 Thomas Clarkson noted that: 'there was no town, through which I passed, in which there was not some one individual who had left off the use of sugar . . .Rich and poor, churchmen and dissenters had adopted the measure. Even grocers had left off trading in the article in some places . . . By the best computation I was able to make from the notes taken down in my journey, no fewer than three hundred thousand persons had abandoned the use of sugar.' Clarkson, *History*, vol. II, pp. 349–50. It has been suggested that Clarkson's estimate of the number of abstainers in Britain is not unreasonable. See Seymour Drescher, *Capitalism and Anti-Slavery: British Mobilization in Comparative Perspective* (Basingstoke: Macmillan, 1986), p. 79.

40 William Allen, *The Duty of Abstaining from the Use of West India Produce*, (London: T.W. Hawkins, 1792), p. 22.

41 See note 26 above.

42 S. T. Coleridge, 'On the Slave Trade', in *The Watchman*, 26 March 1796. Now in *The Watchman*, ed. Lewis Patton (London: Routledge and Kegan Paul, 1972), pp. 139–40.

43 Coleridge, 'On the Slave Trade', p. 140.

44 Hannah More, *The Sorrows of Yamba; or, the Negro Woman's Lamentation* (London: R. White, 1795). Clementina is a character in Richardson's *Sir Charles Grandison*. The daughter of a noble Italian family, and fervently Catholic, Clementina fosters a hopeless and debilitating passion for the English Protestant, Sir Charles. For a related discussion concerning abstention as a form of self-absorptive luxury see anon., *A Plain Man's Thoughts on the Present Price of Sugar* (London: J. Debrett, 1792), which argues that abstainers are parsimonious (they refuse to spend money on an item whose price has risen), indulgent (they revel in the self-gratification of appearing virtuous) and inconsistent (they continue to purchase other items produced by slaves, such as mahogany furniture). 'These tender-hearted antisaccharites have no right to expect credit from the world either for their sincerity or their consistency', p. 11.

45 Anna Laetitia Barbauld, *Epistle to William Wilberforce Esq.* (London: J. Johnson, 1791). All further line references in the text to this edition. Barbauld was an active supporter of the abolition movement – and an abstainer. Maria Edgeworth gives an account of how she 'met at Clifton Mr and Mrs Barbauld. He was an amiable and benevolent man, so eager against the slave-trade that when he drank tea with us he always brought some East India sugar, that he might not share our wickedness in eating that made by

the negro slave.' Quoted in Grace A. Ellis, *A Memoir of Mrs Anna Laetitia Barbauld, with many of her letters* (Boston: James R. Osgood, 1874), p. 222. See also p. 181 for a letter from Barbauld to Mrs. Beechcroft about parliamentary debates on the slave trade. For a favourable review of Barbauld's *Epistle*, see *The Monthly Review* 2nd ser., 6 (1791), p. 226.

46 In an illuminating essay on 1790s polemical writings on women, Harriet Guest identifies the figure of corrupt femininity as a key feature of 1790s anti-commercialism. Guest writes that this figure 'acts as a magnet for gendered characteristics in excess of those necessary to its function as a guarantee of the moral discourses from which it is projected and excluded. It can seem to have assumed the power to characterise not only what is excessive, corrupted and feminised, but those qualities which seem in terms of the discourses of the period to be necessary to femininity itself. In the particular anti-commercial form which. . . is specific to the 1790s, the image of corrupted femininity can seem to embrace and represent all femininity, and thus to identify anti-commercial discourse as misogynistic.' Harriet Guest, 'The Dream of a Common Language: Hannah More and Mary Wollstonecraft', *Textual Practice* 9 (1995), p. 321.

47 William Roscoe, *The Wrongs of Africa* (London: R. Faulder, 1788), p. iii.

48 'Nor less from the gay East, on essenced wings, / Breathing unnamed perfumes, Contagion springs', Barbauld, *Epistle*, ll. 86–7. See Sander Gilman, 'AIDS and Syphilis: The Iconography of Disease', in Douglas Crimp, ed., *AIDS: Cultural Analysis / Cultural Activism* (Cambridge, Mass: MIT Press, 1988), pp. 87–107. Gilman discusses the gender codings of the iconography of disease during the eighteenth century. 'During the enlightenment', he suggests, 'the image of the syphilitic shifts from male to female and with this shift comes another: from victim to source of infection' (p. 96). See also Paula Treichler's compelling discussion of the languages of epidemiology and femininity in 'AIDS, Gender and Biomedical Discourse: Current Contests for Meaning', in Elizabeth Fee and Daniel M. Fox, eds., *AIDS: The Burdens of History* (Berkeley: University of California Press, 1988), pp. 190–266. Triechler explores how the 1980s represented a certain form of upwardly mobile and promiscuous femininity as both host and perpetrator of the AIDS virus.

49 See, for example, anon., *A Monitory Address to Great Britain: A Poem in Six Parts to Which is Added Britain's Remembrancer* (Edinburgh: J. Guthrie, 1792): 'Those who call themselves ladies, but for whom the name of infernal furies is not too bad, have been known to lash their slaves with their own hands, to direct the overseers and drivers where to strike and to see these cruel punishments executed when the husbands refused to witness them' (pp. 324–5). For a similar description see Francis Randolf, *Remarkable Extracts and Observations on the Slave Trade with Some Considerations on the Consumption of West India Produce* (London: J. Johnson, 1792), p. 6. One of the most striking constructions of West Indian feminine corruption earlier in the century is found in Sarah Scott's *The History of Sir George Ellison* (London: A. Millar, 1766). Ellison's first

wife (a Caribbean widow who owns a sugar plantation) indulges her son, weeps at her lap-dog's injuries, but never 'flinched at any punishment' inflicted on her slaves. (vol. 1, p. 25). Curiously enough, Barbauld's 'animated description of the unity and barbarity and voluptuousness in the West Indian woman' was the part of the *Epistle* singled out for praise by Hannah More. Letter from More to Barbauld, July 1791, in Anna Laetitia Le Breton, ed., *Memoir of Mrs Barbauld Including Letters and Notices of her Family and Friends* (London: George Bell and Sons, 1874), p. 67.

PART III

Learned ladies: from Bluestockings to cosmopolitan intellectuals

CHAPTER SIX

Bluestocking feminism

Gary Kelly

Like all feminisms, Bluestocking feminism was historically and socially particular. It had roots in the seventeenth century, it was fully developed among a small group of women and men in the third quarter of the eighteenth century, and it was diffused more widely through the late eighteenth and early part of the nineteenth century in England. Here I first describe the social, ideological and political context and content of Bluestocking feminism. I then read a set of texts published in their own time by first-generation women writers of the Bluestocking circle, namely Elizabeth Montagu, Sarah Scott, Elizabeth Carter and Catherine Talbot. I finish by indicating some of the later developments and appropriations of Bluestocking feminism. I conclude that the significance of Bluestocking feminism for the themes of this book is its contribution to the creation of and dialectic between what came to be considered private and public spheres, as these were foundational for the modern state.

This contribution was directly connected to the fact that Bluestocking feminism was formed in the mid-eighteenth century in England on the dividing line between the gentry and the professional middle class, particularly among the women of those classes, but including male associates, collaborators, mentors, patrons, and clients.[1] For the social formation of Bluestocking feminism was conditioned by particular developments in society, culture, economy and politics during the middle decades of the eighteenth century, especially those developments initiated by and serving the rise of the professional middle class from the 1720s on.[2] These developments included the idea of distinct but connected private and public spheres,[3] serving the construction of an increasingly distinct, detached and oppositional culture for a social group that would eventually, in the early nineteenth century, become dominant in Britain and elsewhere in Europe and its colonies and former colonies. In England, the oppositional culture of this social formation derived largely from anti-court traditions in the upper and middle classes, going back to 1688 and earlier. Significantly, Bluestocking feminism itself had antecedents in the feminist aspects of these traditions.[1] This anti-court culture was produced in the context of an oppositional but close relationship between the gentry and professional middle class that continued through the rest of the eighteenth century and into the nineteenth.

The broad movement of change that eventually transferred hegemony from the historic ruling class of gentry and aristocracy to the middle classes, led by the professions, was expressed and facilitated by a complex cultural revolution that would eventually, among other things, found the modern state.[5] This revolution comprised certain complex and inter-related transformations. One of these was what historians call modernisation, or the transition from social and economic relations based partly or largely on customary practice to relations based on the use of capital. Another major transformation was what historians call the birth of a consumer society and the commercialisation of culture – the elaboration of patterns of consumption based on the hegemonic classes' historic practices of conspicuous consumption, taken on by their social inferiors as a fashion system and social emulation, and including the acquisition of objects and knowledges related to aesthetics and taste in a broad range of fields, from cuisine to the *belles-lettres*.[6] Another important transformation, much commented on in the eighteenth century itself, was the so-called 'rise of civil society', or construction of a social domain of civility and relationships located between the domestic sphere, however defined, and the public, institutional arenas of politics and the state.[7] In civil society, men and women of the middle and upper classes were to meet and mingle in ostensibly egalitarian sociability, supposedly free from the formality and imposed hierarchy of courtly society, and free from the potential imposition of order by force that was thought to have been characteristic of 'barbarous' societies and classes. In civil society the 'civilised' classes could intermarry, construct business and political networks, and so on. Because of historically conventionalised gender identities, women could assume an important and in many ways instrumental role in these and other aspects of the cultural revolution that founded modernity and the modern state. The Bluestocking feminists actively pursued these opportunities, and indeed their feminism was largely directed to securing a place for women within and in certain ways leading the cultural revolution.

In doing so, they were practising roles in the rise of civil society already prescribed for certain kinds of women by male Enlightenment philosophers, especially in Scotland. In the mid-eighteenth century, the Scottish Enlightenment led the theorising of civil society with the work of philosophers such as David Hume, Adam Ferguson and Adam Smith and 'philosophical historians' such as William Robertson. Hume's views on the role of women in creating civil society, set forth in his essays of the early 1740s, are distinctive yet representative, and anticipate and validate the practices of Bluestocking feminism a decade later. In his essay 'Of Refinement in the Arts', for example, Hume argues that the advancement of arts and manufactures is accompanied and facilitated by greater sociability, implicitly among people of various social classes and groups formerly distinct, perhaps distant from or even in conflict with each other. In these new conditions, according to Hume, it becomes impossible for people

to remain in solitude, or live with their fellow-citizens in that distant manner, which is peculiar to ignorant and barbarous nations. They flock into cities; love to receive and communicate knowledge; to show their wit or their breeding; their taste in conversation or living, in clothes or furniture. Curiosity allures the wise; vanity the foolish; and pleasure both. Particular clubs and societies are everywhere formed: both sexes meet in an easy and sociable manner; and the tempers of men, as well as their behaviour, refine apace. So that, beside the improvements which they receive from knowledge and the liberal arts, it is impossible but they must feel an increase of humanity, from the very habit of conversing together, and contributing to each other's pleasure and entertainment.[8]

The Bluestocking circle was precisely one of these ' clubs' – in fact 'club' was an alternative term for the circle at the time.

'Conversation', or a discourse of culture and civility in mixed company, replacing both the formality and masquerade of courtly upper-class society and the supposed roughness and coarseness of male-only society or plebeian society, was a major feature of the 'Bluestocking club'. In his essay 'Of the Rise and Progress of the Arts and Sciences', Hume gives a particular importance to 'conversation', by which he means certain kinds of social interchange, in the progress of civil society:

Among the arts of conversation, no one pleases more than mutual deference or civility, which leads us to resign our own inclinations to those of our companion, and to curb and conceal that presumption and arrogance so natural to the human mind. A good-natured man, who is well educated, practises this civility to every mortal, without premeditation or interest.[9]

According to Hume, in his 'Of Essay Writing', women preside over this 'conversable world', which comprises people who 'join to a sociable disposition, and a taste for pleasure, an inclination for the easier and more gentle exercises of the understanding, for obvious reflections on human affairs, and the duties of common life, and for observation of the blemishes or perfections of the particular objects that surround them'.[10] Just such a conversable world is represented by the Bluestocking meetings, their correspondence networks and their published works. Women have leadership here, according to Hume in 'Of the Rise and Progress of the Arts and Sciences', because conversation between the sexes has a 'polishing' and civilising effect on men, disciplining masculinity that otherwise is naturally rough, aggressive and brutal, especially as developed in the previous age of feudal culture:

What better school for manners than the company of virtuous women, where the mutual endeavour to please must insensibly polish the mind, where the example of the female softness and modesty must communicate itself to their admirers, and where the delicacy of that sex puts every one on his guard, lest he give offence by any breach of decency?[11]

Hume insists, however, that women need a solid education in order to fulfil their historic civilising role, and in this respect he anticipates another major aspect of Bluestocking feminism – its emphasis on and promotion of intellectual life for women. Admittedly, in both Hume and Bluestocking feminism this emphasis is based on conventional historic characterisations of the feminine sphere. Nevertheless, in 'Of Essay Writing' Hume dismisses conventional fear of 'learned ladies'. According to Hume 'all men of sense, who know the world, have a great deference for their [women's] judgment of such books as lie within the compass of their knowledge, and repose more confidence in the delicacy of their taste, though unguided by rules, than in all the dull labors of pedants and commentators'.[12] Therefore 'it is a vain panic, if they [women] be so terrified with the common ridicule that is levelled against learned ladies, as utterly to abandon every kind of books and study to our sex'. Hume even anticipates that the union of the learned and women will bring about a reform in the 'republic of letters', rendering the learned more 'conversable' and women more learned – in effect, a desirable feminisation of culture. Here Hume again anticipates and justifies the Bluestocking programme – in this case, their literary activism as writers of books.

Views echoing those of Hume on the role of what he calls 'women of sense and education' in the advancement of civil society and culture may be found in various forms throughout the social philosophy of the

Enlightenment, and in a wide array of literary works, from *The Spectator* on, at least, but especially through the second half of the eighteenth century.[13] For articulation and management of gender difference was central to the cultural revolution for modernisation. In order to avoid reproducing the characteristics of court society and culture and to establish the new civil society, gender difference and relations had to be reconstructed through education, socialisation and acculturation. The role of women in court society and culture was supposedly, and often in reality, to be an erotic diversion and reward of power in the intertwined sexual and political intrigue of court politics. For the new civil society, woman was reconstructed from traditions of female religious piety and a private, domesticated version of humanist intellectual culture. Bluestocking feminism led this reconstruction.

At the same time, woman was reconstructed to play a new role in the expansion of capitalism, and especially gentry capitalism. On the one hand, courtly woman, supposedly engaged in the fashion system that could threaten the accumulation and maintenance of capital, had to be replaced with a model of woman that facilitated capital. On the other hand, through appropriation of another element of historic gender difference, women were assigned a moderating role in the application of capital and modernisation, ameliorating the socially and economically disruptive effects of capitalism and modernisation. Again, Bluestocking feminism became a focus for this reconstruction of woman, and produced a broad programme of what can be called the feminisation of culture, society, politics and economy, with major diffusions in the late eighteenth-century movement of Sensibility, in Revolutionary feminism of the 1790s, and in post-Revolutionary, Romantic, Victorian, and modern constructions of domestic woman. Bluestocking feminism, in itself and through its various emanations and parallels, had a major role in the cultural revolution that founded the modern state.

The original Bluestockings themselves shared in a broad political tradition and upheld a particular political, social and economic programme. Their personal and published writings show evidence of influence from Whig and classical republican traditions reaching back to the seventeenth century and continued by the so-called eighteenth-century 'commonwealthmen'.[14] Their particular politics, especially as centred in the circle of the 'queen of the Bluestockings', Elizabeth Montagu, could be described as progressive-aristocratic, in being anti-Pittite, irenic, and anti-Wilkesite, and to some extent in accord with anti-court Toryism of the mid-century.[15] In particular, the Bluestockings were drawn to

Bolingbroke's idea of a 'patriot king' as a form of feminised monarchy.
These political traditions and views help to account for what might oth-
erwise seem paradoxical and contradictory – the Bluestockings' counter-
Revolutionary views and opposition to the Revolutionary feminism of
Wollstonecraft and others in the 1790s.

The particularly feminist element in the Bluestockings' politics and
social critique was directed against that aspect of the court system of
government, laws and hegemony that affected women – women such as
the Bluestockings themselves. Bluestocking feminism participated especially in the mid-century critique of the patriarchal court system's trivi-
alisation and eroticisation of women for the processes of court politics
and culture, as these were diffused through society by social emulation.
Bluestocking feminism was designed to detach women from complicity
in court culture and government. Of necessity, Bluestocking feminism
also mounted a critique of patriarchy as it was implicated in the aristocratic and gentry systems of property, patronage, and paternalism –
interlocked systems that required the subordination and oppression of
women. In an economy and social structure still based on the landed
estate, though increasingly diversified into development of industry,
infrastructure and urbanisation, there was strong pressure to pass property intact from generation to generation, preferably between adult
males. A range of legal and social practices sustained this expectation,
and all required restriction of women to the role of providing heirs
whose right to inherit would be free from legal challenge. Social groups
dependent on or allied to the landed classes tended to imitate these
forms, out of social emulation of their 'betters'. Historically, women of
the upper and middle classes were also assigned roles in sustaining the
domestic economy, presiding over the early formation of the succeeding
generation, and supporting or leading the social and cultural life that
would of necessity flow in and through the domestic sphere and, to some
extent, the civil society beyond.

Bluestocking feminism did not aim to overthrow these systems – the
Bluestockings, who were from gentry or upper (professional) middle-
class families, had a large stake in their classes' material interests, even
though they all experienced the subordination and exploitation of
women that helped sustain those interests. Rather, the Bluestocking feminists aimed to modify existing ideology and practice in several ways that
could be described broadly as forms of feminisation. In politics, for
example, they tended to advocate moderation of conflict and confrontation while preserving established order. The Bluestockings seem to

have adopted a version of Whig paternalism in the senatorial republican tradition, designed to sustain a beneficent hierarchical order that would ensure social stability and harmony. Consequently, they opposed the 'democratisation' of politics exhibited in the 'Wilkes and Liberty' movement of the late 1760s and 1770s and in Revolutionary sympathy in the 1790s. In the economic sphere, the Bluestockings promoted and participated in a feminisation of gentry capitalism in order to facilitate the modernisation of customary economic and social relations.[16] They promoted and participated in a wide variety of social, cultural, and economic philanthropy at the local level.[17] In effect, however, these ameliorative attitudes, especially when taken up by more stoutly middle-class women activists later in the century, contributed to the embourgeoisement of upper-class culture and professionalisation of the gentry.

These values and practices of the Bluestockings were validated for them by their particular religious orientation. This orientation served several political and ideological purposes, including differentiation of the Bluestocking intellectual interests from those of the Enlightenment, which was dominated by men, and maintenance of important social distinctions for the Bluestockings themselves. The Bluestocking programme was later paralleled and appropriated by women from middle-class and lower middle-class communities of religious Dissent, such as Anna Laetitia Barbauld, and Evangelicalism, such as Sarah Trimmer. The first-generation Bluestockings, however, were insistently Anglican in a long tradition going back to the Reformation and re-asserted during the Restoration and early eighteenth century. Their religious orientation was feminist in that it opposed the religious scepticism of both libertine court culture and the modernising Enlightenment, and later opposed Dissenting and Revolutionary anti-clericalism and anti-establishmentarianism, all of which were movements dominated by male thinkers and male interests. More broadly, religion had a historic role in female intellectual culture and social practice, seen in the devotional and other-worldly orientation of the female conduct-book tradition and in the injunction to 'good works', or practical philanthropy, as a manifestation of true faith and as a licence to social and economic activism and reform by women otherwise barred from the public political sphere.

In order to carry out their programme, the founding members of the Bluestocking circle adapted elements of courtly and civil society in a particular form of coterie culture, consisting of salons or social meetings, epistolary networks and certain forms of cultural and economic patronage. The term 'bluestocking' itself apparently derives from this programme, referring to an article of the informal and domestic attire of working-class and lower middle-class men, worn at the Bluestocking receptions or salons as a sign of these meetings' semi-domestic, non-courtly character, in contrast to the black silk stockings worn by men at formal and courtly meetings such as levées.[18] Bluestocking salons further revised the courtly salon by replacing cards and gambling with conversation, and formality with informality of manners, and by an aggressively   companionable,   ostensibly   egalitarian,   and   carefully non-eroticised mixing of the sexes. The vulnerability of Bluestocking salons to association with courtly salons is seen in the satires and innuendoes that suggested a hidden agenda of sexual intrigue, actual or displaced.

The Bluestocking coteries and salons became centres for a variety of activities designed to displace forms of patronage practised through court or courtly networks. The orientation of Bluestocking patronage was mainly to literary, cultural and philanthropic activities, and the Bluestockings were critical of patronage for 'mere' material self-interest. Thus Bluestocking ethics and social practice incorporated new ideas of the importance of the 'domestic affections' and friendship as relations of emotional, moral and intellectual intersubjectivity, rather than patronage–client interdependency. These relationships were furthered, appropriately, by the extended and intricate epistolary networks created and maintained by members of the Bluestocking circles among themselves and with others beyond their circles. Selections of this correspondence were published in the post-Revolutionary and Romantic period in order to advance the construction of professionalised and intellectualised domestic woman for the exigencies of that later age of social, cultural and political crisis. This body of writing was recycled again in the late nineteenth and early twentieth century for similar reasons.[19] In addition, the Bluestockings promoted their programme through miscellaneous publications of their own and through patronising publications by others, especially social inferiors.

The Bluestockings' own publications were few, and several leading Bluestocking women did not publish books at all.[20] Direct participation in public print culture was an important but not central activity in the first-generation Bluestocking programme. Nevertheless, the books published by the first generation of Bluestocking women deploy their feminism in a variety of genres and discourses designed to work within, through and against a gendered and hierarchical literary discursive order. The Bluestocking women usually kept to what were at that time considered acceptable 'feminine' genres and themes; works by Bluestocking women that touched the gendered boundaries of discourse were usually published anonymously; and the Bluestockings' works invoke a conventionally feminine religious validation. Yet these works also advance or imply a comprehensive critique of courtly hegemony as diffused through all levels and aspects of society. Thus Bluestocking writers resorted to an increasingly common ploy of women writers engaging with the public political sphere in the decades to come: extending acceptable feminine discourse into that sphere without overtly challenging the gendered character of the discursive order or the gendered separation of cultural and social spheres.

Inevitably, this was a difficult task, demanding and eliciting from the women writers of the Bluestocking circle a variety of stylistic, formal and thematic experimentations. The experimental character of Bluestocking writing has, however, been obscured by three factors. First, there is the later and more prolific literary production of their female successors in the later eighteenth and early nineteenth century.[21] Second, there is the appropriation of the Bluestockings in the reconstructed domestic ideology of the Revolutionary aftermath, Romanticism, and Victorianism. Finally, there is the more overtly experimental and avant-garde character of much late eighteenth- and early nineteenth-century writing by men, for whom such overtness was necessary to establish the authors' 'masculine' character and authority of 'genius'. A brief survey of the first-generation Bluestocking women's literary production will help illustrate these inevitably broad generalisations.

Elizabeth (Robinson) Montagu (1718–1800)[22] was the leading Bluestocking figure. She was the elder of two daughters of a gentry family with estates in Yorkshire and Kent. Her father seems to have resembled the relatively uneducated and uncultivated men of the local gentry, as distinct from the more cosmopolitan county gentry, though he also seems to have had residual traits of the libertine and freethinking upper class of the Restoration period. Her mother seems to have been intellectually and morally superior to her husband, influenced by the education and feminism of the late seventeenth century. This influence seems to have been passed on to her daughters – and, indeed, to her sons, who were successful in a variety of professions. Elizabeth Robinson was beautiful, vivacious and ambitious and soon gained access to fashionable and aristocratic London society. She won the marriage lottery for women of her class with small dowries by marrying a much older but much richer man who, however, generally treated her with respect. At his death, his widow commanded considerable wealth, and she used it and her considerable energy to create and maintain Bluestocking salons and epistolary networks: as anyone will know who has worked with the Montagu papers at the Huntington Library, or with the published selections from this body of writing, she was a voluminous letter-writer. Her published writing in book form was contrastingly small, but it nevertheless reveals central aspects of Bluestocking feminism.

Her three published and anonymous contributions to her friend George Lyttleton's *Dialogues of the Dead* (1760) present different aspects of Bluestocking social and cultural critique. The first dialogue, between Cadmus and Hercules, presents the opposition of feminised and masculinised cultures, as writing and culture (Cadmus) *versus* 'heroic' combative action. The second dialogue, between Mercury and a 'Modern Fine Lady', opposes cultured domesticity to the courtisation of women. The third dialogue, between Plutarch, Charon and a modern Bookseller, attacks the commercialisation of culture and presents the familiar contrast between 'feminine' reading matter, in the form of novels, and the more intellectual and 'masculine' form of historiography.

Montagu's most important work, however, was her much meditated on and anxiously and anonymously published *An Essay on the Writings and Genius of Shakespear, Compared with the Greek and French Dramatic Poets; With some Remarks upon the Misrepresentations of Mons. de Voltaire* (1769).[23] This work has had a twilight existence in literary history, and recent feminist scholarship has been interested in the work mainly as a rare early book-length work of literary criticism by a woman. Like the Bluestocking programme itself, however, the *Essay* had a long agenda, including the promotion of an emergent 'national' literature, cultural modernisation, and classical republican politics in opposition to court culture and politics. For example, Montagu attacks Voltaire's criticism of Shakespeare and promotion of the playwright Corneille as expressions of court culture that is essentially alien to the English literary, and therefore cultural and political, tradition, supposedly represented by Shakespeare. In this way, Montagu gives the central critical technique of comparison and contrast a nationalist and political orientation. In addition, Montagu's literary criticism contains a covert political discourse that promotes classical republicanism and the idea of a patriot king, disparages the mob and advances both anti-Pittite and anti-Wilkesite values – all with implicit topical reference to the political situation in England in the late 1760s, when the book was written and published.

Montagu's sister, Sarah (Robinson) Scott (1720–1795),[24] was never directly involved in the Bluestocking salons and participated in the Bluestocking epistolary networks through her sister. Like her sister, she seems to have had a strong interest in intellectual pursuits, also inherited from her mother, and a commitment to a religiously based but practical philanthropy. She also had an avid and life-long interest in the politics of the day, and a religious piety stronger than her sister's. Afflicted with disfiguring smallpox when approaching marriageable age, and less out-going than her sister, she did not do nearly as well as Elizabeth Robinson in the marriage lottery, marrying late, to a man of uncertain financial prospects; the marriage was sexually unconsummated and brief. Thereafter, Sarah Scott lived with her close friend, Lady Barbara Montagu, until the latter's death, and associated with a small group of modestly philanthropic ladies. These experiences inform her published writings, which she used to raise money for her charitable projects.

For Scott was a more prolific author than her sister, and indeed the most prolific author of the first-generation Bluestockings and their asso-ciates. Aware that women of her class were supposed to avoid publicity, she always published anonymously; nevertheless, she promoted Bluestocking feminism through a number of works of fiction and history. She produced a fictionalised manifesto of the Bluestocking programme in her feminist utopian novel *A Description of Millenium Hall* (1762) and its sequel, *The History of Sir George Ellison* (1766). Together these works rep-resent the creation, from the failure of courtly culture and politics, of a feminised gentry capitalism, spreading from estate to estate and thus modernising and revolutionising England and its empire. Like many women writers, Scott turned her back on the Richardsonian revolution in prose fiction, apparently finding that it embodied a transmuted and disguised form of courtly gallantry. Instead, she experimented with various forms of the early eighteenth-century moralising romance and novel of manners, producing a series of novels each different from the other.[25] In her historiographies Scott promoted the idea of a patriot king as feminised, virtuous monarch and at the same time made oblique comment on the politics of the 1760s.[26]

Elizabeth Carter (1717–1806), close friend of Montagu and of several other Bluestocking writers, came from the professional middle class, like several of the non-publishing Bluestocking figures but unlike the Robinson sisters. Her father was a clergyman in Deal, Kent, and she devoted her life to keeping house for him and serving her family. Nevertheless, she received a classical education, came into contact with Elizabeth Montagu and her upper-class and upper middle-class social world, and was a prominent participant in the Bluestockings' epistolary networks. She was also the most prominently literary and intellectual – indeed, learned – member of the first generation of Bluestocking women.

Carter contributed two letters to Samuel Johnson's *Rambler* (nos. 44 and 100), and she published two collections of poetry, *Poems upon Particular Occasions* (1738) and *Poems on Several Occasions* (1762). As the collections' titles indicate, these were modest in pretensions, being mostly occasional poems, or poems written for specific purposes. This was characteristic of such collections by women of this time. Carter's collections include odes, verse epistles to various female friends, poems marking particular personal moments such as a birthday, meditations on the transitoriness of life, and a few translations from Metastasio (a poet who seems to have been particularly favoured by women readers and writers). The poems are pious, moralistic and mildly feminist, or feminist in a pious vein; an underlying theme is rejection of fashionable and courtly society and preference for quiet and retired life, with a strong emphasis on the domestic affections, and female friendship. By mid-century such collections seem to have acquired a degree of popularity, for *Poems* (1762) went through several editions.

The theme of piety in common life is taken up in a very different kind of discourse in Carter's anonymously published *Remarks on the Athanasian Creed* (1752). It is a rare excursion by a woman into the field of controversial theology, which was decidedly gendered masculine in the eighteenth-century literary discursive order. In what would have been considered at the time as a brisk, rational, and polemical style, Carter enters a local yet long-standing controversy between what may be seen as 'hard-line' and moderate parties in the Anglican church. She denounces the Athanasian creed on the nature of the holy trinity as a theological doctrine that relies upon acceptance of an illogical mystery. She calls instead for a doctrine comprehensible by all. Implicitly, 'all' should include those, such as women and the lower classes, denied advanced education and training in highly professionalised discourses. Carter's intervention is, like the Bluestockings' rejection of libertine and Enlightenment scepticism and anti-clericalism, an attack on a masculinised discourse. Like many advocates of a 'broad' or inclusive national Church, and like many liberal Dissenters, especially later women writers such as Anna Laetitia Barbauld and Mary Wollstonecraft, Carter insists that both reason and 'the heart' are necessary to true faith. Wollstonecraft would turn this assumption into an argument for the professionalised education and ethical emancipation of women. Carter also attacks the view that dogma should be complied with for practical or worldly reasons; the implication here is that such compliance is analogous to that on which despotic court regimes depend.

In her openly acknowledged translation of and commentary on Epictetus (1758),[27] Carter is supposed to have given a rare demonstration that a woman could command classical languages and culture. This in itself was a major contribution to the Bluestockings' attempt to construct a model of woman as intellectual. As usual, however, there is more than an intellectual rarity here. Carter appropriates to the Bluestocking project a major source-text of classical republicanism and the commonwealthman tradition. The stoical tradition represented by Epictetus and others had long been used in constructing an alternative, anti-court patrician culture and politics. At the same time, Carter's extended critique of Epictetus and stoicism in her editorial apparatus, with its frequent references to Biblical authority, attempts to disable the use of Epictetus and stoicism in a masculine aristocratic and heroic tradition and to appropriate them for a feminised, Anglican and even professional middle-class culture.

Carter's close associate, Catherine Talbot (1721–1770), contributed to the Bluestocking project from yet another direction. Talbot was the daughter of a clergyman who died before her birth, and she and her mother lived as permanent guests of Thomas Secker, eventually archbishop of Canterbury and thus ecclesiastical head of the state church. Secker's influence on Talbot was comprehensive and profound, but perhaps surpassed by that of her friend and correspondent, Elizabeth Carter. Talbot published little in her lifetime, probably mindful of social prejudice against women making themselves public. After her death, however, Carter paid for the publication of Talbot's *Reflections on the Seven Days of the Week* (1770), which went through many editions by the early nineteenth century. The work complements Carter's tract on the Athanasian creed by aiming to provide a manual for religion in everyday and common life, and thus would have been seen as an acceptable 'feminine' discourse. In effect, however, it calls for the domestication and thus the feminisation, in terms of contemporary gender difference, of the state religion. Talbot's work, like Carter's, implies that this religion is too often masculinised and professionalised as the discourse of an exclusively male clerical and academic elite. Thus Talbot, like the other Bluestockings, is critical of professionalised discourse and practice for its predominantly masculine character.

Talbot's *Essays on Various Subjects* (1772), also published by Carter, goes further, though it, too, purports to participate in a domain of discourse open to women, that of the *belles-lettres*. The book contains essays, dialogues, 'Occasional Thoughts' (maxims), prose pastorals, a 'Fairy Tale', an imitation of Ossian, allegories, and poetry. The work has, then, the miscellaneous character often adopted by women writers. They did so in order to avoid transgressing boundaries of discourse by publishing a formal treatise of the kind generally considered beyond the intellectual reach of women. Taken all together, however, this miscellany clearly calls for the extension to women of professionalised subjectivity, or moral discipline and intellectual training – forms of moral and intellectual capital with the transcendental legitimation of true, that is Anglican, faith. Whereas men required such capital for professional and public life, and had outlets for such capital there, women of course did not. Talbot, like the other Bluestockings and like the Revolutionary feminists of the 1790s, implies that such capital is still necessary to women if they are to be protected from socialisation to emulation and desire – if, that is, they are to be protected against the processes of courtisation that were the usual kinds of socialisation and acculturation for women of the classes represented by the Bluestockings and their readers.

Another effort of a similar kind by Hester (Mulso) Chapone (1727–1801) became the most frequently reprinted of all books by first-generation Bluestockings. Hester Mulso was a member of the circle of female advisors to the novelist Samuel Richardson, influencing his composition of *Clarissa*. Her husband died nine months after their marriage and, like several other Bluestocking writers, Hester Chapone was left to manage her own life. Like Talbot, Chapone published a number of short pieces of *belles-lettres*, but her most widely read work – and one of the most widely read of its kind – was *Letters on the Improvement of the Mind* (1773). It takes on a genre that had long been used to prescribe subordination for women, that of the female conduct book. Chapone attempts to swing this didactic tradition in the direction of Bluestocking feminism by modifying central points of the tradition. Like the other Bluestocking writers and the conduct writers, male and female, she accepts that women's life is destined, by social practice and prejudice, if not by nature and divine will, to be subordinated to men's. Like the other Bluestocking writers, however, she calls for an intellectualisation and professionalisation of female subjectivity, for the embourgeoisement of upper-class social practice, and a technology of the self with major ethical consequences, through local social amelioration and reform, in and from the domestic sphere.

Chapone supplemented this argument in two further works – *Miscellanies in Prose and Verse* (1775), which is dedicated to Elizabeth Carter and sets forth key points in Bluestocking feminism, and *A Letter to a New-Married Lady* (1777), which is another book in the conduct or advice book tradition.

These are the central texts of first-generation Bluestocking feminism, published during the authors' lifetimes. The field would be extended and complicated by looking at the epistolary dimension of Bluestocking feminism, with letters selected and published after the correspondents' deaths, and the Bluestockings' wide range of activism in literature, culture and philanthropy. The field can be extended again by considering diffusions of and parallels to first-generation Bluestocking work in writers distantly or tangentially associated with the Bluestocking circle, such as Anna Seward, Clara Reeve and Catharine Macaulay Graham; and in second-generation figures associated with the first generation or taking up various aspects of their programme, such as Hannah More, Frances Burney, Anna Laetitia Barbauld, Hester Thrale Piozzi, Mary Wollstonecraft, and Ellis Cornelia Knight.

The dimensions of Bluestocking feminism were extended and altered again in the late eighteenth and early nineteenth century. During the Revolution crisis and debate of the 1790s, the first-generation Bluestockings were vehemently anti-Revolutionary, and counter-feminist in relation to the feminism of Wollstonecraft and others, for reasons I have briefly referred to above. In the Revolutionary aftermath Bluestocking feminism had a further complex potential. On the one hand the Bluestockings were appropriated and institutionalised in a reprogrammed domestic ideology. This ideology tried both to accommodate the counter-Revolutionary rejection of women who were active in the public sphere and to sustain the claim for the professionalisation of women as subjects and as social agents working in and from the domestic and local sphere. This is the significance of the publication, from the 1800s to 1820s, of selected Bluestocking correspondence, including Carter's to Vesey and Talbot (1809) and to Montagu (1817), Montagu's (1810, 1813), Mary Delany's (1820), and Chapone's posthumous works, mainly letters (1807). Yet, as Sylvia Harcstark Myers shows, the Revolutionary aftermath also saw the development of a relentless pejoration of the Bluestockings in the remasculinisation of culture that characterised the Romantic movement.

Further diffusions and appropriations of Bluestocking feminism would be uncovered in Victorian 'women's mission' feminism and suffragism, in nineteenth-century American feminism, in the late

nineteenth-century movement for women's participation in higher education and the professions, in the early twentieth-century Bloomsbury
circle, and of course in the complex, university-based feminist movement of which this essay is a part. Meanwhile, the writings published by
the Bluestocking women during their own time were largely forgotten.
Just as these works were no longer being republished, the Bluestockings
were coming to be known and continued to be known, mainly through
their correspondence which was published in the Revolutionary aftermath to construct a certain figure of intellectualised or professionalised
domestic woman. This figure was designed and continued to be used to
accomplish several kinds of ideological and cultural work in the post-
Revolutionary age. Initially it was a counter to claims made by
Revolutionary feminists. More important in the long term, it was a way
of subordinating women within the cultural revolution that would lead
to the founding of the modern liberal state. This state was based on an
ideology of the sovereign subject to which the Bluestockings' books had
contributed; in fact and in effect, however, the liberal state was based on
adult male suffrage, until the women's suffrage movement, Bloomsbury,
and other diffusions recycled elements of Bluestocking feminism within
modernism and early twentieth-century modernity.

Certainly the original Bluestocking project, like its contemporary and
later diffusions and appropriations, was a feminist one in its time, socially
and historically situated and specific. It was a feminism aimed at alter-
ing the character of the public sphere that was in the process of being
constructed during the Bluestockings' own time. Reproducing the
Bluestockings as they are represented in the published correspondence
of the post-Revolutionary moment, used to constitute and continue a
masculinist liberalism, disguises the nature and extent of this feminism,
however. Recovery of that feminism can help to illuminate not only the
specific historical relations of women writers to particular historical
public spheres, but also the nature, purposes and limits of the idea of the
public sphere as a founding element in the modern liberal state.

NOTES

1 Accounts of the Bluestocking circle may be found in biographies of main
   members of the circle, published collections of their correspondence and
   general studies such as Walter S. Scott, *The Bluestocking Ladies* (London: John
   Green, 1947), and the fullest recent account, Sylvia Harcstark Myers, *The
   Bluestocking Circle: Women, Friendship, and the Life of the Mind in Eighteenth-Century
   England* (Oxford: Clarendon Press, 1990).

2 See Geoffrey Holmes, *Augustan England: Professions, State and Society 1680–1730* (London and Boston: George Allen & Unwin, 1983).

3 See Jürgen Habermas, *The Structural Transformation of the Public Sphere: An Inquiry into a Category of Bourgeois Society*, trans. Thomas Burger (Cambridge, Mass.: MIT Press, 1989).

4 See for example Elaine Hobby, *Virtue of Necessity: English Women's Writing, 1646–1688* (London: Virago Press, 1988); Ruth Perry, *The Celebrated Mary Astell: An Early English Feminist* (Chicago: University of Chicago Press, 1986).

5 See Philip Corrigan and Derek Sayer, *The Great Arch: English State Formation and Cultural Revolution* (Oxford and New York: Basil Blackwell, 1985), and David Lloyd and Paul Thomas, *Culture and the State* (New York and London: Routledge, 1998).

6 Neil McKendrick, John Brewer and J. H. Plumb, *The Birth of a Consumer Society: The Commercialization of Eighteenth-Century England* (London: Europa, 1982).

7 See Jean L. Cohen and Andrew Arato, *Civil Society and Political Theory* (Cambridge, Mass.: MIT Press, 1992).

8 David Hume, *Essays Moral, Political and Literary* (London: Oxford University Press, 1963), p. 278.

9 Hume, *Essays*, pp. 127–8.

10 Ibid., p. 568.

11 Ibid., p. 134.

12 Ibid., pp. 570–1.

13 See Jane Rendall, *The Origins of Modern Feminism: Women in Britain, France and the United States 1780–1860* (Basingstoke and London: Macmillan, 1985), chapter 1.

14 See Caroline Robbins, *The Eighteenth-Century Commonwealthman: Studies in the Transmission, Development and Circumstance of English Liberal Thought from the Restoration of Charles II until the War with the Thirteen Colonies* (Cambridge, Mass.: Harvard University Press, 1959).

15 In this summary of Bluestockings' views, I am drawing to some extent on the published writings of the original Bluestocking women but more on my reading of the Bluestockings' letters, especially in the Montagu manuscripts in the Huntington Library, San Marino, California. I am grateful to the Huntington Library and to the Social Sciences and Humanities Research Council of Canada for fellowships that enabled me to work with these manuscripts.

16 See Gary Kelly, 'Introduction', in Sarah Scott, *A Description of Millenium Hall* (Peterborough, Ont.: Broadview Press, 1995).

17 Edith Sedgwick Larson, 'A Measure of Power: The Personal Charity of Elizabeth Montagu', *Studies in Eighteenth-Century Culture*, 16 (1986), 197–210; see also Betty Rizzo, 'Introduction', in Sarah Scott, *The History of Sir George Ellison* (Lexington: University Press of Kentucky, 1996), pp. xviii, xxvi-xxviii.

18 Myers, *The Bluestocking Circle*, pp. 6–7.

19 For example, *Elizabeth Montagu, the Queen of the Bluestockings: Her Correspondence from 1720 to 1761*, ed. Emily J. Climenson, 2 vols. (London: John Murray, 1906); *Mrs. Montagu, "Queen of the Blues": Her Letters and Friendships from 1762 to 1800*, ed. Reginald Blunt, 2 vols. (London: Constable, 1923).

20 For a selection of these texts, with others by associates of the Bluestocking circle, see *Bluestocking Feminism: Writings of the Bluestocking Circle*, general editor Gary Kelly, 6 vols. (London: Pickering and Chatto, 1999).

21 See Bridget G. MacCarthy, *The Female Pen* (Cork: Cork University Press, 1946–7).

22 Betty Rizzo has determined that 1720, the birthdate formerly given for Elizabeth Montagu, is incorrect; see Rizzo, 'Introduction', p. xxxvii n. 1.

23 See Elizabeth Eger, 'Introduction', in Eger, ed., *Elizabeth Montagu*, vol. 1 of *Bluestocking Feminism: Writings of the Bluestocking Circle*, general editor Gary Kelly, 6 vols. (London: Pickering and Chatto, 1999), pp. lxv–lxxvii.

24 Betty Rizzo has determined that 1723, the birthdate formerly given for Sarah Scott, is incorrect; see note 22.

25 Besides *Millenium Hall* and *Sir George Ellison*, these include *The History of Cornelia*, 1750; *Agreeable Ugliness; or, The Triumph of the Graces; Exemplified in the Real Life and Fortunes of a Young Lady of Some Distinction, from the French*, 1752; *A Journey through Every Stage of Life, Described in a Variety of Interesting Scenes, Drawn from Real Characters*, 1754; and *The Test of Filial Duty; in a Series of Letters between Miss Emilia Leonard and Miss Charlotte Arlington*, 1772.

26 *The History of Gustavus Ericson, King of Sweden; with an Introductory History of Sweden, from the Middle of the Twelfth Century*, 1761; *The History of Mecklenburgh, from the First Settlement of the Vandals in that Country, to the Present Time; including a Period of about Three Thousand Years*, 1762; and *The History of Theodore Agrippa d'Aubigné, containing a Succinct Account of the Most Remarkable Occurrences during the Civil Wars of France in the Reigns of Charles IX., Henry III., Henry IV., and the Minority of Lewis XIII*, 1772.

27 Elizabeth Carter, *The Works of Epictetus, consisting of his Discourses, in Four Books, Preserved by Arrian, The Enchiridion, and Fragments. Translated from the Original Greek by the Late Mrs Elizabeth Carter . . . The Fourth Edition with the Translator's Late Additions and Alterations*, ed. Montagu Pennington, 2 vols. (London: F. C. and J. Rivington, 1807).

CHAPTER SEVEN

Catharine Macaulay: history, republicanism and the public sphere

Susan Wiseman

I

On 20 December 1790 Horace Walpole wrote to Mary Berry of Edmund Burke's *Reflections on the Revolution in France*, 'it has given a mortal stab to sedition, I believe and hope'. Burke's 'foes show how deeply they are wounded by their abusive pamphlets. Their Amazonian allies headed by Kate Macaulay and the virago Barbauld, whom Mr Burke calls our *poissardes*, spit their rage at eighteenpence a head, and will return to Fleet Ditch, more fortunate in being forgotten than their predecessors in the *Dunciad*.'[1] Catharine Macaulay did not slide back into the Fleet Ditch whence Walpole imagined she had crawled. She was, though, for a long time better remembered for her *Letters on Education* than her massive and pathbreaking history of seventeenth-century England. In analysing Macaulay's treatment of seventeenth-century politics this essay suggests some reasons why this hierarchisation might have taken place. It was, I shall argue, Macaulay's place in the politics of English republican historiography and debates on women's relationship to the political sphere, which gave her *History of England* a very particular place in republican patterns of thought.

In 1763, the year of the Peace after the Seven Years War, Macaulay's first volume was published, to acclaim. She was to complete the *History* in 1783 living in obscurity with her second husband, James Graham.[2] Throughout, she was a republican on the model of James Harrington, favouring the rotation of office in a 'democratical system rightly balanced'.[3] Macaulay's narrative closes with the so-called Glorious Revolution, the very moment at which Jürgen Habermas argues that the public sphere emerges in England, facilitated by the development of the coffee-house, periodical and the society. Macaulay's career, however, invites us to complicate Habermas's sense of the public sphere as demarcated by critical reason used by 'private people' whose participation was

guaranteed by propertied citizenship: her participation indicates the very
dynamic relationship between private and public. Similarly, Macaulay's
understanding of republicanism complicates the current picture of civic
humanism. For Macaulay's republicanism is only partially aligned with
the civic humanism delineated by J. G. A. Pocock. Although it is true for
her that the maintenance of civic virtue involved seeing the present
'world of government, commerce, and war as corruption – corruption
essentially the same as that which transformed Rome from republic into
empire', her empathy with earlier histories and forms means that the
other part of the equation of civic humanism, the question of the propertied individual's relationship with commerce, was not the main focus of
her interpretation of English history.[4] In her *History* Harrington's writing
is not understood as offering, exactly, 'a civic morality for market man'
and, for Macaulay, Harrington and Machiavelli do not so much furnish
the categories in which virtue can be discussed as the blueprint for a state
through which virtue could be made possible.[5]

Writing at a moment where Whigs came in many shades and alliances,
Macaulay's position derived clarity and strength from her understanding
of republicanism in the 'true' sense of the term. She was also an historian deeply in sympathy with the struggles of those people and moments
she writes about, seeking to find in them material for the present, though
always conscious of the failure of what she saw as the best enterprises of
English republicanism. However, the world into which Macaulay's
History gradually emerged was about to be transformed; her republican
methods were over-ruled within decades of the final publication of her
History. And if the public sphere into which Macaulay's *History* entered
was soon to see 'the yielding of a world of cities to a world of nations', it
was also one in which the meaning of gender and its relationship to the
writing of history were about to change.[6] This essay, therefore, asks two
interconnected questions. How did Macaulay write the history of the
period 1603–89; what political genres were visible and available to her,
how did she understand her method, shape her history? How can we
trace the changing relationship between women and the public sphere in
the second half of the eighteenth century?

II

'[I]n my opinion, religious and moral turpitude, in a great measure, flow
from political error.' So Macaulay wrote in 1781, when she completed
the Restoration volume of her *History*. Macaulay hoped that her *History*

would reshape the understanding of the English past, and therefore the contours of the contemporary public sphere to usher in the rule of patriotic virtue: 'I vainly hoped that the conviction of uncontrovertible argument, founded on fact, would, in a series of time, extinguish the baneful influence of party spirit; would gradually and almost imperceptibly incline the people to consider the objects of their proper interest.'[7] As her *History*'s concentration on the Civil War years indicates, practical and theoretical republicanism were for Macaulay bound together, and comparison with other histories illuminates Macaulay's methodological interventions.

The intense contemporary importance of regicide, republic and Restoration was signalled by the dominance of historical genres seeming to offer forensic or eyewitness information. Pamphlet collections (like those of George Thomason and John Rushworth), political theory, memoir and secret history transmitted and resurrected political ideals.[8] Some memoirs overlapped with semi-official histories (as in the case of Clarendon) or with scandal and 'secret', counter-histories. Others were suppressed but known (like Lucy Hutchinson's manuscript of the life of her husband, the regicide and republican Colonel John Hutchinson) or printed for political contingency. For generations after the wars political commitment was the key force in history writing; *Eikon Basilike* continued to circulate 'Jacobite . . panegyric'; memoirs and histories, equally partisan, copied from each other to elaborate a political history and, implicitly, theory.[9]

Moreover, history-as-political-opinion was passed on lineally as belief and memory from father to son. At his own request, the Earl of Clarendon's *History of the Rebellion* was not published until after his death, when his son published it with the comment that 'within fifty years since the murder committed on that pious prince [Charles I] [it is] by some men made a mystery to judge on whose side was the right and on which the Rebellion is to be charged'.[10] Gilbert Burnet's *History of my own Times*, like Clarendon's published by a son, opposed Clarendon. It was in turn counterpointed by Laurence Echard's *History of England* which followed up Clarendon in producing a Tory history and legacy of the war. Edmund Calamay responded by justifying the Puritans unjustly attacked by Echard.[11] Although Macaulay's contemporary and rival David Hume claimed impartiality, he too was enlisted for the Tory cause.

As one response to John Oldmixon's *Critical History* makes clear, republican history, when Macaulay came to it, could be caricatured as a lineage of tracts:

Knox begat Buchanan, Buchanan begat Milton, Milton begat Rushworth, Rushworth begat Ludlow, Ludlow begat S-dney, S-dney begat Burnet, Burnet begat B-nnet, B-nnet begat OldM-x-n, OldM-x-n, without Bastardy or Interruption, begat our Critical Historian.[12]

Grey's satire recognises a crucial force in the nature of republican history and historiography as it was understood from within the republican tradition, where printed and manuscript evidence was subordinated to political vision. Sources were often simply copied and accusations of falsification were common, testifying to the politicised valency of memoir; Oldmixon, for example, accused Clarendon's Tory editors of forging large sections of the Earl's *History*.[13]

Macaulay regarded such histories as 'interested' in a way that a republican vision of history, formulated ostensibly outside Whig and Tory lineages, was not. In Macaulay's view the repeated 'general' histories dealing with the previous centuries, crucially the Stuarts, Civil War and Republic, were too infected by 'party' to fulfil their duty to truth; implicitly, too, the continued dominion of interest had failed the calling of history writing. Not only had Britain failed to produce a republic, more miserably England 'was obliged to a foreigner for the best and most faithful narrative of the civil and military atchievements of her gallant sons'.[14] Not that Paul Rapin was even a good historian, he was long popular 'more from the circumstance of having no competitor than from the intrinsic merit of his work'. Although others are numbered 'among the few faithful historians' they are 'too careless writers'.[15] It remained for Catharine Macaulay herself to forge, methodologically and politically, a new history.

The unbroken link Macaulay understood to exist between the painstaking research required by truthful history and her explicit republican commitment determined the account she gave of the seventeenth-century struggles. If her history, too, was part of the political debates of its moment it was different because of the *way* in which it conjoined republicanism and patriotism through sustained and methodologically reinforced interpretation. Macaulay's *History* wore its republican politics on its sleeve rather than in the surname of its author. Furthermore, Macaulay's overt concern with republic as a social and political good both characterised her theory of history and facilitated a clear connection in her writing between examples of virtue and true republicanism. Like her rival David Hume, Macaulay saw herself as studying virtue.[16] But she was insistent about the political system most likely to generate such virtue and the tendency of 'political error' to produce vice.[17]

The most recent test of republican virtue, for Macaulay, was the English Civil War and the hardships suffered by republican patriots after 1660. As she put it in her preface to the volume on the Restoration:

As republican principles and notions have always been too unpopular in this country to found on them any rational scheme of interest or ambition, it was obvious to me, that, however erroneous might be the opinions of the few republicans whom opportunity enabled to take an active part in the affairs of England, their conduct was founded on principle, because diametrically opposed to their interest, and even their safety; accordingly the fate of every one of this party, who did not change with changing times, was banishment, an ignominious death, or the entire ruin of their fortunes: whilst, on the contrary, the men whose conduct was governed either by Whig or Tory principles, were, as the different factions prevailed, in their turn triumphant.[18]

Finished in 1781 when her popularity had waned, the sixth volume also marks a watershed in the affairs Macaulay is recounting. It is with 1660, rather than with 1689, that the legacy with which she is dealing begins. For 1660 saw the defeat of republicanism and the beginning of what was, for her, the start of the writing of winner's history, a history which cruelly distorted the activities of the 'patriots' and, as in 'Mr Hume's very artful narration of facts', valorised Charles I as a martyr.

The importance she gives to the Restoration (as opposed to 1688) and its influence on subsequent events is indicated by the preface to the volume. Produced after a ten-year gap during which she had been heavily criticised, Macaulay justifies her principles and attempts to keep a history of republicanism alive after the complex modifications of Whig alliances in the 1760s and 1770s:[19]

As the Jacobites have carried their panegyric of the first Charles to a height which induced the utter condemnation of all those who opposed this monarch on public grounds, it was impossible to do justice to the patriotic characters which figured in this age, without examining into the conduct and administration of this prince with a degree of rigorous justice and vigilant enquiry which his unhappy fate would otherwise have rendered ungenerous and inhuman: but in this inquiry I was so far from feeling myself the bloody-minded Republican, as I have been termed by the butcherly writers of these days, and so far from possessing the stoicism of the first Brutus, that I shed many tears whilst I was writing his catastrophe, and I have endeavoured to do justice to that part of his conduct which I thought truly great and worthy the imitation of posterity.[20]

The Roman comparison, one of the highest accolades Macaulay allows the characters of her *History*, is especially significant as applied to herself. Were she to be the first Brutus, would Charles I then become the weeping, martyred Lucretia over whose body the republic is established? Or does she also refer to Brutus's consent to the death of his own sons in order that the republic might be founded? Either way, Brutus's conduct is contrasted here not with feminine sentiment but with a more fully engaged, humane, yet still republican response to catastrophe. Anticipating continued conceptual confusion between true republicanism and barabaric cruelty, she concludes that, 'If I have been severe on misguided princes and bad ministers, it is with a view only to the interests of the people.'[21]

As she implies, the wide-ranging resources from which her history is made enables her to see the 'interests of the people'. She uses pamphlets, petitions, including the women's petitions, the Leveller *Agreement of the People*, George Thomason's and John Rushworth's collections.[22] Volumes of Parliamentary History rub shoulders with memoirs such as Clarendon's *History* and those by Whitelock and Ludlow, as well as Harris's *Life of Cromwell* and contemporary historians Hume, Rapin and the critical or scandalous Oldmixon.[23] In March 1765 Thomas Hollis gave her 145 volumes, including many Civil War tracts, and she had at least 6,000 of her own.[24] Macaulay used her sources to offer a pragmatically wide definition of republicanism and the part it played in the Civil War. She includes 'all the different denominations of Republicans', 'Anabaptists, Fifth-monarchy men, and Levellers' as well as classical republicans.[25] Macaulay's emphasis on the detailed use of sources was a methodological advance, but it was also the crucial connection between truth and republican patriotism.

One of Macaulay's chief analytical tools in her *History* is her engagement with the ancient republics as a comparative model for the present and as a prompt to the kind of writing likely to provoke liberty. Although, like Algernon Sidney and others before her she laments the failure of liberty, in that 'the majority of the English nation never engaged in the cause of freedom', the ancient republics remain the model against which English history is to be tested.[26] Macaulay is explicit about the classical model. The opening of the first volume naturalises the use of republican modelling:

From my earliest youth I have read with delight those histories that exhibit Liberty in its most exalted state, the annals of the Roman and the Greek republics. Studies like these excite that natural love of freedom which lies latent in the breath of every rational being, till it is nipped by the frost of prejudice, or blasted by the influence of vice.[27]

Rather than claiming English precursors, the *History* is positioned in relation to classical writing on the ancient republics, and the passage clarifies the role of her *History* as part of a scrupulously documented republican project. Reading on Greece and Rome built her political subjectivity, producing the 'effect which almost constantly attends such reading'; 'Liberty became the object of a secondary worship in my delighted imagination.' Such an education forms a truthful, analytical mind; 'a mind thus disposed can never see through the medium held up by party writers'. The trained and virtuous reader can distinguish between 'the petty virtues of wicked men', 'time-serving placemen' and 'exalted patriots'.[28]

The nature of history and its relation to republicanism was, albeit pessimistically, her theme at the close of her final volume – seeing 1688 as hijacked by power-hungry Court Whigs.[29] Her own role as the model historian, although suggested more tentatively than in the confident opening volume, is proposed:

I appeal to the ingenuous and uncorrupted part of my countrymen, which class of historians have been the real friends of the constitution; those who, by humouring the prejudices of all factions, have left the judgement of the reader in such an embarrassed state as to be incapable of forming any just opinion of men, of measures, or of the true interest of their country; or those writers who, like myself, in an honest contempt of the ill-founded rage and resentment of all denominations of men and interests, have, through the whole course of my narrative, closely adhered to the purest principles of civil and religious freedom.[30]

This account from the 1780s, when she was no longer applauded by the Whigs, presents Macaulay's republicanism as if value-free, unquestionably part of producing a history written within the frame of 'the purest principles of civil and religious freedom'. As Paul Langford points out, though, it also kept in play a continuity of causality and argumentation from the seventeenth century to the present.[31]

For Macaulay, as for other republicans, the theoretical bent of republican history enabled the transportation of visions of republicanism through time: history yielded up the truth of the past but also the blueprint for the future.[32] The *History* engages in a conscious attempt to shape the public sphere through its readers, an attempt reinforced by the distinctions between her *History* and others. Although it is a history motivated by 'belief', while working to politicised ends, Macaulay's history moved the grounds on which the 'true' meaning of the Republic could be decided, from memory (asserted in the reproduction of memoir) to the assessment of virtue and the method of interpretation.[33] Through this new kind of production of history for politics, Macaulay's *History*, while itself (of course) standing in the line of interested histories, reshapes the material of the canon of histories of the seventeenth century by recasting and using the memoirists if not as eyewitnesses, exactly, then as genealogical rather than truthful historians.

In her reshaping we can trace, briefly, the emergence of a community of historians linked horizontally through agreements and disagreements about the nature of the Civil War, history, politics – Hume and Burke were her rivals, and her political community included Richard Price, James Burgh and, most importantly, her adviser Thomas Hollis. However, her careful distinguishing of republican historiography and history from what she represents as Whig typology (for her, as for Civil War republicans, Cromwell was 'the usurper') left her, ultimately, not only documenting a lost history of republicanism, but isolated within the political context and public sphere she and her book inhabited.[34]

III

How did the question of gender impinge on this republican project? I want to examine this firstly through Macaulay's representation of women in relation to republicanism, and secondly through her reception and representation as a female republican, using the instance of her being sculpted as Clio. Macaulay's detailed and tendentious reinterpretation of the English Civil War put her at the centre of debates about the nature of history, but her sex combined with her republicanism to put her in an oblique relationship to the social reproduction of history.[35] Macaulay's position as a woman was of endless interest to those who read her.

The treatment of women within her *History* and the treatment of her gender in its reception offer contrasting illuminations of the sexual, as well as political, place of a woman's republican *History*. That she is tracing republicanism and high politics means that Macaulay focuses on political roles. The part women play in her history is not, in general, that of affective or sentimental objects for the reader's attention; rather, they feature as both villains and patriots within the terms of the *History*. Elizabeth I is no heroine; under her, as under the other Tudors 'the knowledge of Roman and Greek policy' – republicanism transmitted, as Hobbes noted, through the grammar school curriculum and translations of the ancient historians – 'had made no inconsiderable progress', but lacked practical results. Leading up to discussion of the tyranny of Archbishop Laud she points to 'the danger which was to be expected from the king's matrimonial connection'.[36] Queens, Catholic or Protestant, do not fare well.

However, where Macaulay finds women in the republican tradition their roles – in political action and in supporting their husbands – are recognised. Macaulay took an interest, to take two instances, in both Lucy Hutchinson and Rachel Russell. That Macaulay knew Hutchinson's manuscript life of her husband is clear. Julius Hutchinson indicates that the manuscript, when in the possession of 'the late Thomas Hutchinson', 'had been seen by many persons, as well as the editor' and 'he had been frequently solicited to permit them to be published, particularly by the late Mrs Catharine Macaulay, but had uniformly refused'.[37] While to her family Lucy Hutchinson's republican sentiments were an embarrassing legacy, to Macaulay they would have been a useful and sincere record of patriotism.

Rachel Russell appears in the *History* as she had appeared to contemporaries, as the widow of William Russell who had been executed for his part in the Rye House plot. William Russell, whether or not he took part in a plot to assassinate Charles II, or at least his guards, is for Macaulay a republican patriot. Using contemporary sources she traces his insistence on the doctrine of resistance to tyrants, even at the point of execution:

A notion had prevailed among friends of this nobleman, that a pardon might be procured, provided he would acknowledge the doctrine of non-resistance in its fullest extent; and Dr Tillotson and Dr Burnet endeavoured, though in vain, to reason the prisoner into such a confession. 'I can have no conception, says he, of a limited monarchy, which has not a right to defend its own limitations; and my conscience will not permit me to say otherwise to the king.'[38]

It is clear from Rachel Russell's later letters, seen by Macaulay in the edition of 1773, that she wholly shared her husband's view on the centrality of the doctrine of resistance. In 1689 Rachel Russell wrote to John Tillotson, Dean of St Paul's, 'The time seems to be come that you must put anew in practice that submission, you have so powerfully both try'd yourself, and instructed others to'.[39] Clearly, Russell is referring critically here to Tillotson's published encouragement of her husband to retract his statement on resistance.

That Rachel Russell shaped her husband's reputation in correspondence and work in the political sphere after his death is now increasingly recognised by historians; and it is evident from her correspondence with Charles II and Gilbert Burnet immediately after his death. The 1773 *Letters*, like the later publication of Lucy Hutchinson's life of her husband, played a crucial role in making William Russell a patriot hero and in keeping alive a debate over the right of the citizens to reject the rule of a tyrant.

For Macaulay, as for her contemporaries, Rachel Russell's subsequent life was characterised by mourning 'in retirement and continual weeping for her departed lord'.[40] However, Rachel Russell is also 'heroic' and her work for the cause of republicanism in the letters of her widowhood is acknowledged:

> A series of letters to Doctor Fitzwilliam, a clergyman, are very affecting descriptions of the contest between a passionate grief and the principle of pious resignation; and the uninterrupted sorrows of a long life, prove that it was the sense of religion, the duties of a mother, and the promise which she had made Lord Russell in the hour of parting, that she would preserve her life for the sake of his children, which alone prevented her from following the example of the Roman Arria, in that act of conjugal heroism for which this illustrious woman is so justly celebrated.[41]

Macaulay uses Russell as an instance of virtue. Apparently, moral fortitude rather than political opinion ensures her place in the *History*. Yet, once again, the classical allusion is telling. On hearing that her husband was implicated in conspiracy against Claudius, Arria, the wife of Caecina Paetus, stabbed herself with a knife which she then handed to her husband with the words: 'It does not hurt.' Her daughter, also called Arria, was dissuaded from following her mother's example when Nero condemned her husband for treason. Both recalling Lucretia's heroic suicide and alluding to the rule of tyrants, Macaulay deftly uses Arria as an image of feminine political martyrdom and resistance.

In sum, the *History* incorporates women as their lives and virtues are tested by the political arena rather than singling them out either according to a specialised feminine standard of sentimental virtue, or in terms of strictly familial connection. We are a world away from Mary Hays's chronicle of women's achievements as women, in her *Female Biography* and, correspondingly, in some ways closer to the terms on which Macaulay's subjects might have considered women's relationship to politics.[42] That Hays's biographical dictionary includes Rachel Russell and Catharine Macaulay, but excludes the highly politicised Lucy Hutchinson, indicates a discursive distinction in which the relationship between femininity and achievement, rather than politics, are foregrounded.[43]

As Hays notes, however, Macaulay herself was interpreted as an exception: a 'female historian . . . she seemed to have stepped out of the province of her sex . . . The author was attacked by petty and personal scurrilities, to which it was believed her sex would render her vulnerable.'[44] Macaulay, not shy of personal publicity, exploited the female historian's singularity. She several times agreed to have herself represented as the muse of history, Clio, appearing in the frontispiece to vol. I of her own *History*, as 'Libertas' in the frontispiece to volume III of the *History*, and in Richard Samuel's *The Nine Living Muses of Great Britain*, exhibited at the Royal Academy in 1779. Such images, as Elizabeth Eger notes, involved a 'blurring and merging of the real and symbolic in contemporary representations of women' and produced a correspondingly confused response in which sexual satire was the price of Macaulay's public, or semi-public, role.[45]

In September 1777, Thomas Wilson, the older man in whose house Macaulay lived in Bath, had 'a superb white marble statue' executed in the London City church of St Stephen Walbrook and had the pedestal inscribed with a sycophantic motto. The statue represented Macaulay in classical dress, as Clio, to suggest the active role of republican history in provoking, as much as recording, change.[46] This particular statue, however, became the subject of controversy, as did Wilson's inscription, which described Macaulay as 'a kind of prodigy'.[47] The public objected to its presence in a church, and after Macaulay's second marriage to the younger James Graham, this object became caught up in Thomas Wilson's rage against her.[48] The debate about femininity and politics, which reached the pages of *The Gentleman's Magazine*, was crystallised by the question of embodied representation.

As Stephen Bann argues, Clio herself can simultaneously suggest Amazonian freedom, maternal succour and sternness.[49] The iconographic expression of virtues as female, as Marina Warner has noted, derived from the gendering of Greek translated into visual and physical form in assigning 'images a maternal relation to those agents who carry out the principles they represent.'[50] Such ideal figures had a strong place in the political imaginary of the Enlightenment. The implicit elisions of this representation (of muse, liberty, Macaulay) can comment on the relationship between the individual writer and 'the eternal body of history' and could, in the right circumstances, add to the prestige of women themselves, as in the representation of the *Nine Living Muses*.[51]

The reception and subsequent career of Macaulay's embodiment as

History, however, indicates a dynamic between ideal political symbolisation and quotidian sexual and social politics.[52] Macaulay might be willing to represent republicanism, or history, but she had little control over what that representation meant. This statue seems to have prompted the expression of some of the contradictions implicit in Macaulay's already ambiguous participation in highly valued, and politicised, historical writing. Hostile responses to the statue expressed 'contradictory attitudes towards personification' but also a detailed critique of Macaulay's participation in republican history.[53]

In this instance, Macaulay's idealisation, the statue's location and the inscription, called attention to the problematic relations of a woman as writer of history, especially republican history. As Bann has argued, the figural quality of historical discourse is present to text and reader as a kind of invisibility, a Derridean 'white mythology' in which a figure 'is a function both of the text and of the shared knowledge [operating] . . . to engage the mechanism of figural interpretation'.[54] If history presents the reader with truth claims which tend to deny the figural status of their language, then the statue calls attention to the elision of a living figure with the ideal virtues of the art she practised. In the furore around this statue, historical discourse and republicanism were caught up in a debate over the nature of figuration and appropriate public activity.[55] In this instance, the potential for figuration suggested by the statue of Macaulay as History (or vice versa?) points to the problematic dynamic between her project and its reception.

In Macaulay's own writing, republican commitment takes priority over gender. And, as republican *virtu* is highly masculinised, women participate in her *History* as they come close to, or discuss, that ideal with which Macaulay herself strongly identified. The suspension into which this writing strategy put questions of feminine political agency was, however, repeatedly undone by the nature of the attention Macaulay's own republicanism attracted. Her *History* strove to set new, republican standards of history. Yet, as the incident of the statue indicates, such identifications cannot be isolated from other forms of social consciousness, and the *History* existed in a world in which attempts to use femininity as a publicity feature rebounded: her marriage was met by satires which transfer the signifier 'liberty' from republican history to the realm of gender.[56] If republicanism governed Macaulay's interest in women, her own femininity provoked reaction to her politics.

IV

In 1792, Mary Wollstonecraft, writing within a conception of politics that focused on the rights of women, remembered Catharine Macaulay:

When I first thought of writing these strictures I anticipated Mrs Macaulay's approbation, with a little of that sanguine ardour, which it has been the business of my life to depress; but soon heard with the sickly qualm of disappointed hope, and the still seriousness of regret – that she was no more.[57]

The *Vindication of the Rights of Woman* appeared nearly thirty years after the first volume of Macaulay's *History*, but merely eleven years after the last. Yet it seems that by the 1790s the *History* and Macaulay have vanished. At nearly the same time Richard Polwhele, earlier an admirer, could assert that Catharine Macaulay had died in republican America and that he could 'point out numerous femalities, indeed, in Mrs Macaulay's history';[58] How can we assess Catharine Macaulay's place in the political sphere and what are the wider implications of this?

If Macaulay's *History* and career invite us to be more nuanced in models of private and public spheres and to reconsider the dynamic between the two, it also illuminates the changes in the political sphere and in the relationship between femininity and politics towards the end of the eighteenth century. Although it was methodologically innovative and popular when it began to be published, and it continued to be read, the *History* was in significant ways marginal by 1800, and its potential remains, in some ways, unfulfilled. Macaulay wrote of the failure of the English republic, but by the end of the century the American and French republics had come into being. Moreover, within thirty years of the publication of Macaulay's last volume the terms on which she was writing had been substantially replaced. Macaulay's use of classical models was to be replaced by a search for the 'origins' of identity in the land, through Indo-Germanic roots, favouring the 'illusion of organic community'. Macaulay's *History*, though innovative in building a carefully researched historical method, is also situated at the end of a particular tradition of republican history. Her history, looking backwards (to Rome, Sparta and Athens for models to understand early modern actors) and forwards (to the careful research of the emerging discipline of history), is for a twentieth-century reader in some ways a terminus, in others a beginning.

Republicanism and gender shaped Macaulay's career as an historian and changes in these two areas determined the subsequent career and significance of her *History*. I have argued that we can trace Macaulay's political interventions and characterisation in relation to the writing of history and the liberation of republican ideas into the present through the reading of the ancients and the political theory of the Civil War as in the theoretical writings of Algernon Sidney, Harrington and some others. For the writers following Macaulay, though, republicanism, history writing and the place of femininity in the public sphere were all to mean very different things. As Caroline Robbins notes, for all that some were prepared to assert that Thomas Paine thought nothing that Milton and Harrington had not understood before him, a generational chasm in political thinking came into being.[59] Martin Thom sees Chateaubriand's use of republican parallels in his *Essai Historique* of 1797 as disrupted by passages of 'excoriating disillusion'.[60] Although, in the ways I have explored, Macaulay sought self-consciously to change and modernise history, the mode of classical modelling that inhabited her sense of past and present was to be tranformed. Moreover, after the American and French revolutions the status and meaning of English seventeenth-century history was changed.

The relationship between gender and politics was also changing as Macaulay's writing gave way to that of Wollstonecraft. Macaulay's republicanism arguably places her at the end of a tradition in which women's writing on the public sphere was rooted in a discourse of national civic virtue, rather than the place of women in family and home. Political history, for Macaulay as for those she wrote about, began with the relationship between the event and virtue, usually masculine virtue. The writer that Wollstonecraft recovers, in whose 'style of writing, indeed, no sex appears, for it is like the sense it conveys, strong and clear' is the author not of the *History* but of the *Letters on Education*, a text which takes up the questions of civic virtue by concentrating on the shaping of an individual, whilst the *History* analyses the shaping of a state. By the time Wollstonecraft came to write the *Vindication of the Rights of Woman*, what made Macaulay visible was her intervention in the public sphere (characterised as extraordinary) and her discussion of gender and education.

A further point is worth making. For all that she was using the ancient models, Macaulay's society was not governed by an absolute Aristotelian split between *oikos* and *polis*; an intermediary social sphere which mediated virtue existed, a semi-public sphere. Catharine Macaulay could never hold office, yet intervened in high politics. Moreover, the public domain of reason was also that of scurrilous gossip. Macaulay's claims to be a republican historian were both acknowledged and satirised, they existed in the public sphere and experienced sexualised relegation through rumour and print.

That Macaulay was known to subsequent generations as the author of *Letters on Education*, rather than a multi-volume history, speaks of the changing political contexts of her texts. The nature of republicanism, and the narrative of failed republic which organised Macaulay's *History*, were transformed by the French Revolution. When Wollstonecraft comes to search for Macaulay, she looks for a writer analysing political questions from the point of view of women's participation in them under the sign of a feminist teleology. However, Macaulay, in her *History*, was looking back to the politics of the Civil War which shaped her present in terms of the reproduction of states, not the shaping of the female citizen. And, for that reason, Macaulay is doubly lost to Wollstonecraft – as a republican and as a political writer who, in her *History*, takes up a tradition of writing about politics as though gender is not an issue, certainly not the very foundation on which women can claim entry to the political sphere.

By the next generation, it seems, the political imaginary shifted decisively in a change which made Macaulay visible as 'extraordinary' and yet forgot her *History*. By the 1790s republicanism had been transformed, too. For Macaulay the French Revolution promised, 'in theory at least', 'the highest degree of freedom with the highest degree of order'.[61] Her acknowledgment of this, in her lucid critique of Burke's *Reflections*, also almost recognises that revolution's annihiliating transformation of her own patterns of thought. Regarding France, she writes: 'We can gain no light from history; for history furnishes *no example* of any government in a large empire, which, in the strictest sense of the word, has secured to the citizen the *full* enjoyment of his rights.'[62]

NOTES

I am very grateful to Charlotte Grant for reading and commenting on this piece several times.

1 *Letters of Horace Walpole*, ed. Mrs Paget Toynbee, 15 vols. (Oxford: Frowde, 1904–5), vol. XIV, p. 345. I am grateful to Professor Anne Janowitz for this reference.

2 Bridget Hill, *The Republican Virago: The Life and Times of Catharine Macaulay, historian* (Oxford: Clarendon Press, 1992) gives details in full. On Sylas Neville's records of Macaulay's conversation see G. M. Ditchfield, 'Some Literary and Political Views of Catharine Macaulay', *American Notes and Queries* 12 (1974), 70–6.

3 J. G. A. Pocock ed., *The Political Works of James Harrington* (Cambridge: Cambridge University Press, 1977) pp. 155–359. She even recommended a commonwealth modelled on James Harrington's *Oceana* for implementation by the Corsicans. See Catharine Macaulay, *Loose remarks on certain positions to be found in Mr. Hobbes' Philosophical rudiments of government and society* (London: W. Johnston, 1769).

4 Jürgen Habermas, *The Structural Transformation of the Public Sphere* (1962), trans. Thomas Burger (Cambridge: Polity Press, 1989), pp. 27–52, especially p. 51; J. G. A. Pocock, *The Machiavellian Moment* (Princeton and London: Princeton University Press, 1975), p. 466. See also pp. 334, 423, 446. For all its Kantian derivation Habermas's sense of the public sphere retains Aristotelian aspects in its analysis of the relationship between household and polis; for Aristotle women are confined, broadly, to the household (III. iii, 128) in his discussion of the good citizen.

5 Pocock, *Machiavellian Moment*, pp. 432, 446.

6 Martin Thom, *Republics, Nations and Tribes* (London: Verso, 1995), pp. 5, 2.

7 *History*, vol. VI, p. vii. See Barbara Brandon Schnorrenberg, 'The Brood Hen of Faction: Mrs Macaulay and Radical Politics, 1765–1775', *Albion* 11.1 (1979), 33–45, especially pp. 34–6.

8 See Stephen Bann, *The Clothing of Clio* (Cambridge: Cambridge University Press, 1984), p. 1.

9 See Nicholas von Maltzhan, *Milton's History of Britain: Republican Historiography in the English Revolution* (Oxford: Oxford University Press, 1991). Von Maltzhan notes that Milton thought that the Rump was to 'manage the transition' to a republic, not govern (p. 22), a view implicitly echoed in Macaulay's *History* vol. V, where she emphasises the importance of the Leveller programme (pp. 6–10) and the republican aspirations of the friends of liberty. See also David Norbrook, *Writing the English Republic* (Cambridge: Cambridge University Press, 1998).

10 Quoted in R. C. Richardson, *The Debate on the English Revolution* (London: Methuen, 1975), p. 37. *Bishop Atterbury's Vindication* even reprinted Hyde's will proving that he had bequeathed his papers to his sons. *Bishop Atterbury's Vindication* (London: J. Wilford, 1733), p. 29.

11 Richardson, *The Debate*, pp. 40–1.

12 Zachary Grey, *A Defence of Our Ancient and Modern Historians Against the Frivolous Cavils Of a Late Pretender to Critical History in Which the False Quotations . . . of the Anonymous Author are Confuted and Exposed* (London, 1725).

13 Compare Stephen Bann's discovery of a burgeoning of forms utilised to 'express a new vision of the past' in nineteenth-century history, *The Clothing of Clio*, p. 2. See R. C. Richardson, *The Debate on the English Revolution* (London: Methuen, 1975); D. R. Woolf, 'The "Common" Voice: History, Folklore and Oral Tradition in Early Modern England', *Past and Present* 120 (1988), 26–52.

14 *History*, vol. VI, p. vi.

15 Ibid., vol. VI, p. vi.

16 David Hume, 'Essay on History', *Essays and Treatises on Several Subjects* (London, 1758), pp. 26–8.

17 See also Michael McKeon, *The Origins of the English Novel* (Johns Hopkins, 1987; repr. London: Hutchinson, 1988), p. 212. Walpole accuses Macaulay of placing too much emphasis on virtuous men, *Letters*, vol. XIV, p. 332.

18 *History*, vol. VI, pp. vii–viii.

19 See Paul Langford, *A Polite and Commercial People* (Oxford: Oxford University Press, 1989), pp. 370–90, on the remains of the Whig tradition and Wilkesite radicalism.

20 *History*, vol. VI, p. xii. See also *Letters on Education* (London: C. Dilly, 1790), part 2, letter 1, where Macaulay reiterates the view that Brutus's behaviour to his sons was inhumane.

21 *History*, vol. VI, p. xiii.

22 John Rushworth, *Historical Collections* (London, 1659). For example Macaulay uses Rushworth as the source of Lady Fairfax's intervention from the gallery at Charles I's trial. *History*, vol. V, p. 56.

23 This is a sample from vol. V. On the use of sources by real Whigs see Caroline Robbins, *The Eighteenth-Century Commonwealthman* (Cambridge, Mass.: Harvard University Press, 1959), p. 4.

24 Catharine Macaulay, *A Catalogue of Tracts* (1790). See Hill, *Republican Virago*, p. 168.

25 *History*, vol. V, p. 143.

26 *Memoirs of Thomas Brand Hollis*, ed. John Disney (1808), p. 42, quoted in Hill, *Republican Virago*, pp. 182–3. On republican history writing see Norbrook, *Writing the English Republic*.

27 *History* vol. I, p. vii.

28 Ibid., vol. I, p. vii.

29 Langford, *Polite and Commercial*, p. 528.

30 *History*, vol. VIII, pp. 338–9.

31 Langford, *Polite and Commercial*, p. 528.

32 This is the spirit in which Macaulay suggested to the Corsicans that they should run their state according to Harrington's *Commonwealth of Oceana*. Similarly, J. G. A. Pocock tells us that Machiavelli would return to his house in the evening, eat, and then dress himself in formal robes to commune with the ancients.

33 Natalie Zemon Davies contrasts Hume's 'skepticism' as an historian with Macaulay's 'belief'. 'History's Two Bodies', *American Historical Review*, 93.1 (1988), 1–30, p. 9.

34 *History* vol. V, eg. pp. 112, 130, 119, 214.

35 Hill, *Republican Virago*, pp. 74–6.

36 *History*, vol. VI, pp. viii, x.

37 'Preface', *Memoirs of the Life of Colonel Hutchinson* (London: 1806), p. i.

38 *History*, vol. VII, pp. 443–4.

39 Rachel Russell, *Letters of Lady Rachel Russell* (London: Edward and Charles Dilly, 1773), pp. 159–60.

40 *History*, vol. VII, p. 446.

41 Ibid.

42 Mary Hays, *Female Biography*, 6 vols. (London: Richard Phillips, 1803).

43 Hays's *Female Biography* records 'Catherine Macaulay Graham'; she 'dwelt with delight and ardour on the annals of the Greek and Roman republics. Their laws and manners interested her understanding, the spirit of patriotism seized her, and she became an enthusiast in the cause of freedom' (pp. 289–90).

44 Hays, *Female Biography*, vol. V, p. 292.

45 Elizabeth Eger, 'Representing Culture: *The Nine Living Muses of Great Britain*', this volume pp. 104–33.

46 Richardson claims that she is sculpted as 'Dame Thucydides', *The Debate*, p. 53. See also Marina Warner, *Monuments and Maidens* (London: Weidenfeld & Nicholson), p. 361; Iliaria Bignamini and Martin Postle, *The Artist's Model* (Nottingham:University of Nottingham Art Gallery, 1991).

47 Quoted in Hill, *Republican Virago*, p. 100. This section of my argument is indebted to Bridget Hill's research in *Republican Virago*, pp. 99–104.

48 Hill, *Republican Virago*, pp. 78–121.

49 Other roughly contemporary representations of Macaulay, though they hint at her alingnment with History, tend, when not satirical, to blur her relation to Clio and shape her body to emphasise the maternal aspect of the ideal representation of History. For example, the physical hardness of the statue contrasts with other contemporary representations of Macaulay. See Warner, *Monuments*, p. 68; Bann, *Clio*, p. 1.

50 Warner, *Monuments*, p. 68. Vermeer's *The Art of Painting*, discussed by Alpers and Warner, meditates on all the relationships (except perhaps that of the patron) that also, later, went to make up the statue of Catharine Macaulay as History – artist, female model, creative activity, ideal female figure. It analyses the problematic process whereby a 'real' woman is symbolised as an ideal figure, addressing the twin questions of the agency of the sculptor but, also, the willingness of the viewer to enter the discursive realm of idealisation within which the monumental female form is only able to signify. Warner illuminatingly discusses this in terms of the operation of allegory through the willing submission of the viewer to a regime of viewing and system of meaning that can only ever be partially complete and which constantly runs the risk of tripping itself up on the process which it hides, and which Vermeer's painting explores, whereby allegory transposes one set of interpretative relations into another. Warner, *Monuments*, p. 234ff.

51 Davies, 'History's Two Bodies', pp. 15–18.

52 Moreover, portraiture, the antique and the life model were in a complex relation. See Bignamini and Postle, *Artist's Model*, pp. 43–4.

53 Steven Knapp, *Personification and the Sublime: Milton to Coleridge* (Cambridge, Mass.: Harvard University Press, 1985), p. 1.

54 Jacques Derrida, 'White Mythologies', in *Margins of Philosophy*, trans. Alan Bass (Brighton: Harvester, 1982); Dan Sperber, 'Rudiments de rhétorique cognitive', *Poetique* 23 (1975) p. 415, translated and quoted in Bann, *The Clothing of Clio*, p. 4.

55 Bann, *The Clothing of Clio*, p. 5.

56 See, for example, anon., *Female Patriot, An Epistle from C-t-e M-c-y to the Rev. Dr. W-l-n on her late marriage* (London, 1779), p. 6; and anon., *A Bridal Ode on the Marriage of Catherine and Petruchio* (London: J.Bew, 1779), pp. 7–8. On this transfer see Lynn Hunt, *The Family Romance of the French Revolution* (London: Routledge, 1992), pp. xiii-xiv, 1–4. Transposed into the English context Hunt's work might perhaps be considered as according too much to the imaginative dominance of the family.

57 Mary Wollstonecraft, *Vindication of the Rights of Woman* (1792), now in *Works*, ed. Janet Todd and Marilyn Butler (London: William Pickering, 1989), vol. v, pp. 175–6. Thanks to Jane Spencer for discussing this.

58 Richard Polwhele, *The Unsex'd Females: A Poem addressed to the author of the Pursuits of Literature* (London: Cadell and Davies, 1798), p. 37.

59 Robbins, *The Eighteenth-Century Commonwealthman*, pp. 322–3.

60 Thom, *Republics*, p. 3.

61 *Observations on the Reflections of the Right Hon. Edmund Burke on the Revolution in France* (London: C. Dilly, 1790), pp. 76–7.

62 *Observations on the Reflections*, p. 87.

CHAPTER EIGHT

Gender, nation and revolution: Maria Edgeworth and Stéphanie-Félicité de Genlis

Clíona Ó Gallchoir

In France we have a number of women who have acquired reputation merely by the power of conversation, or by writing letters which resembled conversation. Madame de Sévigné is the first of all in this department; but subsequently Madame de Tencin, Madame du Deffant, Madlle. de l'Espinasse, and several others, have acquired celebrity by their mental attractions. I have already said that the state of society in England hardly admitted of distinction in this way, and that examples of it were not to be cited. There are, however, several women remarkable as writers: Miss Edgeworth, Madame D'Arblay, formerly Miss Burney, Mrs. Hannah Moore [sic], Mrs. Inchbald, Mrs. Opie, Miss Baillie, are admired in England, and read with great avidity in the French; but they live in general in great retirement, and their influence is confined to their books.[1]

She [Germaine de Staël] asserts that, though there may be women distinguished as writers in England, there are no ladies who have any great conversational or political influence in society, of that kind which, during *l'ancien régime*, was obtained in France by what they would call their *femmes marquantes*, such as Madame de Tencin, Madame du Deffant, Mademoisselle de l'Espinasse. This remark stung me to the quick, for my country and for myself, and raised in me a foolish, vain-glorious emulation, an ambition false in its objects, and unsuited to the manners, domestic habits, and public virtue of our country. I ought to have been gratified by her observing, that a lady is never to be met with in England, as formerly in France, at the Bureau du Ministre; and that in England there has never been any example of a woman's having known in public affairs, or at least told, what ought to have been kept secret.[2]

Letters for Literary Ladies (1795) and *Helen* (1834) serve as markers for the beginning and the end of Maria Edgeworth's career.[3] Whereas *Letters for Literary Ladies* is generally regarded as somewhat flat and stylistically awkward, *Helen* is perhaps the author's most fluently written and best-plotted fiction. There is, however, a striking continuity of theme between these two works. *Letters for Literary Ladies* consists of three short pieces, 'Letter to a Gentleman on the birth of a Daughter, with a Reply', 'Letters of Julia and Caroline', and 'An Essay on the Noble Science of Self-Justification', whose aim is to argue for women's access to education and equality on the basis of a shared rationality. 'Letter to a Gentleman' in particular, which engages with the works of Edmund Burke and Mary Wollstonecraft, bears striking evidence of its post-Revolutionary context, and focuses specifically on the value of women's literary production.[4] It is evident from the passage from *Helen* cited above that the problematic position of the woman writer in post-Revolutionary society continued to preoccupy Edgeworth. Her veiled citation of Germaine de Staël's reference to her as first among those English women writers 'who live in great retirement', in contrast to the celebrated *femmes marquantes* of pre-Revolutionary France, suggests a consciousness of how crucial it was to maintain this distinction. She herself seems aware that the theme has an almost historical quality: she is, after all, referring to what was *formerly* the case in France. It appears that the debates of the 1790s continued to inform Edgeworth's sense of herself as a woman writer for her entire career. One compelling reason for this, as the passage cited from *Helen* illustrates, is the extent to which gender identity was involved in the discourse of national character. By 1834, this had apparently become so well rehearsed as to need little elaboration.

Edgeworth's recourse above to what might be termed 'the French contrast' as a means of expressing the idea of British national character is a deeply rooted tendency. In Gerald Newman's account of the rise of English nationalism, anti-French antagonism is the key factor in the creation of national character.[5] Linda Colley's more recent work stresses the unifying influence of Protestantism, arguing that 'Protestantism was the foundation that made the invention of Great Britain possible'.[6] However, Colley also states that the presence of France as Britain's seemingly constant enemy had a formative influence on the national identity, and that, to all intents and purposes, Catholicism and France were frequently interchangeable terms.[7] The 'Revolution controversy' of the 1790s was on the one hand an extension of a pre-existing rhetoric and on the other hand an important realignment of its terms. In *Reflections on the Revolution in France*, according to Seamus Deane, Edmund Burke recast the debate on Anglo-French difference, creating a powerful new version of national character which based itself on the conflict between

tradition and modernity.[8] Deane observes that women writers such as
Hannah More, who sought to counter the effects of the Revolution
through writing, employed idealised representations of English woman-
hood energetically as a central image of national difference. According
to Deane, when considering the 'Irish national novel', and Edgeworth's
contributions in particular, 'it is not all suprising to find that its interests
and protocols are similar' to those of More and others like her.[9]
However, Edgeworth's detailed citation of Staël, and her reflection on
the difficulties encountered by women such as *Helen*'s Lady Davenant,
whose intelligence and energy made a narrowly-defined domestic life a
punishing prospect, suggest a much more nuanced approach to the tensions between national and gender identity.

In what follows, I return to the 1790s and the beginning of Edgeworth's
career, focusing specifically on the issues of publicity and 'retirement',
writing and other forms of public presence, arguing that the 'French contrast' referred to in *Helen* was by no means a straightforward response. I
question the terms 'English', 'Irish' and 'French' by arguing that Maria
Edgeworth's position as an Anglo-Irish woman writer leads her to uphold
the ideals of cosmopolitanism, rather than nationalism, and that she
attempts to adhere to the Enlightenment ideal of the Republic of Letters
in the interests of women's authority and intellectual progress more generally. Maria Edgeworth is unquestionably the most significant writer of
the immediate post-Revolutionary era in Ireland. To date, however, there
has been little attention to how her gender, which was a key feature of
post-Revolutionary culture, was influenced by or influenced her response
to the emergent discourse of national character. This is in spite of the fact
that *Letters for Literary Ladies* engages with the ways in which the discourse
of the national was mobilised in order to reinforce the restrictions that
were placed on women's authority and freedom of expression. The origin
of this engagement is Edgeworth's complex sense of identification with
French women writers.

Staël was not the only, and certainly not the first French woman writer
to influence Edgeworth. In 1782 her father, Richard Lovell Edgeworth,
recognising his daughter's literary talent, set her to translate *Adèle et
Théodore*, an educational work by Stéphanie-Félicité de Genlis. The
Edgeworths were remarkably up-to-date: Genlis had at that point published two highly successful and well-regarded works for children, and
in 1782 she achieved a degree of notoriety by taking up the position
of 'Governor' to the sons of the Duke of Orleans, a post never before
held by a woman. In Edgeworth's own biography, 1782 is more readily

recognised as the year in which the fifteen-year-old Maria and her family returned after many years of absence to Ireland, where she was to spend the remainder of her long life. In political terms, it is a landmark date in Irish history, being remembered as the year in which the Irish parliament gained a short-lived measure of legislative independence. The three facts are not as disparate as they might first appear. R. L. Edgeworth's decision to return to Ireland and to resume personal management of his estate at Edgeworthstown, Co. Longford, was expressly motivated by the kind of enlightened patriotism which had a brief flourishing among the Irish ruling classes in the eighteenth century. This movement culminated in demands for the repeal of those acts that had made the activity of the Irish parliament little more than an exercise in rubber-stamping decisions made in London.[10]

1782 was thus a year of great hopes and great optimism in Ireland, not least among the Edgeworth family. R. L. Edgeworth's ambitions for his estate were practical, but also experimental and reforming. He relished the idea of making his estate a 'moral school', in which experiments in agriculture, engineering and education could be pioneered.[11] Given that he chose the translation of Genlis's first work as a suitable first venture into publication for his daughter, we can only expect that he endorsed the views it contained. Genlis's text takes the form of an exchange of letters between a lady who has decided to live in retirement in the country in order to devote herself to her children's education, and a sophisticated friend in the French capital. Marilyn Butler has in fact pointed out how closely the theme and situation of this work matched the Edgeworths' perception of their role and function as landlords in remote Ireland, remarking that it corresponds 'perfectly . . . with their own taste for experimental education in a domestic environment'.[12] In short, R. L. Edgeworth saw himself and his family as active participants in a sphere characterised by progressive and enlightened thought, connected to people of similar aims not only in Britain and Ireland but also in continental Europe. Print was arguably the single most important factor in binding together this particular imagined community. The physical isolation of the Edgeworth family from the metropolitan centre was freely chosen, and was clearly regarded by both Maria and her father as a kind of pattern or example of the way in which lives could be lived locally and practically whilst also acting as experiments in the kind of progressive thought to which print gave access.

Letters for Literary Ladies reflects much of this sense of enlightened optimism. Its interest, however, lies in the fracture of that optimism.

Published first in 1795 and in a revised version in 1798, *Letters for Literary Ladies* is removed in time from the high hopes of 1782. Like progressives across Europe, the Edgeworths were forced to confront the French Revolution as a potent challenge to confident narratives of progress. Closer to home, in Ireland, the Enlightenment patriotism that had characterised the calls for legislative independence was increasingly threatened both by sectarian intransigence and by the rise of radical and revolutionary republicanism, inspired by the French example.

Maria Edgeworth's own sense of the use of print as a medium of social change and improvement had, however, been challenged as early as 1782 when her father's friend, the radical writer Thomas Day, 'who had a horror of female authorship',[13] wrote to congratulate R. L. Edgeworth on the collapse of the plan to publish Maria's translation of *Adèle et Théodore*: a rival translation appeared while only one volume of Maria's was complete, and the project was abandoned. As Maria Edgeworth herself recounts in the *Memoirs* of her father, which she completed after his death, Day's objections had a decisive influence on her subsequent career:

They [*Letters for Literary Ladies*] were not published, nor was anything of ours published, till some time after Mr Day's death. Though sensible, that there was much prejudice mixed with his reasons; yet, deference for his friend's judgment prevailed with my father, and made him dread for his daughter the name of authoress.[14]

Although Edgeworth attempts to make light of what she calls Day's 'eloquent philippic against female authorship',[15] her subsequent remarks suggest that it had a far more disturbing effect on her.

the impression . . . which the eloquence of Mr Day's letter made, though I heard it read only once, at the time it was received, remained for years in my mind; and it was from the recollection of his arguments, and of my father's reply, that 'Letters for Literary Ladies' were written, nearly ten years afterwards.[16]

Letters for Literary Ladies, however, is not a confident and straightforward rebuttal of Day's ideas: its terms are complicated by the ways in which the events of the French Revolution, in the eyes of conservative propagandists, appeared to bear out the misogynistic claims of women's destructive influence in public affairs. One of the more paradoxical effects of the Revolution was the convergence of conservative and radical viewpoints in a shared condemnation of this perceived influence. As Linda Colley observes, the pre-existing perceptions of French culture as feminine or feminised enabled conservatives in the aftermath of the

Revolution to construct it as 'a grim demonstration of the dangers that ensued when women were allowed to stray outside their proper sphere'.[17] Thomas Day's letters from France in the late 1760s indicate, however, that radicals in the eighteenth century used a very similar language. Day wrote to R. L. Edgeworth of the 'disgusting sight' of 'that sex, whose weakness of body, and imbecility of mind, can only entitle them to our compassion and indulgence, assuming an unnatural domination, and regulating the customs, the manners, the lives and the opinions of the other sex, by their own caprices, weaknesses and ignorance'.[18]

As R. L. Edgeworth observed, Day had an 'exaggerated opinion'[19] of Rousseau, who voiced a similar, though less violently expressed view, in *La Nouvelle Héloïse* (1761):

Every thing depends on the ladies; all things are done by them, or for them; Olympus and Parnassus, glory and fortune, are all subject to their laws. Neither books nor authors have any other value than that which the ladies are pleased to allow them. There is no appeal from their decree in matters of the nicest judgment or most trivial taste. – Poetry, criticism, history, philosophy, are all calculated for the ladies, even the Bible itself has lately been metamorphosed into a polite romance. In public affairs, their influence arises from their natural ascendancy over their husbands, not because they are their husbands, but because they are men.[20]

Rousseau's displeasure at the 'universal power' of French women related to his critique of the Paris-dominated Enlightenment, and in particular of the role of the *salonnières* in sponsoring it. Dena Goodman has located the post-Revolutionary hostility to the 'feminised' Enlightenment culture of the Parisian salons in his writing, most specifically his *Lettre à d'Alembert*. She traces the rise of men-only clubs in Paris in the 1780s, arguing that the men who formed them 'denied the need for women as a civilizing force, adopting Rousseau's position that men of letters would be better off without women'.[21] It is at this point that we can see the overlap between the terms in which British national identity was expressed and the manner in which attempts were made to exclude women from the 'republic of letters'. Colley challenges the view that women in Britain were in fact confined more than ever to a restricted sphere of domesticity, suggesting that patriotism enabled women to carve 'out for themselves a real if precarious place in the public sphere'.[22] This place was, however, not only precarious, but highly conditional. The strategic necessity for women to embrace and promote a British national character defined in opposition to that of France entailed an abandonment of the Enlightenment principles that had proved indispensable to women's progress to that date.

The first edition of *Letters for Literary Ladies* exhibits an oscillation between a determined adherence to Enlightenment principles and concessions to post-Revolutionary (and, specifically, post-Burkean) anxieties. Whereas both 'Letters of Julia and Caroline' and 'An Essay on the Noble Science of Self-Justification' were written in 1787 and appear to have remained unchanged before publication, 'Letter to a Gentleman' was written in the changed atmosphere of the 1790s. The earlier pieces, in particular 'Letters of Julia and Caroline', are remarkable for their continued reliance on terms and concepts that by the time of its publication had become tainted by associations with France and the French. In 'Letters of Julia and Caroline' it is proposed that reason is not the enemy but the guarantor of virtue. Caroline, in correspondence with her friend Julia, who is contemplating a separation from her husband, urges her to 'analyse' her notions of happiness, and explain her 'system'.[23] Echoing Rousseau, Julia professes to glory in her 'amiable defects', contrasting herself with Caroline, who, she concludes, is a 'philosopher' (p. 41). Critiques of Rousseau united women writers as diverse as Mary Wollstonecraft and Hannah More, but Edgeworth's response is unusual for its determined countering of Rousseau with a clearly Enlightenment position. Caroline argues that Julia's errors arise from 'the *insufficiency*, not the *fallacy* of theory' and continues:

Your object, dear Julia, we will suppose is 'to please'. If general observation and experience have taught you, that slight accomplishments and a trivial character succeed more certainly in obtaining this end, than higher worth and sense, you act from principle in rejecting the one and aiming at the other. You have discovered, or think you have discovered, the secret causes which produce the desired effect, and you employ them. Do not call this *instinct* or *nature*; this also, though you scorn it, is *philosophy*. (p. 43)

In 'Letter to a Gentleman', however, Edgeworth gave herself the much more difficult task of giving voice to the opinion that, in its questioning of tradition, the sceptical spirit of Enlightenment may have paved the way for social and political disintegration. The topic is women's access to education and writing, but the language alludes to society at large. In writing 'Letter to a Gentleman', therefore, Edgeworth felt the necessity to confront firstly the well-rehearsed Rousseauvian arguments as to women's ineligibility for equality based on a common human capacity for rational thought. But she also addressed a clearly post-Revolutionary agenda which used the 'conspicuous and melancholy examples'[24] of literary women such as Wollstonecraft and Genlis as weapons directed against progressives in general and, specifically, against progressive thinking on gender.

The post-Revolutionary and post-Burkean context is announced on the first page of 'Letter to a Gentleman', in which the Gentleman sketches the disagreement between himself and his friend as follows:

> You are a champion for the rights of woman, and insist upon the equality of the sexes: but since the days of chivalry are past, and since modern gallantry permits men to speak, at least to one another, in less sublime language of the fair; I may confess to you that I see neither from experience nor analogy much reason to believe that, in the human species alone, there are no marks of inferiority in the female. (p. 1)

Edgeworth thus acknowledges that the debate on women and education has, by the 1790s, been placed in the realm of the revolution controversy. However, the author of the 'Answer' later disclaims any interest in women's rights, stating that as a father, he is much more intent on women's happiness. The association of a Burkean position with that of hostility to women's intellectual equality is suggested by allusion to some of Burke's key concepts and phrases. Whereas men have the advantage of 'every assistance that foreign or domestic ingenuity can invent, to encourage literary studies', women are excluded from 'academies, colleges, public libraries, private associations of literary men', 'if not by law, at least by custom, which cannot easily be conquered' (p. 2). Having asserted the entrenched nature of custom, the Gentleman proceeds to declare that he is 'by no means disposed to indulge in the fashionable ridicule of prejudice' (p. 5). Prejudice rather than rational thought is proposed as the only sure guarantor of female virtue:

> Allow me, then, to warn you of the danger of talking in loud strains to the sex, of the noble contempt of prejudice. You would look with horror at one who should go to sap the foundations of the building; beware then how you venture to tear away the ivy which clings to the walls, and braces the loose stones together. (p. 5)

Edgeworth suggests that the invocation of custom is a convenient argument for obstructing women's access to education. What is more, the wider political implications of the dismissal of prejudice are made explicit:

> Morality should, we are told, be founded upon demonstration, not upon sentiment; and we should not require human beings to submit to any laws or customs, without convincing their understandings of the universal utility of these political conventions. (p. 5)

Custom and prejudice are key terms in Burke's *Reflections*, in which he claims that the English are distinguished from the French, and therefore insulated against dehumanising Jacobinical principles, by their adherence to prejudice:

Prejudice is of ready application in the emergency; it previously engages the mind in a steady course of wisdom and virtue, and does not leave the man hesitating in the moment of decision, sceptical, puzzled, and unresolved. Prejudice renders a man's virtue his habit; and not a series of unconnected acts. Through just prejudice, his duty becomes a part of his nature.[25]

As is Wollstonecraft's *Vindication of the Rights of Woman* (1792), the *Letters* are alert to the implications for women and their interests of Burke's anti-revolutionary arguments. However, Edgeworth conflates his voice with that of a more Rousseauvian account of the corrupting effects of female leadership, specifically in relation to France:

Trace the history of female nature, from the court of Augustus to the court of Louis XIV, and tell me whether you can hesitate to acknowledge that the influence, the liberty, and the *power* of women have been the constant concomitants of the moral and political decline of empires; – I say the concomitants: where the events are thus invariably connected, I might be justified in saying they were *causes* – you would call them *effects*; but we need not dispute about the momentary precedence of evils, which are found to be inseparable companions: – they may be alternately cause and effect, – the reality of the connexion is established. (p. 4)

In her initial 'Answer' to this letter Edgeworth did indeed find herself severely restricted in her response to this potent conjunction of reaction and anti-Enlightenment critique. In 1798 a revised edition of *Letters for Literary Ladies* was published, in which the only changes were to the 'Answer' to 'Letter to a Gentleman'. She wrote that it

was thought to weaken the case it intended to support. – That letter has since been written over again; no pains have been spared to improve it, and to assert more strongly the female right to literature.[26]

What strikes one most about the 1795 'Answer' is the extent to which it admits and thereby appears to validate the conservative and reactionary fears of the first letter-writer. In the second paragraph, the enlightened father admits that he is 'sensible that we have no right to try new experiments and fanciful theories at the expence [sic] of our fellow creatures'.[27] Edgeworth here allows the terms 'experiment' and 'theory' to remain under the cloud of their revolutionary connotations, thus more or less conceding defeat for rationalism. Although she almost immediately attempts a defence of rationalism it is indeed weakened by the spectre of female disgrace:

Who can estimate the anguish which a parent must feel from the ruin of his child, when joined to the idea that it may have been caused by an imprudent education: but reason should never be blinded by sentiment, when it is her proper office to guide and enlighten.[28]

Other uncharacteristic concessions to the limitations of reason occur. The enlightened father 'agree[s]' with his conservative friend

in thinking, that the strength of mind, which makes people govern themselves by reason, is not always connected with abilities in their cultivated state. I deplore the instances I have seen of this truth; but I do not despair: I am, on the contrary, excited to examine into the causes of this phaenomenon [sic] in the human mind.[29]

The anguish of a parent over the ruin of a child ('ruin' here specifically implying a daughter) and the deplorable instances of cultivated people acting in an irrational manner suggest the excess and catastrophe which act as signifiers for revolution.

Letters for Literary Ladies negotiates a highly difficult terrain, therefore. These anxious admissions were deleted in the 1798 edition, which also supplied additional examples and anecdotes in order to reinforce the recognition of reason as the infallible principle of human conduct and social organisation. Most significantly, Edgeworth focused her arguments on access to publication and the written word. The enlightened and optimistic father in 'Letter to a Gentleman' counters his friend's prophecies of doom with a confident claim as to the inevitability of progress rooted in print culture:

It is absolutely out of our power to drive the fair sex back to their former state of darkness: the art of printing has totally changed their situation; their eyes are opened, – the classic page is unrolled, they *will* read. (p. 34)

It is, moreover, suggested that women who devote themselves to literary and educational pursuits are *less* likely to become objects of the public gaze:

Unmarried women, who have stored their minds with knowledge, who have various tastes and literary occupations, who can amuse and be amused in the conversation of well-informed people, are in no danger of becoming burthensome to their friends or to society: though they may not be seen haunting every place of amusement or of public resort, they are not isolated or forlorn; by a variety of associations they are connected with the world. (p. 17)

Here we are presented with an Edgeworthian distinction that merits attention: the 'world' to which a literary woman is connected is a network of small communities sustained and held together by print culture.

'CONSPICUOUS AND MELANCHOLY EXAMPLES'

Edgeworth's attempts to distinguish between a woman's access to publication and the unseemly appearance of a woman in the public sphere find an echo in the writing of her first literary model, Stéphanie-Félicité de Genlis. In 1796 Genlis found it necessary to publish *A Short Account of the Conduct of Mme de Genlis since the Revolution*, in the wake of a protracted series of rumours and allegations of improper behaviour and influence arising from her position in the household of the Duke of Orleans. She attempted to do so by making an absolute distinction between the woman of letters (or literary lady), represented through her writing, and the socially prominent and visible 'female politician', asserting a fundamental incompatibility in these positions:

Nobody will believe, that a woman, who has spent her whole life in the cultivation of the arts and sciences, who never solicited a favour at court, nor ever was seen at the house of a minister; who was considered in a manner untameable; one that shut herself up in a cloister when but thirty years of age, that she might complete the education of her daughters, and initiate, in the rudiments of science, some who were yet in their cradles; having renounced, at once, the court and society, hath spent 13 years in teaching, and in the publication of two and twenty volumes; I say, no one will believe that such a woman has been a political intriguer.[30]

But in spite of her protestations it was very widely believed that Genlis had been a political intriguer. She was reputed to wield limitless influence over her employer, the Duke of Orleans; an influence whose origin was sexual. It is accepted that she did in fact conduct an affair with him between 1772 and 1773.[31] Following the outbreak of the Revolution, the Duke of Orleans's manifest enthusiasm for democratic principles was such that he was called 'Philippe-Egalité', a conversion that was attributed to Genlis's success at 'boudoir politics'. The Duke had long been an enemy of Louis XVI's court, and it was claimed that Genlis engineered his revolt against royal authority as a well-timed bid for public popularity. When, however, the Duke refused the regency that was offered to him following Louis XVI's flight to Varennes in 1791, rumour-mongers interpreted the inconsistency by speculating that

Genlis's sexual and political loyalties now lay with her young pupil, the Duke of Chartres, who was by some accounts extravagantly devoted to his teacher. The Duke of Chartres, described by Helen Maria Williams as the 'Democrat Prince', had by then committed himself fully to republican principles, scorning personal decoration, titles and all marks of rank, and becoming, in 1790, a member of the Jacobin Club: inevitably, Genlis's influence was detected behind these actions.[32]

Genlis's reputation as a female politician, with all its negative associations of the manipulation of sexual power, extended to the unstable political atmosphere in Ireland through the marriage of Lord Edward Fitzgerald to her ward, Pamela. Pamela was brought to the Orleans household from England in 1785, along with a younger child named Hermine. From the outset, both girls were rumoured to be Genlis's own illegitimate children, and it was further speculated that Pamela was in fact the product of an affair with the Duke. Later investigations suggest that it is impossible that Genlis was Pamela's mother. Hermine may indeed have been Genlis's daughter, and the two girls may have been brought to the Palais-Royal at the same time to disguise this fact. But it was around Pamela that the whispers circulated, and the idea that she was the natural child of the Duke of Orleans and his female Governor acquired the powerful status of myth. The myth was, moreover, endlessly malleable, varying according to the politics and prejudices of commentators. As Stella Tillyard has commented, 'Pamela's life story was dependent more upon attitudes towards Madame de Genlis than upon anything she herself did'.[33]

Edward Fitzgerald was cashiered out of the British army while in Paris in 1791, for having attended a banquet at which a variety of republican toasts were proposed. He was subsequently introduced to Pamela by the poet and fellow republican, Helen Maria Williams, and the two married after a brief courtship. Fitzgerald and Pamela arrived in Dublin in early 1792, where Fitzgerald became active in the United Irishmen's Society, the group that in 1798 orchestrated a rebellion in Ireland planned with French help. The idea that the radical Irish aristocrat was married to the illegitimate daughter of the democrat Duke of Orleans gave a glamorously high profile to Fitzgerald, and has long been a key myth in the hagiography surrounding the United Irishmen, as the historian Marianne Elliott comments:

the myth [of Pamela's birth] played such a part in creating the reputation of Lord Edward as an advanced democrat that it has survived two centuries of scholarly research, and with Edward's style of dressing and of cropping his hair in the French republican style, long before it became common United Irish practice, [William] Drennan was correct in thinking that 'he and his elegant wife will set the fashion in politics in a short time'.[34]

Before her marriage to Fitzgerald, Pamela had played a similarly iconic role in the early days of the French Revolution: Genlis's biographer describes Pamela being hailed by a crowd of Parisians as she walked in the grounds of the Palais-Royal:

> Mme Vigée-Lebrun . . . relates how she saw the beautiful young girl attired in a riding habit, and wearing a hat decorated with black feathers, proceeding from one end of the gardens to another . . . the crowd dividing into two sections to let her pass, and yelling at the tops of their voices – 'Voilà! Voilà! There is she whom we must have as queen!' And we hear of her again on the 14th of July, dressed in red, making a triumphal progress through the excited populace.[35]

The symbolic role played by the mysterious Pamela in Paris, where she was hailed by the mob as the next queen, and then in Dublin, where again she set the 'fashion in politics', is utterly at odds with the rational and domestic role for women which Edgeworth had found described in *Adèle et Théodore*. The spectacle of Genlis's life and writing must have seemed to Edgeworth a profoundly cautionary tale. While in Paris in 1802–3, however, Genlis was one of the literary figures that Edgeworth and her father were most keen to meet, partly because of their concern for Pamela Fitzgerald, whom they, in common with most others, believed to be Genlis's natural daughter. When Pamela was ordered to leave Ireland, R. L. Edgeworth made a speech on her behalf in the Irish Parliament, and part of the Edgeworths' object in visiting Genlis was to tell her of their sympathy for Pamela, and this evidence of it. Edgeworth's response to Genlis's extraordinary career is surprisingly sympathetic. In spite of the multiple scandals that surrounded Genlis, and in spite of their evident political differences, Edgeworth was 'very eager' to see her, and describes her volume of *Petit Romans* as containing 'beautiful stories'.[36] Having mentioned Pamela Fitzgerald, the Edgeworths were taken aback when Genlis 'diverged into an elaborate and artificial exculpation of Lady Edward and *herself* – proving or attempting to prove that she never knew any of her husbands [sic] plans, that she utterly disapproved of them, or at least of all she suspected of them'. This, according to Edgeworth, was entirely unnecessary, as they 'had no thought of attacking'.[37]

Edgeworth was not taken with Genlis's manner or her personality, however, and it is clear that for the most part she regarded Genlis as the author of her own misfortune:

Her cruelty in drawing a profligate character of the Queen (soon after the Queen's execution) in the *Chevaliers du Cygne*, and her taking her pupils at the beginning of the revolution to the revolutionary clubs – and her connexion with the Duke of Orléans, and her hypocrisy about that connexion – and her insisting on being governess to his children when the Duchess did not wish it, and its being supposed that it was she instigated the Duke of Orléans in all his horrible conduct, and more than all the rest her own *attacks and apologies* have brought her into this isolated state of reprobation. [38]

It is striking that following the litany of allegations made against Genlis, to which Edgeworth clearly gave some credence, she concludes by remarking that Genlis's own insistence on justifying herself in print (by means, for example, of her *Short Account*) has compromised her most. Edgeworth also observes that 'Mme de Genlis seems to have been so much used to be attacked that she has defences and apologies ready prepared as some have books of prayer *suited to all possible situations.*'[39]

Edgeworth's sympathies and loyalties are intriguingly mixed: she admires the talent and intellect of Genlis, while deploring her involvement in political manoeuvring and her counter-productive attempts to take on public opinion; she has great sympathy for Genlis's female victims, the Duchess of Orleans and Marie Antoinette; she also, like her father, has 'no thought of attacking' the unfortunate Pamela Fitzgerald, wife of a man who had helped plan a revolt that drove the Edgeworth family from their home in 1798. The negotiation between apparently incompatible positions that emerges from this correspondence is reflected in the complexity of *Letters for Literary Ladies* and is explored again and again in her later writings.

In her discussion of Jacobin and anti-Jacobin fiction in *Jane Austen and the War of Ideas*, Marilyn Butler observes that Edgeworth's novels 'do not belong unequivocally to one side'.[40] In my view, what Butler refers to as Edgeworth's 'bi-partisan'[41] politics derive in the first instance from a determination to recuperate the image of French femininity in the interests of cosmopolitanism. The conclusion of the 'Answer' to 'Letter to a Gentleman' affirms Edgeworth's attempts to maintain a cosmopolitan ethos even in the aftermath of Revolution: her cosmopolitanism focuses specifically on the refusal to accept the stereotype of French femininity that had come to dominate discussions of revolution and national character in Britain. The voice of the enlightened father pays tribute to the contribution made by French women to their culture and society. The English, it is carefully acknowledged, 'wisely prefer the pleasures of domestic life'. But via the same male persona Edgeworth goes on to argue:

Domestic life, however, should be enlivened and embellished with all the wit and vivacity and politeness for which French women were once admired, without admitting any of their vices or follies. The more men of literature and polished manners desire to spend their time in their own families, the more they must wish that their own wives and daughters may have tastes similar to their own. If they can meet with conversation suited to their taste at home, they will not be driven to clubs for companions; they will invite the men of wit and science of their acquaintance to their own houses, instead of appointing some place of meeting from which ladies are to be excluded. (pp. 36–7)

Implicitly, it is stated that the demonisation of 'Frenchness' that followed the French Revolution will result in an absolute divide between public and private, and in the near total exclusion of women from cultural and intellectual life.

Edgeworth's position as an Anglo-Irish woman writer who entered the public sphere of print in the aftermath of the French Revolution afforded her a unique perspective on contemporary views of national and sexual character. To date, her contacts with and allusions to French women writers have been considered only very briefly. It is clear, however, that these contacts were in some senses formative, and remained significant throughout her career. Her knowledge of the lives and writings of women such as Genlis and Staël provided a complex and often contradictory framework within which she reflected on the ambiguous public presence of the woman writer, and her relationship to the nation. Edgeworth's confrontation of the meanings of post-Revolutionary nationalism for women in general and women writers in particular illuminates not only her own later 'Irish tales', but also the complex cultural condition of the woman writer in the early nineteenth century.

NOTES

1 Germaine de Staël, *Considerations on the Principal Events of the French Revolution*, 3 vols. (London: Baldwin, Craddock and Joy, 1818), vol. III, pp. 296–7.

2 Maria Edgeworth, *Helen*, ed. Susan Manly and Clíona Ó Gallchoir, vol. IX of *The Novels and Selected Works of Maria Edgeworth* (London: Pickering and Chatto, 1999), p. 59.

3 Edgeworth's first publication was a collection of stories for children entitled *The Parent's Assistant*, published a year before *Letters for Literary Ladies*, in 1794. *Helen* was her last novel.

4 For a reading of 'Letter to a Gentleman' which situates it within the context of Edgeworth's writing on Ireland, see my '"The whole fabric must be perfect": Maria Edgeworth's *Literary Ladies* and the Representation of Ireland', in *Gender Perspectives in Nineteenth-Century Ireland: Public and Private*

Spheres, ed. Margaret Kelleher and James H. Murphy (Dublin: Irish Academic Press, 1997), pp. 104–15.

5 Gerald Newman, *The Rise of English Nationalism: A Cultural History, 1740–1830* (London: Weidenfeld and Nicholson, 1987).

6 Linda Colley, *Britons: Forging the Nation, 1707–1837* (London: Vintage, 1996), p. 58.

7 Colley, *Britons*, p. 26.

8 Seamus Deane, *Strange Country: Modernity and Nationhood in Irish Writing since 1790* (Oxford: Clarendon Press, 1997), pp. 8–9.

9 Deane, *Strange Country*, p. 29.

10 See R. B. McDowell, *Ireland in the Age of Imperialism and Revolution, 1760–1801* (Oxford: Clarendon Press, 1991), chapter 5.

11 See Tom Dunne, '"A Gentleman's Estate should be a Moral School": Edgeworthstown in Fact and Fiction, 1760–1840', in *Longford: Essays in County History*, ed. Raymond Gillespie and Gerard Moran (Dublin: Lilliput Press, 1991), pp. 95–121.

12 Marilyn Butler, *Maria Edgeworth: A Literary Biography* (Oxford: Clarendon Press, 1972), p. 149.

13 *Memoirs of Richard Lovell Edgeworth, begun by himself and completed by his daughter*, 2 vols. (London: R. Hunter, 1820), vol. II, pp. 341–2.

14 *Memoirs of R. L. Edgeworth*, vol. II, p. 343.

15 *Memoirs of R. L. Edgeworth*, vol. II, p. 342.

16 *Memoirs of R. L. Edgeworth*, vol. II, p. 343.

17 Colley, *Britons*, p. 252.

18 Thomas Day to *R. L. Edgeworth*, 1769, cited in *Memoirs of R. L. Edgeworth*, vol. I, p. 224. R. L. Edgeworth, in a note which prefaces these letters, emphasises Day's comparative youth at the time of writing, and states that his 'expressions of contempt and horror of French society must not be taken literally or seriously' (vol. I, p. 218). However, in view of his strenuous objection to female authorship voiced in 1782, his opinions appear to have remained relatively constant.

19 *Memoirs of R. L. Edgeworth*, vol. I, p. 218.

20 Jean Jacques Rousseau, *Eloisa, or a series of original letters*, trans. William Kenrick (1803), 4 vols. in 2 (Oxford: Woodstock Books, 1989), vol. II, p. 124.

21 Dena Goodman, *The Republic of Letters: A Cultural History of the French Enlightenment* (London: Cornell University Press, 1994), p. 50.

22 Colley, *Britons*, p. 276.

23 Maria Edgeworth, *Letters for Literary Ladies*, ed. Claire Connolly (London: Everyman, 1993), p. 39. Subsequent references to this edition, which gives the 1798 text, are given parenthetically in the main text.

24 Maria Edgeworth, *Letters for Literary Ladies* (London: J. Johnson, 1795), p. 63. Further references to the 1795 edition will be given in abbreviated form in the footnotes.

25 Edmund Burke, *Reflections on the Revolution in France* (1790), ed. Conor Cruise O'Brien (Harmondsworth: Penguin, 1986), p. 183.

26 *Letters for Literary Ladies*, ed. Connolly (1993), 'Note on the Text'.

27 *Letters for Literary Ladies* (1795), pp. 44–5.

28 Ibid.

29 Ibid., p. 57.

30 Mme de Genlis, *A Short Account of the Conduct of Mme de Genlis since the Revolution* (Perth: R. Morison, 1796), pp. 4–5. An almost identical passage appears in her *Memoirs of the Countess de Genlis*, 8 vols. (London: Henry Colburn, 1825), vol. IV, pp. 74–5.

31 See Jean Harmand, *The Keeper of Royal Secrets: Being the Private and Political Life of Madame de Genlis* (London: Eveleigh Nash, 1913), pp. 88–102. See also Gabriel de Broglie, *Madame de Genlis* (Paris: Librairie Académique Perrin, 1985).

32 Harmand, *The Keeper of Royal Secrets*, p. 188.

33 Stella Tillyard, *Citizen Lord: Edward Fitzgerald, 1763–1798* (London: Vintage, 1998), p. 146.

34 Marianne Elliott, *Partners in Revolution: The United Irishmen and France* (London: Yale University Press, 1982), pp. 25–6.

35 Harmand, *The Keeper of Royal Secrets*, p. 177.

36 Maria Edgeworth to Mary Sneyd (19 March 1803), in *Maria Edgeworth in France and Switzerland*, ed. by Christina Colvin (Oxford: Clarendon Press, 1979), pp. 96, 101.

37 Ibid., p. 100.

38 Ibid., p. 102. *Les Chevaliers du Cynge* was a historical novel replete with analogies to the period of the French Revolution. The 'profligate portrait' of Marie Antoinette is found in vol. II, chapter 22, 'A Queen without understanding, and ill-advised', in *The Knights of the Swan; or, the Court of Charlemagne: A Historical and Moral Tale: to serve as a continuation of* The Tales of the Castle: *and of which all the incidents that bear analogy to the French Revolution are taken from history*, 3 vols. (London: J. Johnson, 1796), pp. 235–41.

39 *Maria Edgeworth in France and Switzerland*, p. 100.

40 Marilyn Butler, *Jane Austen and the War of Ideas* (Oxford: Clarendon Press, 1987), p. 124.

41 Butler, *Jane Austen and the War of Ideas*, p. 124.

CHAPTER NINE

Salons, Alps and Cordilleras: Helen Maria Williams, Alexander von Humboldt, and the discourse of Romantic travel

Nigel Leask

In January 1828 the *Monthly Review* briefly noted that 'Miss Helen Maria Williams died lately in Paris, where she has resided since 1790. She wrote several works connected with France, which obtained for her a considerable deal of popularity in that country, as well as in this; but they have been already forgotten.'[1] 'Notoriety' rather than 'popularity' would perhaps better describe the reception of the thirteen cumulative volumes of Helen Maria Williams's *Letters from France* and *Sketches from France* as they appeared from 1790 through to the final volume in 1819, covering the thirty years of her residence in France. Her passionate, partisan eye-witness account of French history in the making – Gary Kelly has described the composite work as a 'revolutionary prose epic'[2] – had made her an easy target for the anti-Jacobin establishment in Britain. Already a well-known poet and novelist by 1790, both the *Letters from France* and Williams's long, extramarital relationship with the English Jacobin John Hurford Stone dealt her literary reputation a death-blow from which it would never recover. James Boswell famously struck the epithet 'amiable' out of his account of Williams in the second edition of the *Life of Johnson*, and her former acquaintance Hester Piozzi dismissed her in 1798 as 'a wicked little democrat'.[3]

In many ways the veil of obscurity alluded to in the *Monthly* has persisted to the present day, despite excellent recent work on the *Letters* in the context of revolutionary feminism by Gary Kelly, Mary Favret, Vivien Jones, Elizabeth Bohls, Chris Jones and others.[4] In many respects, Williams's career and lifestyle as an English revolutionary feminist in Paris resembles that of Mary Wollstonecraft, her relationship with John Hurford Stone a more successful version of Wollstonecraft's troubled affair with Gilbert Imlay. Yet in contrast to Wollstonecraft, Williams's writings have never been re-edited (despite Janet Todd's useful facsimile edition of the *Letters from France*), and her correspondence has never been collected, let alone published. Her only biography – by Lionel Woodward – was published in Paris in 1930, in French, and is sought in vain in many major libraries.[5]

Given the *Monthly's* investment in a near-contemporary myth of Williams's obscurity, it is ironic that the same periodical had in 1816 praised her to the skies – not on account of her 'several works connected with France' – but for her major literary achievement of the 1810s, a monumental translation of her friend Baron Alexander von Humboldt's *Relation historique du Voyage aux régions équinoxiales du Nouveau Continent* as *Personal Narrative of Travels to the Equinoctial Regions of the New Continent*. Williams's translation of this first part of the Prussian savant's multi-volume account of his expedition to Spanish America in the years 1799–1804 in the company of French botanist Aimé Bonpland, was published in seven volumes between 1814 and 1829, with an introductory preface by Williams. Due to the work's (and the English translation's) chequered publishing career she did not live to see its completion. 1814 also saw the publication of Williams's translation of another important part of the *Voyage de Humboldt et Bonpland*, the 'picturesque atlas' of the expedition entitled *Vues des Cordillères et Monuments des peuples indigènes de l'Amérique* (1810), published in English under the title of *Researches Concerning the Institutions and Monuments of the Ancient Inhabitants of America, with Descriptions and Views of Some of the most Striking Scenes in the Cordilleras*.

Williams's name was prominently displayed on the title page of both the *Personal Narrative* and the *Researches*; addressing her English readership in the preface to the 1810 work, she wrote: 'Long a stranger to my country, I have indeed no critical favour to expect . . . my literary patrons belong to what Ossian calls "the days of other years" . . . but in appealing to an English tribunal, I will not fear injustice, if I have nothing to hope from partiality.'[6] More often than not contemporary reviewers (as well as subsequent Humboldt scholarship) chose to ignore the diffident translator, and no reference was even made to her former reputation as a 'democrat'. The *Monthly Review* was a noteworthy exception, in January 1816 praising the quality of the translation, and regretting that Helen Maria Williams had 'not deem[ed] herself authorised to take the liberty of re-modelling [Humboldt's] arrangement of [his] materials. She has introduced a preface marked equally by taste and sensibility; and we think that the publication would have gained largely on being re-cast by her hands.'[7]

My essay focuses on Williams's Humboldt translations from two related points of view. Firstly, it insists upon taking translation seriously as part of the social mediation of literary texts, and an essential property of the literary public sphere in which Williams, and other women writers like her, participated. The notion of a social mediation of texts is of particular importance in a literary epoch which fetishised the notion of original genius, construing translation as 'woman's work' – secondary, reproductive, literary labour. By considering Parisian salon culture as the social milieu which brought Williams and Humboldt into contact, I will contest the commonly held notion that public women associated with the French *ancien régime* retreated into the private sphere in the Revolutionary aftermath. On the contrary, 'salonnières' like Williams fought to maintain such a public sphere in which both men and women could freely participate through the Napoleonic years and into the Bourbon Restoration. Secondly, it views the Humboldt translations – beyond their status as the 'career move' of a literary woman – in the light of Williams's profound interest in the genre of travel writing in general, and particularly in relation to Latin America. Indeed, if we place *Letters from France* within the category of epistolary travel writing, Williams might be considered as first and foremost a travel writer, even beyond her reputation as a poet of sensibility, and her superb *Tour in Switzerland* (1798) certainly stands comparison with Wollstonecraft's *Short Residence in Sweden*, published two years earlier in 1796. I also contend that Williams's 'Englishing' of Humboldt's *Personal Narrative*, a generically challenging work both at the level of form and of content, is integrally rather than peripherally related to earlier works authored by Williams. Moreover, Williams's mediation of Humboldt's text should properly take its place alongside other better-known British engagements with German romanticism in the 1810s; John Black's translation of A. W. Schlegel's *Lectures on Dramatic Art and Literature*, Carlyle's Goethe translations, or Coleridge's so-called 'plagiarisms' of Schelling, Fichte and Jacobi in the *Biographia Literaria*.

STRUCTURING KNOWLEDGE: HELEN MARIA WILLIAMS, HUMBOLDT AND PARISIAN SALON CULTURE

What then lay behind Williams's endorsement of Humboldt's innovative combination of aesthetic sensibility and scientific precision, and what can it tell us about the transformation of a highly gendered culture of sensibility in the epoch of high romanticism? In reaffirming the significance of the latter part of Williams's literary career, we need to go further than simply praising her intellectual cosmopolitanism. How to get beyond the notion of Williams as passive translator of Humboldt's productive genius for the benefit of an English readership, a notion which genders translation as a feminine activity, either 'beautiful' or 'faithful' to the text which authorises it, as Lori Chamberlain has argued?[8] We need to question the whole discourse of romantic authorship in relation to Humboldt's enormous and problematic oeuvre, in order to re-situate Williams's relationship to the text which she translated.

What was Helen Maria Williams's role in the publication of Humboldt's mammoth thirty-volume *Voyage*, a project which purportedly cost more than 840,000 francs?[9] Given the scattered and uncollected nature of her correspondence, it is hard to find much concrete detail about her relationship with Humboldt, despite the sentimentalised picture she paints of it in her lyric poem 'To the Baron De Humboldt, on his bringing me some flowers in March', published in her 1823 *Poems on Various Subjects*. Yet it appears that she played a much more important role in the genesis of Humboldt's *Voyage* than has been hitherto noticed. The key to Helen Maria Williams's multifaceted involvement with Humboldt lies in the construction of knowledge in early nineteenth-century Paris, notably, the involvement of intellectuals and writers in the female-dominated salons which survived well into the nineteenth century. In her discussion of the salons of pre-Revolutionary Paris, Joan Landes describes how 'a novel pattern of interchange existed between educated men and literate, informed women who functioned not just as consumers but as purveyors of culture . . . the *salonnières* existed as public women outside the institution of marriage'.[10] Whilst Landes is doubtless right that 'the new symbolic order of nineteenth-century bourgeois society was predicated on the silencing of public women'[11] – we will see how Williams's translations were linked to this 'silencing' – the demise of the salons was not as abrupt as she proposes. To understand the context of Williams's involvement with the Humboldt project we need to know more than we do about the survival of salons run by women like Madame Helvetius, Madame de Staël and Helen Maria Williams herself.

Dena Goodman has emphasised the connections between enlightenment salons and correspondence whereby 'the copied and circulated letter, the open letter, the published letter, and the letter to the editor were uniting a vast web of readers into networks of intellectual exchange that began often in the salons of Paris, but spread outward from them into the four corners of Europe and the New World'.[12] This was clearly the seed-bed of Williams's *Letters from France* and other epistolary works, and the milieu of the Parisian salons helps us better understand the peculiarly cosmopolitan nature of Williams's writings. Her roots were in English provincial dissenting culture, and her understanding of a female-dominated intellectual milieu in the pre-Paris years was inspired by Elizabeth Montagu and the English Bluestocking circle. Montagu is the dedicatee of her 1784 poem *Peru*, a sentimental indictment of Spanish conquest based on William Robertson's *History of America* (1777).

Her real intellectual apprenticeship, however, was served in the salons of Revolutionary Paris after her arrival in 1790. She was a regular attender at Madame Roland's salon, where she mingled with other English and American expatriate radicals and Girondin intellectuals, and deepened her interest in Latin America through friendship with the Venezuelan republican and liberator Francisco de Miranda. Two recent studies have cast important new light on the intellectual milieu of Williams and her partner John Hurford Stone in 1790s Paris. David Erdman's *Commerce des Lumières: John Oswald and the British in Paris, 1790–93* describes Williams's activity in the 'British Club' centred on White's Hotel, the members of which on 18 November 1792 drank a toast to 'the Women of Great Britain, particularly those who have distinguished themselves by their writing in favour of the French Revolution, Mrs [Charlotte] Smith and Miss H. M. Williams'. They ended by singing an English version of the 'Marseillaise' penned by Williams, who was herself present at the dinner.[13] In her illuminating essay 'The English Press in Paris and its Successors, 1793–1852', Madeleine B. Sterne has produced the definitive account of the printing business run by John Hurford Stone and Helen Maria Williams in the years between 1793 and the couple's bankruptcy in 1813 – a bankruptcy which, as we will see, was induced by the exorbitant costs of publishing Humboldt's *Voyage*.

Although the 'English Press' bore all the hallmarks of Hurford Stone's mixture of political radicalism and commercial opportunism (its select list included publications by Volney, Joel Barlow, Tom Paine and Joseph Priestley as well as numerous travelogues in both French and English), it was in fact, during its most successful phase, under the financial ownership of Helen Maria Williams. Her financial stake in Stone's earlier press located at the Rue de Vaugirard was substantiated by an 'Acte de Societé' of 1806, which records her astonishing investment of 40,000 livres in the press (presumably emoluments of her highly successful writings and

translations) which now rendered her, and not Stone, its main proprietor.[14] In 1809 the English Press was appointed printer of the 'administration des droits réunis' – the Napoleonic government's excise and tax
papers, and in the years up to 1813, Williams's little printing empire had
fifty-eight presses at its command: it was now one of the leading printing businesses in France. This explains the fact that across from the title
page of Humboldt's 1810 grand folio *Vues des Cordillères* (with its sixty-nine
plates, many of them coloured, amongst the most beautiful and lavish
travel books ever produced) appear the words 'De L'imprimerie de J. H.
Stone'.[15] By 1810, Stone and Williams, in partnership with Maximilien
Schoell – another friend of Humboldt's – had paid 100,000 francs for
the exclusive publishing rights to Humboldt and Bonpland's *Voyage*, of
which the *Vues* made up the fifteenth and sixteenth volumes (the volumes
of the work did not appear in chronological order, the twentieth volume,
for example, entitled *Géographie des plantes équinoxiales*, being the first to
appear in 1807). The following year, they printed the text of Humboldt's
enormously influential *Essai politique sur le royaume de la Nouvelle-Espagne* in
two folio volumes, as well as the *Recueil d'observations de zoologie et d'anatomie
comparée*, 'elaborate, lavishly illustrated, grandiose publications' which
required twenty printing presses.[16] Unfortunately, however, the investment proved to be disastrous, and Humboldt's *Voyage* ruined Stone's and
Williams's short-lived prosperity. The enormous printing expenses
involved together with the cost of preparing the maps and plates ended
up vastly exceeding the profits from the sales of the expensive volumes.
Coinciding with the French political and economic crisis of 1812–13,
Stone and Williams soon went bankrupt, and after 1813 the project was
taken over by Stone's associate, James Smith of Norwich. Between 1814
and 1825 Smith would go on to print Humboldt and Bonpland's *Relation
historique*, the very work which Helen Maria Williams would concur-
rently translate into English as the *Personal Narrative*. Smith was luckier
than Stone (who had been crippled by the economic crisis of 1812–13),
although four more French publishers would be bankrupted before the
completion of Humboldt's ill-starred *Voyage* in 1834. These details of
Williams's business involvement with the Humboldt project cast a dra-
matically new light upon her role as his translator.

   Hurford Stone's and Helen Maria Williams's printing business seems
to have been closely linked to the Parisian salon which Williams initiated
in her apartment in the Rue Helvétius in the autumn of 1792 and which,
surviving all the storms of revolution, war and state surveillance, continued until as late as 1819. Although her principal salon took place on

Sunday nights, the American poet Joel Barlow wrote in 1802, 'I believe she has a party every night – 30 or 40 or 50, chiefly English'.[17] Barlow later complained, 'Helen really runs us down with her great parties . . . It is quite stifling. English lords & ladies, Italian princes and duchesses brought together to inhale each other's exhalations & judge of the state of each other's lungs by a free exchange of expired gasses, compliments and politics.'[18] Also in 1802 Hester Piozzi sneeringly described Williams's salon as 'the resort of a literary côterie, all malcontents, who tell those that get into their circle what a short duration the present order of things [i.e. the Napoleonic consulate] will be granted, and what happy days await France when the next change takes place'.[19] Given that English visitors that same year included Charles James Fox and Lord Holland, Piozzi's party colours are here all too evident.

Salon women were often condemned by opponents of the Revolution as *précieuses* and accused of 'artifice and authorship of stylised discursive practices in conflict with nature'.[20] Elizabeth Bohls describes Williams's prose style – no less than her style of sociability – as 'closer to *précocité* than to the universalist rhetoric of Revolutionary reason. Her calculated refusal to take part in abstract political discourse ironically aligns her with a pre-Revolutionary French type of the powerful public woman',[21] rather than, say, with the rationalism of Wollstonecraft's *Vindication of the Rights of Woman*. We get a sense of the difference of Wollstonecraft's judgement of Williams when she encountered her in Paris: 'her manners are affected, yet the simple goodness of her hearts [sic] continually breaks through the varnish'.[22] Crabb Robinson, visiting her salon in 1814, noted: 'her chin is very long and an almost perpetual smile does not bring it within ordinary bounds . . . She talks freely on political subjects to us without restraint.' He was also surprised to note that she had never heard of William Wordsworth, despite the fact that Wordsworth's first published poem (in 1787) was addressed to 'Helen Maria Williams weep[ing] at a Tale of Distress'.[23]

In the 1800s, then, Williams's salon was 'chiefly composed of liberal republicans and anti-Bonapartists',[24] and she had links with the *ideologue* circle centred on the salon of Madame Helvetius. Regulars at her Sunday night salon at number 38, rue de l'Echiquier (where she had moved from the rue Helvetius – Stone lived in the same street, but not the same house) included Pierre-Louis Ginguené, the painter J.-A. Desrivières Gérard, the political economist J.-B. Say, Benjamin Constant, Carnot, Gregoire de Rostrenen, André-Marie Chénier, Bernardin de Saint Pierre, Tadeusz Kósciuszko, the natural philosopher Georges Cuvier, as well as Alexander von Humboldt and his travelling companion Aimé Bonpland, after their return from the Americas in 1805. After the fall of Napoleon, her salon was visited by a spate of English and American literati, including Samuel Rogers, Robert Southey (who specifically attended in May 1817 in the hope of meeting Humboldt), Wordsworth, Crabb Robinson, John Thelwall and George Ticknor. A clue to the problem of how she managed to finance these large social gatherings after the collapse of the printing business in 1813 is suggested by Lady Morgan's observation (she herself attended Williams's salon in 1816) that the Paris intellectual salon was notable for its lack of social ostentation: 'The women go in *demi-toilette*; and as, in Paris, illumination is extremely cheap, and the apartments always well-lighted, the whole additional expense of the *soirée* is included in tea, or some very slight refreshment, served a little before midnight. Society is therefore not a point of competition, but a source of genuine enjoyment.'[25]

The frequent attendance of Humboldt at Williams's salon suggests a probable source for the connection between Williams and Stone and the Humboldt printing project, although the English Press, from its inception, had anxiously sought travel accounts for its list, as the most lucrative publications of the period.[26] The image of Humboldt as a misogynist workaholic buried in his library is belied by George Ticknor's description of his stellar performances in the Parisian salons. Visiting Madame de Staël's salon (run by her daughter, the Duchess de Broglie) in May 1817, the young American scholar met Benjamin Constant, Jacques de Lacretelle, and A. W. Schlegel, 'assembled to hear the Baron de Humboldt read some passages out of an unpublished volume of his travels'. Ticknor was overwhelmed by Humboldt's 'genius and modesty, and his magical descriptions of the scenery of the Orinoco, and the holy solitudes of nature, and the missionaries'.[27] The unpublished volume from which Humboldt read was probably the fifth volume of the *Personal Narrative*, not published in English until 1821. Did Humboldt perhaps compose the 'autobiographical' portion of his travels based on his field journals (abandoned after five years' intense work, begun almost a decade after his return from America) at the behest of *salonnières* like the Duchess de Broglie or Helen Maria Williams? Was the introduction of a sentimental aesthetic into the highly technical mineralogical, botanical and meteorological treatises composing the major part of the *Voyage*, influenced by the performative context of the salons? We have to be open to the possibility of a collaborative (and through the social milieu of the Paris salons) female sponsorship for at least the public, exoteric portion of Humboldt's work.[28]

If Williams the *salonnière* combined sociability, the exchange of ideas and good business by forging an important author/publisher/printer network, after the bankruptcy she was left with translation alone in order to recoup some of her financial losses incurred in printing Humboldt's work. Judging from a letter of March 1818, Humboldt himself helped Williams out, particularly after Stone's death in the same year, in trying to arrange decent financial terms for her from the publishers of the English translation, Longmans. Unfortunately, as she put it wistfully in a letter of March 1818 to Crabb Robinson, 'the only thing in heaven or earth that M. Humboldt does not understand is business', going on to describe how she had 'acquiesced in conditions with which I was little satisfied'.[29] By this time she had also inherited Stone's debts, and visitors of the 1820s record the poverty in which she lived in the years before her death in 1827. Translating Humboldt must have been an onerous task, despite that fact that she was helped with scientific technicalities by her nephew Charles Coquerel, at the time studying with Parisian savants Joseph-Louis Gay-Lussac, André-Louis Ampère, and François Arago, and her work was corrected by Humboldt himself, by all accounts the most meticulous of critics. But in the very act of translation, Williams appropriated Humboldt's text for non-specialist and women readers, writing proudly in her preface: 'my scanty knowledge of the first principles of science seemed to preclude the full comprehension of many of the subjects which he treats; but a short experience convinced me, that what is clearly expressed must be clearly understood' (vol. I, p. x). The quality of her translation was outstanding, as reviewers in both the *Monthly* and the *Edinburgh Review* acknowledged.[30]

We can now see Williams's translations as rooted in the salon culture which she so actively promoted, but the motive for undertaking the onerous project was financial necessity resulting from the failure of her shared printing business. The picture of post-Revolutionary Williams which is emerging is hardly that of a woman confined to the domestic sphere, confirming Vivien Jones's characterisation of Williams's later work as reflecting 'the pervasive transgression of gendered ideological and generic boundaries'.[31] There seems however to have been another, different, but equally pragmatic reason for her undertaking this immense labour of translation: political repression. In 1795, Williams had published a translation of her friend Bernardin Saint-Pierre's sentimental novel *Paul et Virginie*, during her imprisonment in the Luxembourg under Robespierre's Terror. The novel's tropical setting in Mauritius and the utopian, matriarchal upbringing of the two children offers a powerful

contrast to the dark shades of the masculinist Terror of which Williams
was then a victim. The tragic ending of *Paul et Virginie* indicted the social
vanity and oppressive hierarchies of the *ancien régime*, in many ways rem-
iniscent of the Du Fossé narrative in the first volume of Williams's *Letters
from France*. In a sense the real hero of the Du Fossé story is the French
Revolution; in this light, Williams's translation of the pre-Revolutionary
Paul et Virginie makes out a continuing case in favour of the Revolution at
a time when most of its anti-Robespierre partisans feared it had failed.
In her preface to *Paul and Virginia*, Williams described how under the
Jacobin yoke 'the resources of writing, and even of reading, were encompassed with danger'.[32] Translation remains the sole resource for the
writer in this situation; a form of publication which displaces authorship
thereby avoiding the risks of prosecution. As Gary Kelly puts it 'Williams
[here] turned her translation into an act of political defiance, another
expression of her feminization of Revolution'.[33]

A similar climate of political repression seems to have motivated
Williams's undertaking of the Humboldt translation, begun in the last
four or five years of the Napoleonic Empire. Indeed she would publish
nothing authored by herself between 1803 and Bonaparte's downfall in
1815. As we will see in the next section, Bonaparte had been the hero of
Williams's 1798 *Tour in Switzerland*, but as she put it many years later in
the preface to her 1823 volume of poems, his 'imperial purple at length
cured my enthusiasm, and no odes of my inditing hailed his coronation,
or his marriage'.[34] According to Stone, Bonaparte was outraged by
Williams's refusal to name him in her 1801 *Ode to the Peace*, but clearly the
main problem lay in her republican politics and the dissidents who con-
gregated in her influential salon. After Napoleon's downfall she wrote of
these years, 'the iron rod of despotism crushed my soul and deprived it
of energy'.[35] This was perhaps more than slightly disingenuous given
that Williams's and Stone's printing press was doing lucrative business
printing tax and excise papers for the Napoleonic government in the
years 1809–12, as described above. Nevertheless, turning once again to
translation, and once again (as she had done in *Paul and Virginia*) to a tropical paradise, Williams found in Humboldt's South America, on the eve
of republican liberty, a symbol of hope and a striking contrast to 'the terrible page of our history' (*Personal Narrative*, vol. 1, p. v). The French
Revolution might have suffered terrible set-backs, but the South
American revolutions which she had invoked many years before in her
1787 poem *Peru* were now a reality rather than a dream. As she put in
her preface to the *Personal Narrative*, 'with what soothing emotions, what

eager delight, do we follow the traveller, who leads us from the cares, the sorrows, the joys of ordinary life, to wander in another hemisphere! to mark unknown forms of luxuriant beauty, and unknown objects of majestic greatness – to mark a new earth, and even new skies!' (vol. 1, p. v).

FROM ALPS TO CORDILLERAS: WILLIAMS AND HUMBOLDT AS TRAVEL WRITERS

A famous anecdote describes Humboldt's introduction to Bonaparte. 'So you are interested in botany? So is my wife'; and turning his back, the Emperor walked away. Mary Louise Pratt has criticised the scholarly obfuscation of Humboldt's homosexuality as a 'dirty secret', and linked his wanderlust to 'a need to escape the heterosexist and matrimonialist structures of bourgeois society'.[36] Although the homosocial nature of scientific travel provided cover for Humboldt and Bonpland, contemporaries sometimes surreptitiously drew attention to Humboldt's homosexuality; the *Quarterly Review*, for example, in 1816 punningly referred to Bonpland (rather conspicuously backgrounded by Humboldt in the *Personal Narrative*) as his 'sleeping partner'.[37] One looks in vain for any allusion, however veiled, to the travellers' sexuality in the *Personal Narrative*, although Humboldt's fascination with hermaphroditism is apparent at several points in a narrative which, with its hairy men of the woods, earth-eating Otomac Indians and Amazonian gynocracies, often bears more resemblance to Gabriel Garcia Marquez's *Hundred Years of Solitude* than to scientific ethnography. The third volume, for example, introduces Francisco Lozano, a Venezuelan *campesino* who had suckled a child with his own milk, digressing for four pages on the subject of men with breasts and male breast-feeding (pp. 47–52). Appropriately enough, in her translator's preface to *Personal Narrative*, Williams praised Humboldt's book as itself a form of discursive hermaphroditism, combining 'male' reason with 'female' sentiment: 'the faculty he possesses of raising the mind to general ideas, without neglecting individual facts; and while he appears only to address himself to our reason, he has the secret of awakening the imagination, and of being understood by the heart' (vol. 1, p. ix).

In this respect, Humboldt's whole enterprise can be linked to the philosophical turn taken by the late eighteenth-century culture of sensibility in Weimar Romanticism (in 1795 Humboldt had contributed an allegorical poem on the vital principle entitled *Der Rhodische Genius* to Friedrich

Schiller's journal *Die Horen*, as one of the few scientific contributors). In order better to understand the role of sensibility in the travel writing of Humboldt and Williams, I want to mention briefly Humboldt's experiments with the nervous system and galvanism (animal electricity) in the years before embarking for South America. Michael Dettelbach and Simon Schaffer have recently described these in some detail, particularly Humboldt's masochistic practice of galvanic self-experimentation. In one such experiment (Humboldt was frequently assisted by his lover, the Prussian guardsman Reinhard von Haeften), 'caustic plasters were applied to his back in order to raise large blisters and remove the skin; he then galvanised his wounds and recorded the effects and sensations on his body . . . he reopened the wounds frequently for demonstration'.[38] Schaffer describes how self-experimentation 'patently violated the distance between observer and object so carefully policed by Enlightenment systems of witnessing and authorising [representing] the emergence of a new form of scientific authority, the creative genius'.[39]

Humboldt's South American expedition represented another sort of self-experimentation, the eudiometers, hygrometers and cyanometers which accompanied him the equivalents of the earlier galvanic apparatus, precision instruments designed to gauge his own sensibility in relation to the ever-varying environmental stimuli of the tropics. For Humboldt, aesthetic and emotional responses to natural phenomena counted as data about these phenomena,[40] in contrast to their rigorous exclusion from contemporary practices of naval and military surveying. In her essay 'The Female Thermometer', Terry Castle connects the practice of calibration with the eighteenth-century culture of sensibility, citing Rousseau's desideratum (in *Reveries of a Solitary Walker*) to 'perform upon myself the sort of operation that physicists conduct upon the air in order to discover its daily fluctuations'. Her comment on Rousseau applies equally to Humboldt: 'he makes himself both the observer and the observed – masculine "physicien" and mood-driven woman. This newly self-regarding, ambisexual being might justly be called a female man.'[41] How appropriately, therefore, to find Byron in *Don Juan* borrowing Humboldt's cyanometer (an instrument for measuring the blueness of the sky) to calibrate the English Bluestockings; ('ye, who make the fortunes of all books, / benign ceruleans of the second sex!'[42]):

> Humboldt, 'the first of travellers', but not
> The last, if late accounts be accurate,
> Invented, by some name I have forgot,
> As well as the sublime discovery's date,

An airy instrument, with which he sought
To ascertain the atmospheric state,
By measuring the intensity of blue.
Oh Lady Daphne, let me measure you![13]

The philosophical calibration of sensibility – transgressing gendered boundaries by harmonising the general and the particular, reason and feeling – was an epistemological problem for public women like Helen Maria Williams as well as for feminised male subjects like Rousseau (at least as author of the *Reveries*) and Humboldt. Williams also sought to theorise sensibility as a strategy for revolutionary discourse, rather than subjecting it to critical reason like Mary Wollstonecraft in the *Vindication of the Rights of Woman* (although not, significantly, in her travelogue, *A Short Residence in Sweden*). We saw above how the discursive space opened by salon culture allowed for ongoing public/private discussion between men and women, mediating exchanges between natural philosophy, politics and taste, under the watchful tutelage of the ever-smiling *salonnière*. Although Williams represented her move from sensibility poetry to political polemic in the *Letters from France* as a move from private to public discourse, in fact a considerable number of her early poems had tackled public and historical themes by focusing on sentimental vignettes – a notable example being her 1786 poem *Peru* referred to above.

In the 1790 *Letters* Williams presented her personal, emotional involvement with the Du Fossé family tragedy as the originating motive for her interest in the French Revolution, and her discursive swerve from 'the poetry to the prose of human life'.[44] In the same volume she declared that 'my political creed is entirely an affair of the heart; for I have not been so absurd as to consult my head upon matters of which it is incapable of judging'.[45] Sensibility is the portal through which Williams here approaches the public, political domain, transforming a perceived (gendered) incapacity into a polemical strength. Like the field journals upon which Humboldt based his *Personal Narrative*, 'trac[ing] the first impressions, whether agreeable or painful, which I received from nature, or from man' (vol. i, p. xxxix), and thereby complementing 'nature's own narrative, spoken through his instruments',[46] Williams's *Letters from France* register at first hand her sensitive reaction to political events. If eighteenth-century epistolarity (as Janet Altman suggests) provides 'instruments' which monitor the ebb and flow of (a woman's) passions, Williams's *Letters* go further by analysing her cardiogrammatic fluctuations in relationship to the stimuli of revolutionary France.[47]

Williams's 1798 *Tour in Switzerland* similarly employs sensibility to legit-imise political judgement. Williams, John Hurford Stone and some members of her family had fled Paris for Switzerland in 1793 as political refugees. But the *Tour* was actually written in 1797 in a very different and more auspicious climate for them, on the eve of Bonaparte's invasion of the Swiss Cantons. In many respects it represented an anticipated apology for the French invasion of Switzerland in 1798 which so alien-ated Coleridge and other English republicans. Like Humboldt's Spanish America, Williams's Switzerland is at once a sublime natural spectacle and a cramped, archaic society on the eve of revolutionary change. Williams presents her readers with the conventional awed response to the Swiss Alps. But, as in the *Letters*, sensibility represents a starting point rather than a terminus of her writings: 'I should scarcely have presumed to obtrude that unfinished outline on the public eye, if the other parts of my journal offered nothing new to the observation', namely, 'an attempt to trace the important effects which the French Revolution has produced on that country, and which are about to unfold a new aera in its history'.[48]

Williams is sensitive to the social boundaries of picturesque viewing, noting for instance at the Falls of Schaffhausen that 'the artisan pursues his toil, regardless of the falling river . . . calculated to suspend all human activity in solemn and awful astonishment'.[49] In the mountains Williams suffers the gendered tension between aesthetic and scientific viewing practices, but skilfully manages to invoke the landscape in terms of both at once. Her 'mineralogical companion' (probably Hurford Stone) tries to explain alpine geology for her benefit: 'We had a long physical disqui-sition about quartz, mica, and schorl, which not being perfectly intelli-gible to me, I continued to gaze, with untired delight, on the scene around me, while these naturalists marched off to examine whether an adjoining mountain had most strata of white feld-spar or green granite. Without much knowledge, however, in the science of stones and rocks, the traveller cannot but observe with admiration the diversities of these inanimate objects as he passes along the road.'[50] Without straying over the bounds of allowable female discourse, Williams is here able to display her mastery of geological nomenclature, her disavowal of special knowledge notwithstanding.

In the second volume she follows a similar strategy in relation to the Alpine glaciers; appending her annotated translation of L. F. Ramond de Carbonnières' scientific *Observations on the Glaciers* to the volume, she inserts her *Hymn to the Glaciers* in the main text: 'Leaving to this charming writer the task of philosophical discussion, I shall here transcribe the hymn I composed on those Alpine summits.'[51] Again subscribing to a conventionally gendered division of knowledge, her agency as a translator and intellectual impresario is complemented by her self-presentation as an acute and feeling aesthetic subject. Rather than accepting the limitations of such a private role, however, she incorporates Ramond de Carbonnières' essay, making the *Tour in Switzerland* into a sort of composite text which, looking forward to Humboldt, struggles to harmonise the general and particular, knowledge and sensibility, reason and imagination. As Bohls has written of *Letters from France*, 'Events are refracted through several lenses . . . She embraces multiple authorship as she lets go the single, fixed consciousness of the safely distanced aesthetic spectator. History is no longer linear, but multiperspectival – subject to interpretation by, or negotiation among, any numbers of writers or readers.'[52] Ultimately, the real sublime evoked in the *Tour in Switzerland* is not discovered in the Alps but in the 'commanding genius' of Napoleon, portrayed as a feminised, sensitive liberator and admirer of the poetry of Ossian who is able to combine – in the way Williams's travel book has also sought to combine – aesthetic sensibility with intellectual power.[53] Williams would soon discover how wrong she had been about Bonaparte, that he had only read Ossian for the battle scenes. By this time, however, she had also discovered Humboldt, Napoleon's pacific, hermaphroditic, botanising double, who, 'struggling with the savageness of the untamed wilderness, obtains a victory that belongs to all mankind', as she put it in her preface to the *Personal Narrative*.

Mary Louise Pratt has described how Humboldt's travel narrative 'sought to reframe bourgeois subjectivity, heading off its sundering of objectivist and subjectivist strategies, science and sentiment, information and experience . . . he proposed to Europeans a new kind of planetary consciousness'. Humboldt was troubled by the fact that 'the interests of precision and those of the imagination are so often at odds . . . the accumulation demanded by measurement disturbs the particular repose [*Ruhe*] of the aspect of nature'.[54] In his introduction to the *Personal Narrative*, he explained the difficulties posed by the need to balance description with sequential narrative. Originally, Humboldt admitted that he had wished to avoid 'what is usually called the historical narrative of a journey . . . I had arranged the facts, not in the order in which they successively presented themselves, but according to the relation they bore to each other' (vol. 1, p. xxxviii). Humboldt's precise calibrations of nature seemed to leave little room for literary content, although in his *Relation historique* and other more exoteric parts of the *Voyage* he struggled hard to harmonise measurement and imagination. Yet as a product of Weimar culture and a *habitué* of the female public sphere of the Paris salons, Humboldt lamented the costs to imagination of scientific precision in modern travel writing: 'in proportion as voyages have been made by persons more enlightened, and whose views have been directed towards researches into descriptive natural history, geography, or political economy, itineraries have partly lost that unity of composition, and that simplicity, which characterised them in former ages (vol. I, p. xlii). The reluctant composition of the *Personal Narrative* (Humboldt completed the seven volumes in five years, but apparently suppressed the manuscript describing the final section of his travels in Ecuador, Peru and Mexico) was, he admitted, undertaken as 'a kind of duty owed to the public' (vol. I, p. xxxix). I speculated above that it might have been a duty urged upon him by *salonnières* like Helen Maria Williams, and that Humboldt's particular combination of precision and imagination was stimulated by the performative contexts of the salons.

It is ironic that as the orb of Humboldt's fame mounted during the nineteenth century, the memory of his *unheimlich*, un-English, un-domesticated translator Helen Maria Williams dwindled into the obscurity recorded in the *Monthly Review*'s 1828 obituary. When Thomasina Ross prepared a new translation of the *Personal Narrative* in 1852, this time abridged of the troublesome scientific detail which placed the work beyond the reach of the proper lady reader, she had only a critical word to spare for her predecessor's success in 'Englishing' Humboldt: 'Though faultless as respects correctness of interpretation, it abounds in foreign turns of expression, and is somewhat deficient in that fluency of style without which a translated work is unsatisfactory to the English reader.'[55]

NOTES

1 *Monthly Review* (January 1828), 139.
2 Gary Kelly, *Women, Writing and Revolution 1790–1827* (Oxford: Clarendon Press 1993), p. 77.
3 *The Intimate Letters of Hester Piozzi and Penelope Pennington 1788–1821*, ed. O. G. Knapp (London: Bodley Head, 1914), p. 156.
4 Kelly, *Women, Writing, Revolution*; Mary Favret, *Romantic Correspondence: Women, Politics and the Fiction of Letters* (Cambridge: Cambridge University Press, 1993), chapter 3; Vivien Jones, 'Women Writing Revolution: Narratives of History and Sexuality in Wollstonecraft and Williams' in *Beyond Romanticism: New Approaches to Texts and Contexts 1780–1832*, ed. Stephen Copley and John

Whale (London and New York: Routledge, 1992), pp. 178–99; Elizabeth Bohls, *Women Travel Writers and the Language of Aesthetics 1716–1818* (Cambridge: Cambridge University Press, 1995), chapter 4; Chris Jones, *Radical Sensibility: Literature and Ideas in the 1790s* (London and New York: Routledge, 1993), chapter 5.

5 Lionel Woodward, *Une Anglaise Amie de la Revolution Francaise: Hélène-Marie Williams et ses Amis* (Paris, 1930).

6 Alexander De Humboldt and Aimé Bonpland, *Personal Narrative of Travels to the Equinoctial Regions of the New Continent, During the Years 1799–1804 . . . Translated into English by Helen Maria Williams*, 7 vols. (London: Longman, Rees, Orme et al., 1814–29), vol. I, pp. vi–vii.

7 *Monthly Review* 79 (Jan 1816), p. 15.

8 Lori Chamberlain, 'Gender and the Metaphorics of Translation', *Signs* 13 (Spring 1988), p. 445. Thanks to Gary Kelly for this reference.

9 *Life of Alexander Von Humboldt*, ed. Karl Bruhns, trans. Jane and Caroline Lassell, 2 vols. (London 1873), vol. II, p. 20.

10 Joan Landes, *Women and the Public Sphere in the Age of the French Revolution* (Ithaca and London: Cornell University Press, 1988), pp. 28, 30.

11 Landes, *Women and the Public Sphere*, p. 38.

12 Dena Goodman, 'Enlightenment Salons: The Convergence of Female and Philosophic Ambitions', *Eighteenth Century Studies* 22.3 (1989), 329–50, pp. 340–1.

13 David Erdman, *Commerce des Lumières: John Oswald and the British in Paris, 1792–3* (Columbia: University of Missouri Press, 1986), pp. 230–1.

14 Madeleine B. Sterne, 'The English Press in Paris and its Successors, 1793–1852', *Papers of the Bibliographical Society of America* 74.4 (1980), 307–59, p. 345.

15 It is strange that Lionel Woodward misses this in his account of Stone's involvement in the Humboldt printing industry, although he does acknowledge that Stone's successful printing business at 939 rue de Vaugirard must at least have been co-run by Williams, on account of her frequent reference in correspondence to 'notre imprimerie'. Woodward, *Une Anglaise*, p. 171.

16 Sterne, 'The English Press', p. 349.

17 Quoted in M. Ray Adams, 'Helen Maria Williams and the French Revolution', in *Wordsworth and Coleridge: Studies in Honour of George Mclean Harper*, ed. E. L. Griggs, (Princeton: Princeton University Press, 1939), pp. 87–117, p. 89.

18 Quoted in Sterne, 'The English Press', p. 314.

19 Knapp, *Intimate Letters*, p. 248.

20 Landes, *Women in the Public Sphere*, p. 28.

21 Bohls, *Women Travel Writers*, p. 125

22 Quoted in Kelly, *Women, Writing, Revolution*, p. 49.

23 Woodward, *Une Anglaise*, pp. 178–9.

24 Kelly, *Women, Writing, Revolution*, p. 200.

25 Lady Morgan, *France*, 4th edn, 2 vols. (London 1818), vol. I, p. 419.

26 As early as 1794 Stone was asking his brother to make inquiries about English travel accounts which could be translated into French and published by the Press in Paris for 'a speedy sale'. Sterne, 'The English Press', p. 320.

27 *Life, Letters and Journals of George Ticknor*, 2 vols. (Boston 1876), vol. I, p. 134.

28 This is not to say that Humboldt had not intended from the start to write a 'personal narrative', however reluctant he was to put the plan into action or indeed to bring it to a satisfactory termination. In a letter written in Havana on 21 February 1801 to the German botanist Karl Willdenow, he announced his intention of publishing his scientific observations in separate volumes aimed at the specialist, whereas, by contrast, 'my personal narrative . . . will only contain material of interest to the cultivated reader: physical and moral observations, language, manners, the commercial relations of colonies and cities, landscape description, agriculture, the altitudes of mountains . . . meteorology'. Alejandro de Humboldt, *Cartas Americanas*, ed. Charles Minguet, trans. Marta Traba (Caracas: Biblioteca Ayacucho, 1980), p. 64. The Caracas edition is now the standard scholarly text of Humboldt's American correspondence. My own translation.

29 Woodward, *Une Anglaise*, p. 184.

30 *Monthly Review* 79 (Jan 1816); *Edinburgh Review* 49 (June 1815), p. 111.

31 Vivien Jones, 'Women Writing Revolution', p. 179.

32 *Paul and Virginia, translated from the French by Helen Maria Williams* (London, 1795), p. iv.

33 Kelly, *Women, Writing, Revolution*, p. 56.

34 *Poems on Various Subjects, with Introductory Remarks on the Present State of Literature and Science in France* (London, 1823), p. xlii.

35 Woodward, *Anglaise*, p. 174.

36 Mary Louise Pratt, *Imperial Eyes: Studies in Travel Writing and Transculturation* (London: Routledge, 1992), pp. 111, 240.

37 *Quarterly Review* (Jan 1816), 369. The reviewer was the South African traveller John Barrow. There is in fact no evidence that Humboldt and Bonpland were lovers, although Humboldt's infatuation for the young Ecuadorian nobleman Carlos Montufar, who joined the expedition in 1801, is implicit.

38 Michael Dettelbach, *Romanticism and Administration: Mining, Galvinism and Oversight in Alexander von Humboldt's Global Physics* (unpublished Ph.D. dissertation, Cambridge University, 1994), p. 88.

39 Quoted in Dettelbach, *Romanticism and Administration*. See also Simon Schaffer, 'Genius in Romantic natural philosophy', in Andrew Cunningham and Nicholas Jardine, eds., *Romanticism and the Sciences* (Cambridge: Cambridge University Press, 1990), pp. 82–98, p. 92.

40 Malcolm Nicholson, 'Alexander von Humboldt and the Geography of Vegetation' in Cunningham and Jardine, eds., *Romanticism and the Sciences*, pp. 169–85, p. 180.

41 Terry Castle, 'The Female Thermometer', in *The Female Thermometer: 18th-Century Culture and the Invention of the Uncanny* (New York and Oxford: Oxford University Press, 1995), pp. 21–43, p. 35.

42 Byron, *Don Juan*, ed. T. G. Steffan, E. Steffan and W. W. Pratt (Harmondsworth: Penguin 1973), p. 108.

43 Byron, *Don Juan*, p. 112. Some variants of the last line were 'I'll back a London "Bas" against Peru'; 'A London "bas" will beat thy sky Peru'; 'I'll bet some pair of Stockings beat Peru'. Byron, *Don Juan*, p. 633.

44 Helen Maria Williams, *Letters from France* (8 vols. in 2), facsimile reproduction with an introduction by Janet Todd (Delmar, N.Y.: Scholars Facsimiles, 1975), vol. I, pp. 195–6.

45 Ibid., vol. I, p. 66.

46 Michael Dettelbach, 'Global Physics and Aesthetic Empire: Humboldt's Physical Portrait of the Tropics', in David Miller and Peter Reill, eds., *Visions of Empire: Voyages, Botany, and Representations of Nature* (Cambridge: Cambridge University Press, 1996), pp. 258–92, p. 271.

47 Favret, *Romantic Correspondence*, p. 57, quoting Janet Altman, *Epistolarity: Approaches to a Form* (Columbus: Ohio State University Press, 1982), p. 179.

48 *A Tour in Switzerland*, 2 vols. (London: G. G. & J. Robinson, 1798), vol. I, p. 63.

49 Ibid., vol. I, p. 63.

50 Ibid., vol. I, p. 184.

51 Ibid., vol. II, p. 15.

52 Bohls, *Women Travel Writers*, p. 128.

53 See for example, *Tour in Switzerland*, vol. II, p. 56.

54 Pratt, *Imperial Eyes*, pp. 119, 271.

55 Thomasina Ross, 'Translator's Preface', in Humboldt and Bonpland, *Personal Narrative of Travels to the Equinoctial Regions of America*, 3 vols. (abridged), (London: G. Bohn, 1852). Williams does not come off much better in the introductory remarks to the most recent, 1995 translation of the *Personal Narrative* by Jason Wilson. Wilson describes her translation as 'a faithful version close to [Humboldt's] French except when Humboldt enthused – then his translator interpreted and exaggerated'. One needs to add: *with Humboldt's blessing* – taking account of the fact of the latter's excellent knowledge of English as well as his personal involvement in Williams's translation. Might one not conceive of Williams's work as a *collaboration* with Humboldt rather than simply replicating the gendered metaphor of fidelity or infidelity to a masculine original? *Personal Narrative*, trans. Jason Wilson with an introduction by Malcolm Nicholson (Harmondsworth: Penguin, 1995), p. lix.

PART IV

The female subject

CHAPTER TEN

The most public sphere of all: the family

Sylvana Tomaselli

Our tendency to equate the private with the domestic sphere, and with the family in particular, is at best problematic. More often than not it blinds us to our predecessors' attempts to define or redefine the nature of the public domain, as well as to their analyses of the nature of the family and of membership within it. Above all, it limits our capacity to understand the realm of mores, morals and education with which women have been particularly identified for centuries. To think of the family as an exclusively private domain has very wide-ranging philosophical and political implications. As the idea of relegation to the family retains its currency, it is especially important that the twin issues of the connection between the family and other social institutions and of the family's status in intellectual history be left as open as such matters ever can be. This is particularly true when studying periods in which the possibility and necessity of participation in political life were (or are) themselves open to debate, as was certainly the case during the long Enlightenment.

Much was written in the eighteenth century about the relationship between levels of civilisation, forms of government, economic development and the condition of woman. Her treatment by man, as well as of him, the extent and nature of her contribution to the domestic and market economy, together with her participation in the growth of culture and in various types of government were traced, especially by French and Scottish theorists, in conjectural histories which examined the development of man, woman and their relations at different stages from a primitive condition to commercial society. More widely in Europe, compilations of biographies of eminent women throughout the ages continued to be produced as part of an enduring debate about women's capacity to display the heroic virtues. The ancient world remained the subject of deep interest throughout Europe. Comparisons between it and the modern world were drawn at all levels, including their respective aesthetic achievements, their patriotism, mores, education, religion and family structures.

Moreover, a general fear of population decline amongst political theorists and within government circles, and, in the reading public at large, a passion for the exotic, led to an increased interest in accounts of polygamy, fertility, marital ceremonies and familial arrangements in different parts of the world. Also of great interest throughout the eighteenth century was the alleged correlation between political and domestic freedom, between 'moderate' commercial monarchies and the emancipation of women from violence, denigration and seclusion. This issue was woven into that of the relationship between political and civil liberties and hence also into the debate about the possibility of there being a flourishing civil society in the absence of political participation by the citizenry (however widely or narrowly construed). The question was therefore not only whether, when looking at the history of woman from the state of nature to the present time, her condition could be said to have improved, but also whether the same could be said when looking at history only from ancient (rather than prehistoric) times; it surfaced again when looking at her status under the various forms of governments in different parts of the world.

The extensive literature which these interests and concerns generated provides part of the intricate intellectual context within which the pronouncements of eighteenth-century writers tackling the woman question need to be read. To this sketch much, of course, would need to be added, not least more specifically literary debates, especially those surrounding the cult of sensibility. The same holds for works of a pedagogical nature, as they offer a privileged insight into the kind of human character idealised in the period. Nor can philosophical discussions about the relations between mind and body or about the way of ideas in epistemological treatises be omitted from the grand picture. While many writers benefit from such a backdrop, Mary Wollstonecraft does so more particularly, partly because she was more widely read than might be assumed – if only owing to her need to earn a living as a reviewer and translator – and partly also because she was directly involved in cosmopolitan issues and discussions. As she was an active participant in the controversy surrounding the French Revolution, it would not be amiss to recall the larger canvas of the Enlightenment in which she should be seen as an important figure and within which her views should be placed. This is made more especially necessary given what might otherwise seem her rather unexpected introduction of the subjects of the treatment of children, marriage, female education and the family in her *Vindication of the Rights of Men* (1790), a denunciation of Edmund Burke's *Reflections on the Revolution in France* (1790).

If one forgets for a moment that she was to be the author of the *Vindication of the Rights of Woman* (1792), and succeeds in resisting the considerable power of her rhetoric, the presence of women in her first *Vindication* comes somewhat as a surprise. In fact, few theorists were as effective and clear-minded in the eighteenth century as Wollstonecraft was in placing (or maintaining) the family at the heart of political reform and in pursuing Enlightenment issues within the social and political context of the revolutionary years. While women and the family were ubiquitous in social and political writings in the eighteenth century, Wollstonecraft is noteworthy for her insistence in her first two political works that this continue, and that the political debate not be narrowed as she perceived it had been when she entered the fray. She kept it open to reveal the family at its heart, portraying the family as the unit of the social and moral reproduction of society. This unit consisted of a husband and a wife, a father and a mother, a citizen married to a citizen, a Christian married to a Christian, a companion married to another. What she contended was that husbands' and wives' perceptions of themselves and of each other were the building-blocks of society, and that the condition of women was the true and only starting point of social and political change, however limited or ambitious. In so arguing, she obliterated the separation between the moral and the political, and while she was not alone in this venture, few were as vigorous in it as she was. Moreover, few since then have been as determined to show that women's conception of themselves and of the good life is the decisive factor in the overall nature of the polity. This said, her writings took on the form they did for circumstantial reasons.

Milton apart, the political theorists with whom Wollstonecraft was principally engaged were Richard Price, Adam Smith, Edmund Burke and Jean-Jacques Rousseau. Although Burke remained the most important of these, well beyond her response to his *Reflections*, the person she was in most ardent disagreement with when it came to women and the family was Rousseau. This is patently obvious from the *Vindication of the Rights of Woman* (1792). What is a little less obvious is that the argument between them went beyond pointing to the inanity of Rousseau's prescribed education for Sophie in *Emile* (1762) and the attendant views about women. Wollstonecraft was deeply disappointed with Rousseau, as she was, albeit for different reasons, with other interlocutors, notably

Burke. In Rousseau's case, the disappointment was that peculiar to the disciple. He troubled her. For he had the making, within his own political thought, of the solution to the problem of civilisation, a problem which he had diagnosed as early as 1750 in his *Discours sur les Sciences et les Arts* – a problem and a text which Wollstonecraft took very seriously indeed.[1]

The *Discours* was the award-winning submission to a competition set by the Academy of Dijon. The essay question it had set was: 'Si le rétablissement des Sciences et des Arts a contribué à épurer les moeurs.' In his preface to the published text, Rousseau described it 'as one of the greatest and most beautiful questions which has ever been debated'.[2] It was not, he remarked, a mere metaphysical issue, but one which bore on the happiness of mankind. He also spoke of what he presumed to be his controversial and unexpected stance. Anticipating consternation, he presented himself as independent-minded and courageous. His further declaration of the minor changes he had made to the work allowed him to claim the added virtues of 'equity, respect and gratitude', as these alterations might prove unacceptable to the Academie.[3] This was therefore a grand question, whose answer was given by an author embodying great virtues.

The style of Rousseau's self-presentation is of consequence beyond our understanding of the *Discours*, for Wollstonecraft was to paint herself likewise. It was as a bold champion of virtue addressing men of virtue that Rousseau spoke of those happy nations in which virtue was, or had been, taught as science was taught in theirs (vol. III, p. 11), and it was as such that he bemoaned the growth of modes of politeness which gave individuals the appearance of being virtuous without possessing a single virtue (pp. 5–11). Moreover, the uniformity amongst men engendered by the world of politeness and propriety stifled, he claimed, unadorned but true genius and perverted natural goodness. As health resided in the strength and vigour of the body, so virtue was the strength and vigour of the soul, but the advancement of the arts and sciences, based as they were on falsehood and pretence, weakened both the body and the soul. Human nature, he owned, might not have been better in the age of virtue, but a far greater sense of security prevailed, because men found it easy to know one another and this long-lost advantage spared them many vices (p. 8). The toll which urbanity and decorum exacted was measured in the loss of true friendship, real esteem and trust between men. Whatever might be said in praise of society as it now was could easily be countered by the realisation of the terrible moral cost on which such seeming achievements were grounded. Thus, the modern world of facile but false relations might be one which would see the end of overt hatred not only between individuals (who would resort to more devious means of expressing contempt) but also between nations. With the hatred of other nations, however, the patriotic love of one's country would also be extinguished (pp. 8–9).

Idleness combined with vanity, Rousseau argued, gave birth to the arts and sciences and, worse still for mores, to luxury. Whereas ancient political theory was primarily concerned with mores and virtue, modern political theorists spoke of nothing but commerce and money (p. 19). This degraded the human spirit and made it almost impossible for artists to transcend the mediocrity of their times. They, like everyone else around them, sought only to please, and men sought to please women more especially (p. 21). Luxury, which led to the dissolution of morals, led also to the debasement of taste, to effeminacy and weakness. Only in simple societies were courage, martial virtues and patriotism to be seen. Not all was necessarily entirely lost. The course of luxury, artifice and display might be curtailed. Virtue could be encouraged to blossom again, true merit rewarded, and the sumptuary laws, which had been discarded, might be re-introduced. Women might be instrumental in this reversal, for in a footnote to the passage in which he had deplored the way in which taste was vitiated by men's desire to please women, Rousseau noted that he did not begrudge women their power over men. It could be made to lead to as much good as it had led to evil. Given a better education, women could be of immense advantage to society:

Men will always do what pleases women: if you really want them to be grand and virtuous, teach women what a grand soul and virtue are. The reflections which this subject affords, and which Plato produced in ancient times, would truly merit to be developed at great length by a pen worthy of writing according to such a master and of defending such a great cause. (p. 21n)

The pen was to be Wollstonecraft's, the master she was to follow Aristotle as much as Plato. The prompting, as is surmised below, was not to be entirely Rousseau's.

While Wollstonecraft was not at one with Rousseau on the origins of the arts and sciences and their role in ushering in and fostering artifice and politeness,[1] she condemned contemporary conditions no less vehemently than he. Her criticisms of society were extensive and her longing for a world of virtue ran very deep. For Rousseau, this longing took mostly, although not solely, the form of nostalgia. For Wollstonecraft it became visionary. As she was to put it in her second *Vindication*:

Rousseau exerts himself to prove that all *was* right originally; a crowd of authors that all *is* now right; and I, that all will *be* right.[5]

In her two *Vindications*, she entertained a conception of the world in which man and woman would cease to *appear*; they would *be*. And they would seek to be virtuous and be governed by their sense of duty. They would have a right to what was conducive to their understanding of the nature of their duties and the performance of them. This would be a world in which there was no demarcation of a private from a public sphere. Unlike the society she knew, it would be a state in which human beings would not think of themselves independently of their familial status and the responsibilities which went with it. Men and women would answer to being what they were: fathers, mothers, daughters, husbands, as the case would be. They would be one with themselves and devoid of the elaborate masks which polished society demanded of its members. Crucially, they would be capable of friendship, knowing where they stood and being what they seemed. The world as it was, whether in the closet, the family, the market place or the Houses of Parliament, was a hall of mirrors, in which all sense of appearance's relation to reality had long been lost and with it the trust vital to all meaningful ties between human beings. Vanity ensnared all in a web of deceptions and ruled unchecked. Wollstonecraft wrote to shatter the looking-glass and promote the advent of the age of virtue, Christian and civic combined.[6]

Her thoroughgoing critique of civilisation, consumption and commerce was neither unique nor original. She followed Rousseau, but also took her descriptions and much of her understanding of the psychological, social and economic mechanisms involved in commercial society from Adam Smith, especially his *Theory of Moral Sentiments* (1759). Moved by a belief that things could be otherwise, what she contributed through her *Vindications* was her own comprehension of the genesis and development of the modern self within the context of the family and marriage in a society devoted to increasing material wealth measured in the availability of consumable goods. In deploring the moral consequences of a society unashamedly based on the pursuit of insatiable desires and especially, though not solely, acquisitive ones, her target was women. Like all Enlightenment writers, be they critics or defenders of the progress of commerce and civilisation, Wollstonecraft identified women with the growth of luxury and false needs.[7] They sustained the multiplication of artificial needs and their children grew up to do likewise.

Her stance was that of a Christian and, to some extent, a Stoic. As has been mentioned already, she described the kind of human beings a society of this type fostered in Rousseauvian combined with Smithian terms, that is, as beings who lived *to appear* and who gauged their sense of worth by the approving gaze they met from other similarly fashion-crazed individuals. There was no feeling of sympathy in her account of the behaviour of those who betrayed an obsessive need for approval other than the respect equals pay one another in mutual recognition of a shared common purpose, in this case, the endeavour to live their lives as God-fearing creatures. Her revulsion found a theoretical expression which led her to outline the means for a moral rejuvenation of society, a project which she, *pace* Rousseau or Smith, believed could be effected. Wants could be contracted, and the poor given greater comforts than they presently enjoyed by granting them land or, as she put it, by allowing the industrious peasant 'to steal a farm from the heath'.[8] What is more, she thought she was holding up an inherently desirable model of a human being, for the simple reason that only the pursuit of this ideal would lead to genuine happiness.[9]

To the degree that the two *Vindications* bring to mind a vision of a better world they do so by evoking a predominantly agrarian society, marked by neither an intense division of labour, nor standing armies, nor luxury, nor, in short, any of what were then considered the most salient features of large commercial societies. Wollstonecraft's subsequent and only other major non-fictional works, *An Historical and Moral View of the Origin and Progress of the French Revolution* (1794) and *Letters Written During A Short Residence in Sweden, Norway and Denmark* (1796), force one to think again, but not because Wollstonecraft changed her mind about speculation, wealth and commerce. To understand any aspect of her thought, let alone its overall trajectory, the precise point of her entry into political discourse must always be kept in mind.

In the December 1789 issue of the *Analytical Review*, Wollstonecraft commented on a sermon by an old friend, *A Discourse on the Love of our Country, delivered on Nov. 4, 1789*: Richard Price's address to the Revolution Society in commemoration of the events of 1688. In 1788, three resolutions had been passed by the Society which Price effectively reiterated and Wollstonecraft highlighted in her review article. To begin with, she applauded Price's unaffected style, his account of true patriotism as 'the result of reason, not the undirected impulse of nature, ever tending to selfish extremes', and his defence of Christianity's prescription of universal benevolence against those who argued such sentiment to be incompatible with the love of one's country. She quoted him as saying: 'Our first concern, as lovers of our country, must be to *enlighten* it.'[10] Three lengthy quotations made up the rest of her review. In the first, Price reasserted the gist of the 1788 resolutions by defining liberty of conscience as a sacred right, defending the right of resistance, and describing civil authority as 'a delegation from the people'.[11]

Of Burke's reaction to Price we need only recall that far from narrowing the range of issues which Price's *Discourse* afforded, Burke widened by several orders of magnitude the debate which the preacher had opened. So did Wollstonecraft. Her *Vindication* followed Burke's argument almost point by point. In the thick of it, Wollstonecraft took more than one shot at Burke's manliness and patriotism. This said, the *Vindication of the Rights of Men* is more than an attack on Burke. Through it, and indeed also through the *Vindication of the Rights of Woman*, Wollstonecraft was responding to Price. She was answering his call, as a lover of her country, to enlighten it, and, by the same token, heeding another of his appeals, but not without showing the fundamental moral misapprehension its formulation revealed him to be labouring under. For after impressing on his audience their duty to transmit the blessings obtained by the Glorious Revolution to posterity, 'unimpaired and improved', Price had entreated his listeners in the following terms:

But, brethren, while we thus shew our patriotic zeal, let us take care not to disgrace the cause of patriotism, by any licentiousness, or immoral conduct. Oh! how earnestly do I wish that all who profess zeal in this cause were as distinguished by the purity of their morals as some of them are by their abilities, and that I could make them sensible of the advantages they would derive from a virtuous character, and of the suspicions they incur and the loss of consequence they suffer by wanting it. Oh! that I could see in men who oppose tyranny in the state a disdain of the tyranny of low passions in themselves, or, at least, such a sense of shame and regard to public order and decency as would induce them to *hide* their irregularities and to avoid insulting the virtuous part of the community by an open exhibition of vice! I cannot reconcile myself to the idea of an immoral patriot, or to that separation of private from public virtue, which some think to be possible.[12]

Like Rousseau's first *Discours*, Price's sermon wove patriotism and virtue into one subject. Like Rousseau, Price extended an invitation of sorts in deploring the want of virtue in society. Rousseau's was to consider how women might teach men to be virtuous and great. Price enjoined patriots not to be licentious. *A Vindication of the Rights of Woman* is an answer to both men, one Wollstonecraft had begun to sketch in *A Vindication of the Rights of Men*. The idea of an immoral patriot was to prove more abhorrent still to Wollstonecraft than to Price. Her response to Price, and by the same token to Rousseau, was to give the conditions under which patriots would be moral and the moral patriotic.

In the first *Vindication*, however, it was Burke who bore the brunt of her wider moral indignation at the state of eighteenth-century society. Wollstonecraft, it must be said again, believed that civilisation, despite the evil it generated, was part of God's providence. As mentioned above, she was to take Rousseau to task in her second *Vindication* for thinking otherwise. Endorsing the view that there was a natural order did not mitigate her attack on Burke's rendering of the Settlement of 1689 and his defence of property, social hierarchy and the established Church. From her perspective, Burke was far from respecting God's plan for man in dignifying morally corrupt laws and institutions by presenting them as natural or answering to natural needs. Nor would she let him hold the moral high ground when he attacked Price and fellow sympathisers with the revolution in France as politically inexperienced and irresponsible. Her way of vindicating the rights of men was to vilify him. The strategy she adopted was to undermine his *Reflections'* appeal by showing that it was no more than a self-serving intellectual trick played on readers by a man with a 'mortal antipathy to reason'.[13]

Wollstonecraft's well-known portrait of Burke depicts him as a man enamoured of a fictional Constitution and a glamorised past, infatuated with the French Queen – whom Wollstonecraft then thought to be devoid of both virtue and sense – yet culpable of *lèse-majesté* in relation to the good wife and mother Queen Charlotte, and so besotted with rank as to be contemptuous of the people, blind to the needs of the poor, and silent about the laws and practices which compounded their misery. Whereas she was always proud to assert her own independence of mind, and was to do so most emphatically in the 'Dedication' of her subsequent *Vindication*, she alleged that, for all his claims to the contrary, Burke was in the pay of his political masters. She presented herself as guided solely by the light of reason, while he was led by nothing but desire for glitter and gain. He was vain. She, by contràst, was independent of patronage and her cause was the public good. Like Rousseau in his early *Discours*, she saw herself as the virtuous champion of virtue.[14]

Indeed, her two most famous political works were really vindications of the right of *both* the sexes to the means of understanding the nature of virtue and to the condition in which it might be practicable, namely the development and continued exercise of reason in a strong and healthy body within a society which was devoted to the pursuit of virtue.

They were, to put it in another way, vindications of the right to be dutiful. What she demanded for women was that they be allowed to fulfil their duties as mothers, wives, physicians, nurses, midwives and citizens, and similarly for men. She insisted that rights entailed duties and that those who failed to fulfil their duties forfeited their rights; but none, on the other hand, could be expected to perform duties whose natural rights were not respected. This was to become one of the main premises of her second *Vindication*. While there was no question of a so-called return to nature in either of the two books, she agreed with Burke in thinking of the advance of civilisation as having rendered mankind courteous and polished, only in so far as she considered politeness a thin veneer over callousness and hypocrisy, which established institutions, such as the Church, both nurtured and thrived on. Opposing nature and reason to artifice and politeness, she secured a second reversal (apart from establishing herself as the real man in the affair) by making herself out to be the true patriot and Burke the unreflective Francophile:

our manners, you tell us, are drawn from the French, though you had before celebrated our native plainness. If they were, it is time we broke loose from dependence – Time that Englishmen drew water from their own springs; for, if manners are not a painted substitute for morals, we have only to cultivate reason, and we shall not feel the want of an arbitrary model. Nature will suffice; but I forget myself: – Nature and reason, according to your system, are all to give place to authority.[15]

These were all themes to which she was to return, for her second *Vindication* identifies uncontrolled passions, manners, artifice, hypocrisy, immorality, and lack of cleanliness and delicacy with the French, and reason, morals, nature, plainness and reserve with the English. The task in hand was to bring Englishmen and women back to their true selves, unadorned, commonsensical, trustworthy – real men and women, not images.

A Vindication of the Rights of Men thus reflected a rational and patriotic author fighting against a hysterical Francophile. But Wollstonecraft's show of patriotism led her further. Even Price, although she never addressed him directly on this issue, needed to be enlightened, for the kind of patriot he expected would not be produced by haranguing individuals from the pulpit, nor even by extending political and civil rights. The immorality to which Price was pointing was deeply rooted, and it was exacerbated by women. On this point, she and Rousseau were agreed.[16] Where they differed was on the nature of the remedy. Rousseau, who had so clearly seen the predicament of civilised man, had proved as blind as any other theorist in seeking a solution to it. *Emile* left women more or less as its author had found them. The only society which could produce patriots of the kind Price, and indeed Rousseau, wished for was one in which women were educated to be rational, disciplined and psychologically independent beings. It was a society in which both men and women would be citizens, by enjoying the rights of citizenship and performing its duties. As Wollstonecraft famously summarised her *Vindication of the Rights of Woman*:

if defensive war, the only justifiable war, in the present advanced state of society . . . were alone to be adopted as just and glorious, the true heroism of antiquity might again animate female bosoms. I only recreated an imagination, fatigued by contemplating the vices and follies which all proceed from a feculent stream of wealth that has muddied the pure rills of natural affection, by supposing that society will some time or other be so constituted, that man must necessarily fulfil the duties of a citizen, or be despised, and that while he was employed in any of the departments of civil life, his wife, also an active citizen, should be equally intent to manage her family, educate her children, and assist her neighbours.[17]

The moral depravity of a society devoted to the acquisition of property and its conspicuous display rather than to the pursuit of reason and the protection of natural and social rights found the means of its reproduction in the family. But the domain of perdition could equally be one of salvation, for the family was also the means to social and individual redemption, and patriotism could provide the initial impetus to effect a change in mores:

The personal reserve, and sacred respect for cleanliness and delicacy in domestic life, which French women almost despise, are the graceful pillars of modesty; but, far from despising them, if the pure flame of patriotism have reached their bosoms, they should labour to improve the morals of their fellow-citizens, by teaching men, not only to respect modesty in women, but to acquire it themselves, as the only way to merit esteem. (p. 68)

Patriotism could be the spur. It could provide the emotive force for radical change within women. Patriotism itself did not exist in a social vacuum. Its 'pure flame' had to be kindled and fanned. Patriotism needed the family to sustain itself:

Contending for the rights of woman, my main argument is built on this simple principle, that if she be not prepared by education to become the companion of man, she will stop the progress of knowledge and virtue; for truth must be common to all, or it will be inefficacious with respect to its influence on general practice. And how can woman be expected to co-operate unless she know why

she ought to be virtuous? unless freedom strengthen her reason till she comprehend her duty, and see in what manner it is connected with her real good? If
children are to be educated to understand the true principle of patriotism, their
mother must be a patriot; and the love of mankind, from which an orderly train
of virtues spring, can only be produced by considering the moral and civil interest of mankind; but the education and situation of woman, at present, shuts her
out from such investigations. (p. 68)

The difficulty faced by anyone seeking to make a case along the lines
of Wollstonecraft's argument was that women were thought to be
capable neither of patriotism nor of loving mankind, and much less so
of both, that is, of true patriotism, as Wollstonecraft, following Price,
conceived the matter. He had distinguished true patriotism, Christian
enlightened patriotism, from both the love the Jews bore their nation in
the belief that theirs was a superior people, and that which the Romans
felt for their country, for 'however great it appeared in some of its exer-
tions, it was in general no better than a principle holding together a band
of robbers in their attempts to crush all liberty but their own'.[18] On his
view, and also Wollstonecraft's, we ought to love our country 'ardently,
but not exclusively', 'seek its good, by all the means that our different
circumstances and abilities will allow', 'but at the same time we ought to
consider ourselves as citizens of the world, and take care to maintain a
just regard to the rights of other countries'.[19] True patriotism, rather
than being incompatible with the love of humanity as a whole, was thus
a particular expression of a more expansive love. As for real patriots,
they were, according to Wollstonecraft,

men who have studied politics, and whose ideas and opinions on the subject are
reduced to principles; men who make that science so much their principal
object, as to be willing to give up time, personal safety, and whatever society
comprehends in the phrase, *personal interest*, to secure the adoption of their plans
of reform, and the diffusion of knowledge.[20]

We have already seen how this made Wollstonecraft a true patriot in her
own eyes, since she was independent, and acted, unlike Burke, without
concern for *personal interest* in her dissemination of enlightenment; but by
the same token this account of patriotism most definitely excluded most
other women, who not only did not have any knowledge to impart, but
were unable to transcend personal interest.

That, however, was Wollstonecraft's peculiar charge against her sex,
not the general eighteenth-century outlook on this issue. In fact, as she
herself recognised, there were two overall positions on women and patri-

otism at the time. One saw them as being endowed with too much compassion and humanity to care about or focus on their own country's particular need and interest; the other was that their devotion to their children and immediate kin rendered them incapable of stretching their concern to include the good of their community as a whole, let alone that of the species in its entirety. Curiously enough, Wollstonecraft disagreed. What stood in the way of women's patriotism was not too great a love of mankind or their family. The only love they had in over-abundance was self-love:

Women are supposed to possess more sensibility, and even humanity, than men, and their strong attachments and instantaneous emotions of compassion are given as proofs; but the clinging affection of ignorance has seldom any thing noble in it, and may mostly be resolved into selfishness, as well as the affection of children and brutes. I have known many weak women whose sensibility was entirely engrossed by their husbands; and as for their humanity, it was very faint indeed, or rather it was only a transient emotion of compassion. Humanity does not consist 'in a squeamish ear,' says an eminent orator. 'It belongs to the mind as well as the nerves.'[21]

Not one ever to lessen the charges against women, and using Smith's moral psychology in compounding them, Wollstonecraft was however quick to point to the cause of their baseness:

But this kind of exclusive affection, though it degrades the individual, should not be brought forward as a proof of the inferiority of the sex, because it is the natural consequence of confined views: for even women of superior sense, having their attention turned to little employments, and private plans, rarely rise to heroism, unless when spurred on by love! and love, as an heroic passion, like genius, appears but once in an age. I therefore agree with the moralist who asserts, 'that women have seldom so much generosity as men;' and that their narrow affections, to which justice and humanity are often sacrificed, render the sex apparently inferior, especially, as they are commonly inspired by men; but I contend that the heart would expand as the understanding gained strength, if women were not depressed from their cradles.

I know that a little sensibility, and great weakness, will produce a strong sexual attachment, and that reason must cement friendship; consequently, I allow that more friendship is to be found in the male than the female world, and that men have a higher sense of justice. The exclusive affections of women seem indeed to resemble Cato's most unjust love for his country. He wished to crush Carthage, not to save Rome, but to promote its vain-glory; and, in general, it is to similar principles that humanity is sacrificed, for genuine duties support each other.[22]

To make women more capable of friendship, more just, more generous, in every respect more like Aristotle's ideal of the good man was

Wollstonecraft's proposal. If genuine duties did 'support each other' then women could not be expected to fulfil any one of them without being prepared and orientated towards them all. They needed to be strong in mind and in body, and this required the exercise of both. Just as in Rousseau, the idea of vigour and strength are pervasive in Wollstonecraft's writings. Women could be noble, virtuous and trustworthy. They could rise to the greatest heroism. They could be patriots and citizens.

It may be asked why, if Wollstonecraft was so intent on making Aristotelian citizens out of women, did she think of the household as woman's domain. This leads us back to Wollstonecraft's position on commercial society. Let us recall first that she was in favour of women's being educated to become physicians or farmers or shopkeepers, not least if they preferred celibacy.[23] A second and related point is that she preferred men and women working under one roof. While it is true that she was in favour of women becoming more capable of friendship, the friendships she had in mind were those between men and women, not amongst women. In her view, the more the sexes were kept apart the more susceptible they became to lasciviousness; and with lasciviousness came the appetites' supremacy over reason, and that in turn gave way to unenlightened self-love.[24] She disapproved of girls' boarding schools and all that led to excessive intimacy between women. The same held for standing armies, and she contended in the closing paragraphs of her reflections on the French Revolution:

that all associations of men render them sensual, and consequently selfish; and whilst lazy friars are driven out of their cells as stagnate bodies that corrupt society, it may admit of a doubt whether large work-shops do not contain men equally tending to impede that gradual progress of improvement, which leads to the perfection of reason, and the establishment of rational equality.[25]

The family, the household, and ideally husbandry, or small family workshops or businesses, were the domain of moral probity for both the sexes. They were also the domain of selflessness, the place in which vainglory did not take root, where the mind could, indeed had to, rise above self-interest, and where the passions could be kept under the thumb of reason, books be read, and politics and history studied. In times of peace, when the sword was turned into the ploughshare, the family was the predominant stage on which to exhibit patriotism and civic virtue, and there was more than a little nostalgia when Wollstonecraft explained:

the days of true heroism are over, when a citizen fought for his country like a Fabricius or a Washington, and then returned to his farm to let his virtuous fervour run in a more placid, but not a less salutary, stream. No, our British heroes are oftener sent from the gaming table than from the plow; and their passions have been rather inflamed by hanging with dumb suspense on the turn of a die, than sublimated by panting after the adventurous march of virtue in the historic page.[26]

Strikingly, Fabricius was the Roman hero Rousseau had addressed in his *Discours*. He almost frames the second Vindication, appearing as he does within the first few pages and then again within the last part of the work. The inclusion of George Washington in this evocation of the lives of heroes away from the battlefield brought the recent past to the fore; nothwithstanding her lamentation that the 'days of true heroism' were over, Wollstonecraft was seeking to bring them back, or more accurately, to bring them about for the first time in history. For while she admired what the ancients esteemed, not least self-discipline and frugality, she cast doubt on their motives in war, as we saw in her comments about Cato. Their virtue was questionable, because the nature of their patriotism was. They loved their nation exclusively and engaged in aggressive wars of expansion. Theirs was a bellicose character. True patriotism was enlightened patriotism, and entailed a readiness to fight only just, that is to say, defensive wars.

In times of peace, which in an enlightened age would predominate, men would infrequently be asked the ultimate sacrifice of laying down their lives for their country. Their self-denial and commitment to society would not differ in kind from that of their wives. Working on the farm, assisting neighbours, being a good parent, teacher and fellow-citizen would be expected of all, male and female alike. This would and could only happen in a chaste world, a world in which reason, not the appetites, are cultivated, and in which men and women, far from being separated by the intensification of the division of labour, are brought up together to live and work as friends united in a common interest in history, politics and their family. Wollstonecraft's aim was not to elevate women to a public sphere construed in contrast to a private or intermediary one. Nor, for that matter, to lower men to participation in the domestic sphere. It was instead to show that in a rightly ordered society men and women would be equally capable of true virtue and the highest form of heroism and patriotism; that the qualities required in the household were not different in kind from those required outside of it; that if they were conceived as different, mothers would never be in a position to raise good citizens; and that while women could indeed teach men to be great and virtuous, they needed the means to do so. They needed to be educated, but education understood as the acquisition of knowledge would not suffice in itself. A moral transformation of society, and of women in particular, was required; for it was essential that a woman be at one with herself so as to be one and the same before all – be they parents, husband, children, acquaintances, fellow countrymen or women. To do so she needed to be able to exert control over herself and keep unenlightened self-love in check. Wollstonecraft's prescription to wives not to be overly intimate with their husbands gives an indication of the self-control she thought necessary to maintain all relationships between people.[27] The family, she argued, was the cradle and bastion of a virtuous, heroic and patriotic people. It inculcated generosity, humanity, interest in the well-being of others, love of truth and godliness; thus it made people capable of friendship. It transmitted devotion to duties, if only by the self-denying example of mothers. The family was the most public sphere of all because it made or broke public-spiritedness (or, conversely, selfishness). There could not be a private, different or intermediate sphere for Wollstonecraft as there was no private or different person to inhabit it, nor a private or different virtue or modality to express or experience in it. Indeed, in times of peace, when men do not bear arms, women continue to bear children. As Wollstonecraft's own death from septicaemia following the birth of her daughter Mary was to underline, the nursery was as likely a scene of the ultimate test of citizenship as the battlefield.

NOTES

1 Wollstonecraft's intellectual relation to Rousseau is a complex issue which this chapter will only touch on. Naturally the literature on her has concentrated on her responses to *Emile*. Interestingly, however, the first work of his she refers to in her *Vindication of the Rights of Woman* is the *Discours sur les Sciences et les Arts*. For it is in that work that 'Rousseau celebrates barbarism, and apostrophiz[es] the shade of Fabricius'. See Mary Wollstonecraft, *A Vindication of the Rights of Men* and *A Vindication of the Rights of Woman* and *Hints*, ed. Sylvana Tomaselli (Cambridge: Cambridge University Press, 1995), p. 82. All references to either *Vindication* are taken from this edition.

2 Jean-Jacques Rousseau, *Oeuvres complètes*, ed. Bernard Gagnebin et Marcel Raymond, 4 vols. (Paris: Gallimard, 1964), vol. III, p. 2. All translations are mine.

3 *Oeuvres complètes*, vol. III, p. 2. I mention this because Wollstonecraft was to

depict herself in much the same terms in the dedication to her *Vindication of the Rights of Woman*, pp. 67–70.

4 Even if one only considers the *Vindications* her position on this subject is ambiguous. The matter is made more complex still if one also considers her subsequent political writings, namely her *An Historical and Moral View of the Origin and Progress of the French Revolution* (1794) and her *Letters Written During a Short Residence in Sweden, Norway and Denmark* (1796).

5 *A Vindication of the Rights of Woman*, p. 82.

6 Wollstonecraft does not appear to have thought the two to be conflicting. Indeed, part of the debate between Price, Burke and herself was about the compatibility of the two moralities.

7 See Sylvana Tomaselli, 'The Role of Woman in Enlightenment Conjectural Histories', in Hans Erich Bödeker and Liselotte Steinbrügge, eds., *Conceptualizing Women in Enlightenment Thought. Penser la femme au siècle des Lumières* (European Science Foundation, forthcoming).

8 *A Vindication of the Rights of Men*, pp. 60–1.

9 Editorial introduction, *Vindication of the Rights of Men*, see note 1.

10 Article 11, *Analytical Review*, December 1789, in *The Works of Mary Wollstonecraft*, ed. Janet Todd and Marilyn Butler (London: William Pickering, 1989), vol. VII, pp. 185–7, p. 185.

11 Ibid., p. 186.

12 'A Discourse on the Love of our Country, delivered on Nov. 4, 1789, at the Meeting-House in the Old Jewry, to the Society for Commemorating the Revolution of Great Britain. With an Appendix, containing the report of the Committee of the Society', in *Political Writings*, ed. D. O. Thomas (Cambridge: Cambridge University Press, 1991), pp. 176–96, p. 193. The passage is thought to refer to Charles James Fox.

13 *Vindication of the Rights of Men*, p. 8.

14 It is important to recall that her relationship to Burke was not static. It was not antagonistic prior to the publication of his *Reflections*. Furthermore her *Origin and Progress of the French Revolution* and her *Letters Written during a Short Residence in Sweden* reveal an intellectual *rapprochement* to him.

15 *Vindication of the Rights of Men*, p. 64.

16 For a discussion of Rousseau's views on this matter, see Sylvana Tomaselli, 'The Enlightenment Debate on Women', *History Workshop* 20 (Autumn 1985), 101–24.

17 *Vindication of the Rights of Woman*, p. 236.

18 *A Discourse on the Love of our Country*, p. 179.

19 Ibid., p. 181.

20 *An Historical and Moral View of the Origin and Progress of the French Revolution*, in *The Works of Mary Wollstonecraft*, vol. VI, p. 141.

21 *Vindication of the Rights of Woman*, p. 287.

22 *Vindication of the Rights of Woman*, pp. 287–8. Wollstonecraft cites Smith, *A Theory of Moral Sentiments*, IV.ii.10; see edn ed. D. D. Raphael and A. L. Macfie (Oxford: Clarendon Press, 1976), p. 190.

23 *Vindication of the Rights of Woman*, pp. 238–40.
24 *Vindication of the Rights of Woman*, editorial introduction, pp. ix–x.
25 'An Historical and Moral View', in *The Works of Mary Wollstonecraft*, vol. VI, p. 234.
26 *Vindication of the the the Rights of Woman*, p. 233.
27 *Vindication of the the the Rights of Woman*, pp. 68, 185, 208–18, 260.

CHAPTER ELEVEN

Theorising public opinion: Elizabeth Hamilton's model of self, sympathy and society

Penny Warburton

In *The Structural Transformation of the Public Sphere*, Jürgen Habermas argues that a bourgeois reading public capable of rational, critical debate and competent to form its own opinions emerged over the course of the eighteenth century within the context of a developing market economy. In his seminal account, he claims that there are two forms of public: a literary public sphere and a political public sphere. In general, according to Habermas, these two publics blended together as 'a public consisting of private persons whose autonomy based on ownership of private property wanted to see itself represented as such in the sphere of the bourgeois family'.[1] However, they were divided along class and gender lines:

> The circles of persons who made up the two forms of public were not even completely congruent. Women and dependents were factually and legally excluded from the political public sphere, whereas female readers as well as the prentices and servants often took a more active part in the literary public sphere than the owners of private property and family heads themselves. Yet in the educated classes the one form of public sphere was considered to be identical with the other; in the self-understanding of public opinion the public sphere appeared as one and indivisible.[2]

Habermas's claim that women were 'factually and legally excluded from the political public sphere' needs clarification. He is correct insofar as women were formally excluded from politics – they could neither vote nor stand for parliament.[3] However, in order to comprehend the full range of women's extensive engagement in politics during this period we need to develop a more sophisticated understanding of the political public sphere as a fluid and complex entity whose boundaries were continually shifting. From the electoral canvassing of élite aristocrats such as Georgiana, the Duchess of Devonshire to the food riots of starving plebeian labourers, women of all classes gave voice to their political beliefs through whatever means they could appropriate for this purpose.[4] As Linda Colley and others have argued, although the adherents of the ideology of separate spheres became increasingly prescriptive during the 1790s, at the same time: 'The half-century after the American war would witness a marked expansion in the range of British women's public . . . activities' so that 'even the most conventional British women would come to accept that formal exclusion from active citizenship did not exclude them from playing a patriotic role – and a political role of a kind.'[5]

According to Habermas, the 'self-interpretation of the function of the bourgeois public sphere crystallised in the idea of "public opinion"' during the late eighteenth century. During this process of crystallisation, he claims, the term 'public opinion', first documented in the Oxford English Dictionary in 1781, assumed its modern referent of a public 'competent to form its own opinions'.[6] In Habermas's account of the ideology of the 'public sphere' within the history of 'great thinkers' from Hobbes through to Locke and Rousseau, then Kant, Hegel, Marx and Mill, it is Kant who provides the most developed theory of public opinion as a reasoned form of access to truth. However, Habermas's discussion of the idea of public opinion can be criticised for failing to take into account a more representative group of writers and thinkers. Public opinion was hotly debated during this period in a diverse array of genres including newspapers, political speeches, sermons, novels, plays, criticism, reviews and other writings. For example, Wordsworth's description of an urban public whose 'discriminating powers of the mind' were reduced to a 'state of almost savage torpor' through the 'uniformity of their occupation' in the 'Preface to the *Lyrical Ballads*' clearly reflects a grave concern at the ability of the public to form its own opinions on the value of literature.[7] In this essay I focus on the work of Elizabeth Hamilton, arguing that her reflections on the problem of 'public opinion' via a rethinking of Adam Smith's theory of moral values are an important manifestation of female intervention into the political public sphere during the early nineteenth century.

Hamilton is probably most familiar to us as the author of *Memoirs of Modern Philosophers* (1800), a satire on contemporary radical thinkers, in particular William Godwin and Mary Hays, portrayed unflatteringly as 'Mr. Myope' and 'Bridgetina Botherim'. However, she also wrote on a number of different subjects including education, history, biography, taste and ethics. In her salon at Edinburgh she played host to local literati including Dugald Stewart the philosopher, Joanna Baillie the playwright, and Mrs Grant of Laggan.[8] Gary Kelly has described her project as one of counter-revolutionary feminism, arguing that she intellectualised 'women's culture by popularizing, novelizing, and thereby disseminating philosophy, theology, and history, and doing so in a way that offered herself as model for the new intellectual-domestic woman.'[9] However, Hamilton's engagement in what Kelly has categorised as 'masculine' subjects can also be read within the context of the Scottish common-sense school of philosophy and as a continuation of the Enlightenment project to create a 'science of man'.[10]

A gifted child with a lively intellect, Hamilton demonstrated an early interest in moral philosophy but suffered from considerable social pressure not to display her superior knowledge in case she was accused of pedantry.[11] In her journal she recalls: 'Do I not well remember hiding Kames' *Elements of Criticism*, under the cover of an easy chair, whenever I heard the approach of a footstep?'[12] A philosophical spirit of inquiry pervaded her writing. She experimented with different genres such as historical biography to illustrate the speculative principles that she deduced from her work on education. However, she worried about whether this was the proper vehicle for philosophy. Intending her *Memoirs of Agrippina* (1804) to be read as philosophy, she was disgusted with its reception as a historical romance: 'Agrippina is preposterously classed with novels; and an opinion has been commonly entertained that it is, in reality, a sort of biographical romance.'[13]

In 1813, Hamilton published *A Series of Popular Essays Illustrative of Principles Essentially Connected with the Improvement of the Understanding, the Imagination and the Heart.* Dedicated to her friend Archibald Alison, it was in generic terms her most 'philosophical' book. The work consists of five lengthy essays and an introduction in which she attempts to prove a set of specific axioms. In the first essay she speculates on the purpose of philosophy and suggests that women have a particular contribution to make to the discipline. In the second, she posits that faculties of the mind such as perception are developed in direct proportion to the degree of attention focused on them by the subject's mind. In the third she goes on to argue that this faculty of attention also affects the imagination and thereby produces emotions of taste. It is in the last two essays that her main theme is developed – the idea of the 'selfish principle' and its role in the formation of the self.

Hamilton's theories of the mind and desire were derived from observations she made in her educational writings. Here she argued, firstly, that all knowledge is constructed through associations; secondly, that this process begins in early infancy; and thirdly, that the first ideas generated from association are the strongest and the most permanent. Like Mary Wollstonecraft and Catharine Macaulay, she pushed associationist psychology to its extreme limits, arguing that the mind has no innate sex. Yet at the same time her associationist stance is challenged by her religious beliefs about the existence of original sin, producing an inherent tension in her work.

Throughout the book, Adam Smith is a constant point of reference, and she comments on both the *Wealth of Nations* and the *Theory of Moral Sentiments*, at times directly, at others indirectly. When she agrees with him she tends to mention his name, but when she is critical of his work she is oblique in her references to his ideas. This tentative textual relationship to Smith suggests that Hamilton is anxious to legitimise her writing as part of the Scottish tradition of moral philosophy that she is simultaneously attacking.

In her introduction she makes it clear that her project is philosophical: not 'didactic precept, or grave admonition' but:

a serious examination of the obstacles which impede our progress, and which must be surmounted, before either the heart or the understanding can be effectually improved. The obstacles to which I allude are not created by external circumstances: they are to be found within, and can only be discovered by an actual survey of our common nature; such as may, however, be taken by every person capable of observation and reflection.[14]

Philosophy here becomes, to use Hamilton's expression, 'popular', because in principle philosophy, like science, is a practice open to everyone, including women. It does not have to base itself, theoretically, on a tradition of learned writing but can proceed of and in itself. Indeed, she asserts that her lack of formal philosophical training is a positive advantage, as she is no slavish disciple of any school of thought. Furthermore, she argues that truly great philosophical authorities will respect the integrity of her project and read her without prejudice. While acknowledging the importance of works that diffuse 'the observations or discoveries of superior minds' she claims that her design is an original one:

However I have availed myself of the light derived from the investigations of our eminent philosophers, as the object at which I have aimed is distinct from theirs, the assistance afforded has been only partial. Of my design the prominent feature is an attempt to deduce, from a consideration of the nature of the human mind, proofs, that revealed religion offers the only effectual means of improving the human character. (vol. I, p. xix)

As noted above, her writing can be seen as the continuation of an Enlightenment project to create a 'science of man' founded on experience and observation, through the systematising eye of reason, which would in turn be the foundation of all other sciences. However, Hamilton's philosophy is only scientific insofar as it is part of what she describes as the 'natural progress of society' and the unfolding of providential divine wisdom. As such, her project is curtailed by her religious beliefs, and her hypotheses about the working of the mind are selected in the first place according to how far they support biblical 'truths'.

She calls for a 'revolution in public taste', arguing that philosophy could become part of the general education of both gentleman and ladies, for:

> may it not reasonably be hoped, that when a superficial acquaintance with other branches of science has become too common to confer distinction, the science of mind may be resorted to as a desideratum of polite education? (vol. I, p. 5)

She goes on to suggest that the lack of a classical education, which most women would not have received, is no impediment to instruction in philosophy. Comparing it to other sciences such as chemistry, she argues that in time the results of research into the 'science of mind' will yield comparable benefits to society. Striving to make her work open to all readers she claims that her language will be one sanctioned by custom rather than abstruse metaphysical learning. The central aim underlying Hamilton's project is a pedagogical one: by understanding the working of the mind she posits that it will be possible to use these insights to intervene at an early stage in order to improve pupils' abilities. However, this is not to suggest that 'every village dame, and every parish domine, and every master and mistress of a charity school' should study the philosophy of the human mind, for according to her definition, they should already possess the requisite knowledge through their experience of teaching (vol. I, p. 74).

HAMILTON'S SCIENCE OF MIND: 'A PROPENSITY TO MAGNIFY THE IDEA OF SELF'

In this section I focus on Hamilton's main proposition – the existence of a mental property which she terms the 'selfish principle' and identifies as the 'propensity to magnify the idea of self'. This principle is defined only in negative terms, so its exact meaning is initially elusive (and, I shall argue, subsequently confused). It is not to be equated with self-love, which is defined as:

simply *desire of happiness*; a desire which we may observe to be regulated and controlled by the intellectual powers, and consequently, as to the nature of its operations, dependant on the direction given to the power of attention. (vol. II, p. 120)

Nor should it be conflated with 'selfishness', which she describes as:

inordinate desire of self-gratification, not dependant on the operation of the intellectual faculties . . . but originating in associations that connect the idea of happiness with appropriating the objects that appear desirable to the heart, and thus obtaining enjoyments in which none can participate, and in which none can sympathize. (vol. I, p. 274)

The 'selfish principle', manifested as the propensity to enlarge the idea of self, is distinct from both 'self-love' and 'selfishness' as it operates independent of any 'peculiar direction of attention for its development':

Besides the appetites which direct to the preservation of life, there are certain desires or propensities interwoven in the frame of our nature which operate spontaneously, and arrive at mature strength long before the intellectual faculties . . . this active principle is still without a name . . . I take the liberty of describing it from its operations, as *a propensity to magnify the idea of self*. (vol. I, pp. 271–2)

It is a faculty of mind which is general in its projection outwards onto the world, as every object is potentially an object of desire. As a faculty, the 'selfish principle' is something that is constitutive of the self. Yet Hamilton makes it clear that it is to be resisted. It is tempting to conceptualise it as a precursor to Freud's unconscious as it is both the basis of self-awareness and its debased component. As we shall see, this principle threatens the mechanism of Smith's impartial spectator, since for Hamilton disinterested action is not possible without the impartiality of the divine.

She uses this principle to explain the basis of class, gender and racial conflict, as well as smaller disputes within the domestic sphere and in the local community. Furthermore, she sees it as the prime mover in every instance of an action seemingly motivated by pride or vanity, arguing that there is

not one of the operations of the human mind in which it may not mingle . . . even among notions which we may deem completely virtuous, it may sometimes be found to have insinuated itself. (vol. I, p. 277)

As early as 1808, she writes in her journal that she sees pride as the root of all the passions expressive of hatred, including malice, envy, jealousy and so on. The problem she was struggling to address was how to describe the operation of pride. She writes:

the best I can at present think of, is that of a resistless propensity to extend the idea of self. This propensity leads every man to create around himself a sort of circle, which, in imagination, he completely fills, and which he perpetually endeavours to enlarge, by carefully stuffing into it as many objects as he can possibly find means to appropriate.[15]

Five years later, in the *Series of Popular Essays*, Hamilton sees the 'selfish principle' as distinct from pride but operating alongside it, as a first cause, 'the most active of all the principles inherent in the mind of man' (vol. i, p. 279). Her theory describes a self which is split, does not know itself, and acts from hidden, underlying causes.

She applies it in criticising both barbarian and cultivated societies; for example, she analyses the oppression of women through the lens it provides, writing that:

(women) by the legislators of Europe, have been generally contemplated, as having no other existence than that they have derived from being identified with their husbands, fathers, brothers, or kinsmen . . . for ages an heiress was considered in no other light than as a sort of promissary note, stampt with the value of certain lands, tenements, and hereditaments, and disposable at the will of the sovereign. (vol. i, p. 303)

In effect, she argues that men oppress women in order to magnify their own sense of self. In the eighteenth century property was passed down through a line of male relations, from the father to the first male heir, on whom the estate was entailed. The status of women as legal subjects and property-owners was severely limited, as Susan Staves has shown.[16] Through marriage, the wife became one person in the law with her husband, and as William Blackstone commented, 'the very being or legal existence of the woman is suspended during the marriage'.[17] The marriage settlement or jointure became the most common form of married women's separate property. Gradually over the course of the eighteenth century it came to replace the dower rights women held in common law over their husband's property. Staves argues that this change in property rights was deeply detrimental and disadvantageous for women. Hamilton was deeply critical of a society in which marriage was often no more than a business transaction, and in which the woman was reduced to a mere commodity. She refused her brother Charles's offer to join him in India so that he might find her a husband. In *A Series of Popular Essays* her claim about female oppression is further developed in her analysis of male domination: in early periods she suggests it is exercised through superior strength, and in modern times, through 'a complete subjugation of the intellectual powers of the feebler sex' (vol. ii, p. 84).

Her position is not dissimilar to that of Wollstonecraft's: they both criticise primogeniture and the substandard education offered to women. They differ, however, on the correct response to civil injustice. While Wollstonecraft's *Rights of Woman* suggested change for women through new legislation and political representation, Hamilton was fiercely opposed to party politics of any kind. In particular, she saw women who engaged in party politics as bigoted, because their party zeal encouraged them to accuse all men of injustice and tyranny. She also argued that such women were prevented from being able to see the peculiar privileges of their sex. She writes:

every circumstance which marks their situation in society is considered as a grievance. By looking merely to what would promote the gratification of the selfish principle, they overlook or despise the advantages which the sex, in some respects, in a superior degree enjoys, in this probationary state of existence. (vol. II, p. 81)

Here, in direct contrast to Wollstonecraft, she implies that the double standard of morality and chastity, which discriminates against women, is actually beneficial because it causes women to behave more virtuously than men. Suffering can be advantageous because it directs a penitent mind towards God.

PUBLIC AND PRIVATE IN SMITH'S *THEORY OF MORAL SENTIMENTS*

Hamilton quoted copiously from several Enlightenment figures such as Dugald Stewart, Lord Kames and Edward Gibbon to support her arguments, but, as noted above, she drew more heavily on Adam Smith in *A Series of Popular Essays* than on any other writer in her conceptualisation of 'public opinion'. Sometimes her reading of Smith is confused, but it is not difficult to see how one might read into Smith's impartial spectator a kind of enlightened public opinion, even though, as Maria Luisa Pesante has argued: 'the reflective elaboration of the natural sentiment of sympathy which in Smith's view produces our articulate moral judgements may only with difficulty be subsumed under the law of opinion'.[18] In this section I shall recall Smith's general argument in order to review precisely how Hamilton responds.

Writing against Mandeville's vision of a world ruled by social hypocrisy, Smith contends that moral judgements are not informed solely by self-interest and that we do not behave well simply because it is in our advantage to be seen to do so. For Smith, the ethical is inextricably bound up with the social, and moral judgements are reached through a consensus of public values. Social bonds are created through the operation of sympathy; the word referring not to compassion or pity felt for the other, but to the manner in which we can identify ourselves with each other by imagining ourselves to be in each other's situation. In this way we can sympathise both directly with the motives of the person who acts and indirectly with the gratitude or resentment felt by the recipient of an action. There is, therefore, a kind of relay of sympathy which relates the spectator to the sentiments felt surrounding an action. Sympathy, as Smith defines it, is a complicated concept, which we must be careful to distinguish from the modern term – empathy – a non-intellectual, spontaneous communion of feeling.

It is sympathy which enables Smith to explain how we arrive at a consensus of moral judgements. He introduces the concept of the 'impartial spectator' to elucidate the way people can reach a consensus by envisioning actions from a limited set of perspectives. It explains the work of conscience, as we are said to judge ourselves through the eye of the impartial spectator. He writes:

When I endeavour to examine my own conduct, when I endeavour to pass sentence upon it, and either to approve it or condemn it, it is evident in all such cases, I divide myself, as it were, into two persons; and that I, the examiner and judge, represent a different character from the other I, the person whose conduct is examined into and judged of.[19]

The idea of selfhood draws on a range of metaphors including a language of theatricality in which subjects are figured as spectators who become spectacles for each other.[20] The idiom of theatricality in relation to the self is anticipated by Hume's discussion of identity. In *A Treatise of Human Nature* (1739) he argues: 'The mind is a kind of theatre, where several perceptions successively make their appearance; pass, repass, glide away, and mingle to an infinite variety of postures and situations.'[21] Like Smith, he uses the image of mirrors as a comment on the way that the minds of men 'reflect each other's emotions' and 'sympathize' with each other. According to Hume, sympathy is the sharing of pleasure or pain, though for Smith sympathy is extended to refer to the sharing of any feeling.

Smith's *Theory of Moral Sentiments* constructs a world of social relations in which we depend entirely on others for our happiness, as the correspondence of our emotions with those of others creates our sense of self-esteem. At times, Smith appears to use 'sympathy' in the modern sense of empathy, even though he has said explicitly that sympathy is a purely intellectual operation, in which we relate to others by imagining ourselves to be in their situation. For example, on watching tragedy he writes: 'If we shed any tears, we carefully conceal them, and are afraid, lest the spectators, not entering into this excessive tenderness, should regard it as effeminacy and weakness.'[22] His theory implies that we must practice the virtue of self-command so that others, even complete strangers, can sympathise with us when we suffer an injustice. We must also have a lively imagination so that we can properly participate in the feelings of others and be capable of expressing sensibility. Furthermore, we must be capable of imagining our own actions with as impartial an eye as possible, restraining any tendency to self-deception.

Smith's model is an explicitly gendered one in which men are seen to exert themselves positively in generous, public-spirited actions motivated by rational judgements whereas women merely give in to their natural feelings of sympathy. Thus he distinguishes between the two sexes:

Humanity is the virtue of a woman, generosity of a man. The fair-sex, who have commonly much more tenderness than ours have seldom so much generosity. That women rarely make considerable donations, is an observation of the civil law. Humanity consists merely in the exquisite fellow-feeling which the spectator entertains with the sentiments of the persons principally concerned, so as to grieve for their sufferings, to resent their injuries, and to rejoice at their good fortune. The most humane actions require no self-denial, no self-command, no great exertion of the sense of propriety. They consist only in doing what this exquisite sympathy would of its own accord prompt us to do. But it is otherwise with generosity. We are never generous except when in some respect we prefer some other person to ourselves, and sacrifice some great and important interest. The man who gives up his pretensions to an office that was the great object of his ambition, because he imagines that the services of another are better entitled to it; the man who exposes his life to defend that of his friend, . . . neither of them act from humanity . . . They both consider those opposite interests, not in the light in which they naturally appear to themselves, but in that in which they appear to others.[23]

In *A Vindication of the Rights of Woman* Mary Wollstonecraft later took issue with Smith's depiction of women arguing that they were deficient in both generosity and humanity. Drawing instead on Smith's analysis of the relationship between class and morality, where virtue is rewarded in an upwardly mobile middle class through the acquisition of positions of public responsibility, she posited that the entire female sex was analogous to Smith's obsolete and effeminate aristocracy. Unlike middle-class men, women, she claimed, could not strive to succeed in public office but had to prepare themselves for marriage. As both Lucinda Cole and G. J. Barker-Benfield have argued, the implied subject of the *Theory of Moral Sentiments* is always a middle-class male. Smith's moral philosophy presents us with a vision of society in which the ideal relationships – masculine, heroic and stoic – exist between boys and their tutors.[24]

HAMILTON ON SMITH AND 'PUBLIC OPINION'

Referring indirectly in her *Series of Popular Essays* to the opening passage of the *Theory of Moral Sentiments*, in which Smith describes the identification we feel with our fellow creatures in terms of bodily pains, Hamilton writes:

> some philosophers have been led to conclude, that our sensations on witnessing any species of bodily suffering, is the result of an exercise of the imagination, by which we have placed ourselves in the situation of the sufferer, and made his case our own. (vol. II, p. 279)

Questioning Smith's description of the operation of sympathy, she suggests that the imagination is not a sufficient cause in every case, particularly in those instances when the object of sympathy is one suffering from the sensations of bodily pain. Her contention is that there is a significant difference between the emotions we feel on seeing a moth extinguished in a candle flame, and those we feel in merely hearing about a moth being extinguished. These reflections on the nature of pain were inspired by a visit to the theatre to watch the tragedy of Jane Shore, performed by Sarah Siddons. During the climax of the play when all emotions had been wound up to a pitch, Siddons's fingers were crushed in a doorframe and she uttered a piercing shriek, which destroyed all the 'sympathies of imagination'. In response, the audience transferred their sympathies from the plight of Jane Shore, the part, to the physical agonies of the actress, Sarah Siddons. Clearly, Hamilton has not entirely understood Smith's explanation of the operation of sympathy: it does not matter whether the object is Jane Shore, or the actress who plays her, the mechanism of sympathy as Smith sees it would still work in the same manner. However, Hamilton's reflections on sympathy are interesting not so much because they are philosophically rigorous but rather because of what they indicate about her political and religious beliefs.

Her claim is that 'sympathy' is not always produced through 'imagination', but can occur spontaneously, in and of itself, as a response to the

pain of others. Furthermore, she argues, we are compelled to act immediately to relieve these feelings of pain. Yet this account of sympathy is
not always consistent. Sometimes she makes this distinction between
'sympathy' as a product of the imagination and raw pain as a sensation
over which we have no control:

> the emotions of sympathy may, by a lively imagination, be produced at pleas-
> ure, being invariably consequent on pursuing certain trains of thought: But over
> our sensations we possess no similar power; we can neither excite them by an
> effort of imagination, nor can we destroy them by any effort of the will. (vol. II,
> p. 285)

At other times she lets the distinction lapse, using them equivalently,
as does Smith: again, 'sympathy' is conflated with what is now understood by empathy.

Hamilton claims that sensibility without action is worse than useless.
It is not the degree to which sympathy is experienced but the habitude
with which it is felt and the actions it gives rise to that matter. She chas-
tises women in particular for their inadequacy in the face of suffering,
and commends the actions of a young surgeon who is so intent on operating that he is oblivious to the screams of his patient. Here, her praise
for the virtues of self-command and courage recall the masculine sensibilities of Smith's ideal spectator.

Another point on which Hamilton sought to differentiate her position from Smith's was his model of conscience. As noted above, his
theory of the impartial spectator explains the way our conscience
affects us when we judge ourselves. The 'man within' is said to weigh up
our actions through the eyes of others, and take into account the special
knowledge we have of ourselves that others do not. We then arbitrate
and pass sentence on ourselves. Smith admits that we are often more
biased towards our own actions than we are aware, but insists that this
is how conscience works. For Hamilton, as for Wollstonecraft, conscience cannot be imposed from within by any 'impartial spectator' but
must be enforced from without by the laws of God, the only just tribunal. The false sensibility and sympathy of public opinion aggrieve her
as they impose a false and degraded set of values. In particular, she is
shocked by the treatment of fallen women as still respectable: 'we may
infer', she writes, 'that the period is not far distant when the adulteress
and chaste matron will be universally received upon equal terms' (vol.
II, p. 314). The danger is that with no strict moral code, backed up by
religious laws, public opinion could become subject to the vagaries of

taste, nothing more than the latest fashion. She regards the rise in taste for novels of sensibility as indicative of this dangerous tendency, remarking on the correspondence between poor, dependent and abused heroes and the prevalent sympathy for persons situated in similar positions. 'Public opinion', she claims, 'though a respectable tribunal, is not the highest nor the last tribunal at which those who offend the laws of religion and morality are to appear' (vol. II, p. 321). However, a close reading of Smith's *Theory of Moral Sentiments* suggests that he was also worried about declining standards of taste. The recurrent images of an 'effeminate' culture which does not foster the necessary self-control by which people can 'judge' themselves imply the existence of an educated male élite who will transcend public opinion to produce a more impartial judgement.

Hamilton's conception of the self is intrinsically different from that of Smith. For the latter, the self is often motivated by self-interest or self-love but may have purely disinterested feelings, as well. For the former, the self is deeply motivated by the 'selfish principle', the tendency 'to magnify the idea of self'; the self is egocentric, acting from hidden motives. She suggests that the only solution to the viciousness of the 'selfish principle' is the cultivation of the benevolent affections, which occurs in two ways: via parental affection, and from knowledge of God through divine revelation:

With the knowledge of God communicated by divine revelation, the first idea of perfect holiness was presented to the idea of mind of man; an idea that it is impossible to contemplate without emotions which tend at once to elevate and purify the heart. (vol. II, p. 377)

She asserts that religion has failed for several reasons: religious practice has lapsed, and we have proved fallible as interpreters of the Bible. Faith has been directed away from God towards man-made inventions of religion, represented by the various parties of the Christian church. A more direct relationship with God through prayer is recommended as salutary. In the *Essays* a progressivist, 'Enlightenment' history of religion, corresponding to her vision of the progress of knowledge, is presented, moving from paganism through the heathen theologies to Christianity as the superior religion. Her rejection of the impartial spectator in favour of divine law implies a rejection of public opinion formed through conversation and commerce. Ultimately, this is an extremely conservative ideology, which appears to conflict with her earlier statements about the openness of philosophy as a science for everyone. Hamilton's theory is a hybrid entity, the product of both empirical, rationalist science, and evangelist religion as something always already present.

Hamilton and Smith are to some extent both preoccupied with questions of social reproduction; they ask how moral values are created and then imposed on society. Smith, arguing against Mandeville, emphasised that men act from a variety of motives, and respond with different combinations of self-love and sympathy, to suit a whole range of possible forms of public life. As Edward Hundert writes:

> The primary object of his theory of morals is to show how self-interest, *mitigated* by sympathy and self-command, can result in prudent and sometimes beneficent actions, even . . . in the inescapably utility-maximising exchange relationships of contemporary commercial societies.[25]

Modern commentators on the *Theory of Moral Sentiments* have sometimes misunderstood the work, arguing that the ideas in the earlier work which focus on sympathy are incompatible with the later focus on self-interest in *The Wealth of Nations*.[26] Smith was concerned with sentiments, however, not actions. He admits that beneficence can result from actions motivated purely by self-interest: the rich

> are led by an invisible hand to make nearly the same distribution of the necessaries of life, which would have been made, had the earth been divided into equal portions among all its inhabitants, and thus without intending it, without knowing it, advance the interest of society.[27]

In contrast to Smith, Hamilton was deeply pessimistic in her prognosis and rejected the compatibility of a society driven by commercial activity with one in which virtue counted. In *A Series of Popular Essays* she reviewed the ways in which political economy had effected revolutions in public opinion about 'national wealth'. For example, she points out the impact of Smith's ideas on mercantilist orthodoxy:

> The connexion between national wealth and national happiness, has in all periods seemed so indisputable, that whoever can by his policy augment the national resources, is certain of obtaining the meed of public applause . . . At length, in consequence of attending to circumstances that had before escaped observation, it was discovered that all this labour had been better spared, and that commerce never flowed so prosperously as when left to itself.
>
> When we take a view of these revolutions in opinion, concerning the methods of promoting national happiness and prosperity, it does not seem chimerical to suppose, that a time may arrive when it shall be discovered, that the most inseparable of all connexions is that between happiness and virtue. (vol. II, p. 352)

She appears to end the passage by dismissing political economy – the science which has had so much impact on her own thinking – as ultimately lacking in moral probity with its emphasis on material rather than spiritual gain.

Hamilton's reflections on intellectual history and issues such as the current condition of the public, are, I have argued, a striking example of a woman in the public sphere, reflecting on the nature of that of which she was herself a part. Hamilton's reputation as a writer was considerable and critics and readers alike generally respected her. The *Monthly Review* praised her *Essays* as a work on female education, which could be recommended to mother, daughter and the general public for its 'sage, benevolent and familiar exhortations'. They were suitable to be read 'not merely in the parlour but to be proclaimed from the pulpit' as a work which would simultaneously instruct and entertain.[28] Hamilton's writing can be seen as part of a larger project to recoup 'philosophy' from its association with dangerous, revolutionary ideals. Despite her work's conservatism, however, a conservative 'male' critical public could only digest her philosophy by domesticating it into an acceptable 'female' genre such as that of education.

NOTES

1 Jürgen Habermas, *The Structural Transformation of the Public Sphere: An Inquiry into a Category of Bourgeois Society.* trans. by Thomas Burger (Cambridge: Polity Press, 1989), p. 55. Originally published in German under the title *Strukturwandel der Öffentlichkeit*, in 1962.

2 Habermas, *Structural Transformation*, p. 56.

3 However, women were not legally excluded from voting until the 1832 reform bill which 'by the introduction of the word "male" before the word "person" definitely excluded women from the privileges that Act conferred'. A. E. Metcalfe, *Woman's Effort: A Chronicle of British Women's Fifty Years' Struggle for Citizenship (1865–1914)*, (Oxford, 1917), p. 1.

4 See E. P. Thompson's *The Making of the English Working Class* (Harmondsworth: Penguin Books, 1963), pp. 71–2, and Amanda Foreman's *Georgiana: Duchess of Devonshire* (London: Harper Collins, 1998) for two very different accounts of women and politics.

5 Linda Colley, *Britons: Forging the Nation, 1707–1837* (London and New York: Yale University Press, 1992).

6 Habermas, *Structural Transformation*, pp. 89–90.

7 William Wordsworth, *Selected Prose*, ed. John O. Hayden (London: Penguin Books, 1988), p. 284. Originally published in the 1800 edition of *Lyrical Ballads*.

8 Stewart was Adam Smith's student and chair of moral philosophy at Edinburgh University from 1795 onwards.

9 Gary Kelly, *Women, Writing, and Revolution 1790–1827* (Oxford: Clarendon Press, 1993), p. 265.

10 See David Hume's 'Introduction' to his *A Treatise of Human Nature*, ed. Ernest C. Mossner (London: Penguin Books, 1985). First published in 3 vols. in 1739 and 1740.

11 From now on when I refer to 'philosophy' I will be using the term as shorthand for 'moral philosophy'. In the eighteenth century 'philosophy' was a more fluid and inclusive term which was used to refer to several different areas of inquiry including natural philosophy and moral philosophy.

12 Elizabeth Ogilvy Benger, ed., *Memoirs of Elizabeth Hamilton* (London: Longman, 1818), vol. ii, p. 31.

13 Benger, *Memoirs of Hamilton*, vol. i, p. 160.

14 Elizabeth Hamilton, *A Series of Popular Essays Illustrative of Principles Essentially Connected with the Improvement of the Understanding, the Imagination and the Heart*, 3 vols. (Edinburgh, 1813), vol. i, p. xv.

15 Elizabeth Hamilton, reprinted in Benger, ed., *Memoirs*, vol. iii, p. 83.

16 See Susan Staves, *Married Women's Separate Property in England, 1660–1833* (Cambridge, Mass.: Harvard University Press, 1990), for a discussion of women's property rights in the long eighteenth century.

17 William Blackstone, *Commentaries on the Laws of England*, (Oxford, 1765–69), vol. i, p. 430.

18 Maria Luisa Pesante, 'An Impartial Actor: The Private and the Public Sphere in Adam Smith's *Theory of Moral Sentiments*', in Dario Castiglione and Lesley Sharpe, eds., *Shifting the Boundaries: Transformations of the Languages of Public and Private in the Eighteenth Century* (Exeter: Exeter University Press, 1995), pp. 172–95, p. 181.

19 Adam Smith, *Theory of Moral Sentiments*, ed. D. D. Raphael and A. L. Macfie (Liberty Fund, Minneapolis, 1982), p. 113 (iii.i.6).

20 See David Marshall's 'Theatricality of Moral Sentiments' in *Critical Inquiry*, 10 (June 1984), 592–613, for a detailed reading of the implications this language of theatricality has for Smith's theory.

21 Hume, *A Treatise of Human Nature*, book i, p. 301.

22 Smith, *Theory of Moral Sentiments*, p. 46 (i.iii.9).

23 Ibid., p. 191 (iv.ii.2).

24 See G. J. Barker-Benfield, *The Culture of Sensibility – Sex and Society in Eighteenth-Century Britain* (Chicago and London: University of Chicago Press, 1992), in particular pp. 132–41; and Linda Cole, 'Anti-feminist Sympathies: The Politics of Relationship in Smith, Wollstonecraft and More', *ELH* 58 (1991), 107–40. Wollstonecraft's advocacy of marriage as a friendship between intellectual equals also owes much to Smith's *Theory of Moral Sentiments*.

25 Edward Hundert, *The Enlightenment's Fable: Bernard Mandeville and the Discovery of Society* (Cambridge: Cambridge University Press, 1994), p. 225.

26 This perceived incompatibility between Smith's *Theory of Moral Sentiments* and *The Wealth of Nations* – the so-called Adam Smith problem – was posited by a series of German thinkers in the mid-Victorian period who argued that Smith made a u-turn in his philosophy from altruism as the basis of action to egotism. See the editors' introduction to *The Theory of Moral Sentiments*, p. 20.

27 *Theory of Moral Sentiments*, p. 185 (IV.i.2).

28 *Monthly Review* 74 (August 1814), pp. 402–6.

CHAPTER TWELVE

Intimate connections: scandalous memoirs and epistolary indiscretion

Mary Jacobus

> Subjectivity, as the innermost core of the private, was always already oriented to an audience (*Publikum*). The opposite of the intimateness whose vehicle was the written word was indiscretion and not publicity as such.
>
> (Jürgen Habermas, *The Structural Transformation of the Public Sphere*)[1]

Critical social theory assumes the orientation of private subjectivity towards an audience. Habermas, in the passage above, posits a crucial distinction between intimacy and indiscretion, publicity and scandal – suggesting not only that intimacy takes the written (or printed) word as its vehicle, but that writing creates the very forms of Enlightenment intimacy. I want to explore this assumption about the intimacy of writing, and particularly the intimacy of letters, in relation to one woman who entered the public sphere at the end of the eighteenth century via authorship: Mary Wollstonecraft. My example will be what is often regarded as a case of published indiscretion, Wollstonecraft's *Letters to Imlay*, and their relation to Godwin's 'vindication' of Wollstonecraft, his *Memoirs of the Author of the Vindication of the Rights of Woman* (1798). Godwin's Enlightenment *Memoirs* of Wollstonecraft link radical politics, philosophy and feminist protest during the 1790s, incidentally testifying not only to the struggle over women's access to the supposedly masculine sphere of rationality, but to the existence of a distinctive feminist public sphere.[2] His book, however, had the unintended effect of serving to keep alive the 'scandal' of 1790s feminism, at a time when the private lives of women writers sympathetic to the French Revolution had become the focus of anti-Jacobin political discourse. The publication of Godwin's *Memoirs* undoubtedly jeopardised public perception of Wollstonecraft, both at the time and later. But its interest for us now probably lies less in any revelations about the unconventionality of her personal life, than in exposing the unstable relations between the so-called 'life' and the 'letters' – between publicity and intimacy, or between intimacy and what Habermas calls 'indiscretion'. I also want to suggest that while epistolarity may channel subjectivity towards publicity, as Habermas argues, it equally tends to unsettle assumptions about the discursive relations of private and public spheres.

In his preface to the *Memoirs of the Author of the Vindication of the Rights of Woman*, written during the months immediately after Mary Wollstonecraft's death, Godwin represents himself as a survivor: 'to give the public some account of the life of a person of eminent merit deceased, is a duty incumbent on survivors' (p. 204).[3] His account of Wollstonecraft's agonising post-partum death makes it the last chapter of an unorthodox marriage plot; Godwin's 'We did not marry' deserves its place in the annals of feminist fiction alongside Jane Eyre's 'Reader, I married him.' But Godwin's memoir goes further, not only revealing that Wollstonecraft and Godwin 'did not marry' until after her second pregnancy, but that Wollstonecraft had not married her previous lover, the American wheeler-dealer democrat, Gilbert Imlay (the father of her first child, Fanny). Breaching conventional distinctions between life and work, Godwin insists with utopian candour on 'vindicating' the woman as well as the author – even at the cost of scandalising his readers. His *Memoirs* of Wollstonecraft are notably sensitive to and outspoken about the difficulties for women, whether married or unmarried, imposed by the demands of bourgeois conjugality. But it allowed the anti-Jacobins to represent Wollstonecraft as a 'public' woman with 'French' morals, and to discredit her programme for reforming relations between the sexes (especially marriage) as libertinage.[4] Godwin's aim, to the contrary, had been to trace the intimate connection between what he calls 'those virtues which discover themselves principally in personal intercourse' and the public virtues he sees embodied in Wollstonecraft's writings. According to Godwin, 'There are not many individuals with whose character the public welfare and improvement are more intimately connected, than the author of *A Vindication of the Rights of Woman*' (p. 204). His claim may seem hyperbolic today (how much did the *Vindication* actually contribute to 'public welfare and improvement' during the 1790s, one wonders?). But his *Memoirs* of Wollstonecraft set out to redraw the always fluctuating boundaries between the personal and the public, bringing both intimacy and indiscretion into the realm of political debate.

Feminist critiques of Habermas have pointed out that matters involving women's dissident subjectivities or unconventional sexualities are banished in his work to the margins of the bourgeois public sphere, there to become invisible.[5] By contrast, Godwin never allows us to forget that his own 'connection' to Wollstonecraft is an intimate one. He writes apropos of their relationship: 'I am now led . . . to the last branch of her history, the connection between Mary and myself' (p. 256). His representation of Wollstonecraft as writer, radical and feminist is unthinkable outside the terms of the representation of bodily intimacy and affective connection, and to that extent is corrective of the Habermasian paradigm of rational discourse which can be traced back to Godwin himself. Revisionist accounts of Habermas have regularly criticised *The Structural Transformation of the Public Sphere* (1962) for its unitary, unnuanced, ungendered, disembodied, classless and de-racinated account of the bourgeois public sphere. From this vantage-point, the public sphere seems both an abstraction and an idealisation – at best a mobilising fiction for cultural theorists, at worst a 'phantom public sphere' (as it has recently been renamed), lacking either libidinal investments or a textual unconscious.[6] These accounts of Habermas often attend to the problem by multiplying alternative counter-public spheres or subaltern counter-publics, all competing for articulation within or against the dominant bourgeois public sphere. But the model remains that of communication. Despite assuming its orientation to an audience by way of the written word, Habermas implies that subjectivity is more or less transparent, and that public print-culture is continuous with conversation.[7] Aesthetic categories like 'sensibility' or 'melancholia' ought in any case to complicate any simple view of the relations between Enlightenment subjectivity and what comes to be called 'literature' during the course of the eighteenth century. But the starting point for my argument will be Habermas's well known contention that 'the eighteenth century became the century of the letter' and that 'through letter writing the individual unfolded himself [sic] in his subjectivity'.[8]

For Habermas, the mutual unfolding of subjectivity and epistolarity – 'the literary form of "purely human" relations' – is foundational for print-culture. Letters are the conduit by which a free-floating, freely circulating subjectivity, secreted in the bosom of the conjugal family, enters the public sphere and shapes the terms of rational Enlightenment discourse. As the prototypical form of the domestic and psychological novel, the letter (so Habermas argues) permits its readers to enter into an illusion of intimate connection with author and characters, simultaneously providing privileged access to the writer's subjectivity and to an unmediated literature of 'purely human' relations. Above all, the letter provides the model for what Habermas calls 'experiments with the subjectivity discovered in the close relationships of the conjugal family'. Such subjectivity, he asserts, 'by communicating with itself, attained clarity about itself'.[9] But do such experiments in self-communication necessarily lead to clarity? Surely not. And what about the politics of the conjugal family, which remains unproblematically transparent as well? Suggestive and influential as Habermas's formulation has been for subsequent accounts of the relations between epistolarity and the novel, I want to read Wollstonecraftian epistolarity with an ear for an experiment in subjectivity that may be very far from communicating with itself. In particular, rethinking epistolarity along simultaneously psychoanalytic and feminist lines helps to revise the model of subjectivity proposed by Habermas, implying a critique of the very interiority produced by the conjugal family, while at the same time problematising the question of gender – the gender of an author who was herself a woman, and not just a male-authored heroine (like Rousseau's Julie, or Richardson's Clarissa, Habermas's fictional examples). Epistolarity can also unsettle the communicative Habermasian model in other ways, for instance because it can be thought of as having an *object* (a lost object) rather than an audience. This is an intra-psychic realm that can no longer be adequately described by the terms 'public' or 'private'. Paradoxically, the letter becomes the site for the emergence of what Habermas calls 'the literary' precisely at the point where it coincides with published indiscretion.

'A FEMALE WERTER'

clinical observation shows not only that love is with unexpected regularity accompanied by hate (ambivalence), and not only that in human relationships hate is frequently a forerunner of love, but also that in a number of circumstances hate changes into love and love into hate. (Sigmund Freud, 'The Ego and the Id' (1923))[10]

Freud saw the accompaniment of love by hate as one of the hazards endemic in what he calls the 'displaceable energy' of narcissistic libido; in its unpredictable oscillations, only one thing is certain – that love and hate can and often do turn into their opposite. Even thinking can be included among the energetic displacements of sublimated narcissism; and if thinking, why not writing, particularly letter writing?[11] In positing two classes of instincts – a mischief-making love instinct and a destructive death instinct – *The Ego and the Id* also imagines their dangerous 'defusion' (or turning round of one into the other) and its consequences.

Goethe's *The Sorrows of Young Werter* offers a fictional (and epistolary) narrative of just such a 'defusion' of instincts, in which erotic melancholia
is turned against the self in the form of suicide. This was the epistolary
novel that Godwin invoked apropos of his portrait of Wollstonecraft.
Godwin's *Memoirs* memorialise Wollstonecraft as a woman of exquisite
and potentially self-destructive sensibility. Harnessing her life to an
account of his own conversion into a man of feeling, Godwin feminises
the feminist (Wollstonecraft, the Amazonian author of the *Vindications*)
while humanising the philosopher (Godwin himself, the rationalist
author of *Political Justice*) – but at the price of Wollstonecraft's death.[12]
The radical thrust of his *Memoirs* lies partly in its subversive portrait of
the conjugal family, not only as the foundry for melancholic subjectivity
but, by implication at least, as a source for the connection between love
and destructive (self-)hatred. Godwin describes Wollstonecraft's family
of origin (feckless, rootless and downwardly mobile) as having been ruled
by a domestic tyrant given to drink and domestic violence: 'In his family
he was a despot, and his wife appears to have been the first, and most
submissive of his subjects' (p. 206). This parody of the unreconstructed
family of the *ancien régime* recalls Julie's aristocratic family of origin in *La
Nouvelle Héloise* (similarly a site of paternal violence and of a daughter's
attempted political resistance through her sexuality). The unofficial *telos*
of Godwin's *Memoirs* might, in fact, be described as the transformation
of the despotic, dysfunctional eighteenth-century family into the
Enlightenment ideal of companionate, egalitarian marriage. This trajectory allows Godwin to survey a number of unorthodox alternatives
along the way – same-sex family, Platonic *ménage à trois*, Revolutionary
domesticity, single parenthood; and finally, at the end of his story, the
retrospectively legalised sexual relation that equally scandalised those
who supposed Wollstonecraft previously married to Imlay and those
who believed Godwin opposed to marriage on principle. But at the heart
of Godwin's *Memoirs* there remains the riddle of suicide addressed by
Goethe's novel and, later, by Freud's 'Mourning and Melancholia' (1915).
It was surely to this riddle, as much as to her exquisite sensibility, that
Godwin alluded when he celebrated Wollstonecraft as 'a female Werter'.

Godwin's construction of an alternative, all-female family is a recognisable version of the bourgeois family of sentimental fiction. He com-
pares Wollstonecraft's first sight of Fanny Blood ('the ruling passion of
her mind') to the young Werter's first sighting of Charlotte, imagining
her as a young man viewing a scene in which a woman plays a traditionally nurturing role: 'The first object that caught her sight, was a young

woman of a slender and elegant form, and eighteen years of age, busily employed in feeding and managing some children' (p. 210). Godwin, however, suggests that playing the role of economic provider and would-be home-maker for the consumptive and dependent Fanny – 'a woman of a timid and irresolute nature' (p. 217) – had its drawbacks ('for ten years, [Wollstonecraft] may be said to have been, in a great degree, the victim of a desire to promote the benefit of others', p. 214). But Wollstonecraft did apparently derive one positive benefit from her early passion for Fanny Blood, namely 'an assiduous correspondence'. Godwin notes that she 'had hitherto paid but a superficial attention to literature . . . she had not thought of writing as an art'. It was Fanny who instructed her in the art of writing letters, a form of courtship directed at an object 'contemplated . . . in the first instance, with sentiments of inferiority and reverence' (p. 211; compare Werter's idealisation of Charlotte). The romance of Mary Wollstonecraft and Fanny Blood turns out to be the story of a sentimental correspondence – between women, rather than about them. Although Wollstonecraft tried other careers (lady's companion, school-teacher and governess), she eventually succeeded in earning her living as a writer. Godwin singles out as 'the most active period of her life' the economic independence she achieved from the late 1780s onwards with the help of the radical publisher, Joseph Johnson. The plot of Godwin's *Memoirs* deliberately revises the depressingly straitened career options outlined in Wollstonecraft's *Vindication* (the upper-class woman 'alternately under the despotism of a father, a brother and a husband' and the middle and lower-class woman 'shut out . . . from the very means of an industrious subsistence', p. 231). Significantly, authorship is the one career never mentioned in *The Vindication*. Godwin's Wollstonecraft thus emerges as a new species or 'genus' (as she called herself) – the self-created professional woman of letters.[13]

Apropos of the *Vindication*, Godwin, who also notes what he calls its 'rigid, and somewhat amazonian temper', remarks on 'a luxuriance of imagination, and a trembling delicacy of sentiment' (p. 232) which he associates, fancifully, with Tasso's Armida and Virgil's Dido. His Wollstonecraft – part seductive enchantress, part abandoned heroine – is a literary figure, even a figure for the literature of sensibility. The biographical construction of women of letters often tends to assimilate them to the characters of poetry and fiction (sometimes their own); in this respect, Godwin's *Memoirs* is no exception. But Godwin also shows considerable psychological insight and understanding – for instance, in his account of Wollstonecraft's passion for Fuseli. Although he clearly dislikes Fuseli (regarding him as old-fashioned in his literary tastes, an unreconstructed Rousseauian, and a cynic into the bargain), Godwin understands how passionate intellectual conversations about painting could make Wollstonecraft fall in love with a famous (and sexually ambiguous) artist, and he rises to the challenge posed by recounting Fuseli's role in her erotic life: 'What she experienced in this respect, was no doubt heightened, by the state of celibacy and restraint in which she had hitherto lived, and to which the rules of polished society condemn an unmarried woman. She conceived a personal and ardent affection for him. Mr Fuseli was a married man' (p. 234). Speculating about the difficulties facing celibate unmarried women at the end of the eighteenth century, Godwin acknowledges dryly that although Wollstonecraft tried 'to cultivate . . . a Platonic affection for [Fuseli] . . . she did not in the sequel, find all the satisfaction in this plan, which she had originally expected from it' (p. 237). In his narrative, this unsatisfactory compromise with the forms of bourgeois conjugality propelled Wollstonecraft to France. It was here (so Godwin relates) that she found 'that species of connection for which her heart secretly panted' (p. 239). Her relationship with Gilbert Imlay was facilitated by the social and sexual fluidity surrounding relations between men and women in the pro-Revolutionary expatriate circles she frequented in Paris during the early years of the French Revolution.[14] This, more than any other, was the love affair which made Wollstonecraft, for Godwin, 'a female Werter', not only because of the sentimental and domestic ideals that informed it on her side; and not just because of her attempted suicide when it failed. It was also because it led to the writing of the extended sequence of love letters which he published, with such seeming indiscretion, alongside the *Memoirs*, as part of his four-volume edition of Wollstonecraft's posthumous works.

Godwin remarks in his preface that Wollstonecraft's correspondence with Imlay is superior to 'the celebrated romance of Werter' because it is 'the offspring of a glowing imagination, and a heart penetrated with the passion it essays to describe'.[15] This is no second-hand epistolary fiction, but the thing itself. But his publication of Wollstonecraft's love letters tends to assimilate both her love life and her letters to a literary culture of sensibility. For Godwin, her 'life' is all 'works'; living and writing are equivalent (just as, for Wollstonecraft herself, epistolarity became a form of loving).[16] Godwin's reference to Virgil's Dido – one of the great female lovers and suicides of the classical literary tradition – reminds us that Ovid's *Heroides* had provided a powerful model for epistolary fictions based on the letters of betrayed and abandoned women throughout the eighteenth century.[17] Countless examples of such fictions survive, some in verse, some in prose, but all destined for a public audience. For Godwin himself, Wollstonecraft's love letters clearly belonged to a recognisable literary genre with familiar antecedents. They were to be read as exemplary – as literary – rather than as an indiscretion involving a former lover, to be withheld from the public: 'The following Letters may possibly be found to contain the finest examples of the language of sentiment and passion ever presented to the world.'[18] However ill-judged Godwin's decision may seem in retrospect, given their reception by the anti-Jacobin press, the publication of Wollstonecraft's letters to her former lover was entirely consistent with his Enlightenment (and proto-Habermasian) belief in a public sphere of unimpeded rational communicativeness – or, as Godwin would have called it, in the language of his own day, 'sincerity'.

'CRACK! – CRACK! – AND AWAY YOU GO'

we are driven to conclude that the death instincts are by their nature mute and that the clamour of life proceeds for the most part from Eros. And from the struggle against Eros! (Sigmund Freud, '*The Ego and the Id*')[19]

To read Wollstonecraft's love letters to Imlay at a single sitting (the seventy-seven of them published by Godwin, beginning in Paris in mid-1793 and ending in London in late 1795) is to follow the progress of a love affair lived from the start under the threat, and increasingly the reality, of a separation framed by the events of the French Revolution. But these letters also contain a different history. If epistolarity is the natural expression of intimate life in the conjugal family, how does the intimacy of the conjugal family leaves its mark on the subjectivity of the letter-writer? And is it really possible to read letters like Wollstonecraft's as the unmediated, transparent representation of such an interiority? At once performance of sensibility, an exploration of unsatisfied erotic longing and a form of life-writing, her correspondence with Imlay also simultaneously manages and denies the reality of separation. It allows us to trace the unstable polarities of love and hate, and the 'defusion' in which Freud locates the emergence of an (otherwise mute) death drive. In 'The Ego and the Id' (pp. 46–7) Freud defines the libido as 'the force that introduces disturbances into the process of life'. Noisy in love and in the struggle against it, love letters – as we hear in Wollstonecraft's letters to Imlay – may also enact a mute drama closer to the death instinct than to Eros.

Separation is by definition constitutive of the epistolary mode. For Wollstonecraft, the theme of separation prompts melancholy 'reflections' and brings with it the thought of abandonment from the start: 'I do not know how I fell into these reflections, excepting one thought produced it – that these continual separations were necessary to warm your affection. – Of late, we are always separating. – Crack! – Crack! – and away you go' (letter 4; vol. III, p. 8). The pain of separation becomes the semiotic, sado-masochistic whip that drives her correspondence along; later, she will use her pen as a way to mete out punishment to the absent Imlay. Her lover is always on the go, so she will make use of the vehicle of the written word. The same letter complains that while absence gives life to her erotic imagination, and brings its own satisfactions, presence (according to her) is necessary to arouse his senses:

when I am absent from those I love, my imagination is as lively as if my senses had never been gratified by their presence – I was going to say caresses – and why should I not? I have found out that I have more mind than you, in one respect, because I can, without any violent effort of reason, find food for love in the same object, much longer than you can. – The way to my senses is through my heart; but, forgive me! I think there is sometimes a shorter cut to yours. (letter 4; vol. III, p. 8)

What kind of 'object' feeds love like this, and what kind of nourishment does it provide? Surely, an imaginary object – the absent lover who provides hallucinatory nourishment.[20] When Wollstonecraft writes to Imlay about another 'object, in whom we are to have a mutual interest, you know' (letter 5; vol. III, p. 11) – her unborn baby – she confesses that she has 'more confidence in [Imlay's] affection, when absent, than present' (letter 6; vol. III, p. 16). Her letter tries to sustain the fantasy of eroticised domesticity by recreating a tender interlude from their past together – glistening eyes, soft lips, the 'rosy glow' of cheeks. Memory brings a literary tear to the writer's eye in lieu of an exchange of body fluids, making tears the erotic signifiers of absence. Wollstonecraft's letters suffuse and animate Imlay with the glow of her own lively imagination. But even as she reminds him that he is a man of less 'mind' (and by implication, more body) than herself, her letters defend – fantastically – against the pain of separation, substituting for it her own fiction of their intimate connection.

In reality, Wollstonecraft's denial of absence and her idealisation of Imlay proved increasingly hard to sustain. She starts to imagine two Imlays, one loved, the other hated – one, the domesticated man of feeling whom she tries in vain to recall to her side; the other, the man of commerce to whom she writes as moralist and scold. Unable to admit the meaning of his lengthy absences or to ignore his defection from her fictional idyll, she writes, she tells him, 'to keep alive the sentiments in [his] heart' (letter 20; vol. III, p. 49) – and perhaps in hers too. Often in tears between nursing her baby and letter-writing, she longs to find in him 'that overflowing (*épanchement de coeur*), which becoming almost childish, appears a weakness only to the weak' (letter 22; vol. III, pp. 56–7). Mingled with her demand for overflowing feeling (feelings that overflow onto the page) is what she calls 'the remembrance of old griefs' (letter 4; vol. III, p. 10). Are these, perhaps, griefs too old to be remembered – griefs bound up with her dysfunctional family of origin and her unrecorded history in it? The food that nourishes her imagination may be the memory, not of love overflowing, but of love withheld, refused, or denied; separation makes her imagination lively, but it also recapitulates and preserves past losses and unremembered infant sorrow. Or, as Wollstonecraft puts it, 'sorrow has almost made a child of me' (letter 12; vol. III, p. 31). This is sorrow that feeds, hallucinatorily, on a lost object, defending against pain with erotic fantasy. The underside to the willed liveliness – the lively imagination – of Wollstonecraft's love letters (in particular, the new life represented by the infant Fanny) is agitation, fatigue, obsessive preoccupation with repetitive trains of thought. After Imlay's departure for England ('a separation', Godwin editorialises, 'to which no cordial meeting ever succeeded', vol. III, p. 58n), Wollstonecraft writes: 'I have got a habit of restlessness at night, which arises, I believe, from activity of mind; for, when I am alone, that is, no one near to whom I can open my heart, I sink into reveries and trains of thinking, which agitate and fatigue me' (letter 24; vol. III, p. 64). These trains of thought find their outlet in letter-writing – mutating, however, from imaginary love-making into a record of melancholic (and ultimately suicidal) subjectivity.

Just as Wollstonecraft's fantasy of sexual intimacy seems to mask the memory of old griefs, so her imagined proximity to one 'to whom I can open my heart' seems to imply the wish for a relation that is not so much that of lover and beloved as that of child to mother – an unremembered parental relation, whether of overflowing or (more likely) deprivation. The letter becomes a repository for the 'reveries' that agitate her. The epistolary management of absence contains and makes manageable the anxiety aroused by separation.[21] Imlay is always leaving (never to return), but Wollstonecraft's love letters struggle to transform affective hunger into hallucinatory nourishment, loneliness into imaginary intimacy, painful feelings into the exquisite sensibility celebrated by Godwin as the hallmark of her life and writings. By this time, Wollstonecraft was herself the mother of a nursing infant, recording her feelings as a new mother for Imlay's benefit: 'the sensations before she was born, and when she is sucking, were pleasant; but they do not deserve to be compared to the emotions I feel, when she stops to smile upon me' (letter 27; vol. III, pp. 73–4). The infant stops sucking to smile on the mother (finding herself in her mother's face): the mother finds herself in her baby's smile, and Imlay too. A hostage held against his return ('Bring me then back your barrier-face, or you shall have nothing to say to my barrier girl'),[22] the infant Fanny both looks like him and serves as a metonymy for the erotic feelings he once aroused: 'Pressing her to my bosom, she looked so like you . . . every nerve seemed to vibrate to the touch' (letter 24; vol. III, p. 62). But besides being the bait to recapture Imlay's wandering heart, and besides providing Wollstonecraft's 'only comfort' (letter 27; vol. III, p. 78), her baby becomes a signifier for the letter itself. Wollstonecraft's charming and tender portraits of mother and child at play suggest that the letter can be viewed as a kind of potential space. The mother who finds herself in her baby is also the writer who finds herself in the letter. Idealised as a locus of play – the potential space of self-creation and self-discovery – the letter transforms separation into a crucible for literary production.

But, as the months passed, Wollstonecraft increasingly wrote as a depressed, lonely and ill single mother during the difficult French winter of 1794–95. Significantly, her recognition that Imlay's absence had become the defining condition of their life together ('What! is our life then only to be made up of separations?', letter 37; vol. III, p. 112) coincided with thoughts about weaning Fanny. For Melanie Klein, weaning – the decisive loss of an object (the breast) that is always leaving – necessarily involves the suckling baby's hunger for a lost object and all that it stands for; while for D. W. Winnicott, the disillusionment involved in weaning is the necessary condition for object loss.[23] As if weaning her baby acknowledges the true state of affairs with Imlay (that, for all his protestations, he is lost to her), Wollstonecraft puts herself and Fanny through what she calls 'this inquietude' before her departure for England: 'I thought it best to throw this inquietude with the rest, into the sack that I would fain throw over my shoulder.' But, she goes on, 'after sending her to sleep in the next room for three or four nights, you cannot think with what joy I took her back again to sleep in my bosom' (letter 37; vol. III, p. 116). Perhaps she will take Imlay back too. Soon Wollstonecraft is in London, confronting the unmistakable evidence of

Imlay's unfaithfulness, issuing angry ultimatums, and threatening suicide. From this point on, we can read two parallel, published correspondences. On the one hand, we have the anguished and upbraiding letters Wollstonecraft continued to write to Imlay, oscillating wildly between ill-founded hope, hopelessness, and acceptance of Imlay's defection. On the other hand, we have the quasi-fictional, quasi-autobiographical self-writing – combining the romance of solitary wandering with cultural and political commentary – of *Letters Written during a Short Residence in Sweden, Norway and Denmark* (1796), the epistolary travel book which turns Wollstonecraft's separation from Imlay to both economic and imaginative account.[24] The letters she sends to Imlay grow more recriminatory, more bitterly disillusioned; Imlay becomes a shape-changer, persecutory rather than erotic, in the nightmare drama of shifting identities played out by Wollstonecraft's dreams: 'I do not sleep – or, if I close my eyes, it is to have the most terrifying dreams, in which I often meet you with different casts of countenance' (letter 49; vol. ii, p. 147).

The love letter metamorphoses into a scene of mutual torture, a record of exquisite sensibility given over entirely to pain: 'You tell me that my letters torture you; I will not describe the effect yours have on me' (letter 64; vol. iii, p. 184); and again, 'You tell me "that I torment you." – Why do I? – because you cannot estrange your heart entirely from me' (letter 77; vol. iv, p. 32). Unable to 'estrange' her heart from Imlay, Wollstonecraft wields the letter as an instrument of mingled self-torture and revenge. These are no longer love letters, but hate letters – acts of epistolary self-destruction aimed at an imaginary rejecting or abandoning object. The angry suicide letter Wollstonecraft wrote on her return from Scandinavia threatens, as if before an imaginary tribunal, that 'in the midst of business and sensual pleasure, I shall appear before you, the victim of your deviation from rectitude' (letter 69; vol. iv, p. 12). Even after Imlay tries to make an unequivocal break with her, Wollstonecraft pursues him abroad with spectral epistolary vengeance: 'my image will haunt you. – You will see my pale face – and sometimes the tears of anguish will drop on your heart, which you have forced from mine' (letter 75; vol. iv, p. 24). Her tears are made of ink, but in the epistolary imaginary they become drops of blood; as Wollstonecraft writes in her penultimate letter to Imlay: 'In tearing myself from you, it is my own heart that I pierce' (letter 77; vol. iv, p. 33). Her pen is a weapon that wounds the writer as much as the letter's recipient. To break for good with Imlay (as she repeatedly breaks with him in these rhetorically and emotionally overwrought letters) is not necessarily to let him go. Rather, it is a means of hanging on to him – prolonging the epistolary melodrama for yet another protracted episode.

In recent feminist accounts of Enlightenment and post-Enlightenment epistolarity, women's letters are more usually represented as a means of seduction, or else celebrated as the vehicle for transgressive (read: revolutionary) feminine desire.[25] By contrast, Wollstonecraft reveals the love letter's persecutory potential when the epistolary vehicle is driven by the rage of unremembered infantile abandonment. Far from being an instrument of self-knowledge, her letters to Imlay sustain the illusion of connection at all costs – even at the cost of her own suicide. The second edition of Godwin's *Memoirs* tries to explain how Wollstonecraft could have 'stake[d] her life upon the consequences of her error' – that is, her mistaken idealisation of Imlay. Godwin wonders at her willingness to consign to destruction qualities 'formed to adorn society, and give a relish the most delicate and unrivalled in domestic life, as well as, through the medium of the press, to delight, instruct, and reform mankind' (p. 251n). Perhaps Melanie Klein has the answer to Godwin's (and Freud's) question when she speculates that 'the enigmatic reaction of suicide' is as much an attempt to save loved objects as to murder bad ones – a destructive splitting of the self by way of its internal objects.[26] Confronted by the loss of intimate connection and the collapse of a sustaining fiction, the rational Enlightenment subject disintegrates before our eyes. As Godwin reflects, 'it is perhaps a futile attempt, to think of reasoning with a man [sic] in that state of mind which precedes suicide' (p. 251). His *Memoirs* of Wollstonecraft glimpses that the 'other' of Enlightenment philosophy is not so much the woman of exquisite sensibilities as the melancholic suicide epitomised by Werter. In Wollstonecraft's letters, the semiotics of separation – the 'Crack! – Crack!' that drives her epistolary vehicle careering off course – metamorphose into the sign of a self-punishing and punitive subjectivity. The emergence of the literary coincides with the surfacing of a notoriously silent death drive, the clamour of the struggle against Eros.[27] It is this that constitutes the ultimate revelation – the painful indiscretion – of Wollstonecraft's *Letters to Imlay*.

NOTES

1 Jürgen Habermas, *The Structural Transformation of the Public Sphere*, trans. Thomas Burger (Boston: MIT Press, 1991), p. 49.
2 On women, Romanticism and the public sphere, see the special issue of *Studies in Romanticism* devoted to 'Romanticism and its Publics', and particularly Ann Mellor, 'Joanna Baillie and the Counter-Public Sphere', *Studies*

in Romanticism 33 (winter 1994), 559–67. See also Gary Kelly, *Revolutionary Feminism: The Mind and Career of Mary Wollstonecraft* (London: Macmillan, 1992), esp. chapter 7.

3 This and subsequent page references to Godwin's *Memoirs* are to *Mary Wollstonecraft and William Godwin: A Short Residence in Sweden, Norway and Denmark, and Memoirs of the Author of the Rights of Woman*, ed. Richard Holmes (Harmondsworth: Penguin, 1987).

4 For the reception of Wollstonecraft's *Vindication* and anti-Jacobin attacks provoked by Godwin's *Memoirs*, see R. M. James, 'On the Reception of Mary Wollstonecraft's *A Vindication of the Rights of Woman*', *Journal of the History of Ideas* 39 (1978), 293–302. See also *Anti-Jacobin Review* 1 (1798), 94–102, for the scurrilous attack on Wollstonecraft's life.

5 For feminist reconsiderations of Habermas, see, for instance, Joan Landes, 'The Public and the Private Sphere: A Feminist Reconsideration', and Nancy Fraser, 'What's Critical about Critical Theory?', both in *Feminists Read Habermas*, ed. Johanna Meehan (London and New York: Routledge, 1995), pp. 91–116 and 21–56 respectively.

6 See Bruce Robbins, ed., *The Phantom Public Sphere* (Minneapolis: University of Minnesota Press, 1993), especially Bruce Robbins, 'Introduction: The Public as Phantom', pp. vii–xxvi.

7 See especially the critique by Neil Saccamano, 'The Consolations of Ambivalence: Habermas and the Public Sphere', *Modern Language Notes* 106 (1991), 685–98.

8 *The Structural Transformation of the Public Sphere*, p. 48.

9 Ibid., p. 51.

10 *The Standard Edition of the Complete Psychological Works of Sigmund Freud*, ed. and trans. James Strachey, 24 vols. (London: Hogarth Press, 1953–74), vol. xix, pp. 42–3.

11 See *Standard Edition*, vol. xix, p. 44: 'If thought processes in the wider sense are to be included among these displacements, then the activity of thinking is also supplied from the sublimation of erotic motive forces.'

12 For an account of Godwin's *Memoirs* as an autobiographical as well as biographical project, see Mitzi Myers, 'Godwin's *Memoirs* of Wollstonecraft: The Shaping of Self and Subject', *Studies in Romanticism* 20 (Fall 1981), 299–316.

13 '[I]f I exert my talents in writing I may support myself in a comfortable way. I am then going to be the first of a new genus.' *Collected Letters of Mary Wollstonecraft*, ed. Ralph M. Wardle (Ithaca: Cornell University Press, 1979), p. 164.

14 For the Girondin circle of Helen Maria Williams towards which Wollstonecraft gravitated in Paris, see Gary Kelly, *Women, Writing, and Revolution 1790–1827* (Oxford: Oxford University Press, 1993), chapter 2; for the subversive politics associated with Williams, who lived though the Revolution with her partner, John Hurford Stone, see also Mary A. Favret, *Romantic Correspondence: Women, Politics, and the Fiction of Letters* (Cambridge: Cambridge University Press, 1993), chapters 2 and 3.

15 *Posthumous Works of the Author of a Vindication of the Rights of Woman, in Four Volumes* (London: J. Johnson, 1798), vol. III, preface. Subsequent references are to this original edition. Wollstonecraft's letters to Imlay were republished with a prefatory memoir by C. Kegan Paul in 1879 (*Letters to Imlay*, London: C. K. Paul, 1879). Ralph Wardle's later edition of Wollstonecraft's and Godwin's letters in a single volume, *Godwin and Mary: Letters of William Godwin and Mary Wollstonecraft* (Lawrence: University of Kansas Press, 1966), misses the point: the love letters of an exemplary conjugal couple are not the stuff of this epistolary genre.

16 Would Godwin have gone so far as to publish her letters to Fuseli, one wonders? Unfortunately Wollstonecraft's letters to Fuseli were destroyed when they were returned to the Shelley family after Fuseli's death; see Ralph M. Wardle, *Mary Wollstonecraft: A Critical Biography* (Lawrence: University of Kansas Press, 1951), p. 350.

17 For the genesis of epistolary narrative, see Elizabeth J. MacArthur, *Closure and Dynamics in the Epistolary Form* (Princeton, N.J.: Princeton University Press, 1990), chapter 1, and for the *Heroides*, pp. 44, 66–7. For the eighteenth-century origins of epistolary fiction, see also Ruth Perry, *Women, Letters, and the Novel* (New York: AMS Press, 1980).

18 Godwin, 'Preface', in Mary Wollstonecraft Godwin, *Posthumous Works*, 4 vols. in 2 (Clifton: Augustus M. Kelley, 1972), vol. III, p. 5; subsequent parenthetical references to the letters to Imlay in the text refer to the letter number, the volume number, and page.

19 *The Standard Edition* vol. XIX, p. 46.

20 See Joan Riviere, 'The Inner World in Literature', *The Inner World and Joan Riviere: Collected Papers 1920–1958*, ed. Athol Hughes (London: Karnac Books, 1991), pp. 301–30, p. 310, for an exploration of this hallucinatory denial of the lover's absence.

21 Compare the function of the 'analytic relation'; see Jean-Michel Quinodoz, *The Taming of Solitude: Separation Anxiety in Psychoanalysis* (London and New York: Routledge, 1993).

22 Letter 23; vol. III, p. 61, cf. letter 24; vol. III, p. 65 – as Godwin observes in a footnote, this is a reference to the 'interview' at the Paris barrier that led to Fanny's conception.

23 See 'The Psychogenesis of Manic-Depressive States', in *The Selected Melanie Klein*, ed. Juliet Mitchell (New York: The Free Press, 1986), p. 142: 'the depressive position . . . is stimulated and reinforced by the "loss of the loved object" which the baby experiences over and over again when the mother's breast is taken away from it, and this loss reaches its climax during weaning'. See also D. W. Winnicott, 'The Depressive Position in Normal Development', *Through Pediatrics to Psycho-Analysis* (New York: Brunner and Mazel, 1992), p. 275: 'The child's play at throwing things away . . . is an indication of the child's growing ability to master loss, and it is therefore an indication for weaning.'

24 On Wollstonecraft's travel book, see Favret, *Romantic Correspondence*, chapter 4, and Mary Jacobus, 'In Love with a Cold Climate', in *First Things: The Maternal Imaginary in Literature, Art, and Psychoanalysis* (New York and London: Routledge, 1995), chapter 4.

25 See, for instance, Peggy Kamuf, *Fictions of Feminine Desire: Disclosures of Heloise* (Lincoln and London: University of Nebraska Press, 1982), and Linda S. Kauffman, *Discourses of Desire: Gender, Genre, and Epistolary Fiction* (Ithaca and London: Cornell University Press, 1986).

26 Klein, 'The Psychogenesis of Manic-Depressive States', p. 131.

27 For the relation between Klein's splitting of the object and the ego and Freud's 'defusion of instincts', see Herbert Rosenfeld, 'A Clinical Approach to the Psychoanalytic Theory of the Life and Death Instincts', in *Melanie Klein Today*, ed. Elizabeth Bott Spillius, vol. 1 (London and New York: Routledge, 1987), pp. 239–55.

Bibliography

PRIMARY SOURCES

MANUSCRIPTS

Huntington Library, Pasadena, California

Montagu, Elizabeth, correspondence

Royal Academy Archives, London

Society of Artists papers
Royal Academy papers

Society of Arts (RSA) Manuscript Archives, London

Society Minutes 1754–1954
Committee Minutes 1758–
Dr Templeman's Transactions 1770–1839
Prize winning drawings and engravings 1755–c.1810

BOOKS AND PAMPHLETS

Addison, Joseph and Richard Steele, *The Spectator*, ed. Donald F. Bond, 5 vols., (1st edn 1965; Oxford: Clarendon Press, 1987)

Aikin, Lucy, *Epistles on Women, exemplifying their character and condition in various ages and nations* (London: Joseph Johnson, 1810)

Alexander, William, *The History of Women from the Earliest Antiquity, to the Present Time; giving some Account of almost every interesting Particular concerning that Sex, among all Nations, Ancient and Modern*, 2 vols. (London, 1779)

Allen, William, *The Duty of Abstaining from the Use of West India Produce* (London: T. W. Hawkins, 1792)

Anon., *A Bridal Ode on the Marriage of Catherine and Petruchio* (London: J. Bew, 1779)

A Defence of Our Ancient and Modern Historians Against the Frivolous Cavils Of a Late Pretender to Critical History in Which the False Quotations . . . of the Anonymous Author are Confuted and Exposed (London, 1725)

A Genuine Account of the most Horrid Parricide committed by Mary Blandy, Spinster, upon the Body of her Father Mr.Francis Blandy, Gent. Town-Clerk of Henley upon Thames, Oxfordshire . . . (Oxford: 'Printed and sold by C Goddard, in the High Street: And sold in London by R Walker, in the Little Old Bailey, and by all the Booksellers and Pamphlet-Sellers', 1751)

A Mob in the Pit: or, Lines addressed to the D – ch-ss of A——ll (London: S Bladon, 1773)

A Monitory Address to Great Britain: A Poem in Six Parts to Which is Added Britain's Remembrancer (Edinburgh: J. Guthrie, 1792)

A Plain Man's Thoughts on the Present Price of Sugar (London: J. Debrett, 1792)

A Register of Premiums and Bounties given by the Society instituted at London for the Encouragement of Arts, Manufactures and Commerce, (London: no pub., 1778)

An Address to the Duchess of York Against the Use of Sugar (London: no pub., 1792)

Authentick Memoirs of the Wicked Life and Transactions of Elizabeth Jeffryes, Spinster. Who was Executed on Saturday, March 28, 1752, On Epping-Forest, near Walthamstow. For Being Concerned in the Murder of her late Uncle, Mr Joseph Jeffryes (London, 1752)

Authentick Tryals of John Swan, and Elizabeth Jeffryes, for the Murder of Mr. Joseph Jeffryes of Walthamstow in Essex; with the Tryal of Miss Mary Blandy, for the Murder of her own Father. To which are added, The Particulars relating to those horrid Murders; the Behaviour and Dying Speeches of the Criminals; and whatever else is to be relied on as a true History of those memorable Offenders (London, 1752)

'Essay on History', in *Essays and Treatises on Several Subjects* (London, 1758)

Female Patriot, An Epistle from C-t-e M-c-y to the Rev. Dr. W-l-n on her late marriage (London, 1779)

Genuine Letters that pass'd between Miss Blandy and Miss Jeffries, Before and After Conviction (London: 'Printed for J Scott, in Exchange-Alley; and sold by W. Owen, at Temple-Bar; G. Woodfall, at Charing-Cross; J. Jolliff, in St James's Street; and at all the Pamphlet Shops in London and Westminster', 1752)

Nanny Roc-d's Letter to a member of the B – -f Stake Club; In Vindication of Certain Ladies Calumniated in the Freeholder of March 9th. In the Stile of a Certain Knight (London: J. Roberts, 1716)

Old Truths and Established Facts; Being a Reply to a Very New Pamphlet Indeed (London: no pub., 1792)

Peeping Tom to the Countess of Coventry. An Epithalamium (Dublin: 'Printed for S. Price, opposite *Crane-lane* in *Dame-street*, and R Wilson, in *Eustace-street*', [1752])

Remarks on the New Sugar Bill and on the National Compacts Respecting the Sugar Trade and the Slave Trade (London: J. Johnson, 1792)

The ****-Packet Broke-open; or, a Letter from Miss Blandy in the Shades Below, to Capt. Cranstoun in his Exile Above (London: M. Cooper, 1752)

The Anti-Slavery Scrapbook (London: Bagster and Thomas, 1829)

The Case between the Proprietors of the News-Papers and the Coffee-Men of London and Westminster, (London: E. Smith, 1729)

'The Clubs of London', *National Review* 4.8 (1857), 295–334

The Genuine Trial of John Swan and Elizabeth Jeffreys, Spinster, for the Murder of her late Uncle Mr. Joseph Jeffreys of Walthamstow in Essex (London: C. Corbett, [1752])

The Legal Claim of the British Sugar Colonies to Enjoy an Exclusive Right of Supplying this Kingdom with Sugars in Return for Sundry Restrictions Laid upon these Colonies in Favour of the Products, Manufactures, Commerce, Revenue and Navigation of Great Britain (London: no pub., 1792)

The Life and Character of Moll King, Late Mistress of King's Coffee-House in Covent-Garden, Who departed this life at her Country-House at Hampstead, on Thursday the 17th of September, 1747. Containing A true narrative of this well-known Lady, from her Birth to her Death; wherein is inserted several humorous Adventures relating to Persons of both Sexes, who were fond of nocturnal Revels. Also, the Flash Dialogue between Moll King and Old Gentleman Harry, that was some Years ago murdered in Covent-Garden; and the Pictures of several noted Family Men, drawn to the Life. To the Whole is added, An Epitaph and Elegy, wrote by one of Moll's favourite Customers, And a Key to the Flash Dialogue, (London: W. Price, [1747?])

The Speeches of Mr. Wilberforce, Lord Penrhyn, Mr. Burke, Mr. Pitt &c on a Motion for the Abolition of the Slave Trade in the House of Commons, May the 12th, 1789 (London: John Stockdale, 1789)

The Tryal of Mary Blandy, Spinster; for the Murder of her Father, Francis Blandy, Gent. At the Assizes held at Oxford for the County of Oxford, on Saturday the 29th of February, 1752 . . . Published by Permission of the Judges (London: Printed for John and James Rivington, at the Bible and Crown, in St Paul's Church-Yard, 1752)

The Velvet Coffee-Woman: or, the Life, Gallantries and Amours of the late Famous Mrs. Anne Rochford. Particularly I. The History of Her going by that Name; II. The Adventures of her noted Irish-Lover Mac Dermot; III. An Account of that unparallel Imposter Count Brandenburgh; IV. A Funeral Oration to her Memory, and all Ladies of Industry, as well among the Grecians and Romans, as those of our own Nation, (Westminster: Simon Green, 1728)

The Whole Tryal of John Swann, and Elizabeth Jeffries, for the Murder of her Uncle . . . Second Edition. To which is added, The voluntary Confession of Elizabeth Jeffries, since her Conviction; as also an Account of her incestuous Living with her Uncle, and her Motives for murdering him (London: M. Cooper, 1752)

The Women's Petition Against Coffee. Representing to Publick Consideration the Grand Inconveniences accruing to their Sex from the Excessive Use of that Drying Enfeebling Liquor. Presented to the Right Honourable Keepers of the Liberty of Venus. By a Well-willer, (London: no pub., 1674)

Thoughts on Civilisation and the Gradual Abolition of Slavery in Africa and the West Indies (London: J. Sewell, 1788).

Anti-Jacobin Review 1 (1798)

Astell, Mary, *Political Writings*, ed. Patricia Springborg (Cambridge: Cambridge University Press, 1996)

Ballard, George, *Memoirs of Several Ladies of Great Britain, who have been Celebrated for their Writings or Skill in the Learned Languages Arts and Sciences* (Oxford: Printed by W. Jackson, 1752)

Barbauld, Anna Laetitia, *Epistle to William Wilberforce Esq.* (London: Joseph Johnson, 1791)

Barry, James, *An Account of a Series of Pictures, in the Great Room of the Society of Arts, Manufactures, and Commerce, at the Adelphi* (London: 'Printed for the Author by William Adlard, Printer to the Society and sold by T. Cadell in the Strand', 1783)

 The Works of James Barry, ed. Edward Fryer, 2 vols. (London: Cadell and Davies, 1809)

Benger, Elizabeth Ogilvy, *Memoirs of Elizabeth Hamilton* (London: Longman, 1818)

Bentley, Elizabeth, 'On the Abolition of the African Slave Trade, July, 1787,' in *Genuine Poetical Compositions on Various Subjects* (Norwich: Crouse and Stevenson, 1791)

Biographeum Faemineum, The Female Worthies: or, Memoirs of the Most Illustrious Ladies of Great Britain, 2 vols. (London: S. Crowder, 1766)

Birkett, Mary, *A Poem on the African Slave Trade Addressed to her own Sex* (Dublin: J. Jones, 1792)

Blackstone, William, *Commentaries on the Laws of England*, 4 vols. (Oxford: Clarendon Press, 1765–9)

Blandy, Mary, *Miss Mary Blandy's Own Account of the Affair between Her and Mr. Cranstoun from the Commencement of their Acquaintance in the Year, 1746. To the Death of her Father, in August 1751. With all the Circumstances leading to that unhappy Event. To which is added, An Appendix. Containing Copies of some Original Letters now in Possession of the Editor. Together with An exact Relation of her Behaviour whilst under Sentence; and a Copy of the Declaration signed by herself, in the Presence of two Clergymen, two Days before her Execution. Published at her dying Request.* (London: Printed for A. Millar, in the Strand, n.d.)

Boswell, James, *No Abolition of Slavery, or, the Universal Empire of Love* (London: R. Faulder, 1791)

Bradburn, Samuel, *An Address to the People called Methodists; Concerning the Evil of Continuing the Slave Trade* (Manchester: T. Harper, 1792)

Brown, John, *An Estimate of the Manners and Principles of the Times* (London: printed for L. Davis and C. Reymers, 1757)

Brown, Thomas, *The Works of Mr. Thomas Brown. Serious and Comical, in Prose and Verse* (1707), 4 vols. (5th edn, London: Sam Briscoe, 1715)

Brunton, Mary, *Emmeline* (Edinburgh: Manners & Miller, 1819)

Burke, Edmund, *Reflections on the Revolution in France* (1790), ed. Conor Cruise O'Brien (Harmondsworth: Penguin, 1986)

Burn, Andrew, *A Second Address to the People of Great Britain: Containing a New and most Powerful Argument to Abstain from the Use of West India Sugar* (London: M. Gurney, 1792)

Burney, Fanny, *Evelina* (1778), ed. Edward A. Bloom, (Oxford: Oxford University Press, 1982)

Byron, *Don Juan*, ed. T. G. Steffan, E. Steffan and W. W. Pratt, (Harmondsworth: Penguin, 1973)

Carter, Elizabeth, *The Works of Epictetus, consisting of his Discourses, in Four Books, Preserved by Arrian, The Enchiridion, and Fragments. Translated from the Original Greek by the Late Mrs Elizabeth Carter . . . The Fourth Edition with the Translator's Late Additions and Alterations*, ed. Montagu Pennington, 2 vols. (London: F. C. and J. Rivington, 1807)

   Letters from Elizabeth Carter to Mrs Montagu between the years 1755 and 1800, ed. Montagu Pennington, 3 vols. (London: F. C. and J. Rivington, 1817)

Chapone, Hester, *The Works of Mrs Chapone, containing Miscellanies in Prose and Verse* (Dublin, 1775)

Christina, Colvin, ed., *Maria Edgeworth in France and Switzerland* (Oxford: Clarendon Press, 1979)

Clarkson, Thomas, *The History of the Rise, Progress and Accomplishment of the Abolition of the African Slave Trade by the British Parliament*, 2 vols. (London: Longman, Hurst, Rees and Orme, 1808)

Cockings, George, *Arts, Manufactures, and Commerce: A Poem* (London: the author, 1768)

Coleridge, S. T., 'On the Slave Trade', in *The Watchman* (26 March 1796), ed. Lewis Patton (London: Routledge and Kegan Paul, 1792)

Colman, Goerge and Bonnell Thornton, eds., *Poems by Eminent Ladies*, 2 vols. (London, 1755; revised edn in 1780).

Cooper, Anthony Ashley, Earl of Shaftesbury, *Characteristicks of Men, Manners, Opinions, Times*, 3rd edn (London: John Derby, 1723)

Cowper, William, 'The Morning Dream: A Vision', *The Gentleman's Magazine* 58 (1788)

Cowper, William, et al., *The Anti-Slavery Album: Selections in Verse from Cowper, Hannah More, Montgomery, Pringle and Others* (London: Howlett and Brimmer, 1828)

Crafton, William Bell, *A Short Sketch of the Evidence Delivered before a Committee of the House of Commons for the Abolition of the Slave Trade: To Which is Added a Recommendation of the Subject to the Serious Attention of the People in General*, 3rd edn (London: M. Gurney, 1792)

Delany, Mary, *The Autobiography and Correspondence of Mary Granville, Mrs Delany*, ed. Lady Llanover, 6 vols. (London: Bentley, 1861–2)

Dodd, William, *An Account of the Rise, Progress, and Present State of the Magdalen Hospital*, 5th edn (London: 'Printed by W. Faden, for the Charity. And sold at the Hospital, St George's-Fields', 1776)

   The Sisters; or, the History of Lucy and Caroline Sanson, Entrusted to a False Friend (1754), 2 vols. in 1 (London: Harrison, 1781)

Dossie, Robert, *Memoirs of Agriculture and other Oeconomical Arts* (London: J. Nourse, 1782)

Duncombe, John, *The Feminead, or Female Genius, A Poem*, 2nd edn (London: Printed for R. and J. Dodsley, 1757)

Dyce, Alexander, *Specimens of British Poetesses* (London, 1825)

Edgeworth, Maria, *Belinda* (1801), ed. Eiléan Ni Chuilleanain (London: Dent, 1993)

Letters for Literary Ladies, ed. Claire Connolly (London: Everyman, 1993)

Helen, ed. Susan Manly and Clíona Ó Gallchoir, vol. IX of *The Novels and Selected Works of Maria Edgeworth* (London: Pickering and Chatto, 1999)

Edgeworth, R. L., and Maria Edgeworth, *Memoirs of Richard Lovell Edgeworth, begun by himself and completed by his daughter*, 2 vols. (London: R. Hunter, 1820)

Ellis, Grace A., *A Memoir of Mrs Anna Laetitia Barbauld, with many of her letters* (Boston: James R. Osgood, 1874)

Falconar, Harriet and Maria, *Poems on Slavery* (London: J. Johnson, 1788)

Fielding, Henry, *The Covent-Garden Tragedy. As it is Acted at the Theatre-Royal in Drury-Lane. By his Majesty's Servants* (London: J. Watts, 1732)

The History Of The Adventures Of Joseph Andrews, and of his Friend Mr. Abraham Adams (London: A Millar, 1742)

Finer, Ann and George Savage, eds., *The Selected Letters of Josiah Wedgwood* (Oxford: Clarendon Press, 1965)

Foot, Jesse, *A Defence of the Planters in the West Indies* (London: J. Debrett, 1792)

Fox, William, *An Address to the People of Great Britain*, 10th. edn (London: M. Gurney, 1792)

Genlis, Mme de, *A Short Account of the Conduct of Mme de Genlis since the Revolution* (Perth: R. Morison, 1796)

Memoirs of the Countess de Genlis, 8 vols. (London: Henry Colburn, 1825)

Gerard, Alexander, *An Essay on Taste, with three dissertations on the same subject. By Mr. De Voltaire, Mr. D'Alembert, F. R. S. Mr. de Montesquieu* (London: A. Millar, 1759)

Godwin, William, *Memoir of the Author of the Vindication of the Rights of Woman* (London: J. Johnson and G. G. and J. Robinson, 1798)

Hamilton, Elizabeth, *A Series of Popular Essays Illustrative of Principles Essentially Connected with the Improvement of the Understanding, the Imagination and the Heart* (Edinburgh, 1813)

Harrington, James, *The Political Works*, ed. J. G. A. Pocock (Cambridge: Cambridge University Press, 1977)

Hays, Mary, *Female Biography; or, Memoirs of Illustrious and Celebrated Women, of All Ages and Countries. Alphabetically arranged*, 6 vols. (London: Richard Phillips, 1803)

Heywood, Thomas, *The Generall History of Women, Containing the Lives of the most Holy and Prophane, the most Famous and Infamous in all ages, exactly described not only from Poeticall Fictions, but from the most Ancient, Modern, and Admired Historians to Our Times* (London, 1657)

Hilliar, Anthony, *A Brief and Merry History of Great Britain, Containing an Account of the Religions, Customs, Manners, Humours, Characters, Caprices, Contrasts, Foibles, Factions &c., of the People. Written originally in Arabic by Ali-Mohammed Hadgi,* (London: J. Roberts, J. Shuckburgh, J. Penn and J. Jackson, 1730)

Hollis, Thomas, *Memoirs of Thomas Brand Hollis*, ed. John Disney (London, 1808)

Holmes, Richard, ed., *Mary Wollstonecraft and William Godwin: A Short Residence in Sweden, Norway and Denmark and Memoirs of the Author of the Rights of Woman* (Harmondsworth: Penguin, 1987).

Home, Henry, Lord Kames, *Sketches of the History of Man*, 2 vols. (Edinburgh, 1774)

Humboldt, Alexander de and Aimé Bonpland, *Personal Narrative of Travels to the Equinoctial Regions of the New Continent, During the Years 1799–1804 . . . Translated into English by Helen Maria Williams*, 7 vols. (London: Longman, Rees, Orme et al., 1814–29)

Hume, David, *Essays Moral, Political and Literary* (London: Oxford University Press, 1963)

A Treatise of Human Nature (1739–40), ed. Ernest C. Mossner (London: Penguin Books, 1985)

Hutchinson, Lucy, *Memoirs of the Life of Colonel Hutchinson* (London: J. Hutchinson, 1806)

Keate, George, *An Epistle to Angelica Kauffman* (London, 1781)

Kelly, Gary, ed., *Bluestocking Feminism: Writings of the Bluestocking Circle*, 6 vols. (London: Pickering and Chatto, 1999)

Kippis, Andrew, *The Life of Captain James Cook* (London: G. Nichol and G. J. Robinson, 1788)

Knapp, O. G., ed., *The Intimate Letters of Hester Piozzi and Penelope Pennington 1788–1821* (London: Bodley Head, 1914)

Knipe, Eliza, 'Attomboka and Omaza', in *Six Narrative Poems* (London: C. Dilly, 1787)

Lambert, Anne Thérèse, Marchioness de, *The Works of the Marchioness de Lambert. A new edition from the French*, 2 vols. (London, 1781)

Le Breton, Anna Laetitia, ed., *Memoir of Mrs Barbauld Including Letters and Notices of her Family and Friends* (London: George Bell, 1874)

Lyttleton, George (Baron Lyttleton), *Dialogues of the Dead* (London: W. Sandby, 1760)

M. P., *A Character of Coffee and Coffee-Houses. By M.P.* (London: John Starkey, 1661)

Macaulay, Catharine, *The History of England, from the Accession of James I to that of the Brunswick Line*, 8 vols. (London: J. Nourse, 1763–83)

A Modest Plea for the Protection of Copyright (Bath: Edward and Charles Dilly, 1774)

The History of England, from the Revolution to the Present time, in a series of letters (Bath: R. Crutwell, 1778), vol. 1

Observations on the Reflections of the Right Hon. Edmund Burke on the Revolution in France (London: C. Dilly, 1790)

Letters on Education, with Observations on religious and metaphysical subjects (London: C. Dilly, 1790)

Macky, John, *A Journey Through England. In Familiar Letters. From a Gentleman Here, to his Friend Abroad*, 3rd edn (London: J. Hooke, 1723)

Miller, Rev. James, *The Coffee-House. A Dramatick Piece. As it is Perfom'd at the Theatre Royal in Drury-Lane* (London: J. Watts, 1737)

Misson de Valberg, Henri, *Mémoirs et observations faites par un voyageur en Angleterre*, (La Haye, 1698); trans. Ozell, *Memoirs and Observations in his Travels over England. With some account of Scotland and Ireland. Dispos'd in Alphabetical Order* (London: D. Browne et al., 1719)

Montagu, Elizabeth, *An Essay on the writings and genius of Shakespear, compared with the Greek and French dramatic poets. With some remarks upon the misrepresentations of Mons. de Voltaire* (London: J. Dodsley, 1769)

    Elizabeth Montagu, the Queen of the Bluestockings: Her Correspondence from 1720 to 1761, ed. Emily J. Climenson, 2 vols. (London: John Murray, 1906)

    Mrs. Montagu, 'Queen of the Blues': Her Letters and Friendships from 1762 to 1800, ed. Reginald Blunt, 2 vols. (London: Constable, 1923)

More, Hannah, *The Slave Trade: A Poem* (London: T. Cadell, 1788)

    The Sorrows of Yamba: or, the Negro Woman's Lamentation (London: R. White, 1795)

    'Bas Bleu, or Conversation. Addressed to Mrs Vesey', in *Selected Writings of Hannah More*, ed. Robert Hole (London: Pickering & Chatto, 1996)

Morgan, Lady, *France*, 4th edn, 2 vols. (London, 1818)

Ovid, *Metamorphoses*, trans. Mary Innes (London: Penguin Classics, 1955)

Pennington, Montagu, ed., *A Series of Letters between Mrs. Elizabeth Carter and Miss Catherine Talbot, from the year 1741 to 1770. To which are added, Letters from Mrs. Elizabeth Carter to Mrs. Vesey, between the Years 1763 and 1787; Published from the origininal manuscripts in the possession of The Rev. Montagu Pennington, M.A.*, 2 vols. (London: F. C. and J. Rivington, 1808)

Polwhele, Richard, *The Unsex'd Females: A Poem addressed to the author of the Pursuits of Literature* (London: Cadell & Davies, 1798)

Pratt, Samuel Jackson, *Humanity, or, The Rights of Nature: A Poem in Two Books*, part 1 (London: T. Cadell, 1788)

Price, Richard, 'A Discourse on the Love of Our Country, delivered on Nov. 4, 1789, at the Meeting-House in the Old Jewry, to the Society for Commemorating the Revolution of Great Britain. With an Appendix, containing the report of the Committee of the Society', in *Political Writings*, ed. D. O. Thomas (Cambridge: Cambridge University Press, 1991)

Randolf, Francis, *Remarkable Extracts and Observations on the Slave Trade with some Considerations on the Consumption of West India Produce* (London: J. Johnson, 1792)

Richardson, Samuel, *Pamela* (London: C. Rivington and J. Osborn, 1740)

    Clarissa, 7 vols. (London: S. Richardson, 1747–8)

Robinson, Mary, *Sappho and Phaon. In a Series of Legitimate Sonnets, with Thoughts on Poetical Subjects, and Anecdotes of the Grecian Poetess* (London: Printed by S. Gosnell, 1796)

    A Letter to the Women of England, on the Injustice of Mental Subordination (London: T. N. Longman and O. Rees, 1799)

Roscoe, William, *The Wrongs of Africa* (London: R. Faulder, 1788)

Roughead, William, ed., *Trial of Mary Blandy*, Notable English Trials series (Edinburgh and London: William Hodge, 1914)

Rouquet, André, *The Present State of the Arts in England* (1755), ed. R. W. Lightbown (London: Cornmarket Press, 1970)

Rousseau, Jean-Jacques, *Oeuvres complètes*, ed. Bernard Gagnebin et Marcel Raymond (Paris: Gallimard, 1964)

[*La Nouvelle Héloïse*, 1761] *Eloisa, or a series of original letters*, trans. William Kenrick (1803), 4 vols. in 2 (Oxford: Woodstock Books, 1989)

Rushworth, John, *Historical Collections*, 7 vols. (London: T. Newcomb, 1659)

Samuel, Richard, *Remarks on the Utility of Drawing and Painting. To the Society Instituted at London for the Encouragement of Arts, Manufactures and Commerce* (London: printed by Thomas Wilkins, Aldmanbury, 1786)

Scott, Mary, *The Female Advocate; a poem occasioned by reading Mr Duncombe's Feminead* (London: Joseph Johnson, 1774)

Scott, Sarah, *The History of Cornelia* (London: A. Millar, 1750)

   A Journey through Every Stage of Life, Described in a Variety of Interesting Scenes, Drawn from Real Characters, 2 vols. (London, 1754)

   Agreeable Ugliness; or, The Triumph of the Graces; Exemplified in the Real Life and Fortunes of a Young Lady of Some Distinction, from the French (London, 1754)

   The History of Gustavus Ericson, King of Sweden; with an Introductory History of Sweden, from the Middle of the Twelfth Century (London: A. Millar, 1761)

   A Description of Millenium Hall, and the country adjacent: together with the characters of the inhabitants, and such historical anecdotes & reflections, as may excite in the reader proper sentiments of humanity . . . By a Gentleman on his travels (London, 1762)

   The History of Mecklenburgh, from the First Settlement of the Vandals in that Country, to the Present Time; including a Period of about Three Thousand Years (London, 1762)

   The History of Sir George Ellison (London: A Millar, 1766)

   Filial Duty; in a Series of Letters between Miss Emilia Leonard and Miss Charlotte Arlington (London: the author, 1772)

   The History of Theodore Agrippa d'Aubigné, containing a Succinct Account of the Most Remarkable Occurrences during the Civil Wars of France in the Reigns of Charles IX., Henry III., Henry IV., and the Minority of Lewis XIII (London: E. & C. Dilly, 1772)

Seward, Anna, *The Letters of Anna Seward: Written between the Years 1784 and 1807* (Edinburgh: E. Ramsay, 1811)

Seward, Thomas, 'The Female Right to Literature', in *A Collection of Poems in Several Hands* (London: Printed for R. Dodsley, 1748) vol. II, pp. 295–302

Smith, Adam, *The Theory of Moral Sentiments* (1764), ed. D. D. Raphael and A. L. Macfie (Oxford: Clarendon Press, 1976) reprinted by the Liberty Fund in 1982

Smollett, Tobias, *The Adventures of Roderick Random* (1748), ed. Paul-Gabriel Boucé (Oxford: Oxford University Press, 1981)

Staël, Germaine de, *Considerations on the Principal Events of the French Revolution*, 3 vols. (London: Baldwin, Craddock and Joy, 1818)

Stevens, George Alexander, *The Adventures of a Speculist; or, A Journey Through London¼ exhibiting a Picture of the Manners, Fashions, Amusements, &c. of the Metropolis at the middle of the eighteenth century*, 2 vols. (London: for the editor, sold by S. Bladon, 1788)

The Critical Review, 1788

The Gentleman's Magazine, 1788–9

The Monthly Review, 1789

Thrale, Hester Lynch, *Thraliana: The Diary of Mrs Hesther Lynch Thrale 1776–1809*, 2nd edn, ed. Katherine C. Balderston (Oxford: Clarendon Press, 1965)

Ticknor, George, *Life, Letters and Journals of George Ticknor*, ed. G. S. Hillard, 2 vols. (London: Sampson Low, 1876)

Walpole, Horace, *Letters of Horace Walpole*, ed. Mrs Paget Toynbee, 15 vols. (Frowde: Oxford, 1904–5)

The Yale Edition of Horace Walpole's Correspondence, ed. W. S. Lewis, 48 vols. (London: Oxford University Press, 1937–83)

Ward, Edward, *The London Spy Compleat, in Eighteen Parts*, 2nd edn (London: J. How, 1704)

Wardle, Ralph, *Godwin and Mary: Letters of William Godwin and Mary Wollstonecraft* (Lawrence: University of Kansas Press, 1966)

Wardle, Ralph M., ed., *Collected Letters of Mary Wollstonecraft* (Ithaca: Cornell University Press, 1979)

Williams, Helen Maria, *A Poem on the Bill Lately Passed for Regulating the Slave Trade* (London: T. Cadell, 1788)

Paul and Virginia, translated from the French by (London: G. G. & J. Robinson, 1795)

A Tour in Switzerland; or, A view of the present state of the governments and manners of those cantons, with comparative sketches of the present state of Paris, 2 vols. (London: G. G. & J. Robinson, 1798)

Sketches of the state of manners and opinions in the French Republic towards the close of the eighteenth century. In a series of letters (London, 1801)

Poems on Various Subjects, with Introductory Remarks on the Present State of Literature and Science in France (London, 1823)

Letters from France (8 vols. in 2), Facsimile Reproduction with an introduced by Janet Todd (Scholars Facsimiles, Delmar, NY 1975)

Wollstonecraft, Mary, *Posthumous Works of the Author of a Vindication of the Rights of Woman, in Four Volumes* (London: J. Johnson, 1798)

Letters to Imlay (London: C. K. Paul, 1879)

Posthumous Works, 4 vols. (Clifton: Augustus M. Kelley, 1972)

The Works of Mary Wollstonecraft, ed. Janet Todd and Marilyn Butler (London: William Pickering, 1989)

A Vindication of the Rights of Men and *A Vindication of the Rights of Woman* and *Hints*, ed. by Sylvana Tomaselli (Cambridge: Cambridge University Press, 1995)

Wordsworth, William, *Selected Prose* ed. John O. Hayden (London: Penguin Books, 1988)

Yearsley, Ann, *A Poem on the Inhumanity of the Slave Trade* (London: C. G. & J. Robinson, 1788)

SECONDARY SOURCES

Abrams, M. H., *A Glossary of Literary Terms*, 6th edn (Fort Worth: Harcourt Brace Jovanovich College Publishers, 1993)

Adams, M. Ray, 'Helen Maria Williams and the French Revolution', in E. L. Griggs, ed., *Wordsworth and Coleridge: Studies in Honour of George Mclean Harper* (Princeton: Princeton UP, 1939)

Alexander, Sally and Barbara Taylor, 'In defence of patriarchy', *New Statesman* 21 (Dec. 1979)

Allan, D. G. C., *William Shipley Founder of the Royal Society of Arts: A Biography with Documents* (London: Scolar Press, 1968)

'Artists and the Society in the 18th Century: (ii) Members and Premiums in the First Decade, 1755–64', *Journal of the Royal Society of Arts*, (March 1984), 271–5

RSA: A Chronological History of the Royal Society for the Encouragement of Arts, Manufactures and Commerce (London: RSA, 1998)

Altman, Janet, *Epistolarity: Approaches to a Form* (Columbus: Ohio State University Press, 1982)

Ashfield, Andrew, ed., *Romantic Women Poets, 1770–1838: An Anthology* (Manchester: Manchester University Press, 1995)

Romantic Women Poets, 1788–1848, vol. II (Manchester and New York: Manchester University Press, 1998)

Babington, Thomas, Lord Macauley, *The History of England from the Accession of James the Second (1848–55)*, 6 vols (London: Macmillan, 1913)

Ballaster, Ros, et al., *Women's Worlds: Ideology, Femininity and the Woman's Magazine* (London: Macmillan, 1991)

Bann, Stephen, *The Clothing of Clio* (Cambridge: Cambridge University Press, 1984)

Barker, Hannah and Elaine Chalus, eds., *Gender in Eighteenth-Century England: Roles, Representations and Responsibilities* (London and New York: Longman, 1997)

Barker-Benfield, G. J., *The Culture of Sensibility: Sex and Society in Eighteenth-Century Britain* (Chicago and London: University of Chicago Press, 1992)

Barrell, John, *The Political Theory of Painting from Reynolds to Hazlitt: 'The Body of the Public'* (New Haven and London: Yale University Press, 1986)

'The public prospect and the Private View: The Politics of Taste in Eighteenth-Century Britain', in his *The Birth of Pandora and the Division of Knowledge* (Basingstoke and London: Macmillan, 1992) pp. 41–63

Barrell, John, ed., *Painting and the Politics of Culture: New Essays on British Art 1700–1830* (Oxford: Oxford University Press, 1992)

Barty-King, Hugh, *The Baltic Story: Baltick Coffee House to Baltic Exchange, 1744–1994* (London: Quiller Press, 1994)

Baumgärtel, Bettina, ed., *Retrospektive Angelika Kauffmann* (Düsseldorf: Verlag Gerd Hatje, 1999)

Belanger, Terry, 'Publishers and Writers in Eighteenth-Century England', in Isabel Rivers, ed., *Books and their Readers in Eighteenth-Century England* (New York: St. Martin's Press, 1982), pp. 5–25

Bennett, Judith M., 'Feminism and History', *Gender and History* 1 (1989)

Bermingham, Anne, 'Elegant Females and Gentleman Connoisseurs: The Commerce in Culture and Self-Image in Eighteenth-Century England', in

Bermingham and John Brewer, eds., *The Consumption of Culture 1600–1800: Image, Object, Text* (Routledge: London and New York, 1995), pp. 489–514

Bermingham, Anne and John Brewer, eds., *The Consumption of Culture, 1600–1800: Image, Text, Object* (London and New York: Routledge, 1995)

Berry, Christopher, *The Idea of Luxury, A Conceptual and Historical Investigation* (Cambridge: Cambridge University Press, 1994)

Bignamini, Iliaria and Martin Postle, *The Artist's Model. Its Role in British Art from Lely to Etty*, ed. Martin Postle and Joanne Wright (Nottingham: University of Nottingham Art Gallery, 1991)

Bleackley, Horace, *The Beautiful Duchess: Being an Account of the Life and Times of Elizabeth Gunning, Duchess of Hamilton and Argyll* (London: John Lane The Bodley Head and New York: Dodd, Mead, 1907)

Bock, Gisela, 'Women's History and Gender History: Aspects of an International Debate', *Gender and History* 1.1 (1989), 7–30

Bohls, Elizabeth, *Women Travel Writers and the Language of Aesthetics 1716–1818* (Cambridge: Cambridge University Press, 1995)

Bramah, Edward and Joan Bramah, *Coffee Makers: 300 Years of Art and Design* (London: Quiller, 1989)

Breen, Jennifer, ed., *Women Romantic Poets, 1785–1832: An Anthology* (London: Everyman, 1992)

Brewer, John, 'This, That and the Other: Public, Social and Private in the Seventeenth and Eighteenth Centuries', in Dario Castiglione and Lesley Sharpe, eds., *Shifting the Boundaries: Transformations of the Language of Public and Private in the Eighteenth Century* (Exeter: Exeter University Press, 1995)

The Pleasures of the Imagination: English Culture in the Eighteenth Century (London: HarperCollins, 1997)

Brissenden, R. F., *Virtue in Distress: Studies in the Novel of Sentiment from Richardson to Sade* (London: Macmillan, 1974)

Brodsky, Joseph, 'The Muse is Feminine and Continuous', *Literary-Half-Yearly* (Mysore) 32.1 (1991) 21–3

Broglie, Gabriel de, *Madame de Genlis* (Paris: Librairie Académique Perrin, 1985)

Bruhns, Karl, ed., *Life of Alexander Von Humboldt*, 2 vols., trans. Jane and Caroline Lassell (London: Longman, 1873)

Bryan, Michael, *Bryan's Dictionary of Painters and Engravers*, new edition revised and enlarged under the supervision of George L. Williamson (London: George Bell, 1905)

Butler, Judith, *Bodies that Matter: On the Discursive Limits of 'Sex'* (New York and London: Routledge, 1993)

Butler, Marilyn, *Maria Edgeworth: A Literary Biography* (Oxford: Clarendon Press, 1972)

Jane Austen and the War of Ideas (Oxford: Clarendon Press, 1987)

Butler, Marilyn, ed., *Burke, Paine, Godwin and the Revolution Controversy* (Cambridge: Cambridge University Press, 1984)

Calhoun, Craig, ed., *Habermas and the Public Sphere* (Boston: Massachusetts Institute of Technology, 1992)

Castiglione, Dario and Lesley Sharpe, eds., *Shifting the Boundaries: Transformations of the Language of Public and Private in the Eighteenth Century* (Exeter: Exeter University Press, 1995)

Castle, Terry, *The Female Thermometer: 18th-Century Culture and the Invention of the Uncanny* (New York and Oxford: Oxford University Press, 1995)

Chamberlain, Lori, 'Gender and the Metaphorics of Translation', *Signs* 13 (Spring 1988)

Clark, Anna, 'Gender and Politics in the Long Eighteenth Century: A Review Essay', *History Workshop Journal* 48 (Autumn 1999), 252–7

Clery, Emma J., 'Women, Publicity and the Coffee-House Myth', *Women: A Cultural Review* 2.2 (1991), 168–77

Clifford, Helen, 'Key Document from the Archives: The Awards of Premiums and Bounties by the Society of Arts', *Royal Society of Arts Journal* (August/September 1997), 78–9

Cohen, Jean L. and Andrew Arato, *Civil Society and Political Theory* (Cambridge, Mass.: MIT Press, 1992)

Cole, Linda, 'Anti-Feminist Sympathies: The Politics of Relationship in Smith, Wollstonecraft and More', *ELH* 58 (1991), 107–40

Coleman, Deirdre, 'Conspicuous Consumption: White Abolitionism and English Women's Protest Writing in the 1790s', *ELH* 61 (1994)

Colley, Linda, *Britons: Forging the Nation, 1707–1837* (London and New York: Yale University Press, 1992)

Colson, Percy, *White's, 1693–1950* (London: William Heineman, 1951)

Compston, H. F. B., *The Magdalen Hospital. The Story of a Great Charity* (London: SPCK, 1917)

Copley, Stephen, ed., *Literature and the Social Order in Eighteenth-Century England* (London: Croom Helm, 1984)

Corrigan, Philip and Derek Sayer, *The Great Arch: English State Formation and Cultural Revolution* (Oxford and New York: Basil Blackwell, 1985)

Cunningham, Andrew and Nicholas Jardine, eds., *Romanticism and the Sciences*, (Cambridge: Cambridge University Press, 1990)

Davidoff, Leonore, 'Regarding Some 'Old Husbands' Tales': Public and Private in Feminist History', in her *Worlds Between: Historical Perspectives on Gender and Class* (Cambridge: Polity, 1995)

Davidoff, Leonore and Catherine Hall, *Family Fortunes: Men Women and the English Middle Class, 1780–1850* (London: Hutchinson, 1987)

Davies, Natalie Zemon, 'History's Two Bodies', *American Historical Review* 93.1 (1988), 1–30.

de Saussure, César, *A Foreign View of England in the Reibns of George I & George II: the letters of Monsieur César de Saussure to his Family, translated and edited by Madame Van Muyden* (written 1729, 1st edn, London: John Murray, 1902)

Deane, Seamus, *Strange Country: Modernity and Nationhood in Irish Writing Since 1790* (Oxford: Clarendon Press, 1997)

Delia Gaze, ed., *Dictionary of Women Artists*, 2 vols. (London and Chicago: Fitzroy Dearborn Publishers, 1997)

Derrida, Jacques, 'White Mythologies', in *Margins of Philosophy*, trans. Alan Bass (Brighton: Harvester, 1982)

Dettelbach, Michael, 'Romanticism and Administration: Mining, Galvinism and Oversight in Alexander von Humboldt's Global Physics' (unpublished PhD dissertation, Cambridge University, 1994)

'Global Physics and Aesthetic Empire: Humboldt's Physical Portrait of the Tropics', in David Miller and Peter Reill, eds., *Visions of Empire: Voyages, Botany, and Representations of Nature* (Cambridge: Cambridge University Press, 1996), pp. 258–92

Dictionary of National Biography (DNB) (Oxford: Oxford University Press, 1995)

Ditchfield, G. M., 'Some Literary and Political Views of Catherine Macaulay', *American Notes and Queries* 12 (1974), 70–6

Dood, G., 'Public Refreshment', in Charles Knight, ed., *London*, 6 vols. (London: Charles Knight, 1843), vol. IV, pp. 305–20

Drescher, *Capitalism and Anti-Slavery: British Mobilization in Comparative Perspective* (Basingstoke: Macmillan, 1986)

Dunne, Tom, '"A Gentleman's Estate Should be a Moral School": Edgeworthstown in Fact and Fiction, 1760–1840', in Raymond Gillespie and Gerard Moran, eds., *Longford: Essays in County History* (Dublin: Lilliput Press, 1991), pp. 95–121

Eagleton, Terry, *The Function of Criticism* (London: Verso, 1984)

Earle, Peter, *The Making of the English Middle Class: Business, Society and Family Life in London, 1600–1730* (London: Methuen 1989)

Edelstein, T. J., *Vauxhall Gardens* (New Haven: Yale Center for British Art, 1983)

Eger, Elizabeth, 'Fashioning a Female Canon: Eighteenth-Century Women Poets and the Politics of the Anthology', in Isobel Armstrong and Virginia Blain, eds., *Women's Poetry in the Enlightenment: The Making of a Canon, 1730–1820* (London: Macmillan, 1999), pp. 201–15

Eimer, Christopher, *The Pingo Family and Medal-Making in Eighteenth-Century Britain* (London: British Art Medal Trust, 1998)

Elias, Norbert, *The Civilising Process*, trans. Edmund Jephcott, (1st edn 1938; Oxford: Blackwell, 1994)

Ellis, Frank H., *Sentimental Comedy: Theory and Practice* (Cambridge: Cambridge University Press, 1991)

Ellis, Markman, *The Politics of Sensibility: Race, Gender and Commerce in the Sentimental Novel* (Cambridge: Cambridge University Press, 1996)

Elshtain, Jean Bethke, *Public Man, Private Woman: Women in Social and Political Thought* (Oxford: Robertson, 1981)

Erdman, David, *Commerce des Lumières: John Oswald and the British in Paris, 1790–3* (Columbia: University of Missouri Press, 1986)

Ezell, Margaret, *Writing Women's Literary History* (Baltimore and London: Johns Hopkins University Press, 1993)

Favret, Mary A., *Romantic Correspondence: Women, Politics, and the Fiction of Letters* (Cambridge: Cambridge University Press, 1993)

Feldman, Paula, ed., *British Women Poets of the Romantic Era: An Anthology* (Baltimore: Johns Hopkins University Press, 1997)

Fergus, Jan and Janice Farrar Thaddeus, 'Women, Publishers, and Money, 1790–1820', *Studies in Eighteenth-Century Culture* 17 (1987), 191–207

Folger Collective on Early Women Critics, eds., *Women Critics 1660–1820* (Bloomington and Indianapolis: Indiana University Press, 1997)

Foreman, Amanda, *Georgiana: Duchess of Devonshire* (London: HarperCollins, 1998)

Fraser, Nancy, 'What's Critical about Critical Theory?', in Johanna Meehan, ed., *Feminists Read Habermas* (London and New York: Routledge, 1995), pp. 21–56

Gallagher, Catherine, *Nobody's Story: The Vanishing Acts of Women Writers in the Marketplace, 1670–1820* (Berkeley: University of California Press, 1994)

Gantz, Ida, *The Pastel Portrait: The Gunnings of Castle Coote and Howards of Hampstead* (London: The Cresset Press, 1963)

Gilman, Sander, 'AIDS and Syphilis: The Iconography of Disease', in Douglas Crimp, ed., *AIDS: Cultural Analysis / Cultural Activism* (Cambridge, Mass.: MIT Press, 1988)

Gleadle, Kathryn and Sarah Richardson, eds., *The Power of the Petticoat: Women in British Politics, 1760–1860* (Basingstoke: Macmillan, 2000)

Goodman, Dena, 'Enlightenment Salons: The Convergence of Female and Philosophic Ambitions', *Eighteenth Century Studies* 22.3 (1989), 329–50

The Republic of Letters: A Cultural History of the French Enlightenment (London: Cornell University Press, 1994)

Gordon, Scott Paul 'Voyeuristic Dreams: Mr. Spectator and the Power of Spectacle', *The Eighteenth Century* 36.1 (1995), 3–23

Greer, Germaine, *Slip-Shod Sibyls* (London: Viking, 1995)

Grundy, Isobel and Susan Wiseman, eds., *Women, Writing, History: 1640–1740* (London: Batsford, 1992)

Guest, Harriet, 'The Dream of a Common Language: Hannah More and Mary Wollstonecraft', *Textual Practice* 9 (1995)

Habermas, Jürgen, *The Structural Transformation of the Public Sphere: An Inquiry into a Category of Bourgeois Society*, trans. Thomas Burger (Cambridge: Polity, 1989); originally published in German under the title *Strukturwandel der Öffentlichkeit*, (Darmstadt and Neuwied: Hermann Luchterhand Verlag, 1962)

'Further Reflections on the Public Sphere', in Craig Calhoun, ed., *Habermas and the Public Sphere* (Cambridge, Mass. and London: The MIT Press, 1992), pp. 421–62

Harmand, Jean, *The Keeper of Royal Secrets: Being the Private and Political Life of Madame de Genlis* (London: Eveleigh Nash, 1913)

Hemingway, Andrew, 'The Political Theory of Painting without the Politics', *Art History* 10.3 (1987), 381–95

Hewitson, Anthony, ed., *Diary of Thomas Bellingham* (Preston, 1908)

Hill, Bridget, *The Republican Virago. The Life and Times of Catharine Macaulay, Historian* (Oxford: Clarendon Press, 1992)

Hilton, Boyd, *The Age of Atonement: The Influence of Evangelicalism on Social and Economic Thought, 1785–1865* (London: Oxford University Press, 1988)

Hobby, Elaine, *Virtue of Necessity: English Women's Writing, 1646–1688* (London: Virago Press, 1988)

Hohendahl, Peter, *The Institution of Criticism* (Ithaca: Cornell University Press, 1982)

Holmes, Geoffrey, *Augustan England: Professions, State and Society 1680–1730* (London and Boston: George Allen and Unwin, 1983)

Homans, Margaret, *Women Writers and Poetic Identity* (Chicago: University of Chicago Press, 1980)

Honour, Hugh, *The Image of the Black in Western Art*, vol. IV (Cambridge, Mass.: Harvard University Press, 1989)

Hont, Istvan and Michael Ignatieff, eds., *Wealth and Virtue: The Shaping of Political Economy in the Scottish Enlightenment* (Cambridge: Cambridge University Press, 1983)

Howson, Gerald, *The Macaroni Parson: A Life of the Unfortunate Dr. Dodd* (London: Hutchinson, 1973)

Hudson, Derek and Kenneth Luckhurst, *The Royal Society of Arts 1754–1954* (London: John Murray, 1954)

Hundert, Edward, *The Enlightenment's Fable: Bernard Mandeville and the Discovery of Society* (Cambridge: Cambridge University Press, 1994)

Hunt, Lynn, *The Family Romance of the French Revolution* (London: Routledge, 1992)

Hunt, Tamara L., 'Elizabeth Nutt: An Eighteenth-Century London Publisher', *Antiquarian Book Monthly* (December 1996), 20–4

Hutchison, Sidney C., *The History of the Royal Academy 1768–1968* (London: Chapman and Hall, 1968)

Italia, Iona, 'Philosophers, Knight-Errants, Coquettes and Old Maids: Gender and Literary Self-Consciousness in the Eighteenth-Century Periodical (1690–1765)' (unpublished PhD dissertation, University of Cambridge, 1997)

Jacobus, Mary, *First Things: The Maternal Imaginary in Literature, Art, and Psychoanalysis* (New York and London: Routledge, 1995)

James, R M, 'On the Reception of Mary Wollstonecraft's *A Vindication of the Rights of Woman*', *Journal of the History of Ideas* 39 (1978), 293–302

Jay, Peter and Caroline Lewis, eds., *Sappho through English Poetry* (London: Anvil Press Poetry, 1996)

Johnson, Pauline, 'Feminism and the Enlightenment', *Radical Philosophy* 63 (1993), 3–13.

Jones, Chris, *Radical Sensibility: Literature and Ideas in the 1790s* (London and New York: Routledge, 1993), 3–13

Jones, Rica, 'The Artist's Training and Techniques', in *Manners and Morals: Hogarth and British Painting 1700–1760* (London: Tate Gallery, 1987) pp. 19–28

Jones, Robert, *Gender and the Social Formation of Taste in Eighteenth-Century Britain* (Cambridge: Cambridge University Press, 1998)

Jones, Vivien, *Women in the Eighteenth Century: Constructions of Femininity* (London: Routledge, 1990)

'Women Writing Revolution: Narratives of History and Sexuality in Wollstonecraft and Williams', in Stephen Copley and John Whale, eds., *Beyond Romanticism: New Approaches to Texts and Contexts 1780–1832* (London and New York: Routledge, 1992)

Jones, Vivien, ed., *Women and Literature in Britain, 1700–1800* (Cambridge: Cambridge University Press, 2000)

Jordanova, Ludmilla and Peter Hulme, eds., *The Enlightenment and Its Shadows* (London: Routledge, 1990)

Kamuf, Peggy, *Fictions of Feminine Desire: Disclosures of Heloise* (Lincoln and London: University of Nebraska Press, 1982)

Kauffman, Linda S., *Discourses of Desire: Gender, Genre, and Epistolary Fiction* (Ithaca and London: Cornell University Press, 1986)

Kelly, Gary, *Revolutionary Feminism: The Mind and Career of Mary Wollstonecraft* (London: Macmillan, 1992)

Women, Writing, and Revolution 1790–1827 (Oxford: Clarendon Press, 1993)

'Introduction', in Sarah Scott, *A Description of Millenium Hall* (Peterborough, Ont.: Broadview Press, 1995)

Kerber, Linda, 'Separate Spheres, Female Worlds, Woman's Place: The Rhetoric of Women's History' *JAH* 75.1 (1988)

Klein, Lawrence, 'The Third Earl of Shaftesbury and the Progress of Politeness', *Eighteenth Century Studies* 18.2 (1984–5), 186–214

'Gender, Conversation and the Public Sphere in Early Eighteenth-Century England', in Judith Still and Michael Worton, eds., *Textuality and Sexuality* (Manchester: Manchester University Press, 1993), pp. 100–15

'Gender and the Public/Private Distinction in the Eighteenth Century: Some Questions about Evidence and Analytic Procedure', *Eighteenth Century Studies* 29 (1995), 92–109

'Coffeehouse Civility, 1660–1714: An Aspect of Post-Courtly Culture in England', *Huntingdon Library Quarterly* 59.1 (1997), 30–51

Knapp, Steven, *Personification and the Sublime: Milton to Coleridge* (Cambridge, Mass.: Harvard University Press, 1985)

Kowaleski Wallace, Elizabeth, *Consuming Subjects: Women, Shopping and Business in the Eighteenth Century* (New York: Columbia University Press, 1997)

Landau, Leya, 'Reading London: the Literary Representation of the City's Pleasures, 1700–1782' (unpublished PhD dissertation, University College, University of London, 1999)

Landes, Joan B., *Women and the Public Sphere in the Age of the French Revolution*, (Ithaca: Cornell University Press, 1988)

'The Public and the Private Sphere: A Feminist Reconsideration', in Johanna Meehan, ed., *Feminists Read Habermas* (London and New York: Routledge, 1995), pp. 91–116

Landes, Joan B., ed., *Feminism, the Public and the Private* (Oxford and New York: Oxford University Press, 1998)

Langford, Paul, *A Polite and Commercial People: England 1727–1783* (Oxford: Oxford University Press, 1989)

Larson, Edith Sedgwick, 'A Measure of Power: The Personal Charity of Elizabeth Montagu', *Studies in Eighteenth-Century Culture* 16 (1986), 197–210

Lerner, Gerda, *The Majority Finds its Past: Placing Women in History* (New York: Oxford University Press, 1979)

The Creation of Patriarchy (Oxford and New York: Oxford University Press, 1981)

Lillywhite, Bryant, *London Coffee-Houses* (London: George Allen & Unwin, 1963)

Lloyd, David and Paul Thomas, *Culture and the State* (New York and London: Routledge, 1998)

Lloyd, Sarah, '"Pleasure's Golden Bait": Prostitution, Poverty and the Magdalen Hospital in Eighteenth-Century London', *History Workshop Journal* 41 (1996), 50–70

Longe, Julia G., *Martha Lady Giffard: Her Life and Correspondence (1664–1722)*, (London: George Allen, 1911)

Lonsdale, Roger, *The Oxford Book of Eighteenth-Century Women Poets* (Oxford: Oxford University Press, 1989)

MacArthur, Elizabeth J., *Closure and Dynamics in the Epistolary Form* (Princeton, N.J.: Princeton University Press, 1990)

MacCarthy, Bridget G., *The Female Pen*, 2 vols. (Cork: Cork University Press, 1946–7)

Maltzhan, Nicholas von, *Milton's History of Britain: Republican Historiography in the English Revolution* (Oxford: Oxford University Press, 1991)

Marshall, David, 'Theatricality of Moral Sentiments', *Critical Inquiry* 10 (June 1984), 592–613

McCalman, Iain, 'Ultra-Radicalism and Convivial Debating-Clubs in London, 1795–1838', *English Historical Review* 102 (1987), 309–33

McDowell, Paula, *Women of Grub Street: Press, Politics, and Gender in the Literary Marketplace, 1678–1730* (Oxford: Clarendon Press, 1998)

McDowell, R. B., *Ireland in the Age of Imperialism and Revolution, 1760–1801* (Oxford: Clarendon Press, 1991)

McGann, Jerome, ed., *The New Oxford Book of Romantic Period Verse* (Oxford: Oxford University Press, 1993)

McKendrick, Neil, John Brewer, and J. H. Plumb, *The Birth of a Consumer Society: The Commercialization of Eighteenth-Century England* (Bloomington: Indiana University Press, 1982)

McKeon, Michael, *The Origins of the English Novel* (Johns Hopkins, 1987; repr. London: Hutchinson, 1988)

Meehan, Johanna, ed., *Feminists read Habermas – Gendering the Subject of Discourse* (London: Routledge, 1995)

Mellor, Ann, 'Joanna Baillie and the Counter-Public Sphere', *Studies in Romanticism* 33 (winter 1994), 559–67

Metcalfe, A. E., *Woman's Effort: A Chronicle of British Women's Fifty Years Struggle for Citizenship (1865–1914)* (Oxford, 1917)

Midgley, Clare, *Women Against Slavery: The British Campaigns 1780–1870* (London: Routledge, 1994)

Miller, John, *The Glorious Revolution*, 2nd edn (Longman: London and New York, 1997)

Mintz, Sidney, *Sweetness and Power: The Place of Sugar in Modern History* (Harmondsworth: Penguin, 1985)

Mitchell, Juliet, *Women's Estate* (New York: Pantheon, 1972)

Mitchell, Juliet, ed., *The Selected Melanie Klein* (New York: The Free Press, 1986)

Moore, Frank Frankfort, *A Georgian Pageant* (New York: E. P. Dutton and Company, 1909)

Myers, Mitzi, 'Godwin's *Memoirs* of Wollstonecraft: The Shaping of Self and Subject', *Studies in Romanticism* 20 (1981), 299–316

Myers, Sylvia Harcstark, *The Bluestocking Circle: Women, Friendship, and the Life of the Mind in Eighteenth-Century England* (Oxford: Clarendon Press, 1990)

New Monthly Magazine and Literary Journal 16 (1826)

Newman, Gerald, *The Rise of English Nationalism: A Cultural History, 1740–1830* (London: Weidenfeld and Nicholson, 1987)

Nichols, John, Thomas Percy and John Calder, eds., *The Spectator*, 1788–89, 8 vols.

Norbrook, David, *Writing the English Republic* (Cambridge: Cambridge University Press, 1998)

Nussbaum, Martha, 'Through the Prism of Gender: How Scholarship About Women's Lives is Changing our Understanding of the Past – and the Present', *Times Literary Supplement*, 20 March 1998, pp. 3–4

Ogborn, Miles, *Spaces of Modernity; London's Geographies 1680–1780* (New York: The Guilford Press, 1988)

Outram, Dorinda, *The Enlightenment* (Cambridge: Cambridge University Press, 1995)

Pateman, Carole, 'The Fraternal Social Contract', in John Keane, ed., *Civil Society and the State: New European Perspectives* (London: Verso, 1988)

    The Sexual Contract (Cambridge: Polity Press, 1988)

    The Disorder of Women: Democracy, Feminism and Political Theory (Cambridge: Polity Press, 1989)

Paulson, Ronald, *Hogarth*, 3 vols., (Cambridge: The Lutterworth Press, 1992–3)

Pearson, Jacqueline, *Women's Reading in Britain, 1750–1835: A Dangerous Recreation* (Cambridge: Cambridge University Press, 1999)

Percival, Alicia C., 'Women and the Society of Arts in its Early Days', *Journal of the Royal Society of Arts* 125 (December 1976–November 1977), 266–9, 330–3, 416–18

Perry, Gill, '"The British Sappho": Borrowed Identities and the Representation of Women Artists in late Eighteenth-Century British Art', *The Oxford Art Journal* 18.1 (1995), 44–57

Perry, Ruth, *Women, Letters, and the Novel* (New York: AMS Press, 1980)

    The Celebrated Mary Astell: An Early English Feminist (Chicago: University of Chicago Press, 1986)

Pincus, Steven, "'Coffee Politicians Does Create'": Coffeehouses and Restoration Political Culture', *Journal of Modern History* 27 (1995), 807–34

Pocock, J. G. A., *The Machiavellian Moment: Florentine Republican Thought and the Atlantic Tradition* (Princeton: Princeton University Press, 1975)

Virtue, Commerce and History (Cambridge: Cambridge University Press, 1985)

Pocock, J. G. A., ed., *The Political Works of James Harrington* (Cambridge: Cambridge University Press, 1977)

Pointon, Marcia, *Hanging the Head: Portraiture and Social Formation in Eighteenth-Century England* (New Haven and London: Yale University Press, 1993)

Strategies for Showing. Women, Possession, and Representation in English Visual Culture, 1665–1800 (Oxford: Oxford University Press, 1997)

Porter, Roy, 'Material Pleasures in the Consumer Society', in Roy Porter and Marie Mulvey Roberts, eds., *Pleasure in the Eighteenth Century* (Basingstoke: Macmillan, 1996), pp. 19–36

Porter, Roy and M. Teich, eds., *The Enlightenment in National Context* (Cambridge: Cambridge University Press, 1981)

Pratt, Mary Louise, *Imperial Eyes: Studies in Travel Writing and Transculturation* (London: Routledge, 1992)

Pressly, William J., *The Life and Art of James Barry* (New Haven and London: Yale University Press, 1981)

Quinodoz, Jean-Michel, *The Taming of Solitude: Separation Anxiety in Psychoanalysis* (London and New York: Routledge, 1993)

Reinhold, Helmut, 'Zur Sozialgeschichte des Kaffees und des Kaffeehauses', *Kölner Zeitschrift für Soziologie und Sozialpsychologie* 10 (1958), 151–4

Reiss, Timothy, *The Meaning of Literature* (New York: Cornell University Press, 1992)

Rendall, Jane, *The Origins of Modern Feminism: Women in Britain, France and the United States 1780–1860* (Basingstoke and London: Macmillan, 1985)

'Virtue and Commerce: Women in the Making of Adam Smith's Political Economy', in Ellen Kennedy and Susan Mendus, eds., *Women in Western Political Philosophy* (Brighton: Harvester Wheatsheaf, 1987)

Reynolds, Sir Joshua, *Discourses on Art*, ed. Robert R. Wark (New Haven and London: Yale University Press, 1975)

Richardson, R.C., *The Debate on the English Revolution* (London: Methuen, 1975)

Richetti, John J., *Popular Fiction before Richardson: Narrative Patterns 1700–1739*, (Oxford: Clarendon, 1969)

Riley, Denise, *'Am I that Name?' Feminism and the Category of 'Women'* (London: Macmillan Press, 1988)

Rivière, Joan, 'The Inner World in Literature', *The Inner World and Joan Rivière: Collected Papers 1920–1958*, ed. Athol Hughes (London: Karnac Books, 1991)

Rizzo, Betty, 'Introduction', in Sarah Scott, *The History of Sir George Ellison* (Lexington: University Press of Kentucky, 1996)

Robbins, Bruce, *The Phantom Public Sphere*, (Minneapolis and London: University of Minnesota Press, 1993)

Robbins, Caroline, *The Eighteenth-Century Commonwealthman: Studies in the Transmission, Development and Circumstance of English Liberal Thought from the Restoration of Charles II until the War with the Thirteen Colonies* (Cambridge, Mass.: Harvard University Press, 1959)

Roberts, William, *Memoirs of the Life and Correspondence of Mrs. Hannah More* (London: R. B. Seely and W. Burnside, 1834)

Robinson, Edward Forbes, *The Early History of Coffee Houses in England, With Some Account of the First Use of Coffee and a Bibliography of the Subject* (London: Kegan, Paul, Trench and Trübner, 1893)

Robinson, Henry and Walter Adams, eds., *The Diary of Robert Hooke, 1672–1689* (London, 1935)

Rosaldo, Michelle Zimbalist and Louise Lamphere, eds., *Women, Culture and Society* (Stanford, Calif.: Stanford University Press, 1974)

Rosenfeld, Herbert, 'A Clinical Approach to the Psychoanalytic Theory of the Life and Death Instincts', in Elizabeth Bott Spillius, ed., *Melanie Klein Today*, vol. 1 (London and New York: Routledge, 1988), pp. 239–55

Ross, Angus, 'Introduction', in Angus Ross, ed., *Selections from The Tatler and The Spectator* (London: Penguin, 1982)

Ross, Marlon B., *The Contours of Masculine Desire: Romanticism and the Rise of Women's Poetry* (New York and Oxford: Oxford University Press, 1989)

Roughead, William, ed., *Trial of Mary Blandy*, Notable English Trials series (Edinburgh and London: William Hodge, 1914)

Rowbotham, Sheila, 'The trouble with patriarchy', *New Statesman* 21 (Dec. 1979)

Roworth, Wendy Wassyng, ed., *Angelica Kauffman: A Continental Artist in Georgian England* (Brighton and London: Reaktion Books, 1992)

Russo, Mary, *The Female Grotesque: Risk, Excess and Modernity* (New York and London: Routledge, 1994)

Saccamano, Neil, 'The Consolations of Ambivalence: Habermas and the Public Sphere', *Modern Language Notes* 106 (1991), 685–98

Schiebinger, Londa, 'Feminine Icons: The Face of Modern Science', *Critical Inquiry* (Summer 1988), 661–91

Schnorrenberg, Barbara Brandon, 'The Brood Hen of Faction: Mrs Macaulay and Radical Politics, 1765–1775', *Albion* 11.1 (1979), 33–45

Scott, Walter S., *The Bluestocking Ladies* (London: John Green, 1947)

Shapiro, Ann-Louise, ed., *Feminists Revision History* (New Brunswisk, N.J., 1994)

Shevelow, Kathryn, *Women and Print Culture: The Construction of Femininity in the Early Periodical* (London: Routledge, 1989)

Siltanen, Janet and Michelle Stanworth, eds., *Women and the Public Sphere: A Critique of Sociology and Politics* (London: Hutchinson, 1984)

Silver, Larry, 'Step-Sister of the Muses: Painting as Liberal Art and Sister Art', in Richard Wendorf, ed., *Articulate Images. The Sister Arts from Hogarth to Tennyson* (Minneapolis: University of Minnesota Press, 1983) pp. 36–70

Smith, Hilda, ed., *Women Writers and the Early Modern Political Tradition* (Cambridge: Cambridge University Press, 1998)

Solkin, David H., *Painting for Money: The Visual Arts and the Public Sphere in Eighteenth-Century England* (New Haven and London: Yale University Press, 1992)

Sombart, Werner, *Luxury and Capitalism* (1919) (Ann Arbour: University of Michigan Press, 1967)

Spencer, Jane, *The Rise of the Woman Novelist: From Aphra Behn to Jane Austen* (Oxford and New York: Oxford University Press, 1986)

Sperber, Dan, 'Rudiments de rhétorique cognitive', *Poetique* 23 (1975)

Stallybrass, Peter and Allon White, *The Politics and Poetics of Transgression* (London: Methuen, 1985)

Staves, Susan, 'British Seduced Maidens', *Eighteenth Century Studies* 14 (Winter 1980–81), 109–34

  '"The Liberty of a She-Subject of England": Rights Rhetoric and the Female Thucydides', *Cardozo Studies in Law and Literature* 2 (1989), 161–83

  Married Women's Separate Property in England, 1660–1833 (Harvard University Press, 1990)

Steeves, Harrison R., *Before Jane Austen: The Shaping of the English Novel in the Eighteenth Century* (London: George Allen & Unwin, 1966)

Stephen, Leslie, *English Literature and Society in the Eighteenth Century* (1903) (London: Methuen, 1966)

Sterne, Madeleine B., 'The English Press in Paris and its Successors, 1793–1852', *Papers of the Bibliographical Society of America* 74.4 (1980), 307–59

Sussman, Charlotte, 'Women and the Politics of Sugar, 1792' *Representations* 48 (1994), 48–69

Sutherland, Kathryn, and Stephen Copley, eds., *Adam Smith's Wealth of Nations: New Interdisciplinary Essays* (Manchester: Manchester University Press, 1995)

Taylor, Barbara, 'Work in Progress: Feminism and the Enlightenment, 1650–1850. Research Agenda for a Comparative History', *History Workshop Journal* 47 (Spring 1999), 261–72

Thom, Martin, *Republics, Nations and Tribes* (London: Verso, 1995)

Thompson, E. P., *The Making of the English Working Class* (Harmondsworth: Penguin Books, 1963)

Tillyard, Stella, *Citizen Lord: Edward Fitzgerald, 1763–1798* (London: Vintage, 1998)

Timbs, John, *Club Life of London with Anecdotes of the Clubs, Coffee-Houses and Taverns of the Metropolis During the 17th, 18th, and 19th Centuries*, 2 vols. (London: Richard Bentley, 1866)

Todd, Janet, ed., *A Wollstonecraft Anthology* (Cambridge: Polity Press, 1989)

Tomaselli, Sylvana, 'The Enlightenment Debate on Women', *History Workshop Journal* 20 (Autumn 1985)

  'The Role of Woman in Enlightenment Conjectural Histories', in Hans Erich Bödeker and Liselotte Steinbrügge, eds., *Conceptualizing Women in Enlightenment Thought. Penser la femme au siècle des Lumières* (European Science Foundation, forthcoming)

Tomeroy, Peter, 'Angelica Kauffman ("Sappho")', *The Burlington Magazine* 63 (1971) 275–6

Trevelyan, G. M., *English Social History: A Survey of Six Centuries from Chaucer to Queen Victoria* (London, 1944)

Triechler, Paula, 'AIDS: Gender and Biomedical Discourse: Current Contests for Meaning', in Elizabeth Fee and Daniel M. Fox, eds., *AIDS: The Burdens of History* (Berkeley: University of California Press, 1988)

Uglow, Jenny, *Hogarth: A Life and a World* (London: Faber, 1997)

Uphaus, Robert W. and Gretchen M. Foster, eds., *The 'Other' Eighteenth Century. English Women of Letters, 1660–1800* (East Lansing: Colleagues Press, 1991)

Van Sant, Ann Jessie, *Eighteenth-Century Sensibility and the Novel: The Senses in Social Context* (Cambridge: Cambridge University Press, 1993)

Verrückt nach Angelika: Porzellan und anderes Kunsthandwerk nach Angelika Kauffmann (Düsseldorf: Hetjens-Museum, 1999)

Vickery, Amanda, 'Golden Age to Separate Spheres? A Review of the Categories and Chronology of English Women's History', *Historical Journal* 36.2 (1993)

A Gentleman's Daughter (New Haven and London: Yale University Press, 1998)

Wardle, Ralph M., *Mary Wollstonecraft: A Critical Biography* (Lawrence: University of Kansas Press, 1951)

Warner, Marina, *Monuments and Maidens* (London: George Weidenfield & Nicholson, 1985)

Waterhouse, Sir Ellis, 'The Bourgeois Sentimental Decade: 1740–1750', in *Three Decades of British Art 1740–1770* (Philadelphia: American Philosophical Society, 1965), pp. 1–23

Wilson, Angus, *A Bit Off the Map, and Other Stories* (New York: The Viking Press, 1957)

Wilson, Kathleen, 'Empire of Virtue. The Imperial Project and Hanoverian Culture, c. 1720–1785', in Lawrence Stone, ed., *An Imperial State at War: Britain, 1689–1815* (London: Routledge, 1994)

Winnicott, D. W., 'The Depressive Position in Normal Development', *Through Pediatrics to Psycho-Analysis* (New York: Brunner and Mazel, 1992)

Woodward, Lionel, *Une Anglaise Amie de la Revolution Francaise: Hélène-Marie Williams et ses Amis* (Paris 1930).

Woolf, D. R., 'The "Common" Voice: History, Folklore and Oral Tradition in Early Modern England', *Past and Present* 120 (1988) 26–52

Wright, Charles and C. Ernest Fayle, *A History of Lloyd's from the Founding of Lloyd's Coffee House to the Present Day* (London: Macmillan, 1928)

Yolton, John et al., eds., *The Blackwell Companion to the Enlightenment* (Oxford: Blackwell, 1991)

Index

abolition 10–12, 133–51
  sugar, abstention from 135, 143, 144–6
  see also slavery
Addison, Joseph 33
  see also *The Spectator*
aesthetics
  and muses 108
  and women 11, 106, 112–13
Altman, Janet 229
anthologies 13, 22 n. 41
Antoinette, Marie 213, 247
Apollo 107, 108, 111, 120
Armstrong, Nancy 12, 13
Arria 190
Ashfield, Andrew 13
associationism 259–60
Astell, Mary 5
  A Serious Proposal to the Ladies 54

Baillie, Joanna 200, 258
Ballard, George 113
Bann, Stephen 191, 192
Barbauld, Anna Laetitia 13, 18, 107, 169, 177
  and James Barry 116, 117
  and educational writing 15
  Epistle to William Wilberforce Esq. 12,
    147–150
  and female literary critics 122
  and religion 174
  as virago 181
Barbon 83
Barker-Benfield, G. J. 267
Barlow, Joel 221, 223
Barrell, John 77, 106
Barry, James 106, 107,108, 116, 118
  Letter to the Dilettanti Society 11,104, 105
  Progress of Human Knowledge and Culture 76, 95,
    96, 116
belles-lettres 176
Berry, Chistopher 83
Berry, Mary 181

biography 17
Blackstone, William 263
Blandy, Mary 9, 54, 55, 56, 57, 60, 61, 66
Bleackley, Horace 59
Bluestockings
  assemblies 16
  calibration of by Byron 228–229
  correspondence of 177, 178
  cultural authority of 6
  feminism of 15, 163–78
  influence on Bloomsbury 178
  influence on Helen Maria Williams 221
  patronage 170
  and philanthropy 169, 173
  politics of 167–9
  publications of 170
  religious orientation of 169, 174–175
  see also women, networks of
Bohls, Elizabeth 217, 223, 231
Bolingbroke, *see* patriot king
Bonpland, Aimé 218, 224, 227
Boswell, James
  Life of Johnson 217
Bramah, Edward 31, 47 n.16
breast-feeding, male 227
Brewer, John 8, 76
Britannia 111, 124
Broglie, Duchess de 224
Brown, John
  *An Estimate of the Manners and Principles of the
    Times* 81, 82
Brunton, Mary 1, 2, 12
Brutus 185
Burgh, James 188
Burke, Sir Edmund 188, 201, 241, 246, 247
  Reflections on the Revolution in France 17, 181,
    195, 201, 208
Burnet, Gilbert 183, 184, 189, 190
Burney, Frances 177, 200
  Evelina 80
Butler, Marilyn 203, 213

Byron, George Gordon, Lord
  Don Juan 228, 229

Calamay, Edmund 183
Carter, Elizabeth 14, 55, 107, 122, 124, 163,
    173–5, 177
  Epictetus 175
  Poems 174
  Remarks on the Athanasian Creed 174
Castle, Terry 228
Chamberlain, Lori 220
Chambers, William 115
Chapone, Hester 14, 18, 125, 176–7
  Letters on the Improvement of the Mind 176
charity 8, 83, 173
Charles II 189–90
Chartres, Duke of 211
Chateaubriand 194
Cheere, Sir Henry 83, 84
Cibber, Colley 39
citizens 18
civic humanism 10–11, 16, 17, 81, 82, 83, 85,
    106, 182
  and the arts 104
civic virtue 8, 16, 194
  see also virtue
civil society 116, 164, 240
Civil War, English 183, 185
Clarendon 183, 186
Clarkson, Thomas 135, 140
Cleopatra 148
Clery, Emma 31, 46 n.7, 47 n. 16
Clifford, Helen 94
Clio 188, 191–2
  see also muses
clubs 165, 214
  'British Club' in Paris 221
coffee-houses 27–45
  as counter-culture 31
  female 42
  Habermas's account of 8, 9, 27–8
  politeness in 30
  sociability in 29
  transformation into clubs 43
  women in 27, 31–43
coffee-women 9, 31–43
Cole, Linda 267
Coleridge, S. T. 230
  'plagiarisms' in *Biographia Literaria* 219
  The Watchman 145
Colley, Linda 2, 201, 204, 205, 257
commerce 10–11, 81, 140, 149, 182, 243
  and abolition 133–51
  civic humanist distrust of 85
  commodity exchange 134, 135

humanity of 133
  see also culture, commercialisation of
Compston, H. F. B. 63
Constant, Benjamin 223, 224
contract theory 4–5
conversation 6, 165, 170, 200, 209, 214
Copley, Stephen 76
copyright
  engravers' 76
  literary 14, 15
Coram, Thomas 80
cosmopolitanism 17, 202, 220, 240
Cosway, Maria 120
Covent Garden 32, 35
Cowper, William
  'Morning Dream' 134
Crabb Robinson, William 223, 224, 225
Crafton, W. B. 143
culture
  feminisation of 166
  commercialisation of 164, 172

Davidoff, Leonore 1
Day, Thomas 204, 205
Deane, Seamus 201, 202
Declaration of Independence, American 5
Declaration of the Rights of Man, French 5
Deffant, Mme du 200
De Grey 184
Delany, Mary 118
Devonshire, Georgiana, Duchess of 257
Dodd, William 64, 65
  The Sisters 62
domestic ideology 13, 15, 17, 171, 177, 213–14
domestic sphere 176, 239
Dossie, Robert 92
Duncombe, Susanna 14

Eagleton, Terry 27
Echard, Laurence 183
Edgeworth, Maria 1, 2, 12, 17, 200–14
  Belinda 88
  Helen 200–1, 202
  Letters for Literary Ladies 17, 200–14
Edgeworth, Richard Lovell 202, 203, 204, 205
  Edinburgh Review 225
education 125, 201, 203, 207, 253–4, 259
  philosophy and 271
Elias, Norbert 30
Elizabeth I 188
Elliott, Marianne 211
Ellis, Markman 65
empire 138, 173
  and aesthetics 113–15, 129 n. 36
  and women 208

Enlightenment 5, 7, 15, 17, 191, 106, 261,
    269
    and coffee-house sociablity 30
    epistolarity 286
    philosophy 286
    reason 208–9
    and scientific authority 228
    'science of man' 260
    Scottish 117, 127 n. 7
    see also cosmopolitanism
Erdman, David 221
Eubulus 28–30
Eve 104
execution 56
exhibitions 75, 84, 87, 92
    women artists in 106

family, the 17, 18, 239–54
    alternative, all-female 278
    conjugal family 276, 281
    and political reform 241
    and population 240
fashion 140, 167
fathers
    and daughters 55, 62
    incest 57
    see also parricide
Favret, Mary 217
Female Spectator, The 10
    see also Eliza Haywood
Fergus, Jan 14
Ferguson, Adam 165
Fielding, Henry 122
    Covent Garden Tragedy 35–6
    Joseph Andrews 38
Filmer, Sir Robert
    Patriarcha, or the Natural Power of Kings 4
fine arts 104
Fitzgerald, Edward, Lord 211
Fitzgerald, Pamela 211, 212
Florini, Rosa 120
Foundling Hospital, The (London) 11, 75, 78,
    80, 81, 84
Fox, Charles James 223
Franklin, Benjamin 140
French Revolution, the 15, 16, 195, 204, 229,
    230, 240
    'Revolution controversy' 201, 240
    the Terror 226
Freud, Sigmund
    'The Ego and the Id' 277, 281
    libido 281
    'Mourning and Melancholia' 278
    unconscious 262
Fuseli, Henry 280

Gainsborough, Thomas 94
Gallagher, Catherine 13
Garrick, David 88, *89*
Genlis, Stéphanie-Félicité de 17, 202, 203, 207,
    210, 211, 212
    *A Short Account of the Conduct of Mme de Genlis
    since the Revolution* 210
Gentleman's Magazine, The 56, 141, 191
gentry capitalism 15, 167
George III 4
Gerard, Alexander 75
Gibbon, Edward 264
Glorious Revolution, the 4, 181, 246
Godwin, William 258
    *Memoirs of the Author of the Vindication of the
    Rights of Woman* 274, 275, 278
Goethe, J. W.
    The Sorrows of Young Werther 278
    translated by Carlyle 219
Goodman, Dena 205, 220
gossip 10, 38, 194–5
Gower, Lady 58
Graham, James 181, 191
Graves, Robert 109
Greer, Germaine 108
Greville, Lady Louisa Augusta 94
Griffith, Elizabeth 107
Guest, Harriet 13
Gunning Sisters 9
    Elizabeth, Duchess of Hamilton and
    Brandon 57, 58, 59, 66, 67
    Maria, Lady Coventry 57, 58, 59
    see also mobs

Habermas, Jürgen 7–9, 12, 16, 18, 28, 32, 45,
    152 n. 8, 181
    *The Structural Transformation of the Public
    Sphere*, 7, 27, 257
    counter-public spheres in 276
    feminist critiques of 275–6
    intimacy and indiscretion in 274
    'public opinion' in 258
    'purely human' relations in 135,
        276
    revisionist accounts of 276
Hall, Catherine 1
Hamilton, Elizabeth 18
    Edinburgh salon 258
    Memoirs of Agrippina 259
    Memoirs of Modern Philosophers 258
    political economy 270
    religion 269
    'selfish principle' 269
    A Series of Popular Essays 259–61
    sympathy 267–8

Hampton Court
 Beauty Room 60
Harrington, James 181, 182, 194
Hayman, Francis 80, 87
Hays, Mary 111, 125, 191, 258
 Dictionary of Female Biography 111, 190
Haywood, Eliza
 British Recluse 54
 The Female Spectator 10
Hegel, G. W. F. 258
Helvetius, Mme 220, 223
Hemans, Felicia 13
Hercules, choice of 76–8, 88, 119
Hermes 77
Heywood, Thomas
 Generall History of Women 109
 *Nine Bookes of Various History Concerninge
  Women* 109
Highmore, Joseph 14, 80
 Pamela 80
 Hagar and Ishmael 80
Hilliar, Anthony 28
history, conjectural 17, 239–40
Hobbes 188, 258
Hogarth, William
 Four Times of the Day 37
 The Harlot's Progress 76, 78, 80, 83, 84, 94
 Moses Brought before Pharoah's Daughter 80
Hohendahl, Peter 27, 46 n. 1
Hollis, Thomas 186, 188
Homans, Margaret 109
Horace
 Ars Poetica 119
Howson, Gerald 63
Humboldt, Alexander von 16, 17, 231, 224
 galvinsim and masochism 228
 and hermaphroditism 227
 homosexuality of 227
 Relation Historique [*Personal Narrative*] 16, 218,
  224, 227, 229, 231–2
 Vues des Cordillères 218, 222
Hume, David 83, 85, 97, 115, 116, 165, 183,
  184, 186, 188
 Of Essay Writing 116
 Of Luxury, later *Of Refinement in the Arts* 11,
  85–6, 114, 165
 Of the Rise and Progress of the Arts and Sciences
  166
 A Treatise of Human Nature 265
Hundert, Edward 270
Hutchinson, John, Colonel 183
Hutchinson, Julius 189
Hutchinson, Lucy 183, 189, 190
Hutchinson, Sidney 89
Hutchinson, Thomas 189

icons, feminine 109, 111, 212
imagination 259
Imlay, Gilbert 217, 275, 280
Inchbald, Elizabeth 14, 200
Ireland 203

James II 4
Jeffries, Elizabeth 9, 54, 56, 57
Johnson, Joseph 111, 122, 279
 *Johnson's Ladies New and Polite Pocket
  Memorandum for 1778* 111
Johnson, Samuel 87, 97, 116
Jones, Chris 217
Jones, Vivien 217, 225

Kames, Henry Home, Lord 113, 264
 Elements of Criticism 259
Kauffman, Angelica 89, 107, 118, *120*, 121
 Calypso Mournful after the Departure of Ulysses
  118
 Sappho 119, 120, *121*
 *Self-Portrait in the Character of Painting Embraced
  by Poetry* 119, *120*
 *Self-Portrait: Hesitating Between the Arts of Music
  and Painting* 88, *90*, 119
Keate, Georgiana 121
Kelly, Gary 217, 226, 258, 259
King, Moll 35–9
Kirby, Joshua 94
Kirby, Sarah 94
Klein, Lawrence 8, 92
Klein, Melanie
 on meaning 284
 on suicide 286
Kneller, Sir Godfrey 83, 125
Knight, Ellis Cornelia 177
Kowaleski-Wallace, Elizabeth 38

Lambert, Marchioness de 111
Landau, Leya 32, 45, 47 n. 25
Landes, Joan 220
Langford, Paul 4, 187
Leapor, Mary 124
'learned ladies' 166
Lennox, Charlotte 107
L'Espinasse, Mlle de 200
letters 200, 286
 as courtship 276
 and Enlightenment salons 220
 epistolary networks 169, 170
 and intimacy 274
 public and private 8, 275
 and separation 282
liberty 134, 186, 187, 191
Linley, Elizabeth 107

literary sphere 16
see also public sphere
literary tradition 123
Locke, John 258
  Two Treatises on Government 4
  see also contract theory
Lucretia 186, 190
luxury 11, 12, 81, 82, 85, 106, 114
  'de-moralisation' of 11, 83
  and effeminacy 106, 243
  of feeling 141, 142, 145
  oriental 149
  and women 244

Macaulay, Catharine 14, 15, 16, 18, 107, 111,
  177, 181–99, 259
  History of England 16, 181–95
  A Modest Plea for the Property of Copyright
  14, 15
Macaulay, Lord 44
Machiavelli 182
Macky, John
  Journey Through England 34
Magdalen Hospital 9, 63, 65
Manchester Mercury, The 133, 134
Mandeville 83, 85, 264, 270
Marx, Karl 258
Matthaeis, Paolo de 78, 79
McCalman, Iain 43
Mellor, Anne 13
Midgely, Claire 135
Miller, James
  The Coffee-House 39–49
Milton, John 194, 241
Minerva 78, 104, 106, 108, 116
Miranda, Francisco de 221
Misson, Henri 28
mobs 58, 66, 67
Montagu, Elizabeth 76, 96, 97, 107, 116, 122,
  123, 163, 167, 171–2, 221
  Dialogues of the Dead 172
  An Essay on the Writings and Genius of
  Shakespeare 172
  and Helen Maria Williams 221
Monthly Review 136, 217, 218, 225, 232, 271
More, Hannah 6, 14, 15, 107, 125, 177, 200,
  206
  'The Slave Trade' 137–9
  'The Sorrows of Yamba' 146–7
Morgan, Lady 224
Moser, George Michael 94
Moser, Mary 89, 94
muses 104–32
  Clio 188, 191
  history of allegory 108–9

models of female intellect 111
relation between mythical and real 111
Urania 118
Myers, Sylvia Harcstark 177

Napolean Bonaparte
  and Humboldt 227
  and Helen Maria Williams 226, 231
nation 16
  British 205
  national character 17, 111, 201
  national identity and gender 202
  see also cosmopolitanism; patriotism
Newman, Gerald 201

Oldmixon, John 183, 184, 186
Opie, Amelia 200
Orleans, Duke of 202, 210, 211, 213
Ossian 218
  admired by Bonaparte 231
Ovid
  Metamorphoses 109
  Heroides 280

Paine, Thomas 194, 221
Pandora 116
parricide 54
Pateman, Carole 1, 5
patriarchy 168
patriot king 168, 172
patriotism 245–6, 249
patronage 170
Paulson, Ronald 76
Pears, Iain 6
Perry, Gill 119
Pesante, Maria Luisa 264
philanthropy 169, 173
philosophy 259, 260, 272 n. 11, 286
  see also under women
Pincus, Stephen 31, 47 n. 16
Piozzi, Hester Thrale 177, 217, 223
Pocock, J. G. A. 182, 100 n. 13
Pointon, Marcia 94
polite arts 92
  and civic virtue 106
polite culture 76
politeness 92, 242, 248
politics, and femininity 193
  see also public sphere, political
Polwhele, Richard 193
Poussin, Nicolas
  Apollo and the Muses on Parnassus 107
  Inspiration of the Epic Poet 120
Pratt, Samuel Jackson 141
Pressly, William 105

Price, Richard 188, 241, 246, 247, 248
  A Discourse on the Love of our Country 245
private sphere 12, 17, 28, 61, 135
  see also separate spheres; public sphere;
    women, retreat
property, literary 14
  see also copyright; women, property
prostitutes 9, 76, 63
  penitent 63, 64
public
  definition of term 5-6
  opinion 18
public sphere
  civic virtue in 16
  in history and theory 3-9
  literary 219, 257
  and modern state 178
  political 18, 193, 195, 257
  and print 203
  and public opinion 258
  and republicanism 181-2
  semi-public sphere 194
  women's place in 1-3
  see also separate spheres; private sphere
public spaces 6, 7, 8, 11, 30, 207
public virtue 15
  see also civic humanism, civic virtue

Quarterly Review 227

Raphael 107
  Madonna 112
  Parnassus 107
Rapin 184, 186
Reeve, Clara 122, 177
Renaissance
  court and education 109
'republic of letters' 166, 205
republicanism 16, 181-99, 211
  classical 175, 187
  republican historiography 181
  Helen Maria Williams and 226
  women and 188
Reynolds, Sir Joshua 11, 87, 115
  Discourses 85
  Garrick between Tragedy and Comedy 88, 89
Richardson, Samuel 122, 176
  Clarissa 56, 277
  Clementina 146
  Pamela 78, 79
Robbins, Caroline 194
Robertson, William 165
Robinson, Mary
  *A Letter to the Women of England on the Injustice
    of Mental Subordination* 122

Poems from Sappho to Phaon 122
Rochford, Anne 34, 37, 48 n. 35
  The Velvet Coffee-Woman 34-5
Roland, Mme, salon of 221
Roscoe, William
  The Wrongs of Africa 147
Rouquet, André 81
Rousseau, Jean-Jacques 229, 241, 258
  critiques of 206
  Discours sur les Sciences et les Arts 242
  Emile 241, 249
  Lettre à d'Alembert 205
  La Nouvelle Héloïse 205, 277, 278
  Reveries of a Solitary Walker 228
Royal Academy, The 11, 75, 85, 88, 105, 115,
    116, 117
  annual exhibition 83
  'Instrument of Foundation' 83
  life classes in 90
  and Richard Samuel 111
  Somerset House 118
  and women artists 106, 119
Rush, Hannah
  Compartment with Cattle 93
Rushworth, John 183, 186
Russell, Rachel 189, 190
Russell, William 189, 190
Russo, Mary 53

St Martin's Lane Academy 83
salonnières 16, 205, 219, 220, 223-5, 229, 232
salons 109
  Bluestocking 123
  Edinburgh 258
  female-dominated 220
  as described by Habermas 8, 123, 169, 229
  Parisian 205, 219, 221, 222-225, 232
Samuel, Richard 11, 107, 108, 111, 113, 116, 125,
    126
  The Nine Living Muses of Great Britain 11,
    104-32, 191
  description of painting's subjects 107
Sappho 107, 108, 111, 119-22
Saussure, César de 32
scandal 17, 34, 38
Schiebinger, Londa 109
Schlegel, A. W. 219, 224
Scotland 117
Scott, Mary
  'The Female Advocate' 125
Scott, Sarah 163, 173
  The History of Sir Goerge Ellison 173
  Millenium Hall 54, 173
sensibility 12, 13, 79, 167, 229, 240
  and abolition 134, 143

'false and bastard' 145
sympathy and femininity 135, 137, 251
and travel writing 228, 230
in Weimar Romanticism 227
in Wollstonecraft's love letters 285
separate spheres 1, 3, 13, 18, 171, 258
see also public sphere; private sphere;
domestic sphere
Sévigné, Mme de 200
Seward, Anna 177
Seward, Thomas
'The Female Right to Literature' 124
sexuality 13
and the coffee-woman 35–9, 42–3
and intimacy 283
Shaftesbury, third Earl of 78
Shelley, Mary 13
Siddons, Sarah 267
Sidney, Algernon 186, 194
sister arts, the 108
slavery 147
anti-slavery artefacts 140–1
african slaves 138, 149
women's identification with 122
women's anti-slavery verse 136, 139
see also abolition
Smith, Adam 18, 83, 85, 165, 241, 260
humanity 266
'impartial spectator' 264, 265
public and private 264–7
sympathy 265
The Theory of Moral Sentiments 18, 142, 145, 244
The Wealth of Nations 270
Smith, Charlotte 14, 221
Smollett, Tobias 122
Society for the Encouragement of Arts,
Manufactures, and Commerce 11, 75, 84,
85, 86, 88, 90, 97, 113, 117
George Cockings's poem in praise of 95
exhibitions of artists at 87
honorary premiums 94
premiums 86, 90, 92, 93
Solkin, David 77, 80, 81
Spectator, The 6, 27, 29, 33, 43, 167
see also *The Female Spectator*
Spencer, Jane
The Rise of the Woman Novelist 12
Staël, Germaine de 201, 202, 220, 224
Stallybrass, Peter 27, 46 n. 1
Staves, Susan 263
Steele, Richard 55
see also *The Spectator*
Stephen, Leslie 44
Sterne, Laurence 63, 79
A Sentimental Journey 79

Sterne, Madeleine B. 221
Stevens, George Alexander
The Adventures of a Speculist 36
Stewart, Dugald 258, 264, 272 n. 8
Stone, John Hurford 217, 221, 230
printing business with Helen Maria
Williams 221–2, 226
Sussman, Charlotte 135

Talbot, Catherine 55, 163, 175
Reflections on the Seven Days of the Week 175
Essays on Various Subjects 176
tea
drinking in gaol 60
tea tables 135, 145
Tencin, Mme de 200
Thaddeus, Jamie Ferrar 14
Thom, Martin 194
Thomason, George 183, 186
Thornhill, Sir James 83
Tickner, George 224
Tillotson, John 189
Tillyard, Stella 211
Todd, Janet 217
Tomeroy, Peter 119
translation 6, 16, 219, 220
as act of political defiance 226
travel 17
Trevelyan, G. M. 44
Trimmer, Sarah (see also Kirby) 169
Tyers, Jonathan 80

Van Sant, Ann 65
Vauxhall Gardens 11, 75, 78, 79, 80
Vigée-Lebrun, Elisabeth 212
virtue 10, 11, 13, 15
Christian and civic 244
and the family 254
gender and heroic virtue 239
in Macaulay's *History* 184
republican 185
in Wollstonecraft 243–4, 247

Walpole, Horace 58, 60, 63, 181
Ward, Ned
The London Spy 32
Warner, Marina 108, 191
Wedgwood, Josiah 11, 140
Wentworth, Hon. Thomas Watson 81
Wheateley, Phillis 125
Whigs 182
Churchmen 4
Court 187
government 4
paternalism 169

White, Allon 27, 46 n. 1
Wilberforce, William 136, 137, 147
Wilkes, Wetanhall
 Essay on the Pleasure and Advantages of Female Literature 111
William of Orange 4
Williams, Helen Maria 16, 17, 151 n. 3, 211, 214
 'English Press' in Paris 221, 223, 226
 and geology 230
 Humboldt's *Personal Narrative* 219, 224
 Letters from France 217, 229
 Ode to the Peace 226
 Paul and Virginia 226
 Peru 221, 226, 229
 Poems on Various Subjects 220
 salon run by 223–5
 Sketches from France 217
 Tour in Switzerland 219, 230, 231
Wilson, Angus 45
Wilson, Thomas 191
Winnicott, D. W. 284
Wither, George
 A Collection of Emblems 77
Wollstonecraft, Mary 5, 7, 14, 17, 18, 104, 174, 177, 193, 194, 201, 206, 207, 217, 239–54, 259
 on family 254
 'female Werther' 280
 on friendship 244, 251
 as represented by Godwin 275, 278, 279, 286
 An Historical and Moral View of the Origin and Progress of the French Revolution 245
 as icon 104, 279
 Letters to Imlay 18, 274, 281–86
 as mother 284
 passion for Fuseli 280
 patriotism 246, 249, 250–251
 and political discourse 245
 and Rousseau 242
 Short Residence in Sweden 219, 245, 285
 The Wrongs of Woman 54
 Vindication of the Rights of Men 241, 246, 248
 Vindication of the Rights of Woman 5, 17, 193, 194, 208, 223, 229, 246, 264, 266
 boarding schools 252

 as champion of virtue 247
 citizenship and gender 252, 253–4
 heroism 253
 rights and duties 248
 women's career options 279
women
 and authorship 125, 204
 and business 38
 as objects of display 12, 209
 domestic 167
 and the fine arts 106
 intellectuals 15, 107, 109, 166
 as legal subjects 5, 263
 and marriage 263, 275
 networks of 2, 107, 112, 164, 166, 210
 and the novel 12–13
 and patriotism 205, 258
 and performance 66, 68
 and philosophy 206, 259
 and poetry 13
 and the political sphere 135, 257, 258
 and print culture 123, 210, 225
 as printers and publishers 15, 23 n. 50
  see also Williams, Helen Maria
 and property 13, 38, 168, 263
  see also copyright
 as public spectacle 2, 9, 62
 and public virtue 66
 and retreat 53–4, 202
 suffragism 177
 visibility of 6, 133
 and visual representation 11, 105
 writers 12–15
  diversity of literary genres 13
  politics of literary genre 176
Woodward, Lionel 218
Wordsworth, William 223, 224
 Preface to *Lyrical Ballads* 258

Yearsley, Anne 14, 151 n.3

Zenobia 111
Zoffany, Johan
 The Academicians of the Royal Academy 89
 The Tribuna of the Uffizi 112